22 Microcomputer Projects to Build, Use, and Learn

DANIEL METZGER

Prentice-Hall, Inc., Englewood Cliffs, New Jersey 07632

Library of Congress Cataloging in Publication Data
Metzger, Daniel L., (date)
  22 microcomputer projects to build, use, and learn.

  Includes index.
  1. Microcomputers—Amateurs' manuals. I. Title.
  II. Title: Twenty-two microcomputer projects to build,
  use, and learn.
  TK9969.M47   1985   621.3819'58   84-18306
  ISBN 0-13-934720-8
  ISBN 0-13-934712-7 (pbk.)

Editorial/production supervision: Virginia McCarthy
Cover design: Lundgren Graphics, Ltd.
Manufacturing buyer: Anthony Caruso

© 1985 By Prentice-Hall, Inc., Englewood Cliffs, New Jersey 07632

All rights reserved. No part of this book may be
reproeduced, in any form or by any means,
without permission in writing from the publisher.

Printed in the United States of America

10 9 8 7 5 4 3 2 1

ISBN 0-13-934720-8
ISBN 0-13-934712-7 {PBK.} 01

Prentice-Hall International, Inc. *London*
Prentice-Hall of Australia Pty. Limited, *Sydney*
Editora Prentice-Hall do Brasil, Ltda., *Rio de Janeiro*
Prentice-Hall Canada Inc., *Toronto*
Prentice-Hall Hispanoamericana, S.A., *Mexico*
Prentice-Hall of India Private Limited, *New Delhi*
Prentice-Hall of Japan, Inc., *Tokyo*
Prentice-Hall of Southeast Asia Pte. Ltd., *Singapore*
Whitehall Books Limited, *Wellington, New Zealand*

I was fortunate to spend the early part of my youth in a time and place where "building it yourself" implied necessity, not an educational or recreational experience. Most Saturday mornings I would scurry through breakfast and then run down the stairs to investigate the sounds of pounding and sawing from the basement. There would be my father, bending over a board with a hammer in his hand and a row of nails between his lips.

"What you makin', Daddy?"

He would somehow manage to answer loudly without dropping any of the nails.

"Why, I'm buildin' a chicken coop."

The answer was the same every weekend, and repetitions of the question were useless. Of course, there were no chickens. He simply meant that I would have to wait and watch until the table or cupboard—or perhaps toy stilts—took shape. Then, with my curiosity satisfied, I could go out to play while he finished the project.

Well, Dad, chicken coops have changed a little since those times, but we're still building them. This one's for you.

for my Father
Leonard Joseph Metzger

Contents

Preface ix

Microcomputer-Project Components List x

1 Warmup Exercises for a Microprocessor Chip 1

- **1.1** WHAT GOES ON INSIDE A COMPUTER? 1
- **1.2** THE ADDRESS BUS: HALF OF THE COMPUTER CONQUERED IN A SINGLE BLOW 2
- **1.3** THE DATA BUS AND DATA TYPES 5
- **1.4** PROGRAM SEQUENCING 7
- **1.5** THE CLOCK AND OTHER PIN FUNCTIONS 9
- **1.6** PROJECT ONE: A SINGLE-INSTRUCTION PROGRAM 12
- **1.7** A TWO-INSTRUCTION PROGRAM 12
- **1.8** MORE SELF-PROGRAMMED LOOPS 16
- **1.9** SUMMARY REMARKS 19
  CHAPTER SUMMARY 20

2 Building an EPROM Memory Programmer 21

- **2.1** MEMORY TYPES 21
- **2.2** THE TRI-STATE DATA BUS 24
- **2.3** CHIP SELECT BY ADDRESS DECODING 25
- **2.4** THE 2716 EPROM 27
- **2.5** THE EPROM PROGRAMMER 29
- **2.6** THE PROGRAMMER CIRCUITRY 30

2.7 CONSTRUCTION DETAILS 32
CHAPTER SUMMARY 34

3 Adding the Memory: Lights and Sirens 35

3.1 THE MEMORY CONNECTION 35
3.2 IMMEDIATE-MODE ADDRESSING 37
3.3 A DIAGNOSTIC PROGRAM 38
3.4 THE RELATIVE ADDRESSING MODE 41
3.5 A PROGRAMMABLE LAMP FLASHER 42
3.6 FLOWCHARTING AND A POLICE SIREN 44
3.7 AN AMBULANCE SIREN 46
3.8 THEME AND VARIATIONS: MORE PROGRAM IDEAS 50
CHAPTER SUMMARY 50

4 Output Interfaces: Waveform Generators and Number Games 52

4.1 THE OUTPUT DATA LATCH 52
4.2 A WAVEFORM GENERATOR 53
4.3 THIRTEEN/NINETEEN: A NUMBER GAME 57
4.4 AN EIGHT-BIT WAVEFORM GENERATOR AND DATA GENERATION WITH *BASIC* 63
4.5 INDEXED ADDRESSING FOR THE WAVEFORM GENERATOR 65
4.6 HEX DRILL: A COMPUTER TUTOR 67
CHAPTER SUMMARY 74

5 Troubleshooting: Single-Step and Bus-Display Hardware 75

5.1 HALT AND DISPLAY ADDRESS! 75
5.2 A SINGLE-STEP CIRCUIT 76
5.3 DATE-BUS DISPLAY 78
5.4 ADDRESS RECOGNITION 80
5.5 MICROCOMPUTER TROUBLESHOOTING TIPS 82
5.6 CORRECTING SOFTWARE ERRORS 84
CHAPTER SUMMARY 86

6 Input Interfacing: Two Games of Skill 87

6.1 MEM: A COMPUTER MEMORY GAME 87
6.2 SUBROUTINES AND THE STACK 93
6.3 THE PROGRAMMER'S MODEL 96
6.4 INTERRUPTS AND THE STACK 97
6.5 MORE ABOUT BRANCH COMMANDS 99
6.6 MEM GAME WITH SUBROUTINES AND INTERRUPT 102
6.7 AIR RAID: AN ACTION GAME 106
6.8 PROGRAMMING PHILOSOPHY AND A SECOND AIR RAID 110
6.9 SOUND EFFECTS AND OTHER GAME MODIFICATIONS 120
CHAPTER SUMMARY 124

Contents vii

7 A Logic Analyzer to Build 126

7.1 INTRODUCTION TO LOGIC ANALYZERS 126
7.2 TRIGGERING AND USING A LOGIC ANALYZER 127
7.3 CIRCUIT DESCRIPTION 128
7.4 CONSTRUCTION DETAILS 130

8 An IC Tester: Introducing the 6821 Programmable I/O Chip 134

8.1 TESTER OPERATION AND OVERVIEW 134
8.2 THE 6821 PROGRAMMABLE I/O CHIP: BASIC FUNCTION 136
8.3 INTERRUPTS AND HANDSHAKING WITH THE PIA 140
8.4 IC-TESTER HARDWARE 145
8.5 IC-TESTER SOFTWARE 149
8.6 DATA DEVELOPMENT 158
CHAPTER SUMMARY 164

9 Microchicken: A General-Purpose Computer with Monitor 165

9.1 COMPUTER OVERVIEW AND OPERATION 165
9.2 SYSTEM HARDWARE 167
9.3 MONITOR PROGRAM OVERVIEW 174
9.4 KEYBOARD ROUTINES 176
9.5 DISPLAY ROUTINES 180
9.6 THE MONITOR SINGLE-STEP FUNCTION 183
9.7 PROGRAM DEBUGGING WITH SST 186
9.8 THE EPROM ROUTINES 188
9.9 THE MICROCHICKEN TAPES: SAVE AND LOAD ROUTINES 193

10 Chicken Pickin': An Industrial Microcomputer Application 205

10.1 THE PROBLEM AND THE PROGRAM 205
10.2 ANALOG CHICKEN: ADDING AN A/D CONVERTER 208
10.3 SERIAL CHICKEN: THE RS-232 INTERFACE 214
10.4 THE ACIA SERIAL INTERFACE CHIP 216
10.5 THE APPLE CONNECTION 220
10.6 LINEAR CHICKEN: A COMPUTER BRAIN TRANSPLANT 223
10.7 PROGRAM PROLIFERATION 230

11 Video Chicken: Adding a TV Monitor 232

11.1 THE 6847 VIDEO DISPLAY GENERATOR 232
11.2 STAND-ALONE VDG TEST CIRCUITS 235
11.3 INTERFACING THE COMPUTER AND THE VIDEO DISPLAY 240
11.4 VIDEO CHICKEN 243
11.5 THINGS LEFT UNDONE 250

Appendices 253

A MICROCOMPUTER WIRING TECHNIQUES 255

B IC PACKAGE-PINOUT LABELS 258

C CYCLE-BY-CYCLE OPERATION OF 6802 INSTRUCTIONS 260

D OBJECT CODE FOR *Ambulance Siren* (CHAPTER 3) 264

E PROGRAM LISTING FOR *Air Raid* SOUND (CHAPTER 6) 265

Index 271

6802 Programmer's Reference 275

Preface

Probably, you have picked up other books on microcomputers before this one. If so, you will have noticed that they all try to introduce you to microcomputers "head first": hundreds of pages of number systems and logic operations, instruction sets and flow charts, interrupt vectors and stack pointers—with a small chapter somewhere near the end dealing with the actual microcomputer chips, and no chapter anywhere that actually tells you how to wire up the chips to do something useful or interesting.

This book will introduce you to microcomputer chips "feet first," with specific directions for building working microcomputer circuits in every chapter, starting with the very first chapter. The necessary headwork is all there, but it has been sandwiched in between the projects in the belief that you are not really ready to understand it until you have something tangible to which it can be related. The projects should be followed in sequence, since the later ones depend on knowledge (and often make use of test circuits) that you have built up in the earlier projects.

We have chosen the Motorola 6802 microprocessor for our projects because it is inexpensive (about $7) and it requires fewer external chips and less wiring than most anything else on the market. The 6802 is an easier-to-use version of the original Motorola 6800, and is a perfect lead-in to the more advanced 6801, 6809, and 68000 processors which seem to be dominating in new designs. In addtion, it is strikingly similar to the 6502, which has long been the most popular chip in desktop personal computers.

The projects have been carefully designed to lead from the simple to the sophisticated, and to cover the most frequently used programming techniques and support chips seen in current industry practice. For example, the first project uses only six components and 21 pin connections, but later projects culminate in a complete microprocessor-based industrial control system with interfacing to a master computer and video display.

Some of the early projects require the use of a triggered oscilloscope. This is a great aid in visualizing what the computer is doing when it executes your programs, but it is not required in the later projects. If you don't have a 'scope, there are alternative projects listed to help you get through the first chapters. Of course, you will need a regulated supply to deliver the +5 V and occasional other voltages required in the projects. Triple-output supplies (fixed 5-V and dual variable 20-V outputs) are ideal, but for most of the projects the simple home-built supply of Figure 9-7(a) will be adequate. For prototyping you will want one solderless IC breadboard with at least 200 sets of contact points (five contacts per set) for the early projects, and a pair of these for more advanced projects. You will find a detailed list of the components required for the projects following this preface. Most of these can be obtained at local electronics stores, but better prices can usually be obtained by checking the mail-order ads in the back of some of the electronics and computer magazines. Happy computing!

MICROCOMPUTER-PROJECT COMPONENTS

Item	Approx. Cost Each	EPROM Programmer (Ch 2)	Logic Analyzer (Ch 7)	Early Projects (Ch 1-6)	Extra for IC Tester (Ch 8)	Extra for Computer (Ch 9)	Computer Add-Ons (Ch 10, 11)
74LS00 NAND	0.25	1	2	3			
74LS02 NOR	0.25						1
74LS04 inverter	0.25		1	1			
74LS20 4-NAND	0.25			1			
74LS47 7-segment decoder	0.75			1			
74LS73 JK FF	0.40			1			
74LS75 Latch	0.40			1			
74LS76 JK FF	0.40		1				
74LS86 EOR	0.40		2	2			
74LS125 buffer	0.50			1			
74LS133 13 NAND	0.60		1				
74LS138 address decoder	0.60			1			
74LS193 decade counter	0.80	2	2				
74LS244 buffer	1.30		2				2
74LS373 latch	1.40			1		1	1

Preface   xi

MICROCOMPUTER-PROJECT COMPONENTS (*Continued*)

Item	Approx. Cost Each	EPROM Programmer (Ch 2)	Logic Analyzer (Ch 7)	Early Projects (Ch 1–6)	Extra for IC Tester (Ch 8)	Extra for Computer (Ch 9)	Computer Add-Ons (Ch 10, 11)
78M05 5-V reg.	1.25	1	1			1	
741 op amp	0.35					1	
1372 TV mod.	7.00						1
1408 D/A conv. (L7 or L8)	3.00			1			
2016 RAM (or 6116)	4.50					1	1
2716 ROM	3.50			2		1	
6802 μP	7.00			1			
6810 RAM	3.00		2				
6821 PIA	3.00				1		
6847 VDG	11.00						1
6850 ACIA	3.50						2
Crystal	4.50			2.0 MHz		4.0 MHz	3.58 MHz
TIL 311 (hex)	11.00		4	2			
MAN 72 (7-segment)	1.00			1	2		
Discrete (LED)	0.15	19	8	8		1	
HEX thumb switch	3.00	2					
8 DIP switch	1.50		1				
P.B. SPST N.O.	1.00	2		4			
P.B. DPST N.O.	1.50		1				
P.B. SPDT	2.00	1	2	1			
TOG SPST	1.00	5	1			1	
TOG SPDT	1.25	3	1		1		
TOG DPDT	1.50	1					
Breadboard (1200-contact)	22.00			1	2		
Transformer, 18 V CT, 0.3 A	5.00	1	1			1	
1000 μF, 15 V	0.60	1	1			1	
25 μF, 25 V	0.20						2
1.0 μF, Mylar	0.75	1					
0.1 μF, ceramic	0.15	2	6	3	3		
33 pF	0.10			2			
10 kΩ	0.05	8		4	12	3	3

MICROCOMPUTER-PROJECT COMPONENTS (*Continued*)

Item	Approx. cost Each	EPROM Programmer (Ch 2)	Logic Analyzer (Ch 7)	Early Projects (Ch 1-6)	Extra for IC Tester (Ch 8)	Extra for Computer (Ch 9)	Computer Add-Ons (Ch 10, 11)
1.5 kΩ	0.05			2	8		
1 kΩ	0.05		8	8			
680 Ω	0.05	8		8			8
220 Ω	0.05					7	

In addition you will need a supply of No. 22 solid PVC insulated hookup wire (preferably in all 10 colors), IC sockets for permanently wired projects, and small quantities of various resistors and capacitors.

The EPROM memory chip with the Microchicken monitor program (Chapter 9 project) is available from the author for $20. The double-sided printed-circuit board for the Microchicken computer is also available at $25. Write:

> D. L. Metzger
> P.O. Box 466
> Temperance, MI 48182

ACKNOWLEDGMENTS

The author wishes to acknowledge his very great debt to a good friend and colleague, Timothy J. Maloney, whose detailed proofreading of the manuscript and programs for this book has improved greatly its accuracy and clarity. Only those who have themselves attempted to trace a 1000-word machine-language program can appreciate how large a debt this is.

1

Warmup Exercises for a Microprocessor Chip

1.1 WHAT GOES ON INSIDE A COMPUTER?

Everyone knows what computers do. They predict election results on TV, play championship-level chess, handle the inventory and billing for your company, and beguile you of your quarters at the video arcade. But how do computers do these things? What goes on inside a computer?

Actually, a computer predicts election results in about the same sense that a typewriter writes books. A typewriter is a machine for making very regularized marks on paper; a computer is a machine for switching sets of voltages at a very fast rate. A typewriter is capable of making only a few dozen different marks (letters), although a person skilled in the use of language can combine these letters into words, sentences, and paragraphs with infinite variations of meaning. Similarly, a computer is capable of performing only a few dozen different switching patterns (instructions), but a person skilled in the art of programming can combine these instructions into programs to implement an infinite variety of control and computational tasks.

Extending the analogy, a typewriter has no built-in character or mechanism that represents the feline animal, but we have fairly widespread agreement that the marks CAT will represent such an animal. This set of marks is quite arbitrary. Another group of people has chosen the marks GATO to represent the same concept. The typewriter has only these few dozen marks. Meaning is assigned to groups of marks by the writers who make them.

Extending the analogy, a computer has nothing inside it which represents Democrats or Republicans or pawns or rooks. A computer, quite literally, doesn't know 1 from 2. A computer has only a certain number of voltage patterns. Meaning is assigned to those patterns by the programmers who make them.

Still, a computer is quite a bit more impressive than a typewriter. There must be some area where the analogy breaks down. In fact, there are at least two. First, computers are fast to a degree that defies human comprehension. The slow ones perform 1 million operations per second; the fast ones do a hundred times that. To get an idea of what this means, imagine a store clerk who takes one year to calculate your change if you give him a dollar for a 68-cent purchase. That's about how slow a human seems compared to a computer.

The second difference is that a computer, once programmed, can complete its task without human supervision. If the programmer has anticipated all of the sets of voltage patterns that the computer will encounter, and if he has provided instructions to be implemented in each case, the computer will complete a very extensive series of voltage switchings. It will encounter various input voltage patterns and produce various intermediate results, and depending on these it will follow one or another set of instructions, as designated by the programmer. If the program is well written, the final result may be a checkmate or a printed inventory list. But this depends quite a bit more on the program than on the computer, just as the success of a book depends quite a bit more on the author than on his typewriter. The computer is, after all, only a machine.

1.2 THE ADDRESS BUS: HALF OF THE COMPUTER CONQUERED IN A SINGLE BLOW

A computer follows its program by fetching an instruction from memory, executing that instruction, and then fetching the next instruction from the next memory location. These instructions are fetched, one at a time, by signals which the microprocessor sends out via the address bus.

All of the projects in this book are designed for the Motorola 6802 microprocessor. Like most microprocessor chips, this one comes in a 40-pin package. Sixteen of these pins are output lines from the processor to the memory. The voltage pattern on these lines is used to select the location in memory that the processor is going to access.

Each individual line conveys one *bit* of information. It may have only two different values: a low voltage (about 0.1 V, represented by the symbol ∅) or a high voltage (about +4 V, represented by the symbol 1).

A group of lines acting together is called a *bus* in computer terminology. Each unique voltage pattern, which selects a unique location in memory, is spoken of as an *address*. Thus the 6802 has a 16-bit address bus, as shown in Fig. 1-1.

Two of the pins of the 6802 are simply grounds and two must be con-

Sec. 1.2 The Address Bus

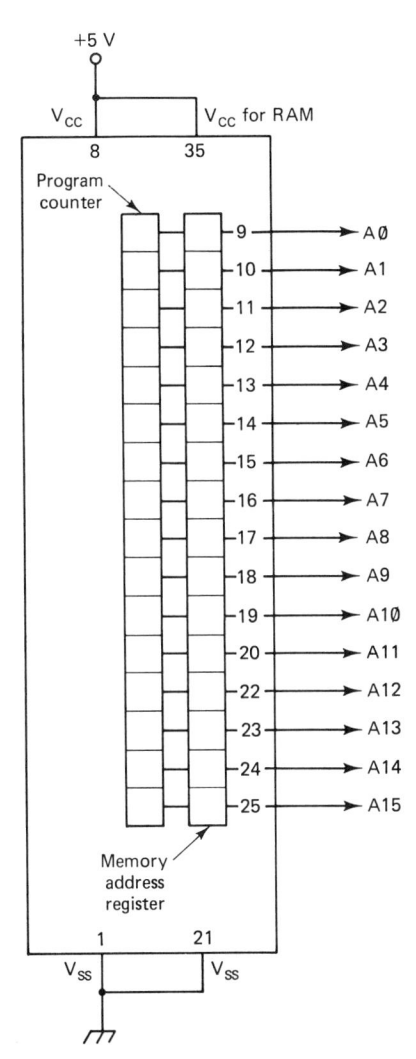

Figure 1-1 Sixteen of the 40 pins of the microprocessor are used to select the memory address being accessed. Four others are simply supply and ground pins.

nected to the V_{CC} supply (+5 V). So now you know what half of the pins on the microprocessor are for!

In the actual memory chip these individual locations will be only a few thousandths of an inch apart, but the term *address* makes it clear that each one contains data that is separate from that at any of the other addresses.

Counting in binary. A single line could be used to access only two different memory addresses; one for logic ∅ on the line (0.1 V), and another for logic 1 on the line (+4 V). If we used two lines (call them A∅ and A1), we could make four different combinations to select four different memory addresses.

A1	AØ
Ø	Ø
Ø	1
1	Ø
1	1

With three address lines we could select eight different addresses, and with four lines we could select 16 addresses.

Although the voltages appearing on one address line are inherently no different from the voltages on any other, we find it helpful to assign place values to each line so that each voltage pattern is identified by a unique number. Thus line AØ is understood to represent units. A logic 1 (+4 V) means that we have one unit (one), and a logic Ø means that we have no units (zero). Line A1 represents groups of two, A2 represents groups of four, and A3 represents groups of eight. The following table shows all possible combinations of a 4-bit address bus. Note that the numbers 10 through 15 are alternatively listed as *A* through *F* in the last column. This allows us to represent any combination of four binary values with a single digit. More on this later.

Groups of 8 A3	Groups of 4 A2	Groups of 2 A1	Units AØ	Decimal Total	Hexadecimal Representation
Ø	Ø	Ø	Ø	0	Ø
Ø	Ø	Ø	1	1	1
Ø	Ø	1	Ø	2	2
Ø	Ø	1	1	3	3
Ø	1	Ø	Ø	4	4
Ø	1	Ø	1	5	5
Ø	1	1	Ø	6	6
Ø	1	1	1	7	7
1	Ø	Ø	Ø	8	8
1	Ø	Ø	1	9	9
1	Ø	1	Ø	10	A
1	Ø	1	1	11	B
1	1	Ø	Ø	12	C
1	1	Ø	1	13	D
1	1	1	Ø	14	E
1	1	1	1	15	F

The total number of combinations of four lines, each one of which can assume two states, is 2^4 or 16. Each time another line is added the number

Sec. 1.3   The Data Bus and Data Types   5

of combinations increases by another factor of 2. The 16 address lines on our microcomputer can access 2^{16} or 65 536 different memory locations. We will use only a few of these addresses in our first projects, and never more than a few hundred in any of the projects in this book.

Hex notation.   A typical signal on the address bus is represented below, with 1 standing for voltages near 4 V and Ø standing for voltages near 0:

$$Ø111Ø1ØØ11Ø11Ø1Ø$$

Although we do occasionally have to deal with digital information in this binary form, we would very much prefer to express it in a more convenient way. With some labor we can determine that the number above represents (from right to left) no 1s, a 2, no 4s, an 8, a 16, no 32s, a 64, a 128, no 256s, no 512s, a 1024, no 2048, a 4096, an 8192, a 16 384, and no 32 768, which equals 29 914 in our usual decimal system of numbers.

However, if we use a hexadecimal system (16 basic symbols instead of 10), we can represent any 16-bit binary number with just four of these symbols. And we can change from binary to hexadecimal (hex for short) immediately, without any calculation at all. It's done by grouping the binary digits in fours and writing the hex value for each group:

Ø111	Ø1ØØ	11Ø1	1Ø1Ø
7	4	D	A

To make it clear that a number is hexadecimal and not decimal, we place a dollar sign in front of it. The number above is thus written $74DA.

Computer programs are almost always written with hex numbers representing the binary digits that the machine actually deals with. To work with hex numbers you just have to get used to the idea that what you have been calling 10, 11, 12, 13, 14, and 15 are now called, respectively, A, B, C, D, E, and F.

The program counter, shown in Fig. 1-1, is a 16-bit storage register within the microprocessor which holds the address of the next memory location to be accessed. Normally, the program counter increments (increases its count by one) each machine cycle and sends the result out the address bus. There are special instructions that can cause the contents of the program counter to jump to an entirely new value. The memory-address register makes it possible to access memory locations that are not in the program counter's sequence without disturbing the program counter.

1.3 THE DATA BUS AND DATA TYPES

Eight of the pins on the 6802 microprocessor are dedicated to the data bus, as shown in Fig. 1-2. (That leaves only 12 pins to explain, if you've been keeping track.) The "width" of the data bus defines the "word length" of

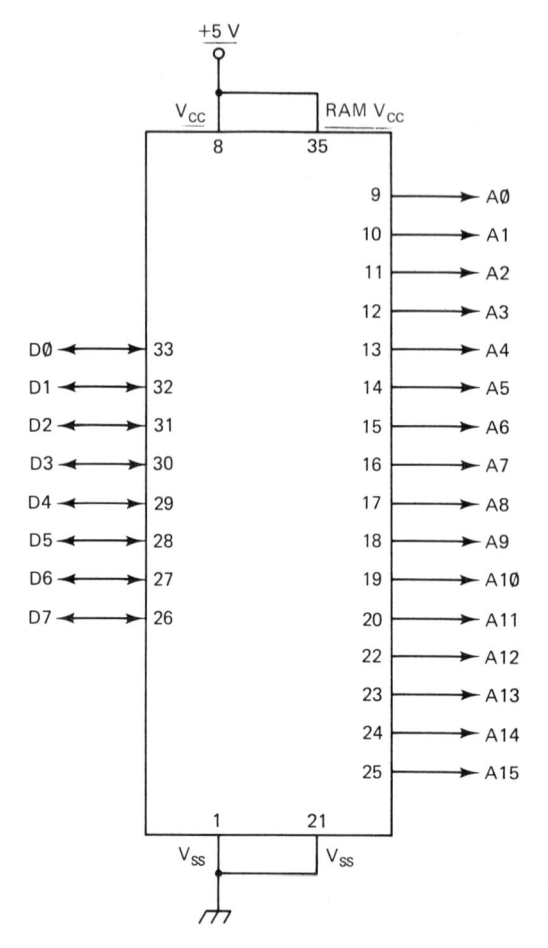

Figure 1-2 The data bus can be used to read data into or write data out from the microprocessor.

a computer. Eight-bit word length has been the most common with microcomputers since their beginning, although microprocessors with 16-bit word lengths are now common. Large computers have 32- or 64-bit word lengths.

Bits, bytes, and nibbles. We have seen that a binary digit is called a bit. Microprocessor hardware is most commonly designed to handle 8 bits of data at a time, and an 8-bit block of data is called a *byte*. One hex digit represents 4 bits or a half a byte, and a half a byte, of course, is called a *nibble*.

Unlike the address bus, the microprocessor data bus is bidirectional; that is, it can send data out to an external chip or it can read data in from an external chip. Whereas the address bus handles binary signals representing address locations only, the data bus handles binary signals representing a number of different things. Since these *data types* are often a source of confusion, we will stop right now to sort them out.

Sec. 1.4 Program Sequencing 7

1. Instructions. The data bus may be used to read instruction codes from the program memory to the processor. For example, the code 0111 1111 ($7F) tells the processor to clear (set to zero) the contents of a specified memory location.

2. Addresses. The data bus may be used to read an address into the microprocessor. This may be for the purpose of jumping the program counter to a new series of addresses, or simply to access an out-of-sequence address without disturbing the program counter. Since the address bus is 16 bits wide, the data bus will have to read two 8-bit bytes from two successive memory locations and piece them together (concatenate them) to form a full address. The 6802 reads the left 8 bits (most significant byte or MSB) first and the least significant byte (LSB) second.

Try to keep the distinction clear between a *memory location*, the *address of that memory location*, and the *contents* of two such memory locations which may be concatenated to form another address.

3. Numeric data. The data bus may be used to read or write 8-bit patterns which represent numeric data. Since only 2^8 or 256 different patterns are possible on an 8-bit binary bus, only the numbers from 0 to 255 (decimal) can be represented. We will represent this as hex 00 through hex FF. Larger numbers and fractional values can be represented by concatenating several 8-bit words.

4. User codes. The data bus may be used to read or write 8-bit codes to activate certain pieces of equipment. For example, in ACSII (American Standard Code for Information Interchange), the binary pattern 0101 0001 ($51) represents the letter Q. The other typewriter characters are similarly represented. As another example, in designing an in-plant telephone system you may decide quite arbitrarily to use the code 0111 1100 ($7C) to access the shipping department's phone.

1.4 PROGRAM SEQUENCING

Since the data bus handles several different data types, how does the processor know how to interpret the data it is receiving? For example, the binary pattern 0100 1111 ($4F) is a 6802 instruction telling the processor to clear an internal register called accumulator A. But it may also be the LSB of address $F84F, and it is the ASCII code for the letter O, and we may have chosen it as the code to ring the telephone in the plant medical examiner's office. When the processor reads this data, how does it know what to do?

The answer is that the processor doesn't know—it *assumes*. At every point in its program the processor is expecting one or another of those data types. It is up to the programmer to know which one, and to supply it at the proper point. If you try to tell the processor to print a letter O when it is looking for an instruction, the processor is going to clear its register A, regardless of what you intended for it to do. Doesn't this make programming a tedious and error-prone business? Yes, it certainly does. Tracking down errors—debugging—is by far the biggest part of a programmer's job, and confused data types is one of the bugs to watch out for.

Instruction codes. Upon starting a program the processor places a 16-bit pattern on the address bus. This accesses a selected location in the program-memory chip, and the chip responds by placing an 8-bit pattern on the data bus. The processor reads this pattern and *assumes* that it is an instruction code.

These 8 bits are sent to an *instruction-decoder* circuit within the processor, as shown in Fig. 1-3. One of the results of the decoding will be to activate selected logic circuits within the processor to perform the desired

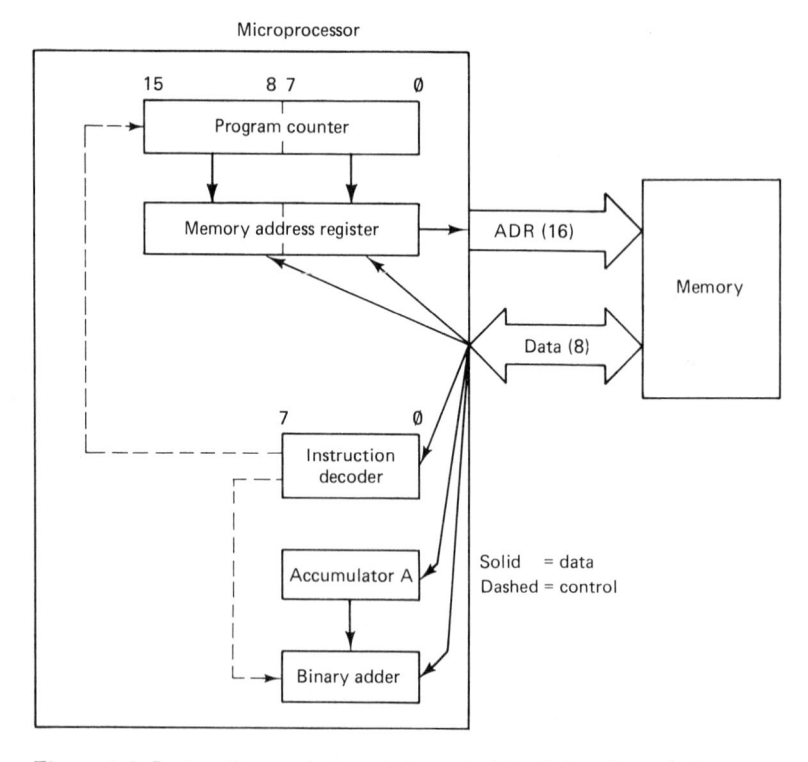

Figure 1-3 Instruction codes are interpreted to determine what operation to perform and whether any more data is needed to specify the operand.

Sec. 1.5 The Clock and Other Pin Functions 9

operation. Typical operations are *Clear* accumulator A, *Jump* the program counter to a new address, and *Add* the contents of a specified memory location to the contents of accumulator A. However, before any operation can be completed the decoder must decide whether the instruction is complete or whether more information is needed.

Addressing modes. The instruction to Increment Accumulator is *inherently* complete in that one byte. It leaves no questions unanswered, and can be implemented without requiring any more data. Actually, there are four more internal processor registers besides accumulator A, and there are 51 *inherent* instructions permitting the data in these registers to be cleared, incremented, decremented, complemented, added, shifted, or transferred in various ways. All of these inherent-mode instructions are complete in one byte, and the processor assumes that the next byte coming in the data bus will be another instruction code.

The instruction to Jump the program counter to a new address is given by the code $7E, and it obviously requires an answer to the question "Which address?" Upon receiving such an instruction the processor assumes that the next two bytes fetched by the program counter will be the high and low address bytes, respectively, of the operand. (The *operand*, by the way, is the answer to the question: What data does this instruction operate on?) The next (fourth) byte will then be another instruction code. These three-byte instructions are called *extended mode* because they extend the processor's access to the entire 65 536 words of memory. There are 40 extended-mode instructions in the 6802 instruction set.

It is interesting to note from the programming card (last two pages) that all the inherent-mode instruction codes begin with the hex digits 0, 1, 3, 4, or 5 and all the extended-mode instructions begin with $7, $B, or $F. There are four more instruction modes besides *inherent* and *extended*, but we will explain them as they come up. For now it is enough if you understand that some instructions are complete in one byte while others require additional bytes to specify the operand.

1.5 THE CLOCK AND OTHER PIN FUNCTIONS

Now it is time to deal with the 12 remaining pins on the 6802 package. Then we will be ready to wire up our first microcomputer project.

The clock signal is called E (for enable) and is available at pin 37. The address lines change states about 25 ns after E goes low. Data being written (output) by the processor is applied to the data bus shortly after E goes high. Data being read into the processor is sampled while E is high, although the memory chip may have applied the data to the data bus shortly after E went low, causing a new address to appear on the address bus. Clock timing is illustrated in Fig. 1-4.

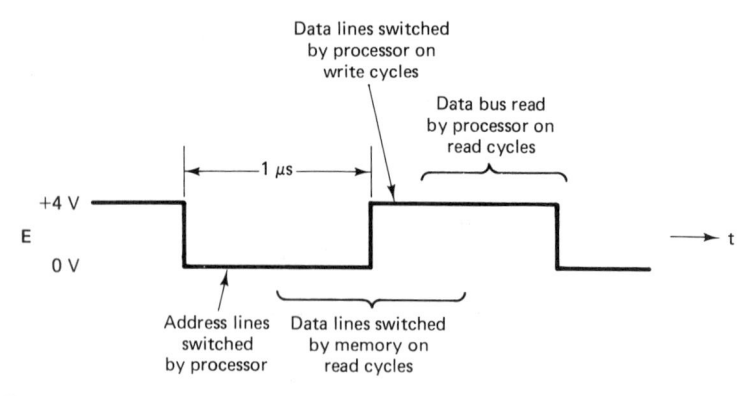

Figure 1-4 Address lines switch after the fall of E. The processor reads (or switches) the data lines after the rise of E.

A **crystal** is connected between XTAL (pin 38) and EXTAL (pin 39) to set the frequency of the clock. The frequency of E will be one-fourth the frequency of the crystal. We use a 2-MHz crystal for most of the projects in this book. This is slower than normal to allow us to see the bus signals on the 'scope more clearly and to make the projects less sensitive to stray wiring capacitance. The usual crystal is 4.0 MHz (an inexpensive 3.58-MHz TV color-burst crystal can be used), and the 68B02 will run at 2 MHz with an 8-MHz crystal for higher-speed computation. A pair of 33-pF capacitors must be connected from pins 38 and 39 to ground to ensure proper oscillation.

$\overline{\text{RESET}}$, pin 40, is brought low (grounded) to stop the processor and pulled high to start running the program from the beginning.

RE (**Read/write-memory Enable**), pin 36, is held high to allow the processor to use its 128 bytes of internal read/write memory. Holding RE low disables the internal memory.

R/$\overline{\text{W}}$ (**Read/Write-not**), pin 34, is an output telling external read/write memory chips whether the processor is reading data from them (high level) or writing data to them (low level).

$\overline{\text{IRQ}}$ (**Interrupt Request not**), pin 4, and $\overline{\text{NMI}}$ (Non-Maskable Interrupt not), pin 6, can interrupt the processor in its current computations and cause it to jump to a new routine when these pins are brought low. We will hold them high until we begin to use the interrupt feature.

$\overline{\text{HALT}}$, pin 2, halts the processor without resetting it when brought low. It can be used to make the processor execute a single instruction at a time. We will hold it high until we need the single-step feature.

MR (**Memory Ready**), pin 3, is an input that can be brought low by an external memory chip that is too slow to have its data ready by the next rise of the E clock. The processor will then wait for the data. We won't be using any slow memories, so we will keep pin 3 tied high.

VMA (**Valid Memory Address**), pin 5, is an output that goes low when

Sec. 1.5   The Clock and Other Pin Functions   **11**

the processor is doing an internal operation and the signals on the address bus are not valid. It will be used to prevent an improper access of memory.

BA (Bus Available), pin 7, is an output which can be used to indicate that the processor is halted, leaving the address and data buses free for use by another system. We will leave this line unconnected.

Figure 1-5 illustrates the 6802 pin functions.

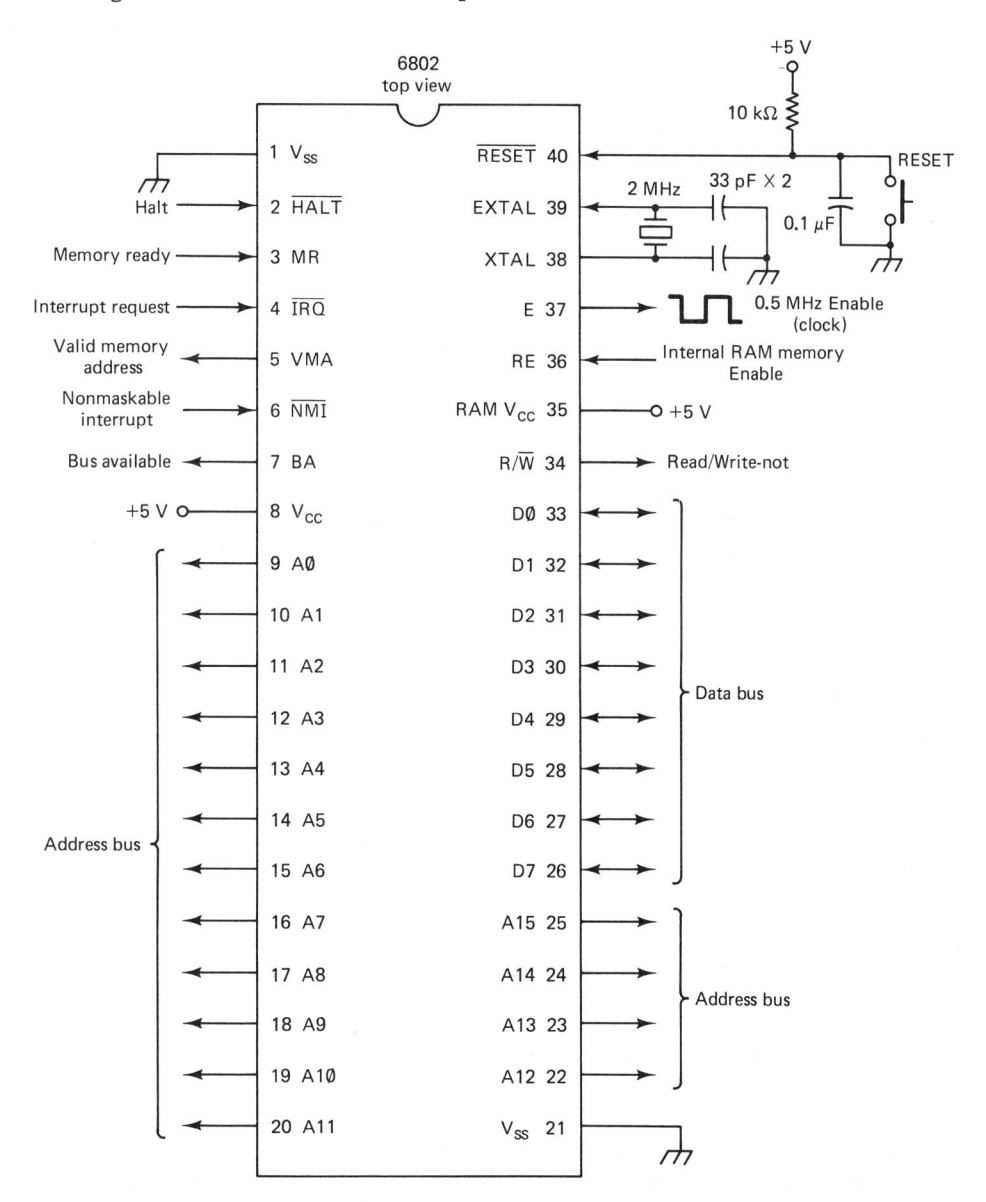

Figure 1-5 Pin functions of the 6802 microprocessor.

1.6 PROJECT ONE: A SINGLE-INSTRUCTION PROGRAM

For our first project we will use an oscilloscope to follow the microprocessor through a single JUMP instruction, executed repetitively. To keep things simple we will not use a memory chip, but will hard-wire the data bus with the binary pattern for the JMP instruction, which is 0111 1110, or $7E. The processor will then read $7E every time it fetches data from the data bus.

We will also have to wire up the V_{CC}, ground, reset, and crystal pins, as shown in Fig. 1-6, but we can leave the address pins unconnected since there is really no memory for them to access.

Program operation. When the RESET pin is grounded and released, the processor will read the data bus, and of course it will find 7E, which it will decode as the JMP instruction. This is an extended-mode instruction, so the processor will increment its program counter and read the data bus twice more to pick up the most-significant and least-significant bytes of the address that it is to jump to. It will read $7E both times, so the program counter will be jumped to address $7E7E, and the binary equivalent of this will appear on the address bus.

At this point the processor will again be expecting an instruction followed by two address bytes, and it will again be told to JMP ($7E) to address $7E7E. The address bus will be sending out $7E7E, $7E7F, and $7E80 to read these three bytes. This is futile in the setup of Fig. 1-6 since there is really no memory chip receiving the address signals, and the data bus is going to read $7E regardless of what address the processor tries to access. The sequence of data on the buses, endlessly repeated, looks like this:

Cycle	Binary Address 15 14 13 12	11 10 9 8	7 6 5 4	3 2 1 0	Binary Data 7 6 5 4	3 2 1 0	Hex Address	Hex Data	Meaning
1	0 1 1 1	1 1 1 0	0 1 1 1	1 1 1 0	0 1 1 1	1 1 1 0	7 E 7 E	7 E	JMP
2	0 1 1 1	1 1 1 0	0 1 1 1	1 1 1 1	0 1 1 1	1 1 1 0	7 E 7 F	7 E	MSB
3	0 1 1 1	1 1 1 0	1 0 0 0	0 0 0 0	0 1 1 1	1 1 1 0	7 E 8 0	7 E	LSB

Project procedure. Set up the system of Fig. 1-6 on an IC breadboard. A microcomputer on a breadboard can grow into an awesome mess, so unless you have quite a bit of experience in digital breadboarding, turn now to Appendix A for some hints on how to avoid breadboard disasters.

Trigger the 'scope from address line A1 (pin 10), external trigger, positive slope, and set the sweep time to 2 μs per division. Observe address line A0 and note that it has a low voltage for the first division (2 μs or one ma-

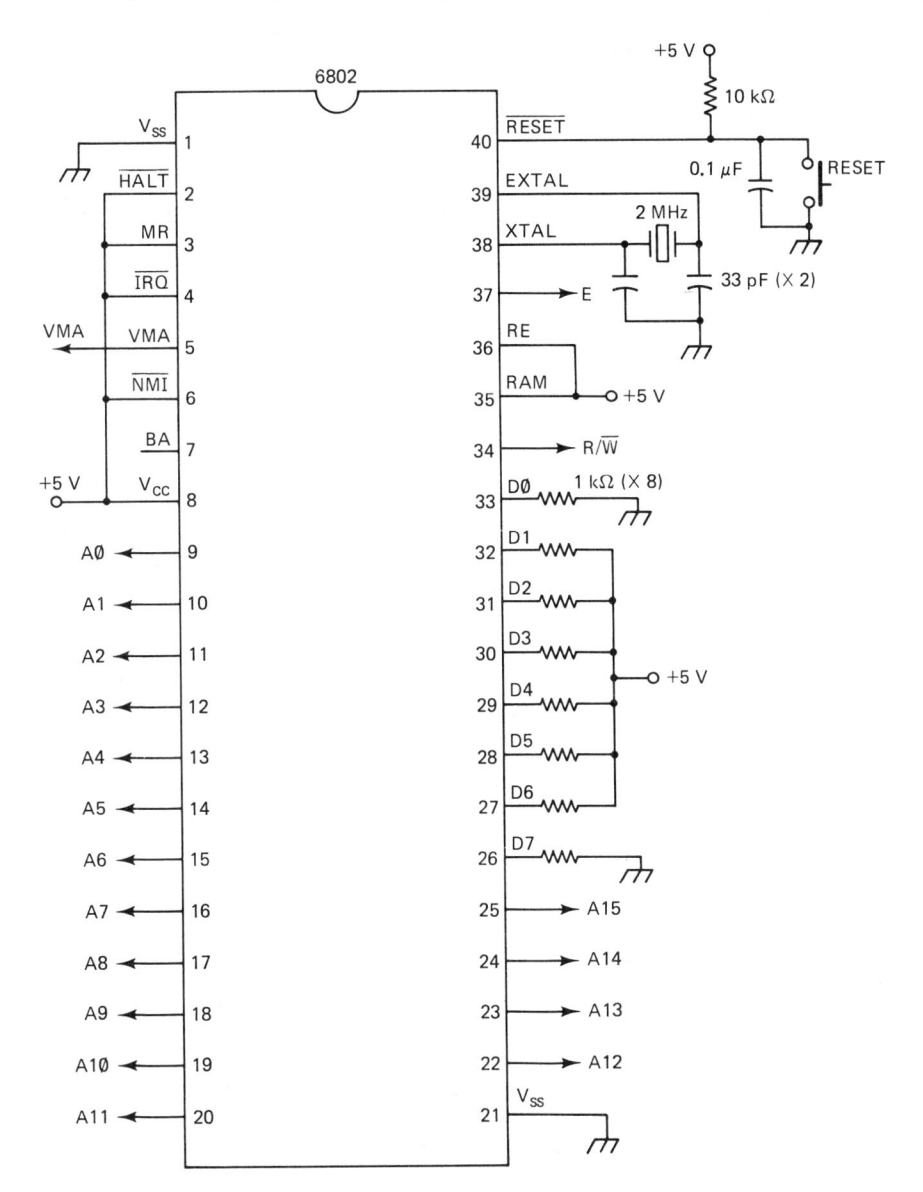

Sec. 1.6 Project One: A Single-Instruction Program 13

Figure 1-6 Project One hardware connections. The processor reads data $7E on each machine cycle.

chine cycle), followed by a division of logic-1 data (about +4 V), and then a division of logic-0 data. This pattern repeats every three divisions, and is predicted in the *binary address 0* column of the table above. Now move the probe to lines A1 through A15 and confirm that the data is as predicted in the table. Data lines D0 through D7 hardly need to be checked, since they are hard-wired, but they are listed to set the stage for the next section, in which the data does change.

Observe the E clock (pin 37) and measure its period (it should be 2 μs). Observe the timing relationship between the fall of E and the transitions of lines A0 through A7. The specs for the 6802 say there is a minimum delay of 20 ns between the fall of E and the address transition. Speed up the sweep and measure the delay in your system.

1.7 A TWO-INSTRUCTION PROGRAM

By wiring certain address lines back to certain data lines, instead of hard-wiring all the data lines, we can cause the data being read from the data bus to change as the address is incremented by the program counter. This will allow us to observe the 6802 as it executes a somewhat more complex loop. Figure 1-7 shows a connection in which line A1 keeps changing line D1 from a logic 0 to a logic 1. The instruction fetched is thus alternately 7E (Jump to a specified address) and 7C (Increment the contents of a specified address).

Internal operations. The programming card (last two pages) shows that the extended-mode increment instruction (7C) requires six machine cycles for its completion. Here is a breakdown of what is happening during each cycle:

1. On the negative half of E, 16 bits are placed on the address bus. On the positive half of E, the processor reads $7C (INC extended) on the data bus.

2. The next higher address is placed on the address bus and the processor reads the MSB of the operand address from the data bus. (The operand is the 8-bit data to be incremented. The operand address is the 16-bit address which contains this data.)

3. The third higher address is placed on the address bus and the processor reads the LSB of the operand address from the data bus.

4. The MSB and LSB are concatenated to form the full operand address, which is placed on the address bus. The processor reads the operand from the data bus and stores it in an internal register.

5. The operand address remains on the address bus, but the VMA line (which is normally high) goes low to indicate that memory is not to be accessed during this machine cycle. The processor increments (adds one to) the operand data in its internal register.

Sec. 1.7 A Two-Instruction Program

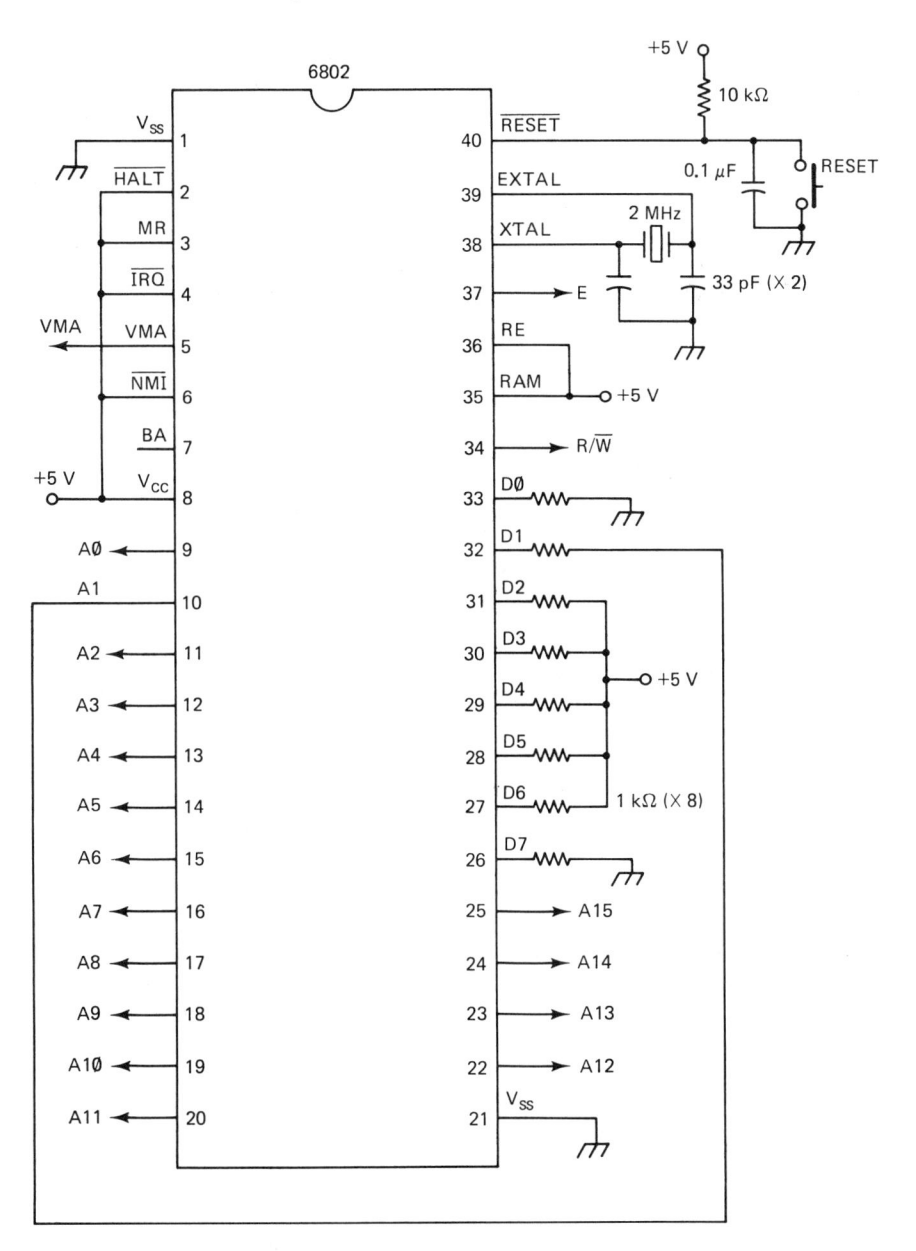

Figure 1-7 Address line A1 changes the data-bus word from $7E to $7C, putting the processor in a two-instruction loop.

6. The operand address remains on the address bus and VMA goes high. R/$\overline{\text{W}}$ goes low to indicate that the processor is writing data to memory. The incremented operand data is placed on the data bus.

For the complete command to function it must, of course, access a readable/writable memory device. The seventh machine cycle will fetch the next instruction code.

The above cycle-by-cycle description is summarized for each 6802 instruction in Appendix C.

Project procedure. Set up the system of Fig. 1-7. The 1-kΩ resistors on the data lines pull them high or low on data-read cycles, while allowing them to output either level on write cycles. Only D$\emptyset$ outputs a different level than its input level in this setup. Trigger your 'scope from line A7, negative slope. Set the sweep speed to 5 μs/div and determine the number of 2-μs machine cycles it takes to complete a program loop. The D$\emptyset$, VMA, or R/$\overline{\text{W}}$ lines are good ones to check to observe the repetition rate.

Switch to 2 μs/div and fill in the chart on page 17 with the binary data for each machine cycle on lines VMA, R/$\overline{\text{W}}$, A$\emptyset$-A15, and D$\emptyset$-D7. You may notice that the "high" logic levels may be as low as +3.5 V on some lines and that some lows are as high as 0.4 V. This is due to the loading of the 1-kΩ resistors, but it presents no problem. The processor reads anything over +2.0 V as a logic 1 and anything under +0.8 V as a logic $\emptyset$. Change the binary data to hex representation and interpret the meaning of each data byte.

D$\emptyset$ switches only as a result of a processor write to the data bus. Remember that the write data is switched after the rise of E, and is thus present only during the last half of the machine cycle. Increase the sweep speed and measure the time from the rise of E to the transition of D$\emptyset$. Also measure the time of the rise and fall of VMA and R/$\overline{\text{W}}$ with respect to the E clock.

1.8 MORE SELF-PROGRAMMED LOOPS

If you want more practice at unraveling microcomputer programs, you may try some of the connections that follow. First, here is a list of the 6802 instructions you may encounter, with their hex codes and the number of bytes and machine cycles required by each. The three-byte instructions are extended-mode, and the letter M is used to designate the memory location specified by the second two bytes. The one-byte instructions are inherent-mode.

Cycle	VMA	R/W	Binary Address 15 14 13 12 11 10 9 8 7 6 5 4 3 2 1 0	Binary Data 7 6 5 4 3 2 1 0	Hex Address	Hex Data	Meaning
1							
2							
3							
4							
5							
6							
7							
8							
9							
10							
11							
12							
13							
14							
15							

Op Code	Hex Code	Bytes	Cycles	Operation
ASL	78	3	6	Shift bits of M left one place, 0 entering rightmost bit
CLR	7F	3	6	Clear contents of M to zero
CLRA	4F	1	2	Clear internal register accumulator A to zero
CLRB	5F	1	2	Clear internal register accumulator B to zero
DEC	7A	3	6	Decrement (decrease by 1) contents of M
INC	7C	3	6	Increment (increase by 1) contents of M
INX	08	1	4	Increment internal 16-bit register X by 1
JMP	7E	3	3	Jump program counter to address M
RTI	3B	1	10	Return from interrupt (details later)
TST	7D	3	6	Test M to see if it contains zero (all bits 0)

First, try connecting A1 to D0 and A7 to D5 through the 1-kΩ resistors, leaving the other data lines connected for $7E, as in Fig. 1-6. This makes a five-cycle loop with two instructions, one inherent-mode and one extended-mode. We will leave it to you to determine what the instructions are. Trigger on line A7, negative slope. Make a new chart like the one given in the preceding section and record the binary data. Convert to hex and interpret the meaning of the data on each cycle.

A **15-cycle program** with three instructions can be implemented by connecting A1 to D1 and A2 to D2. Trigger on A7, negative slope, to start the 'scope trace at the start of the program.

A 21-cycle program with four instructions can be created by connecting A0 to D1 and A1 to D2 (again, trigger on A7, negative slope). For a real challenge you can run and decipher a 23-cycle program with five instructions (four extended and one inherent) by connecting to A0 to D1, A1 to D0, and A7 to D5 through the 1-kΩ resistors, triggering on A7, negative slope.

You may experiment with other combinations of address lines feeding data lines without fear of damage to the processor, but unless the Jump instruction ($7E) comes up fairly often the program will probably not repeat in a short enough time to be read from the 'scope. Also, if you hit a WAI or SWI instruction, you may halt the processor.

If you don't have a 'scope, you can still get some feeling for what the microprocessor is doing by hard-wiring the data bus with an instruction that permits the program counter to increment through all 65 536 addresses. Figure 1-8 shows the CLRA instruction (clear accumulator A to zero, $4F, or binary 0100 1111) wired to the data bus. This is a two-cycle inherent-mode instruction, so the processor will take 2 × 2 μs, or 4 μs, to implement it and then advance to the next address. The total time to cycle through all 65 536 addresses is thus 4 μs × 65 536, or 0.26 second. An LED on line A15 will thus flash at a rate of 1/0.26, or about four flashes per second. A14 will flash at about 8 Hz, and A13 at 16 Hz. You can wire the data bus for $08 (the four-cycle *Increment Internal Register X* instruction) to slow the flashes to one-half the rate above.

Sec. 1.8   More Self-Programmed Loops

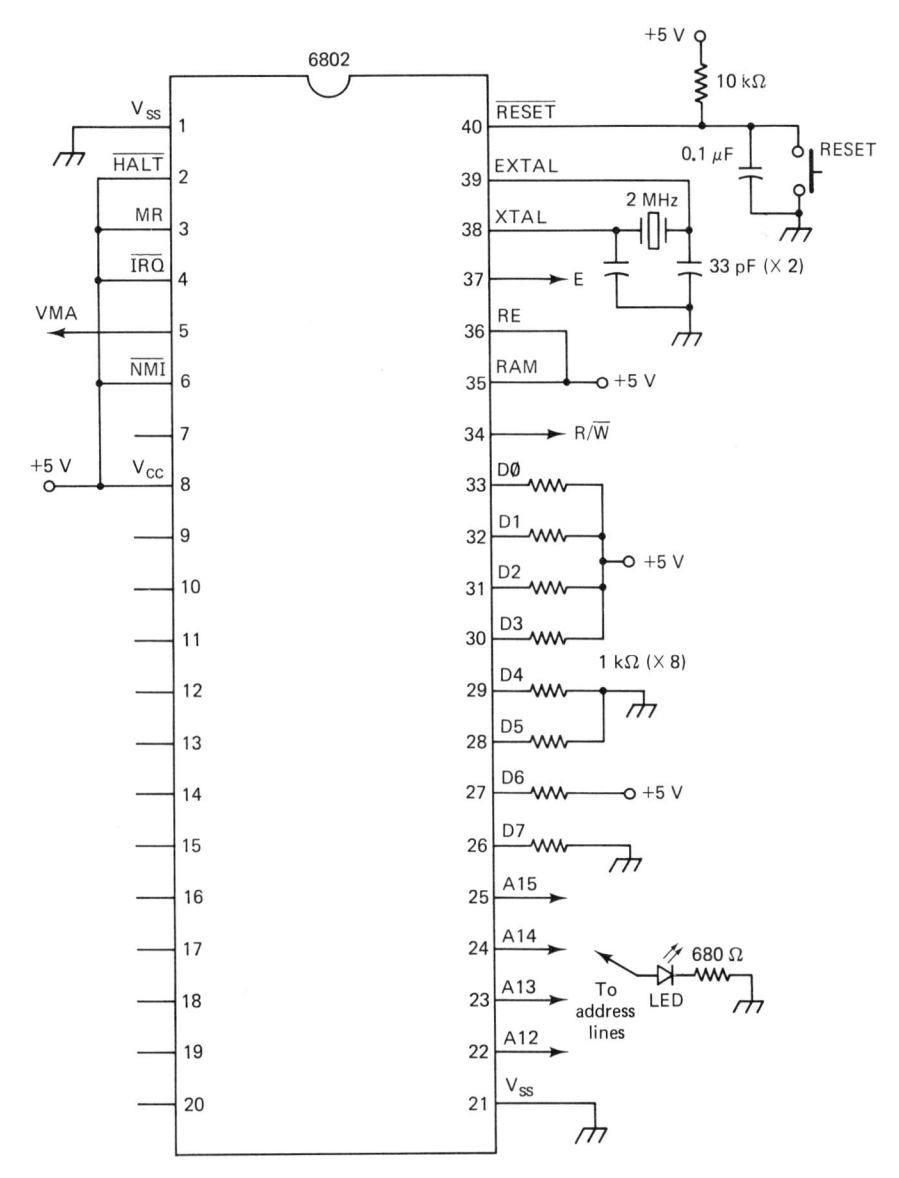

Figure 1-8 The program counter runs through all 65 536 addresses with this connection. The higher-order address lines flash the LED at an observable rate.

1.9 SUMMARY REMARKS

This chapter has presented an intimate look at some of the basic operations performed by a microcomputer. It may be necessary to reassure you that nothing spectacular has been left out. The operations that you have seen thus far really are typical of what computers are doing when they guide rockets to the moon and beat you at chess. There are other internal registers besides the program counter and accumulator A, but they are much the same. There are many other instructions, but none of them are much more impressive than the ones you have already seen. Some of the newer microprocessors, such as the 6809, have an 8-bit unsigned multiply instruction, which some people find impressive, but there are no instructions like "Seek and destroy aliens" or "Isolate opponent's king."

All of the power of computers is due to the patience and cleverness of programmers who are able to string thousands of these idiot-level instructions together to implement useful tasks, and to the incredible speed and reliability of the electronic hardware.

CHAPTER SUMMARY

1. A bit is a binary digit; low or ∅ is about 0.1 V and high or 1 is about +4 V in microcomputer systems. A nibble is 4 bits and can be represented by one hex digit (∅ through F). A byte is 8 bits. A word is the number of bits transferred at a time on the data bus.

2. The 6802 processor uses an 8-bit word and a 16-bit address bus. It can access up to 65 536 addresses, each containing a data word which has one of 256 possible values.

3. Data is stored in memory locations which are accessed, generally sequentially, by the program counter. Each memory location has a unique address, and contains data which may represent any of four types of things:

   - Instruction codes
   - Addresses (only half an address can fit into each location)
   - Numeric data (0 through 255 in decimal or ∅∅ through FF in hex)
   - User codes, such as ASCII or programmer-defined codes

4. The processor assumes the first word it reads to be an instruction code. If that code is inherent-mode, it assumes the next word is another instruction code. If the code is extended-mode, it assumes the next two words to be the MSB and LSB of the operand address.

5. The 6802 E-clock frequency is one-fourth of the crystal frequency. The processor switches the address lines after the fall of E. The processor reads (or switches) the data lines after the rise of E. VMA goes low when the processor is not accessing memory on that cycle. R/$\overline{W}$ goes low on write cycles only.

2

Building an EPROM Memory Programmer

Before we can get our microprocessor to do anything really useful, we will have to connect its address and data buses to a memory chip, and we will have to program that memory with a fairly extensive set of instructions and operands. In this chapter we examine a number of general memory types and take a closer look at the type 2716, which we will be using for program storage in our projects. We will then build a 2716 programmer which we will use for the rest of our projects.

2.1 MEMORY TYPES

Memories may be broadly divided into RAMs, ROMs, and bulk-storage devices. Figure 2-1 illustrates the types available.

RAMs are random-access memories, which means that every word in them can be accessed as quickly as any other word. This is not a good name, since most ROMs are also random-access. The defining feature of the chips we call RAMs is that they can be written to and read from equally as fast. Thus they should be called read/write memories, but "RWMs" doesn't make a good acronym. Almost all present-day RAMs are *volatile*. This means that if the power supply is disconnected, the data in the RAM is lost. Manufacturers are using battery backup and even integrated in-package batteries to overcome the volatility problem. RAMs are generally used for data storage or temporary program storage.

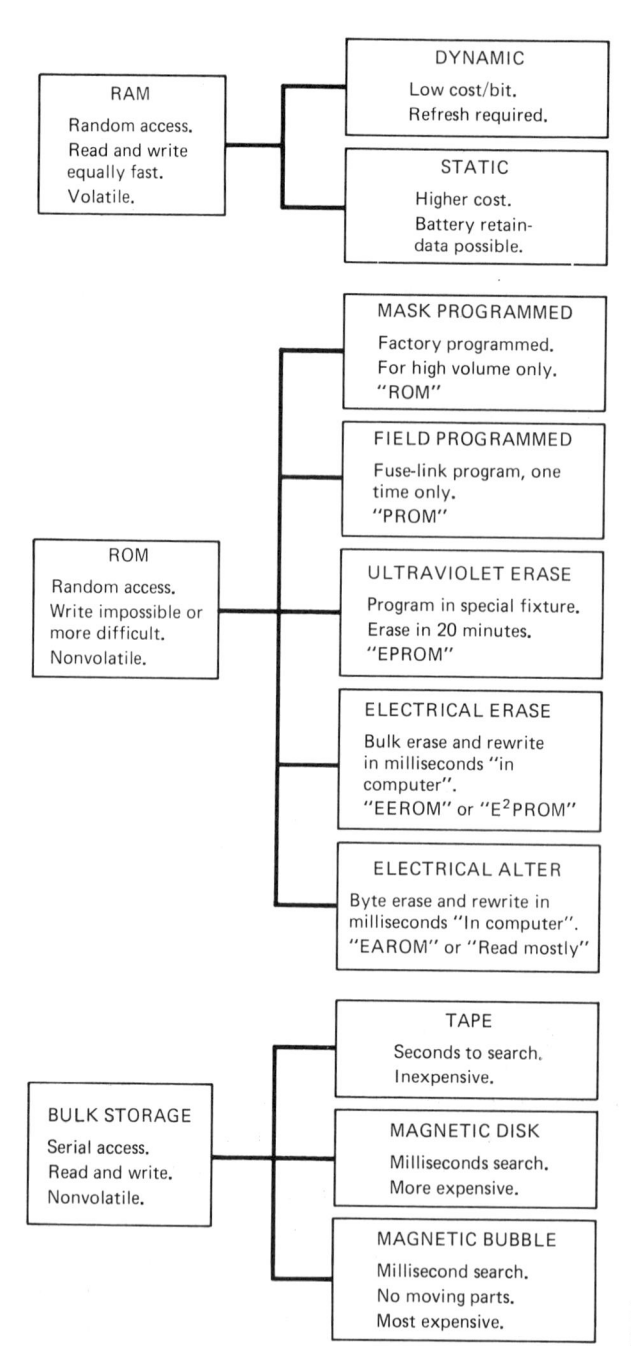

```
RAM                    DYNAMIC
Random access.         Low cost/bit.
Read and write         Refresh required.
equally fast.
Volatile.              STATIC
                       Higher cost.
                       Battery retain-
                       data possible.


                       MASK PROGRAMMED
                       Factory programmed.
                       For high volume only.
                       "ROM"

                       FIELD PROGRAMMED
                       Fuse-link program, one
                       time only.
                       "PROM"

ROM                    ULTRAVIOLET ERASE
Random access.         Program in special fixture.
Write impossible or    Erase in 20 minutes.
more difficult.        "EPROM"
Nonvolatile.
                       ELECTRICAL ERASE
                       Bulk erase and rewrite
                       in milliseconds "in
                       computer".
                       "EEROM" or "E²PROM"

                       ELECTRICAL ALTER
                       Byte erase and rewrite in
                       milliseconds "In computer".
                       "EAROM" or "Read mostly"


                       TAPE
                       Seconds to search.
                       Inexpensive.

BULK STORAGE           MAGNETIC DISK
Serial access.         Milliseconds search.
Read and write.        More expensive.
Nonvolatile.
                       MAGNETIC BUBBLE
                       Millisecond search.
                       No moving parts.
                       Most expensive.
```

Figure 2-1 Common memory types for microcomputer systems.

Sec. 2.1   Memory Types 23

- Static RAMs hold their data intact as long as the supply voltage is present.
- Dynamic RAMs use stored charge to hold their data and must be *refreshed* (read and written back with the same data), typically every 5 ms. Dynamic RAMs can get more memory into fewer chips at a lower price than static RAMs, but the refresh process takes time away from the processor's primary tasks.

ROMs are read-only memories, and are generally used for storage of instructions and data that will not be modified during the running of the program. All ROMs are nonvolatile. Their data remains intact when the supply voltage is removed. Programs stored in ROM are sometimes called *firmware*, and ROMs may be classified according to how firm their data is.

- Mask-programmed ROMs have a permanent program installed during the photomask operation of their manufacture. They are used where 1000 or more chips with the same program are required. The program can never be changed.
- PROMs are field-Programmable Read-Only Memories. They are programmed by special devices which blow tiny fuse links at selected locations in the chip. Once programmed they cannot be changed.
- EPROMs are Erasable and field-Programmable. They are programmed by applying an overvoltage which injects a charge behind a nearly-perfect insulator. They have a window in the top of the package exposing the chip itself. The program is bulk-erased by shining a strong ultraviolet light on the chip. We will use this type for program storage in our projects.
- EEROMs or E^2ROMs are Electrically Erasable, for some types only in bulk, but for some, word by word. The erasing process generally takes much longer than the memory read. They are sometimes called read-mostly memories.

Bulk-storage devices for microcomputers are not random-access, but they are nonvolatile and readable/writable. They permit the inexpensive storage of large quantities of data, but the access time to this data is much slower than it is with RAMs and ROMs.

- Magnetic tape is one form of bulk storage. Microcomputer systems generally use standard cassette tape cartridges. Access to different points on the tape is not automatic, and manual search may take several minutes.
- Floppy disks $5\frac{1}{4}$ inches in diameter can store over 100 kilobytes of data for about $2.50, and are consequently very popular in the microcom-

puter world. Access time to any random data is typically a few tens of milliseconds, and the search is automatic. Quite a bit of mechanics, interface circuitry, and programming is required to get them to work.

- Bubble memories offer many of the features of floppy disks in a system with no moving parts. They also require extensive interface circuitry. They cannot yet store 100 kilobytes in a portable package for $2.50, however.

2.2 THE TRI-STATE DATA BUS

In a real microcomputer system, the processor will be exchanging data with one or more RAMs, ROMs, and input/output (I/O) devices, all via the same data bus, as shown in Fig. 2-2. Obviously, only one of these devices can be

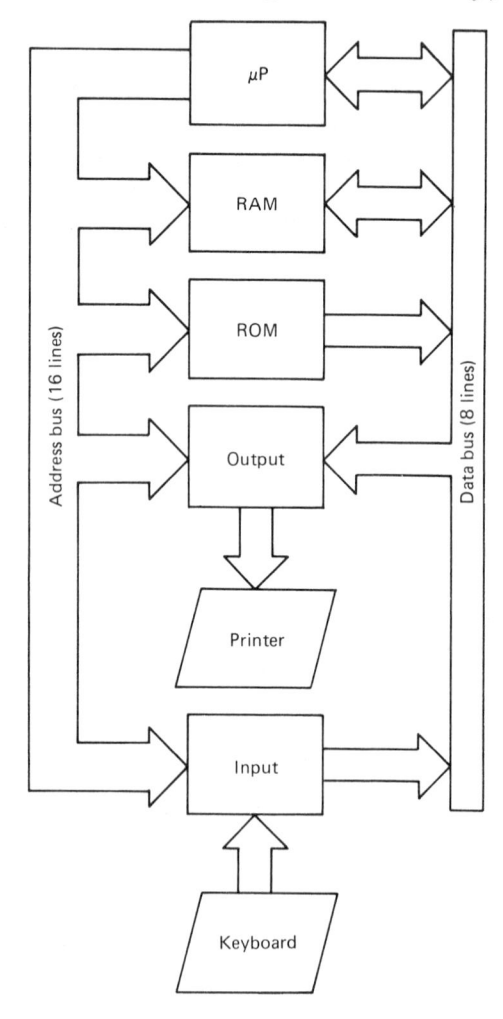

Figure 2-2 Only one device can be writing to the data bus at a time. The others must be reading or in the high-Z (floating) state. The processor does all the writing to the address bus.

allowed to write data onto the bus at a time. If, for example, the RAM tries to output a logic 1 on the D0 while the processor is trying to output a 0 on the same line, we have a *fight for the bus*. The voltage on line D0 may then assume a value that is neither a logic 1 nor 0 (between +0.8 and 2.0 V), with unpredictable results.

To prevent a fight for the bus, all logic pins connected to the microcomputer data bus must either be input-only or tri-state output. Input-only devices read data from the bus, presenting a relatively high impedance to it. An example would be an output-port chip which reads the data bus and outputs the data read to an external device, such as a printer.

A tri-state device can output a logic 0 or a logic 1 if its output is enabled. If its output is disabled, it presents a high impedance, like an input-only device. This third state is called the high-Z or floating state, and it permits another device to output data to the bus. Whether the first chip actually reads the data on the bus or not depends on whether the chip has a read function and whether this function is enabled. Tri-state devices permit the data bus to be *bidirectional*; that is, data can be sent from chip A to chip B or from chip B to chip A.

2.3 CHIP SELECT BY ADDRESS DECODING

The EPROM chip that we will be using for program storage can hold 2048 eight-bit words. Eleven address lines are required to form 2048 different combinations, since $2^{11} = 2048$. The 6802 has 16 address lines, so five lines

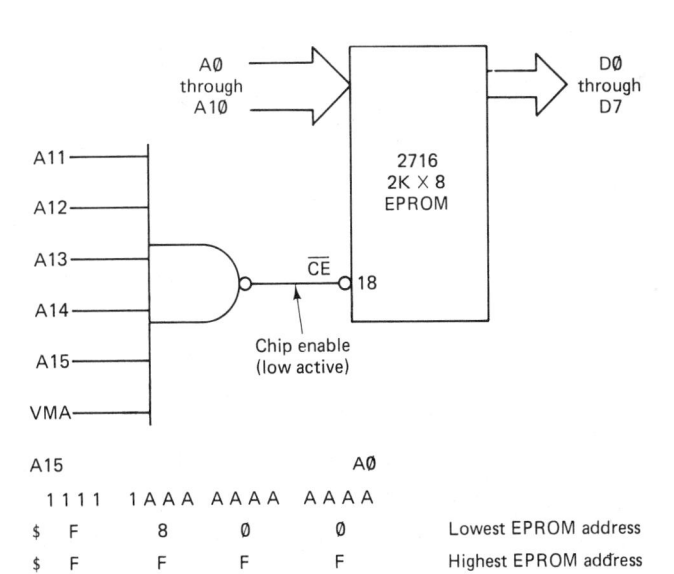

Figure 2-3 The 2-K EPROM is selected by *high* levels on the five most-significant address lines, and occupies the address space from $F800 to $FFFF.

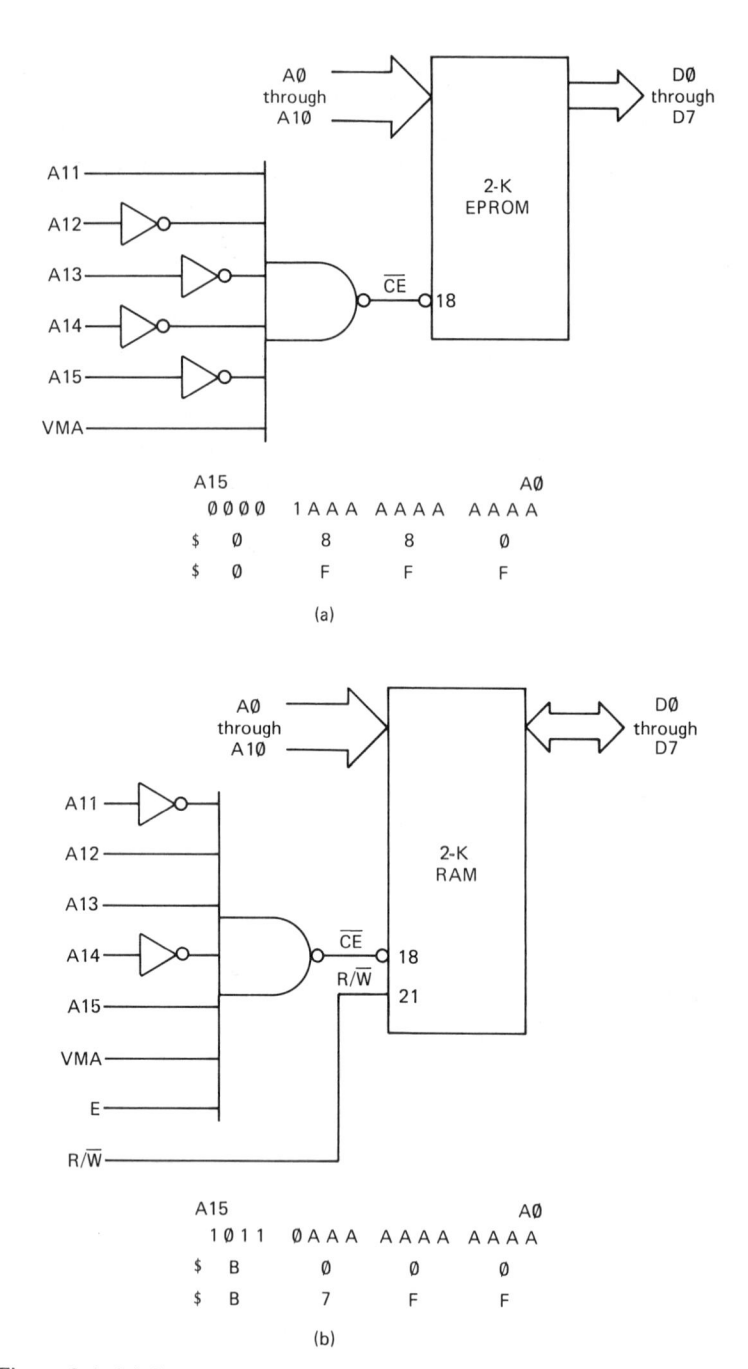

Figure 2-4 (a) Inverting selected address lines places the memory at a different 2-K block in the processor's 64-K addressing range. (b) RAMs require an E-clock input and a separate Read/Write-not input to prevent false writes.

(A11 through A15) are not required for address selection. We may use any or all of these lines for chip selection, that is, for determining whether or not we are accessing the EPROM.

Figure 2-3 shows how a six-input NAND gate selects the EPROM for all addresses in which A11 through A15 are high. This is the 2-K block from $F800 to $FFFF. (In microcomputing a "K" is 1024 words.) Notice that the low-order 11 address lines are used to select locations within the 2-K block.

Since there are five address lines used for chip decoding, it would be possible to select one from a total of 2^5 or 32 different devices, each device having 2 K locations. Figure 2-4(a) and (b) shows decoding for the 2-K blocks from $0800 to $0FFF, and from $B000 to $B7FF, respectively.

Notice that the VMA line from the processor has been ANDed into the chip-select logic to prevent the memories from being accessed while the processor is performing an internal operation.

In Fig. 2-4(b) the memory is a RAM, so the processor's Read/Write-not line is connected to control whether the processor is reading from the memory or writing data to the memory via the bus. The *E*-clock is also connected to prevent a spurious write to the RAM while the address lines are in transition. A write cannot occur until the second half of the *E* cycle.

2.4 THE 2716 EPROM

This popular EPROM is available for about $3.50 at the time of this writing. Check the back pages of the electronic and computer magazines for the best mail-order prices, but avoid any "deals" on parts that are not guaranteed or are listed as "no chance to test." Strangely enough, there are two very different EPROMs sold under the designation 2716. The one we want operates from a single +5-V supply. The other type requires multiple supplies—be sure you don't order this type by mistake.

The 2716 comes in a 24-pin package, as shown in Fig. 2-5. Eleven of these pins are address inputs, eight are tri-state data input/ouput lines and two are devoted to the +5-V supply and ground. Of the remaining three pins, two are low-active *enable* inputs and one supplies the overvoltage (+25-V) used in programming the chip.

Memory read. Pin 18 ($\overline{CE}$ or chip enable, low) is used to select the chip among other devices, as shown in Fig. 2-4. With $\overline{CE}$ high the 2716 cannot be read and requires about 10 mA from V_{CC}, compared to typically 60 mA with $\overline{CE}$ low.

Pin 20 ($\overline{OE}$ or output enable, low) can be used to place the data outputs in their high-impedance (high-Z) states. Placing $\overline{OE}$ high does not decrease the current drain, but the data lines do respond several times faster to $\overline{OE}$

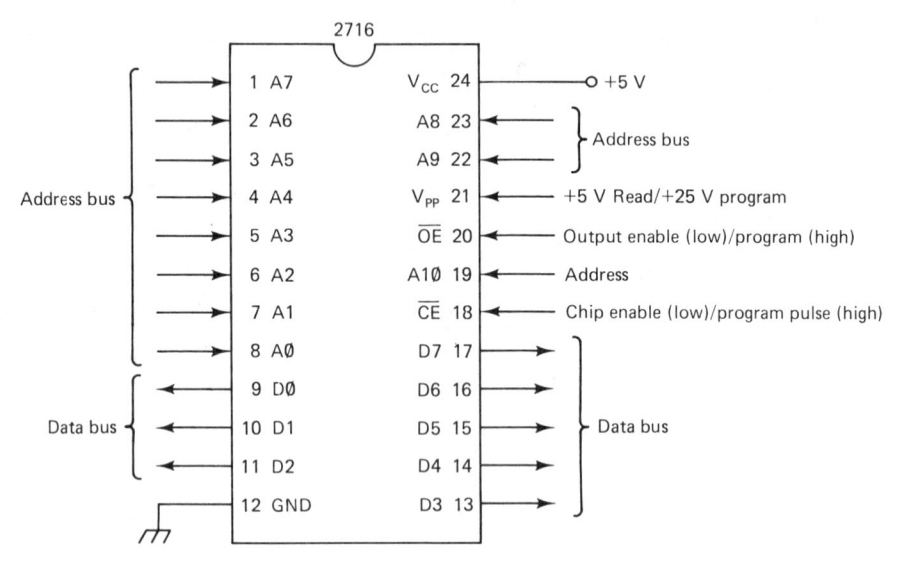

```
                    2716
              ┌──────────┐
         1  A7│          │Vcc  24 ──o +5 V
         2  A6│          │A8   23
         3  A5│          │A9   22     } Address bus
         4  A4│          │Vpp  21 ── +5 V Read/+25 V program
         5  A3│          │OE   20 ── Output enable (low)/program (high)
         6  A2│          │A10  19 ── Address
         7  A1│          │CE   18 ── Chip enable (low)/program pulse (high)
         8  A0│          │D7   17
         9  D0│          │D6   16
        10  D1│          │D5   15     } Data bus
        11  D2│          │D4   14
        12 GND│          │D3   13
              └──────────┘
```

Figure 2-5 Pin functions for the 2716 EPROM.

than to $\overline{CE}$ (120 ns compared to 450 ns for the "slow" versions of the 2716). Normally, pin 20 is tied low.

Pin 21 (V_{PP}) must be held at 5 V during memory read.

Memory programming. The programming mode is entered when pin 21 (V_{PP}, the programming supply) is at +25 V and pin 20 ($\overline{OE}$) is high. *Note that V_{PP} must never be applied without V_{CC} being present.*

To program, data is applied to the data "output" lines, which are in a high-Z state. Voltages below +0.8 V will be interpreted as logic 0 and voltages above +2.0 V as logic 1. Current drain will be less than 10 μA per data line. A +5-V, 50-ms pulse is then applied to pin 18 ($\overline{CE}$, now called PGM) to "burn" the data into the selected address. The current supplied by V_{PP} to pin 21 will rise from 5 mA to 30 mA (maximum) during the programming pulse.

A 2716 can be erased by placing it about 3 cm from a strong ultraviolet source (such as a sunlamp or ultraviolet fluorescent tube) for about 30 minutes. You may already have such a lamp for making printed-circuit boards by the photonegative process. Regular fluorescent lamps and sunlight are not effective substitutes. Ordinary room light will not erase the memory, but you can put a piece of black tape over the window if you're nervous about having your program zapped by a strong light source.

A clean (erased) 2716 has data which is all binary 1-level, or $FF, at every address. Binary 1s can be changed to binary 0s at any time with the programmer, but 0s can be changed back to 1s only by erasing the whole memory. A 2716 can be erased and reprogrammed dozens of times, but it is quite sensitive to misapplied voltages. There is little chance of it surviving if

Sec. 2.5   The EPROM Programmer

you plug it into the socket the wrong way or apply the wrong voltage to a pin.

2.5 THE EPROM PROGRAMMER

This is a true stand-alone programmer. The only thing you have to connect it to is the 117-V wall socket. Programmers that are driven by a computer are much faster to use, but connecting them to the computer can be a major project. For short programs this programmer will do quite nicely, and it will help you firm up your understanding of binary and hex numbers, the address and data buses, and the program counter. If you are a judicious shopper, you should be able to build it, complete with power supply and cabinet, for less than $40.

Programmer operation. Figure 2-6 shows the front panel of the programmer and Fig. 2-8 the interior. The 2716 has 2048 memory locations to which we assign addresses $000 through $7FF. Let us say that we wish to use the programmer to store data $7E in memory location $456. Here is the procedure:

1. Turn the power switch off and insert the 2716 EPROM. *Be sure not to put it in backward.* Never insert or remove the EPROM with the power on. Check that the power plug is connected to the ac line and switch the power on. Never turn the power switch on with the line plug disconnected.
2. Set the high three switches to the binary equivalent of the most-significant address digit (1ØØ for $4 in this case).

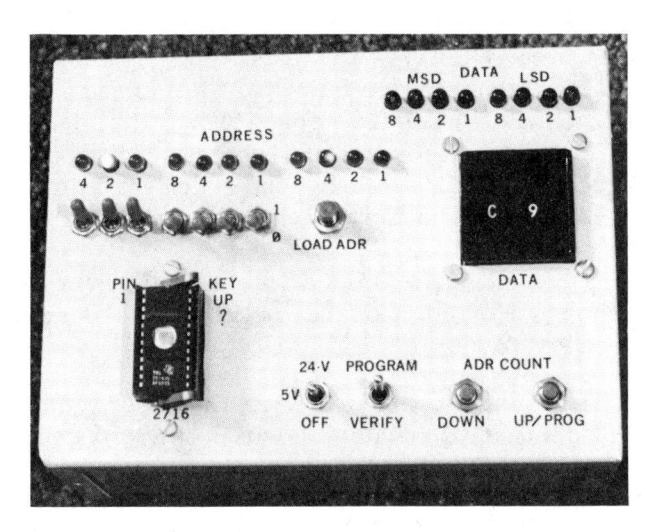

Figure 2-6 The prototype 2716 EPROM programmer.

3. Set the group of four switches to the middle address digit (0101 for $5) and press LOAD ADR.
4. With S3 on VERIFY, press S1 (UP) as needed to count the low four LEDs to the low hex digit (0110 for $6 in this example).
5. Set S3 to PROGRAM.
6. Set the thumbwheel switches to the desired hex digit ($7E in this example).
7. Press S1 (UP/PROGRAM). The data is stored and the address is incremented (to $457 in this case).
8. Note that the low two hex digits count automatically, but the high digit must be switched manually. After programming location $4FF you would otherwise jump to $400, so you must manually set the high three switches to 101 to make it $500.
9. To examine addresses, set S3 to VERIFY and count UP or DOWN with S1 or S2. To make larger jumps in address, use the toggle switches and LOAD ADR.

2.6 THE PROGRAMMER CIRCUITRY

Figure 2-7 shows the complete schematic diagram of the EPROM programmer. The circuitry generates the 50-ms programming pulses, automatically increments to the next address, and provides binary readout of the data and address lines via discrete LEDs.

Debounce. U1 A and B comprise a standard switch-debounce circuit to ensure the generation of a single pulse for each press of S1. (Pushbutton and toggle-switch contacts generally make and break a dozen or more times over a period of a few milliseconds when the switch is operated.)

Normally, pin 6 is high because pin 5 is low, making it impossible to satisfy the AND condition at the input of gate B. When S1 is pressed, pin 1 is pulled low, making pin 3 go high, while pin 5 is pulled high by the internal pull-up resistor. Thus both inputs to gate B (4 and 5) are high and the output (6) goes low. This happens on the first touch of the switch armature to the upper (pin 1) contact. Similarly, the first touch of the switch to the lower contact snaps pin 3 low and pin 6 high.

The switch armature may bounce on and off of either contact with no effect on the output. Of course, it may not bounce *between* the contacts. U1 C and D provide debounce for S2.

Pulse generator. U2 is a one-shot which accepts the positive-going edge from the S1 debounce circuit and generates a 50-ms positive 5-V pulse at output Q in response. The 50-kΩ trimpot adjusts the pulse length, which should be set with the aid of a 'scope to a tolerance of ±5 ms. It is this pulse

Sec. 2.6   The Programmer Circuitry

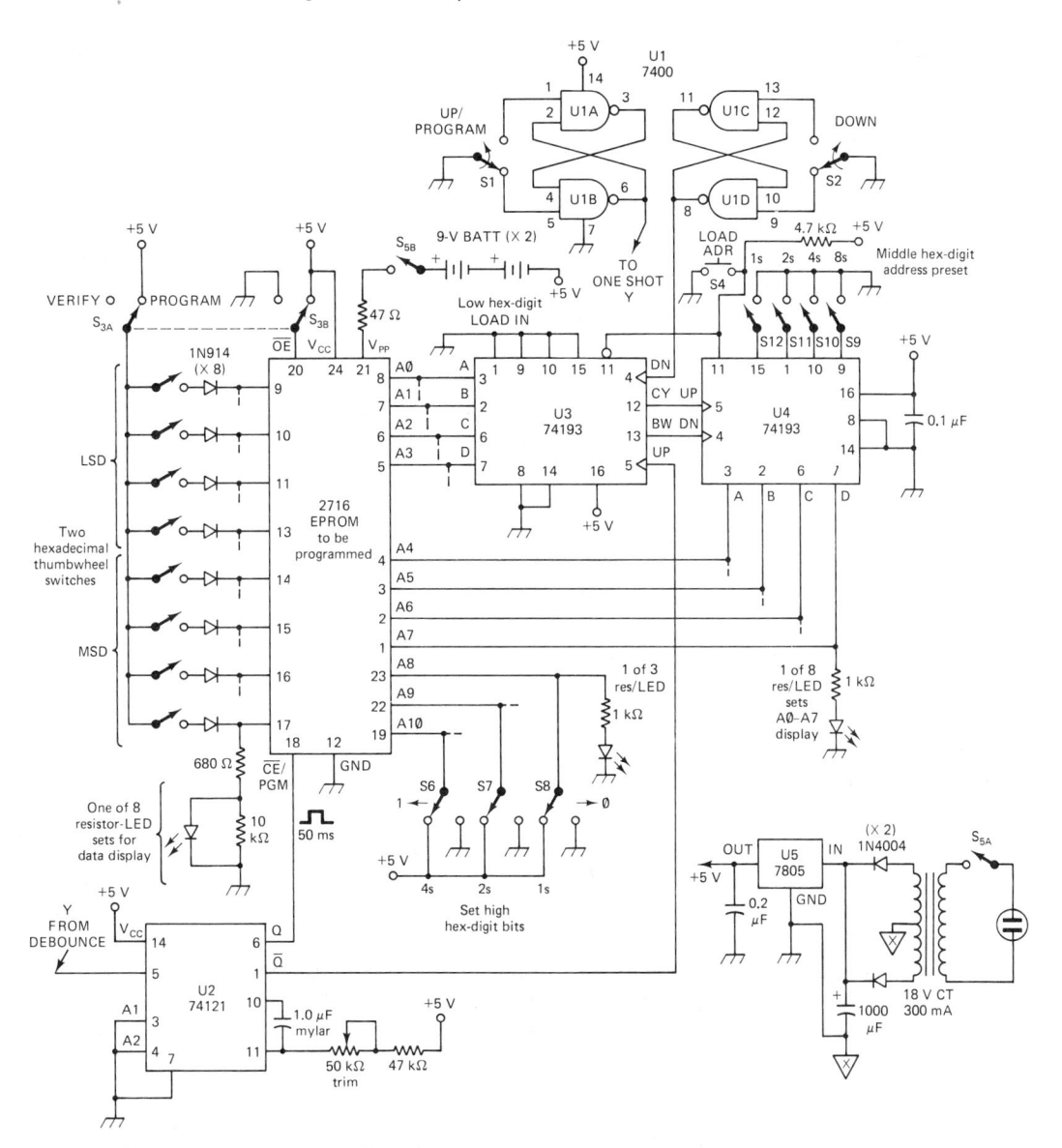

Figure 2-7 Wiring diagram of the 2716 EPROM programmer.

which causes the data on the data bus to be loaded into the address on the address bus of the 2716, provided that the programming voltage is applied to pin 21.

Address counter. U3 is a 4-bit binary couter (16 counts) which increments upon receiving a positive-going edge at pin 5 and decrements upon receiving a positive-going edge at pin 4. The $\bar{Q}$ output of the one-shot provides such an edge for UP count at the *end* of the 50-ms pulse. The S2 debounce provides a positive-going edge for DOWN count when S2 is released. The four binary outputs of this counter feed A0 through A3 of the 2716. The carry and borrow outputs drive the second counter, U4.

U4 continues the binary counting sequence from U3 through four more binary digits, feeding lines A4 through A7 of the 2716. U3 is always set to 0000 by S4 (LOAD ADR), but U4 can be set to any desired count by the four switches on pins 15, 1, 10, and 9. Thus any specific address can be reached with no more than eight presses of S1 or S2.

The highest-order address lines (A8, A9, and A10) are controlled manually by three toggle switches. One manual address change for every 256 automatic changes is felt not to be too unreasonable.

Data is applied to the data bus by two hexadecimal (4-bit binary) thumbwheel switches. Separate toggle switches could be used, but setting them is time consuming and error prone. Sixteen-key pushbuttons are used in more advanced programmers, but this would double the complexity of our project.

The 680-Ω resistors give LED currents of about 5 mA each when the data lines are pulled high by the switches (on program) or the 2716 (on verify). The 10-kΩ resistors in parallel with the LEDs hold the data inputs near 0 V on PROGRAM; the LEDs alone would only pull the inputs down to about 1.2 V. The diodes in series with the data switches prevent the chip's outputs from being shorted together through the switches on the VERIFY function.

2.7 CONSTRUCTION DETAILS

Figures 2-6 and 2-8 show the physical construction of the prototype programmer. This unit was built in a cabinet for permanent use. If you intend to build the development system (Chapter 9) fairly soon, you may prefer to build the programmer on a single 5 inch × 10 inch piece of perforated fiberglass board, since the development system includes a programming function. This construction technique is illustrated in Chapter 7. It would make the project easier to build and disassemble, but the finished product would be less durable.

Components. Few of the components are critical and many substitutions are possible. The ICs may be any of the 74/54, LS, S, or regular TTL series. Any silicon diodes can be used at the data inputs. A *type 340* 5-V regulator can be substituted for the 7805. The 680-Ω, 1-kΩ, and 10-kΩ resistors can be 1.5 times higher or lower if this will let you take advantage of parts on hand.

A few of the components do need special attention. Make sure to get hexadecimal thumbwheel switches. BCD (binary-coded decimal) types count 0—9 and will not work. S1 and S2 are SPDT nonshorting (form-C) pushbutton switches. S3 is a DPDT toggle and S6 through S8 are SPDT toggles.

Sec. 2.7 Construction Details

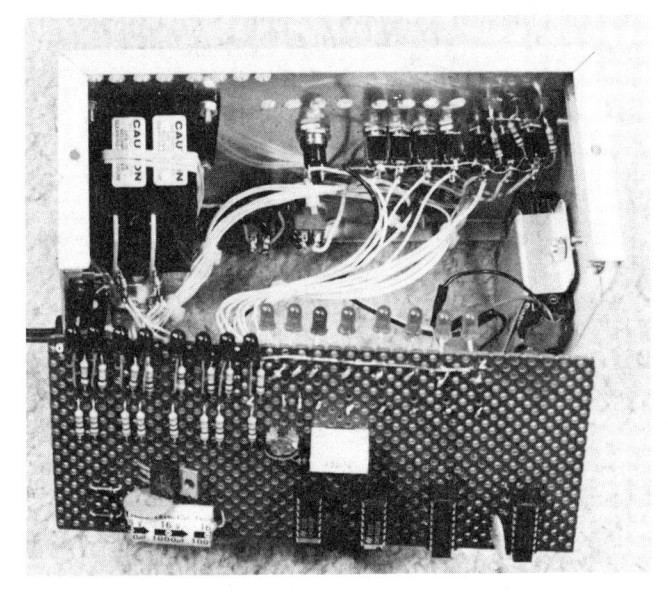

Figure 2-8 Inside the EPROM programmer.

The 1-μF capacitor must be a stable type; do not use electrolytic or disk ceramic.

Component placement and wiring. Mount as many of the components as possible on the board to minimize interconnecting wiring. In the prototype the LEDs were mounted on the board and positioned to fit through holes in the cabinet. The switches and transformer were mounted on the cabinet. Interconnections were made with No. 26 stranded wire, except for V_{CC} and ground, which were done with No. 22. All components and wiring are kept on one half of the cabinet shell; the other half serves only as a cover. A 3-inch × 7-inch × 5-inch minibox was used in a prototype.

A $2\frac{7}{8}$-inch × $6\frac{3}{4}$-inch piece of perfboard in a pair of card slides holds most of the components. Connections between ICs were made with wirewrap. (Be sure to get wirewrap sockets, a hand wrap tool, and the proper wire.) Connections to other components were soldered.

Troubleshooting and calibration. Do not plug in an EPROM until the programmer has been checked and calibrated. Pin 6 of U1 should snap low, then high, as S1 is pushed and released. S2 should affect pin 8 similarly. Check U1 wiring if this is not so.

Pin 6 of U2 should rise for 50 ms each time S1 is released. Using your 'scope on driven (not auto) trigger, positive slope, set this pulse time to exactly 50 ms by adjusting the 50-kΩ trimmer. If you cannot obtain an oscilloscope you may, with some risk, start with the trimmer at maximum resistance and decrease it by 5-kΩ steps until reliable EPROM programming results. Then decrease it 5 kΩ below this value.

U3 pin 3 should change levels each time S1 is released; pin 2 should change every other time, and pin 6 every fourth time. Check for a 50-ms *low* pulse at pin 5, a high level at pin 11, and a low at pin 14 if this is not so. The outputs of U4 (pins 3, 2, 6, and 7) should assume the states set by S9, 10, 11, and 12, respectively, when S4 is pressed.

With S6 through S8 in their 1 positions and S9 through S12 in their ∅ positions press LOAD ADR, and then press DOWN (S2) once. All 11 address LEDs should be on. If any are dim, try the corresponding switch in the opposite position to see if the switch is wired backward. If the LED cannot be made to light, the LED itself is probably wired backward. Set the thumbwheel switches to FF and check that all eight data LEDs light in the PROGRAM position of S3. Check that +23 V appears on pin 21 only, and that +5 V appears on pins 20 and 24 only. Now you may try programming an EPROM.

CHAPTER SUMMARY

1. RAMs are volatile memories used primarily for data storage. They are more correctly called read/write memories.
2. ROMs are nonvolatile, also random-access, and used mainly for permanent program storage.
3. Disks and tape are used for bulk read/write storage but they are slow access (not random access).
4. The third (high-impedance) output state permits many devices to reside on the same bus, and to send or receive data as selected by the processor.
5. The higher-order address lines are commonly decoded to select among several memory and I/O devices. The low-order lines, of course, select memory locations within an individual chip.
6. The 2716 EPROM is a 2-kilobyte (2048-byte) ROM, programmable with a special fixture and erasable by ultraviolet light.

3

Adding the Memory: Lights and Sirens

In this chapter we connect the 6802 processor to the 2716 program memory and run some simple but useful programs. We also encounter two new addressing modes and acquire an introduction to a program-development technique called *flowcharting*.

3.1 THE MEMORY CONNECTION

The basic system connections for the projects in this chapter are shown in Fig. 3-1. Most of the wiring consists of connecting the eight data pins and 11 address pins of the memory to the corresponding pins of the processor. Note that we begin here to use two simplifying techniques for drawing microcomputer schematics. First, the data- and address-bus lines are represented as single heavy lines and split into individual lines only at the IC symbol. Second, the pins are placed around the chip symbols for convenience in drawing the lines, rather than in order as they are on the actual chip.

Partial address decoding. In Section 2.3 we saw that five NAND-gate inputs (A11-A15) were required to select a unique 2-K block of memory addresses for the 2716 EPROM, and that 32 such blocks were available. However, it is not necessary to provide a unique address space for each memory device; it is only necessary to provide a number of blocks equal to or greater than the number of devices the processor will be accessing. Two

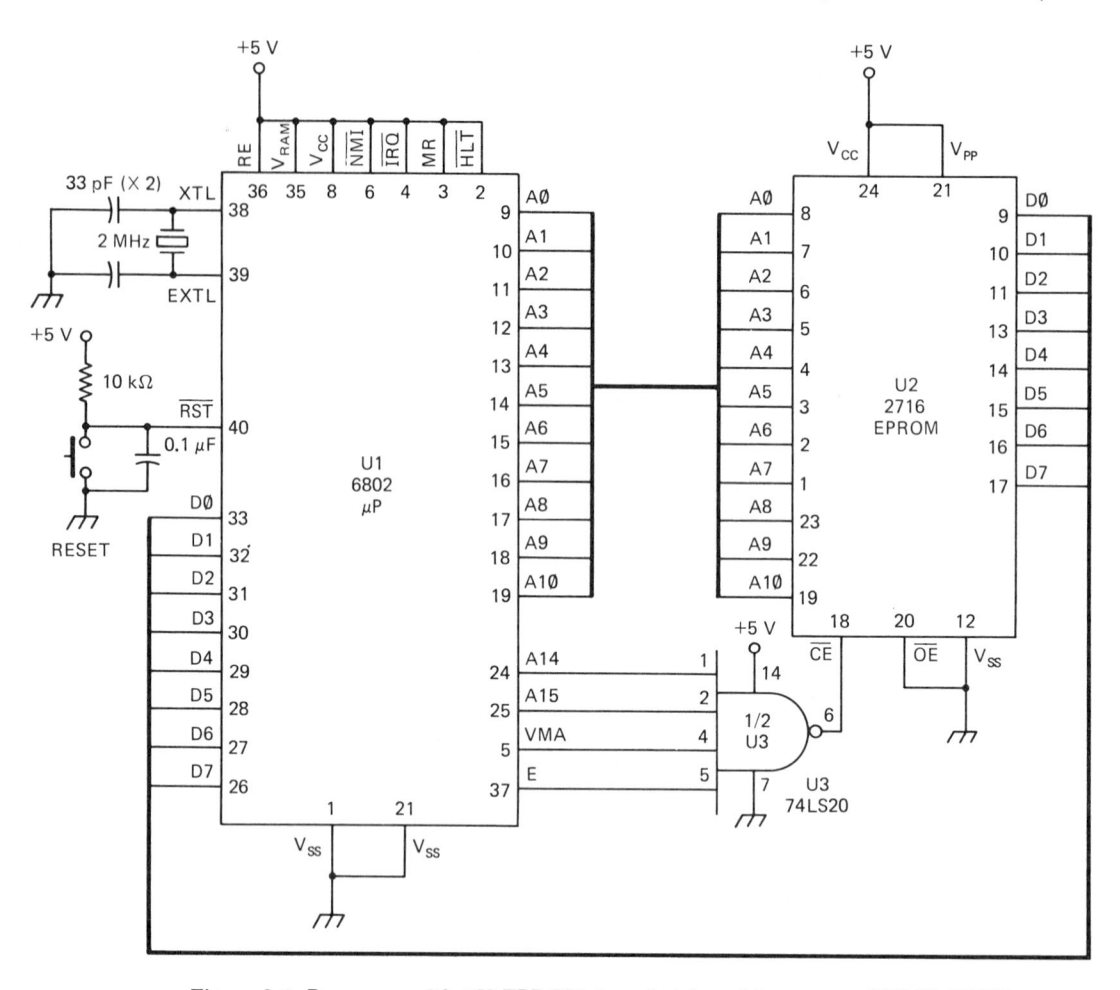

Figure 3-1 Processor with 2K EPROM decoded for address range $F800-FFFF.

NAND-gate inputs at each device (A14 and A15) could select 2^2 or 4 different devices. This is shown in Fig. 3-1.

If A0 through A10 are used for address selection, and A14 through A15 are used for chip selection, the three lines A11-A13 are not used for anything, and they can assume any of 2^3 or 8 different states without affecting the chip or address selection of the EPROM. There are, in fact, eight "mirror images" of each EPROM address, all equally valid. The following table shows how the address lines are decoded for the EPROM, and the eight 2-K ranges at which it can be accessed. The symbol X means "don't care," and "A" means "address select." The A lines are set to all 0s and then to all 1s for each of the eight binary counts of the three X lines.

A15 1 1 X X	A11 X A A A	A7 A A A A	A3 A A A A
C000 to C7FF C800 to CFFF	D000 to D7FF D800 to DFFF	E000 to E7FF E800 to EFFF	F000 to F7FF F800 to FFFF

Internal RAM. The 6802 has 128 bytes of internal RAM (read/write memory) which is fully decoded for addresses $0000 to $007F. This RAM is enabled if pin 36 is high and disabled if pin 36 is grounded. The low 32 bytes of RAM are separately powered from pin 35 (5 V at 8 mA) to permit a battery supply to save critical data during power down.

It is to avoid conflicts with this internal memory device that partial decoding for the EPROM is necessary. A single AND-gate input would have sufficed in this case, providing for two devices with 16 mirrors for the EPROM. However, future projects will use four devices.

3.2 IMMEDIATE-MODE ADDRESSING

Two of the most frequently used microcomputer instructions are *Load Accumulator* from a memory location and *Store Accumulator* in a memory location. There are two accumulators, *A* and *B*, so there are four such instructions in the extended mode.

> LDAA $B6   STAA $B7
> LDAB $F6   STAB $F7

Each of the four requires three bytes. The *loads* require four, and the *stores* require five machine cycles.

Often enough the data to be loaded into the accumulator is a constant value, not to be changed as the program runs. There is, in that case, no reason to keep the data in RAM, and no reason to store it in a separate data table to be accessed by the two operand bytes following the instruction. In fact, the most convenient place to put the operand data, when the data is a constant, is *immediately* after the instruction code.

Immediate-mode instructions are two bytes long. The first byte is the operation code and the second byte *is the operand data*. This is in contrast to the extended mode, in which the two bytes following the op code give the *address* of the operand data. Immediate mode is indicated by a number sign (#) in front of the operand data when writing program mnemonics. To load the data 16 (decimal) into accumulator A, we would write

> LDAA #$10

The machine code for LDAA # is $86 and for LDAB # it is $C6. The in-

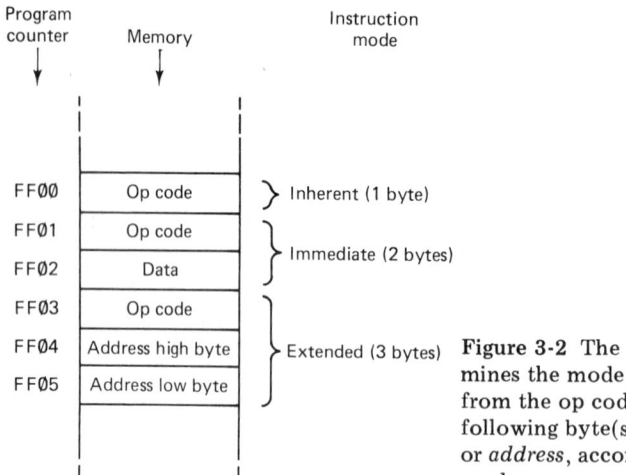

Figure 3-2 The processor determines the mode of each instruction from the op code and interprets the following byte(s) as *op code*, *data*, or *address*, according to instruction mode.

struction above is thus given in machine code by two 8-bit words, expressed in hex as 86 1∅. Figure 3-2 illustrates the inherent, immediate, and extended addressing modes.

There are no Store Immediate instructions because the op code would have to be followed by two operands—one giving the operand data and another giving the address to be written to.

3.3 A DIAGNOSTIC PROGRAM

It is common practice to troubleshoot computer hardware by running a short diagnostic program, which may simply access each memory and I/O device and switch each line of the address and data buses. This section describes an elementary version of such a program.

The reset vector. In order to allow your program to start anywhere in memory, the 6802 has a routine permanently programmed into it which it executes when the $\overline{\text{RESET}}$ pin is brought from low to high. As part of this routine the processor reads two bytes from addresses $FFFE and $FFFF and interprets them, respectively, as the high and low bytes of the address of the start of the program. The processor then fetches what it assumes to be the first instruction of your program from that address.

The test program will start at address $FFF∅, so the high 12 lines will be driven high and the low four lines will be driven low each time the program loops back to start. The program will then store data into RAM location $∅∅∅F, driving all address lines to the *opposite* state, thus assuring that all lines do switch. The data stored will be alternately $FF and $∅∅, forcing

Sec. 3.3 A Diagnostic Program

all data lines to switch. The Store instructions will cause the VMA line to low on the fourth cycle and the R/W̄ line to go low on the fifth cycle of its execution. Here is a listing of the program:

Object Code			Source Code			Comments
Address	Op code	Operand	Label	Mnemonic	Operand	Cycles
FFF0	86	FF	START	LDAA	#$FF	2	Drives A0–A3 low, A4–A15 high (first cycle)
FFF2	B7	00 0F		STAA	RAM	5	Drives D0–D7 high, while driving
FFF5	4F			CLRA		2	A0–A3 high, A4–15 low (seventh cycle)
FFF6	B7	00 0F		STAA	RAM	5	Drives D0–D7 low (fourteenth cycle)
FFF9	7E	FF F0		JMP	START	3	Repeats loop of 17 machine cycles
FFFE	FF	F0		ORGIN			Reset vector

The program listing is in the standard form used in industry. The middle (*source code*) columns are written first. Every line contains a mnemonic (memory aid) abbreviation for the instruction code. An operand is supplied unless the instruction is inherent-mode. Notice that the operands in the source code are usually names descriptive of function rather than numeric addresses. Labels are supplied only in front of instructions that are entry points accessed by some form of Jump instruction.

The *comments* are written next. The program can be written and run without any comments at all, but there is no way anyone else will be able to understand the function and strategy of the routines without comments. You won't be able to figure it out yourself six months after you write it.

Industrial microcomputer programs today typically run to *tens of thousands of words*. They are written by teams, not by individuals. These people have to be able to understand each other's program routines, so it is essential that you make it an ironclad rule to finish the comments before you start to troubleshoot your program.

Good comments explain the end result and strategy of a group of program lines. Comments that simply translate the source code, line by line, are useless. Try to group about three to six lines together and identify a single objective for them as a step toward better comments.

The *object code* is written last. This is the hex representation of what actually appears on the address and data buses. Producing object code from source code is a purely mechanical matter, and computer programs called *assemblers* are normally used to do it. It will be instructive to do it by hand a few times though.

Programming the EPROM with the data from the object-code listing above requires an adjustment for the fact that the processor has 16 address lines, whereas the EPROM has only 11. Thus, when the processor sends out the binary address

$$1111\quad 1111\quad 1111\quad 0000\quad (\$FFF0)$$

the EPROM will pick up

$$111\quad 1111\quad 0000\quad (\$7F0)$$

and the programmer must load address $7F0 to have the processor access it as $FFF0.

Here is a list of processor and corresponding EPROM hex addresses, together with the program size (number of words to end of EPROM) in decimal. The list assumes that the 2716 is decoded for the highest 2-K block of memory in order to hold the reset vector at FFFE and FFFF.

2716 Address	6802 Address	Bytes Left	2716 Address	6802 Address	Bytes Left
0000	F800	2048	0600	FE00	512
0100	F900	1792	0700	FF00	256
0200	FA00	1536	0780	FF80	128
0300	FB00	1280	07C0	FFC0	64
0400	FC00	1024	07F0	FFF0	16
0500	FD00	768	07FE	FFFE	2

Project procedure. Program a 2716 EPROM with the diagnostic-program data at addresses $07F0 through 07FF. (Leave the unspecified bytes at $07FC and $07FD unprogrammed.) Place this EPROM in the system of Fig. 3-1. Observe the E clock on the 'scope and adjust the sweep-time variable to display 20 cycles in the 10 horizontal divisions. Observe each address and data line and VMA and R/$\overline{W}$ to be sure that it transitions to valid logic levels. The data bus may have invalid levels (between 0.8 and 2.0 V) during the first half of some machine cycles if both the EPROM and the processor are in the high-Z state. This causes no problem because the bus is read only during the second half of the cycle.

There is no single bit which switches only at the beginning of the program, but an inspection of the binary addresses will show that A4, A3, and A1 are high together only during the final JMP instruction ($FFFA and $FFFB). The second NAND gate of the 74LS20 can thus be connected as shown in Fig. 3-3 to provide a triggering signal which goes high as the program transitions from address $FFFB to $FFF0. Set up this trigger circuit and verify the address and data states predicted in the program comments for the first and seventh machine cycles. Also check for a low VMA during the sixth and thirteenth cycles and a low R/$\overline{W}$ during the seventh and fourteenth cycles.

Sec. 3.4 The Relative Addressing Mode

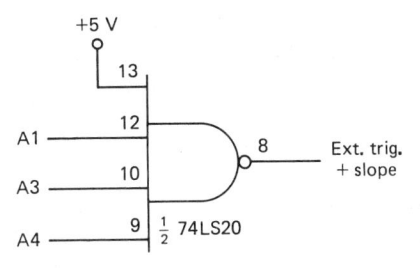

Figure 3-3 A logic gate to provide a unique trigger at the start of the diagnostic program.

3.4 THE RELATIVE ADDRESSING MODE

The feature that distinguishes a computer from a calculator is its ability to branch to one set of instructions or another, depending on the results of certain tests on the data. In the 6802 all of these "test and branch" instructions are in the *relative* addressing mode.

Branch instructions jump the program counter to a new location if the results of the test are positive, but the new location is specified *relative* to the normal program-counter location, rather than in absolute terms. For example, the BEQ command ($27) tests the results of the previous instruction for a zero result. If a zero result is detected, the program counter is advanced by the number of counts given in the second byte (the byte following the op code). This skips past certain instructions to a new set of instructions. If a nonzero result is found, the program counter is simply advanced to the third byte, which is the next instruction op code.

All branch instructions require two bytes and four cycles (except BSR, which takes eight cycles). Forward branching is limited to 127 bytes ($7F) from the following op-code address. Branch operands (second bytes) from $80 to $FF are interpreted as *negative* or back branches, with $FF equaling -1 and $80 equaling -128 (decimal). A table of forward and back branching operands appears on page 100.

A **time-delay routine** is one of the simplest and most commonly encountered applications of the Branch instruction. Here is an example:

Address	Op Code	Operand	Label	Mnemonic	Operand	Cycles	Comments
FF80	B6	40 00		LDAA	INPUT		This routine places a delay of
FF83	7F	00 10		CLR	RAM		(2 μs/cycle) X (13 cycle/
FF86	7C	00 10	LOOP	INC	RAM	6	loop) X (256 loops) or
FF89	27	03		BEQ	DONE	4	6.7 ms between LOAD
FF8B	7E	FF 86		JMP	LOOP	3	and STORE operations
FF8E	B7	60 00	DONE	STAA	OUTPUT		

The loop consists of the three commands INC, BEQ, and JMP. Normally, the INC will cause RAM location $0010 to contain some nonzero value, the BEQ instruction will not detect a zero result, and the program counter will simply advance to the JMP instruction. The JMP sends the program counter back through another INC and BEQ, taking 13 machine cycles each time.

When the Increment finally makes the contents of the RAM location roll around from $FF to $00 (this takes 256 increments), the BEQ will detect a zero and jump the program counter 03 bytes ahead, bypassing the JMP command.

Notice that we wrote *one* loop of the delay routine, but the machine executes that loop 256 times, each time with a different value in RAM location $0010. It may not seem like much in this application, but we have tapped the source of the computer's power. It is the ability to have the machine execute hundreds of times a routine that we have to write only once.

3.5 A PROGRAMMABLE LAMP FLASHER

The X register is a 16-bit register within the 6802 microprocessor. Its primary function will not be explored until the next chapter, but we will begin to make its acquaintance here. It can be incremented or decremeted through 65 536 counts and can be tested for zero with the BEQ command.

The X register can be loaded in the immediate mode, but because it is two bytes long, two bytes are required after the op code to contain the operand data. The second byte is the high-order half and the third byte is the low-order half of the data to be loaded into X.

The X register can be loaded and stored in the extended mode, in which case the second and third bytes of the command are the high- and low-order halves, respectively, of an *address* which we call M. The high-order byte of X is loaded or stored at M. The low-order byte of X is loaded or stored at the next sequential address, $M + 1$.

Here is an example of a Load X, immediate, followed by a Store X, extended, command:

Address	Op Code	Operand	Mnemonic	Operand
FFA0	CE	0A 57	LDX	#0A57
FFA3	FF	00 25	STX	0025

This procedure would cause X to be loaded with $0A57, after which data $0A would be stored into address location $0025 and $57 would be stored into address location $0026.

The schematic for a programmable lamp flasher is given in Fig. 3-4. The second section of the 74LS20 NAND gate is used simply as a driver for

Sec. 3.5   A Programmable Lamp Flasher

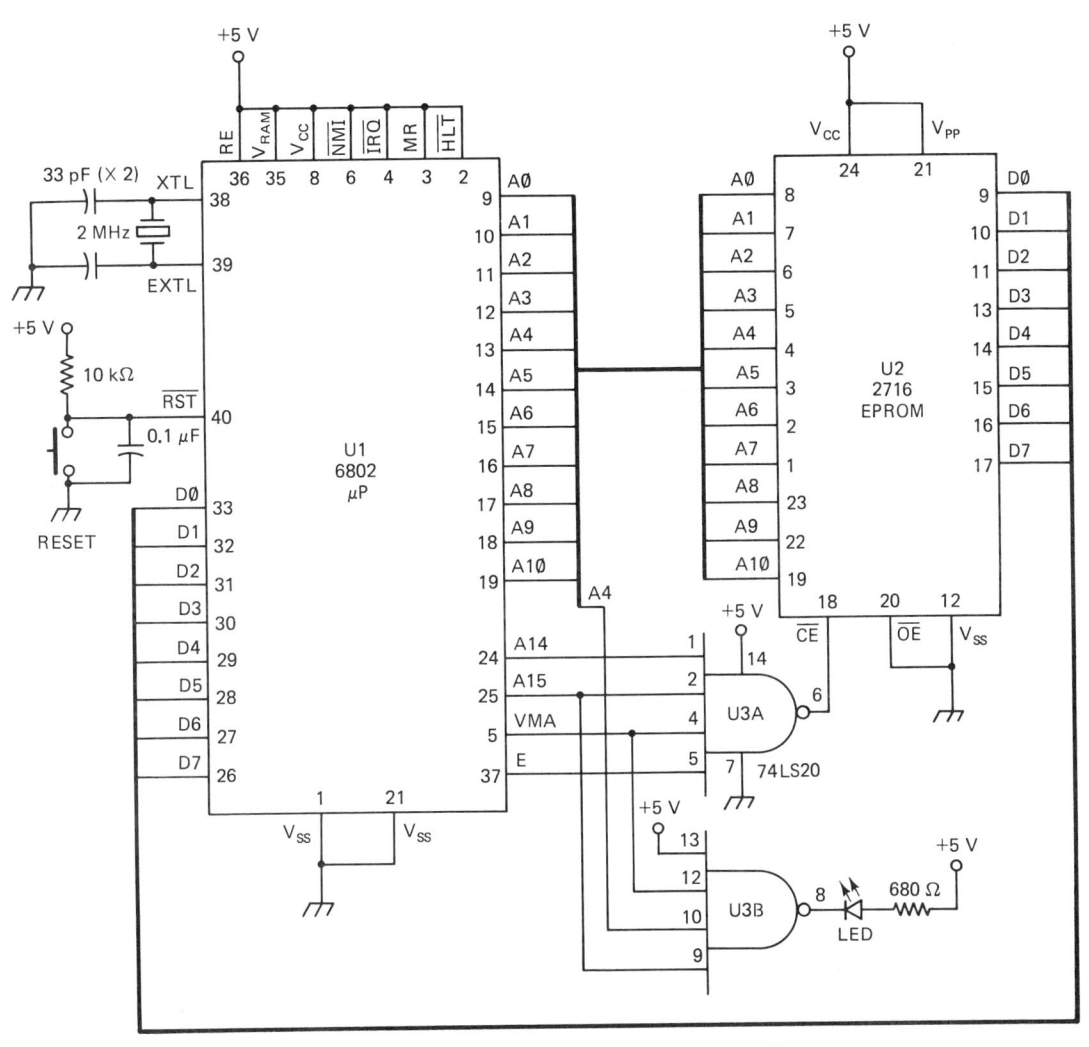

Figure 3-4 Programmable light flasher. The same hardware is used for programmable sirens by replacing the LED with an earphone or speaker.

the LED. The rest of the hardware is identical to the diagnostic system of Fig. 3-1.

The program for the basic lamp flasher is given below. It consists of two delay loops, one which keeps address line A4 high and a second which keeps A4 low. The loops count down the X register to produce longer delays than are possible by counting 8-bit RAM locations. The length of the ON and OFF times can be changed independently simply by changing the immediate values that are loaded into X before the first and second loops, respectively. The maximum delay is about 1.4 seconds in each loop.

Address	Op Code	Operand	Label	Mnemonic	Operand	Cycles	Comments
FFD7	CE	40 00	ON	LDX	#$4000		This loop holds line A4 high,
FFDA	09		LOOP1	DEX		4	turning LED on for 16 384
FFDB	27	03		BEQ	OFF	4	loops or 0.36 second.
FFDD	7E	FF DA		JMP	LOOP 1	3	
FFE0	CE	80 00	OFF	LDS	#$8000		This loop is twice as long, and
FFE3	09		LOOP2	DEX			holds A4 low, turning LED
FFE4	27	03		BEQ	GOON		off.
FFE6	7E	FF E3		JMP	LOOP 2		
FFE9	7E	FF D7	GOON	JMP	ON		Go back to first loop.

3.6 FLOWCHARTING AND A POLICE SIREN

Flowcharting. If you are experienced at reading schematic diagrams, you know that they can be "scanned" rather quickly for an overview of the system operation, and then analyzed in great detail for troubleshooting a particular part of the circuit. Nothing like this "zoom lens" view is possible with computer program listings. You usually have to go through a program line by line to gain an understanding of what it is doing.

Flowcharts, however, do provide a kind of bird's-eye view of a program. In addition, flowcharts can be made pretty nearly machine independent by the use of generalized terms instead of specific instruction mnemonics. They thus provide a good means for starting a new program, starting to learn an existing program, or translating a program from one machine's language (instruction set) to another's.

Figure 3-5 shows a flowchart for the *Police Siren* program. In flowcharting, circles are used for beginning and end points, rectangles are used for data operations, and diamonds are used for decision or branch points. It is a good idea to label the destination of each branch and *use that same label* when writing the source code.

Program description. This program produces a tone that sweeps from a low to a high audio frequency in the familiar "whooping" manner of a police siren. This is done by establishing delay loops to switch an address line high and low at an audio rate (approximately 1 ms in each state), with a decrement instruction used to decrease the delays (increase the audio frequency) after each audio cycle. Accumulator A is used to hold the current number of loops for the delay routine, and accumulator B is counted down to zero to determine the end of each delay. The program is placed in mem-

Sec. 3.6   Flowcharting and a Police Siren   45

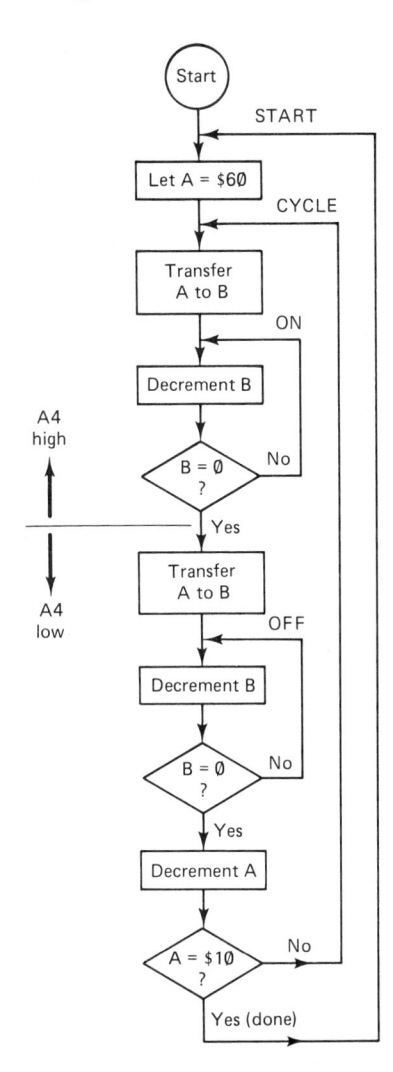

```
                    ┌───────┐
                    │ Start │
                    └───┬───┘          START
                        │        ◄──────────────┐
                        ▼                       │
                ┌──────────────┐                │
                │ Let A = $60  │                │
                └──────┬───────┘   CYCLE        │
                       │       ◄────────────┐   │
                       ▼                    │   │
                ┌──────────────┐            │   │
                │  Transfer    │            │   │
                │   A to B     │            │   │
                └──────┬───────┘     ON     │   │
                       │        ◄──────┐    │   │
                       ▼               │    │   │
                ┌──────────────┐       │    │   │
  A4            │  Decrement B │       │    │   │
  high          └──────┬───────┘       │    │   │
   ▲                   │               │    │   │
   │                   ▼               │    │   │
   │                 ╱     ╲   No      │    │   │
   │                ╱ B = 0 ╲──────────┘    │   │
   │                ╲   ?   ╱              │   │
   │                 ╲     ╱               │   │
   ▼                   │ Yes               │   │
  A4                   ▼                   │   │
  low           ┌──────────────┐           │   │
                │  Transfer    │           │   │
                │   A to B     │           │   │
                └──────┬───────┘  OFF      │   │
                       │      ◄─────────┐  │   │
                       ▼                │  │   │
                ┌──────────────┐        │  │   │
                │  Decrement B │        │  │   │
                └──────┬───────┘        │  │   │
                       │                │  │   │
                       ▼                │  │   │
                     ╱     ╲   No       │  │   │
                    ╱ B = 0 ╲───────────┘  │   │
                    ╲   ?   ╱              │   │
                     ╲     ╱               │   │
                       │ Yes               │   │
                       ▼                   │   │
                ┌──────────────┐           │   │
                │ Decrement A  │           │   │
                └──────┬───────┘           │   │
                       │                   │   │
                       ▼                   │   │
                     ╱     ╲   No          │   │
                    ╱A = $10╲──────────────┘   │
                    ╲   ?   ╱                  │
                     ╲     ╱                   │
                       │ Yes (done)            │
                       └───────────────────────┘
```

Figure 3-5 The *Police Siren* program consists of two delay loops, with the value in accumulator A causing progressively shorter delays (higher frequencies).

ory so that line A4 is high while the first loop is being executed and low while the second loop is being executed.

Accumulator A establishes an initial delay of 96 ($60) loops for each half of the audio cycle. Accumulator B is counted down from this value to zero with line A4 high (addresses $FFDX). When B = 0 a similar loop is entered with A4 low (address $FFEX). Accumulator A is then decremented, so the next pair of loops will have a shorter delay (higher frequency). The last decision diamond checks to see if the delay has been reduced to 16 ($10) loops, and restores it to $60 loops if so.

Here are the object code, source code, and comments for the *Police Siren* program:

Address	Object Code	Label	Mnemonic	Operand	Cycles	Comments
						Police Siren
FFD7	86 60	START	LDAA	#$60		Start delay with 96 loops.
FFD9	16	CYCLE	TAB			Count down via accumulator B.
FFDA	5A	ON	DECB		2	(2 µs/cycle) (9 cycles/loop)
FFDB	27 03		BEQ	SWITCH	4	(96 loops) = 1.7 ms/half-cycle;
FFDD	7E FF DA		JMP	ON	3	2890 Hz, minimum frequency
FFE0	16	SWITCH	TAB			A4 low in first loop.
FFE1	5A	OFF	DECB			A4 high in second loop.
FFE2	27 03		BEQ	NEWF		
FFE4	7E FF E1		JMP	OFF		
FFE7	4A	NEWF	DECA			Reduce delay to minimum of
FFE8	81 10		CMPA	#$10		(2 µs/cycle) (9 cycles/loop)
FFEA	27 03		BEQ	DONE		(17 loops) = 0.31 ms/half cycle
FFEC	7E FF D9		JMP	CYCLE		or 1634 Hz.
FFEF	7E FF D7	DONE	JMP	START		Then start 96 loops again.
FFFE	FF D7					Reset vector

Project procedure. Set up the system breadboard as shown in Fig. 3-4, but replace the LED with a high-impedance earphone or speaker. Program a 2716 with the object code fom the listing above. Insert the EPROM in the system and press Reset.

3.7 AN AMBULANCE SIREN

The past several years have witnessed a spectacular shift from analog to digital techniques in electronic systems. This is due primarily to two characteristics of digital devices.

First, digital signals possess an integrity which analog signals cannot match. The analog voltage 1.0169 V may be stable only to ±0.1 mV, and the meter used to read it may have an uncertainty of ±0.2 mV, placing the value between 1.0166 and 1.0172 V. In the presence of noise the integrity of the signal may be further deteriorated. The digital signal whose binary representation is 10 0111 1011 1001 will be interpreted as 10169 exactly, unless there is a clear-cut error in the reading of a digit. Digital systems thus tend to be more fixable than analog systems because the signals do not deteriorate by degrees; they are either correct or incorrect.

The second advantage of digital systems, in particular microprocessor systems, is that they are reprogrammable. As long as the basic input/output devices remain the same, simply changing the program-memory chip can change the function of the system. This often makes it possible for automated machinery to adapt to new production models and new safety require-

Sec. 3.7   An Ambulance Siren   47

ments without any hardware changes at all. This project illustrates the second advantage by changing the police siren to an ambulance siren by changing only the EPROM program.

The ambulance siren alternates between low- and medium-pitched tones, switching about twice a second. Figure 3-6 is a flowchart of the program. The 16-bit X register holds the number of cycles to be made at each frequency, and is decremented at the end of each cycle. Accumulator A holds the current delay (number of loops), and accumulator B is counted down to zero to determine when to end the delay for each half-cycle, as in the police siren. This time, however, the delay is switched between 80 ($5∅) and 64 ($4∅) loops, rather than continuously decremented.

The program is listed below without the object code. This will give you a chance to try your hand at assembling source code into object code. A simplified programming card is given in Fig. 3-7. You may use this card for this chapter and the next, by which time you should be ready to graduate to the complete programming card on the last two pages. The correct object code for the ambulance siren is given in Appendix D.

Address	Object Code	Label	Mnemonic	Operand	Cycles	Comments
						*Ambulance Siren
FFD4		START	LDDA	#$4∅		Start delay with 64 loops.
		TONE	LDX	#$∅∅B∅		Make 176 cycles per tone.
		CYCLE	TAB			(2 µs/cycle) (9 cycles/loop)
		ON	DECB		2	(64 loops) = 1.2 ms/half-cycle
			BEQ	SWITCH	4	or 434 Hz, high frequency
			JMP	ON	3	80 loops → 347 Hz, low frequency
		SWITCH	TAB			First loop keeps A4 high.
		OFF	DECB			This loop
			BEQ	LAST?		keeps
			JMP	OFF		A4 low.
		LAST?	DEX			Last cycle?
			BEQ	NEWF		Yes; change frequency.
			JMP	CYCLE		No; make another AF cycle.
		NEWF	CMPA	#$4∅		A set for high frequency?
			BEQ	LOWER		Yes; make delay longer.
			JMP	START		No; start with high frequency
		LOWER	ADDA	#$1∅		Add 16 loops to delay.
			JMP	TONE		Start 176 AF cycles.
FFFE	FF D4					Reset vector

Project procedure. Generate the object code and check that each loop places line A4 in a different state. Program the EPROM and test the ambulance siren.

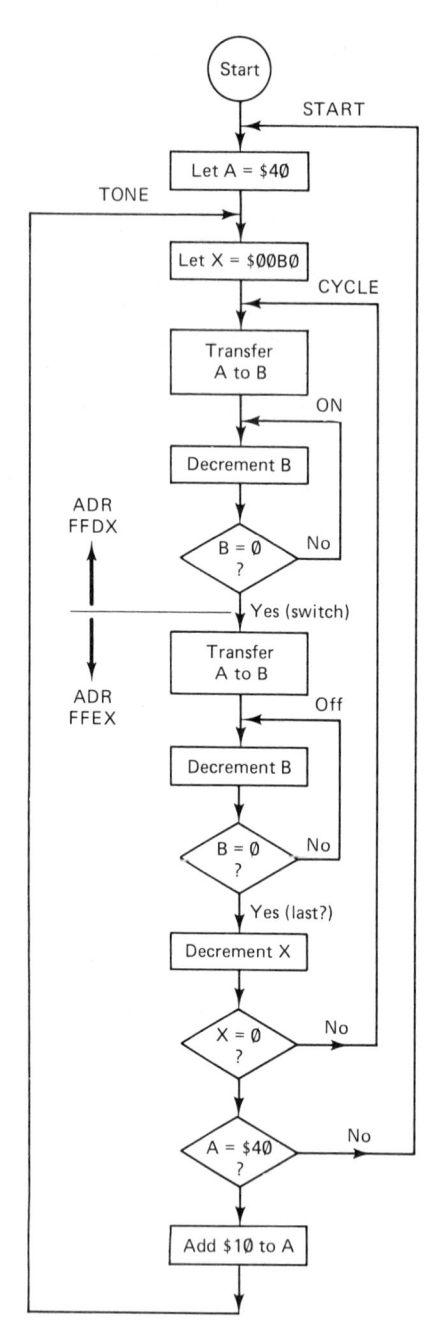

Figure 3-6 The *Ambulance Siren* makes $B0 number of audio cycles with $40 delay loops per half-cycle, then $B0 cycles with delays of $50.

48

ABBREVIATED 6802 INSTRUCTION SET

Operation	Mnemonic	Inherent (1 byte) Opcode	Inherent (1 byte) Cycles	Relative/ Immediate (2 bytes) Opcode	Relative/ Immediate (2 bytes) Cycles	Extend (3 bytes) Opcode	Extend (3 bytes) Cycles	Effects Logic	Z flag
Add	ABA ADDA ADDB	1B	2	8B CB	2 2	BB FB	4 4	$A + B \to A$ $A + M \to A$ $B + M \to B$	✓ ✓ ✓
AND, bit by bit, logic	ANDA ANDB			84 C4	2 2	B4 F4	4 4	$A \cdot M \to A$ $B \cdot M \to B$	✓ ✓
Arithmetic shift left, one position	ASL ASLA ASLB	48 58	2 2			78	6	M A } C 7 ← 0 B] □←□□□□□□□□←0	✓ ✓ ✓
Branch if equal 0	BEQ			27	4			} Senses last instruction affecting Z (zero) flag	
Branch if not equal 0	BNE			26	4				
Clear	CLR CLRA CLRB	4F 5F	2 2			7F	6	$00 \to M$ $00 \to A$ $00 \to B$	1 1 1
Compare (pseudo-subtract)	CMPA CMPB CBA CPX	11	2	81 C1 8C*	2 2 3	B1 F1 BC	4 4 5	$A - M$ $B - M$ } Sets flag bits only $A - B$ $(X_H, X_L) - (M, M+1)$	✓ ✓ ✓ ✓
Decrement	DEC DECA DECB DEX	4A 5A 09	2 2 4			7A	6	$(M-1) \to M$ $(A-1) \to A$ $(B-1) \to B$ $(X-1) \to X$	✓ ✓ ✓ ✓
Increment	INC INCA INCB INX	4C 5C 08	2 2 4			7C	6	$(M+1) \to M$ $(A+1) \to A$ $(B+1) \to B$ $(X+1) \to X$	✓ ✓ ✓ ✓
Jump	JMP					7E	3	byte 2, byte 3, $\to PC_H, PC_L$	
Load	LDAA LDAB LDX			86 C6 CE*	2 2 3	B6 F6 FE	4 4 5	$M \to A$ $M \to B$ $(M, M+1) \to X_H, X_L$	✓ ✓ ✓
Logic shift right	LSR LSRA LSRB	44 54	2 2			74	6	M A } 7 → 0 C B] 0→□□□□□□□□→□	✓ ✓ ✓
Store	STAA STAB STX					B7 F7 FF	5 5 6	$A \to M$ $B \to M$ $(X_H, X_L) \to (M, M+1)$	✓ ✓ ✓
Subtract	SUBA SUBB SBA	10	2	80 C0	2 2	B0 F0	4 4	$A - M \to A$ $B - M \to B$ $A - B \to A$	✓ ✓ ✓
Transfer	TAB TBA	16 17	2 2					$A \to B$ $B \to A$	✓ ✓
Test (pseudo-subtract zero)	TST TSTA TSTB	4D 5D	2 2			7D	6	$M - 0$ $A - 0$ } Sets flag bits only $B - 0$	✓ ✓ ✓

*3 bytes

A, B = accumulator contents; M = memory or immediate-byte contents; X = index register contents; H, L = high, low bytes of 16-bit word; M + 1 = contents of the following memory location; C = carry bit. ✓ indicates set to 1 if result = 0, cleared to 0 if result nonzero.

Figure 3-7 A beginner's programming card for the 6802 processor. The complete card appears on the last two pages.

3.8 THEME AND VARIATIONS: MORE PROGRAM IDEAS

Countless sound patterns can be generated using the techniques of this chapter, although the techniques are certainly primitive compared with what you will learn in chapters to come. If you have the time and feel that it will improve your understanding, try writing your own programs for some of the following tasks. But *don't* skip the flowcharts or the comments to the source code.

The police siren "whoops" a bit rapidly, don't you think? How about modifying it to generate two cycles at each delay count before decrementing A. You may want to output via line A5, keeping it high for the first half and low for the second half of *both* cycles.

Music is too much to hope for with square-wave outputs, but a recognizable tune might be achieved. The tune and rhythm of "Dixie" are a bit complicated, but "Yankee Doodle" is simple enough. Try 100 cycles at the following frequencies using the technique of the ambulance siren, extended to seven tones with no looping back to repeat: 262, 262, 294, 330, 262, 330, and 294 Hz.

Morse code can be generated using a single 400-Hz tone of varied lengths. Use 200 cycles for a dash, 50 cycles for a dot, a dot-length space between parts of a letter and a dash-length space between letters. Spaces are made by simply not switching the address line during the delay.

CHAPTER SUMMARY

1. If n address lines are left unused for either chip selection or addressing, each address is mirrored in 2^n places.
2. Immediate-mode instructions have the operand data following the instruction code in the program memory. This requires one operand byte for instructions referencing the A or B accumulators and two operand bytes for index-register instructions.
3. The reset vector is at addresses $FFFE (high-byte) and $FFFF (low-byte). The starting address to which the machine goes upon *Reset* is stored there.
4. Source code consists of an instruction mnemonic (three or four letters), followed by an *operand* (except for inherent-mode instructions), and preceded by a label if the instruction is referenced by a Jump or Branch.
5. Comments explain the larger purpose of a group of instructions.
6. Object code consists entirely of hexadecimal digits. Each instruction will include four digits for the address of the op code, two for the op

code itself, and none, two, or four for the operand, depending on the instruction.
7. Relative addressing is used only for branch instructions. In this mode a single operand byte following the op code tells the number of bytes to be skipped over if the branch condition is fulfilled.
8. Flowcharts provide a bird's-eye view of program operation. Circles represent start and end points, rectangles represent data operations, and diamonds represent decision blocks (branches).

4

Output Interfaces: Waveform Generators and Number Games

In Chapter 3 we took a single output line from one of the address pins. That was cheating, but it kept things simple. In this chapter we will see the standard technique for outputting digital data, and we will see how digital data words can be converted into analog signals. In addition, we will see how a desktop microcomputer can assist in developing lengthy programs, and we will introduce the powerful and important *indexed* addressing mode.

4.1 THE OUTPUT DATA LATCH

In the course of executing a program dozens or hundreds of instruction codes, address words, and data words flit by on the data bus. Some few of these words may be data destined to be output from the computer to some external device. It is the function of the data latch to catch these particular words at its input (data-bus) side and retain them at its output side until the next output word appears on the data bus. This is illustrated in Fig. 4-1.

The 74LS75 latch is a standard TTL chip; a quad type D flip-flop. It is only 4 bits wide, so it outputs only the low-order nibble of a data word, but that is all we will need for our first two projects in this chapter.

The latch is selected or *enabled* by a pulse at its chip-enable input. This pulse is obtained by decoding the address, VMA, and R/$\overline{\text{W}}$ lines, as was shown for memory selection in Fig. 2-4. The microprocessor clock, E, must also be ANDed into the decoding for outputs, since the processor does not output data on the data bus until the second half of the clock cycle (high E). If

Sec. 4.2 Waveform Generator

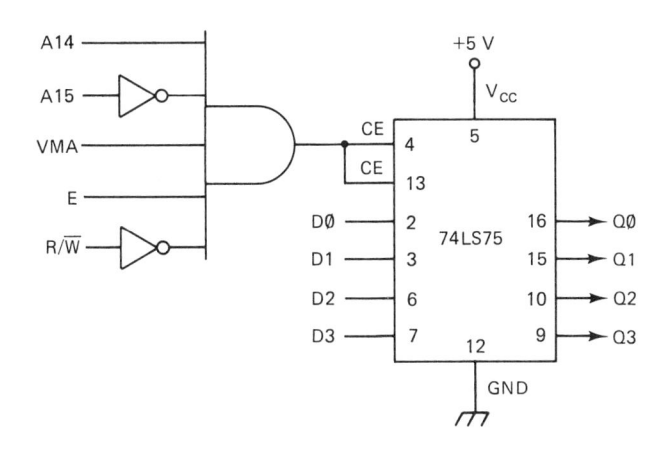

Figure 4-1 The 74LS75 quad latch reads the data bus when E pulses high on a write to the selected address. This data is held at the Q outputs until changed by another write to the latch.

E were not included in the decode logic, the latch would output the previous cycle's data for the first half of the cycle.

The output port thus responds to the accessing of a particular memory location. It is up to the system designer to decode the address lines so that each memory device and output port responds to a *different* set of memory addresses. To decode an output port *uniquely* it would be necessary to use a 16-input AND gate or its equivalent to feed the CE line of the latch. This is seldom done in simple systems because it is only necessary to provide a *distinct block* of addresses for each memory or I/O device.

The highest two address lines will decode four devices; the highest three will decode eight, and simple systems seldom have a total of RAMs, ROMs, and I/O devices exceeding eight.

The latch in Fig. 4-1 is enabled whenever A14 is high and A15 is low. This may be expressed in binary as

$$01XX \quad XXXX \quad XXXX \quad XXXX$$

where X indicates address bits which have no effect on the selection of the latch. The addresses to which the latch responds (setting all Xs to 0, then to 1) are \$4000 to \$7FFF, a total of 2^{14} or 16 384 (decimal) addresses. To minimize confusion we will make it a practice to access I/O devices by their lowest address (all X bits = 0) in our projects.

4.2 A WAVEFORM GENERATOR

A digital-to-analog converter produces a single output voltage level proportional to the binary count on its several digital input lines. An elementary D/A converter is shown in Fig. 4-2. One volt at the "8s" input D3 produces 9.90 mV out, but 1 V at D2 (the 4s digit) produces 4.96 mV out, or just about half as much. D1 and D0 produce one-fourth and one-eight of the

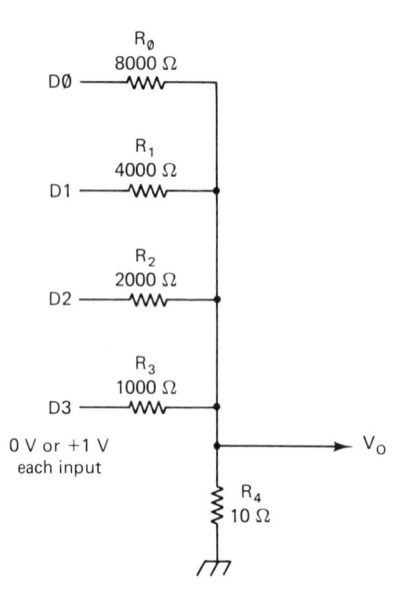

Figure 4-2 A simple D/A converter. Each higher-order data input produces twice the output of the next lower-order data input.

voltage of D3, respectively, corresponding to their weight in the binary number system.

It is necessary that R_4 be very much smaller than the other resistors to minimize changes in the current supplied by one input as the other inputs are turned on. For example, with only D0 ON, V_O is 1.248 mV, and the current supplied by R_ϕ is

$$I_\phi = \frac{V_{IN} - V_O}{R_\phi} = \frac{1\text{ V} - 1.248\text{ mV}}{8\text{ k}\Omega} = 124.8\text{ }\mu\text{A}$$

However, with all four inputs ON, V_O is 18.41 mV and the current supplied by R_ϕ is

$$I_\phi = \frac{V_{IN} - V_O}{R_\phi} = \frac{1\text{ V} - 18.41\text{ mV}}{8\text{ k}\Omega} = 122.7\text{ }\mu\text{A}$$

This error from voltage buildup across R_4 would increase if R_4 were increased to gain a higher V_O.

A complete system for generating 16-step waveforms using a microcomputer, output latch, and D/A converter is shown in Fig. 4-3. The processor and program memory are connected as they were for the projects in Chapter 3, but a 4-bit latch has been added to hold data bits D0 through D3 when address $4000 is accessed. Here is a table showing how the system

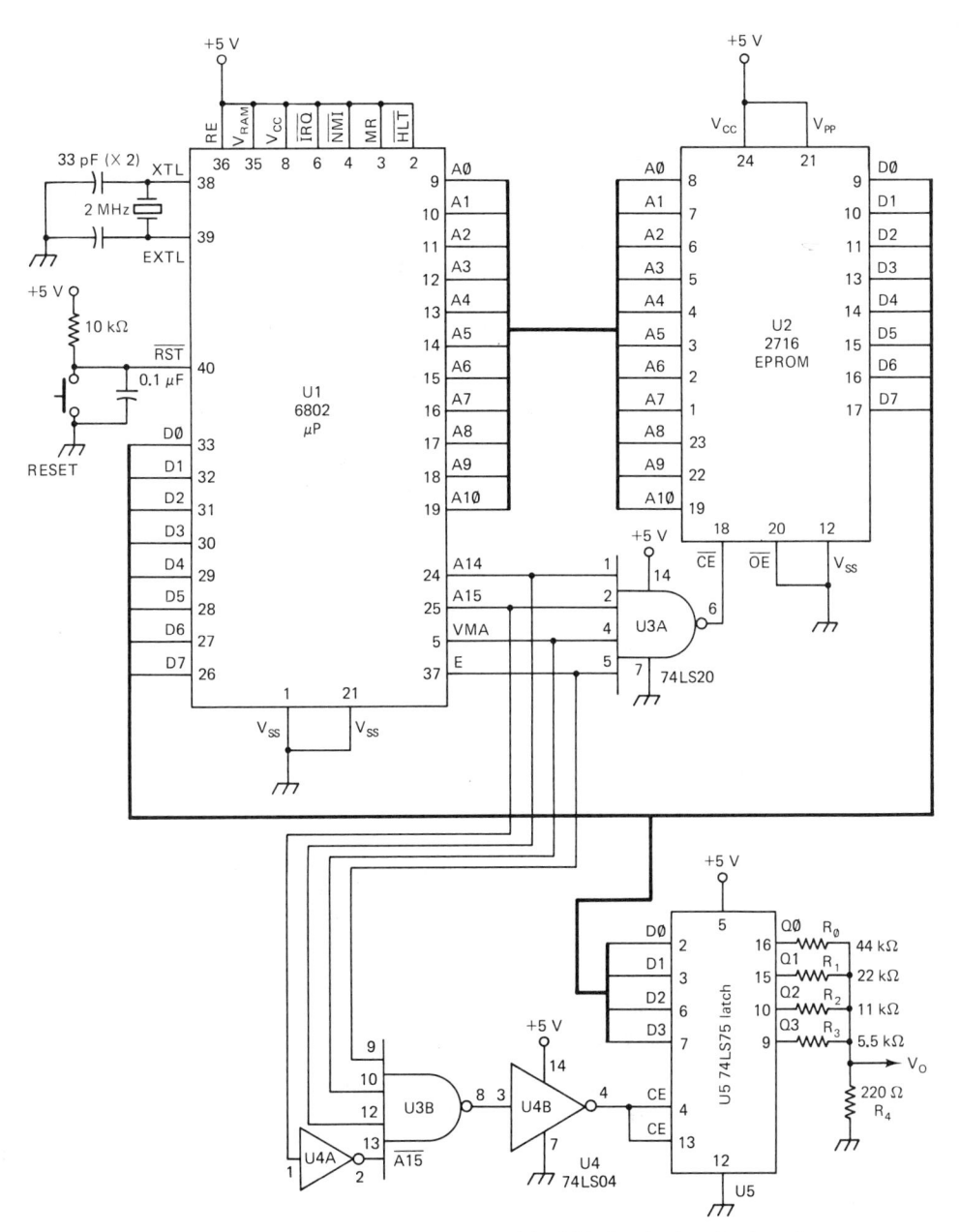

Figure 4-3 A microcomputer system with 4-bit latched output and an elementary D/A converter.

addresses are decoded:

A15	A14	Device Selected
0	0	Internal RAM (6802)
0	1	Output latch (74LS75)
1	0	Available (not used)
1	1	Program ROM (2716)

R/$\overline{\text{W}}$ is not included in the decoding. Any access of the latch address (even a read, such as LDAA $4000) will thus output data via the latch. The program must take care that all accesses to latch addresses are intentional writes. The output of the 74LS20 NAND gate is low-active, but the $\overline{CE}$ inputs of the latch are high-active. This is the reason for the inverter at the 74LS20 output.

A **ramp-generator program** is listed below. It is quite straightforward. Values from 0 to 15 are stored successively in the output latch via accumulator A. When the count of 16 is reached, the accumulator is immediately restored to zero.

Address	Object Code	Label	Mnemonic	Operand	Comments
					*Ramp Generator
FFEA	B7 40 00	START	STAA	OUTPUT	This program stores values
FFED	4C		INCA		increasing from 0 succes-
FFEE	81 10		CMPA	#$10	sively to 15 (decimal) in the
FFF0	27 03		BEQ	CYCLE	output, and then returns the
FFF2	7E FF EA		JMP	START	output to zero and runs up
FFF5	4F	CYCLE	CLRA		again.
FFF6	7E FF EA		JMP	START	
FFFE	FF EA				Reset vector

Project procedure. Set up the system of Fig. 4-3. It is especially important that the ratio of R_2/R_3 be 2.0 ± 5%. Program a 2716 with the object code above and observe V_O on your 'scope. Analyze the program to determine the period of one cycle (16 output levels) and compare to the measured period.

Slow-speed ramps or triangle waves of various frequencies and rise/fall ratios can be produced using the same circuit (Fig. 4-3) and the program listed below. These analog outputs are slow enough to be observed on a voltmeter, and can be used to position mechanical devices such as machine tools and robotic arms.

Sec. 4.3   Thirteen/Nineteen: A Number Game   57

Address	Object Code	Label	Mnemonic	Operand	Cycles	Comments
						Slow Ramps
FFC0	B7 40 00	UP	STAA	OUTPUT		Output to latch.
FFC3	CE 1A 00		LDX	#$1A00		Make 6656 delay loops
FFC6	09	DELAY1	DEX		4	at 11 cycles/loop,
FFC7	27 03		BEQ	DONE1	4	2 μs/cycle,
FFC9	7E FF C6		JMP	DELAY1	3	16 steps/ramp =
FFCC	4C	DONE1	INCA			2.3 sec runup time.
FFCD	81 10		CMPA	#$10		Increase output voltage,
FFCF	27 03		BEQ	DOWN		If count = 16, go to
FFD1	7E FF C0		JMP	UP		down counts; other-
FFD4	E3	DOWN	DECA			wise, count up more.
FFD5	B7 40 00		STAA	OUTPUT		Decrease output.
FFD8	CE 0D 00		LDX	#$0D00		Delay half as long
FFDB	09	DELAY2	DEX			as up ramp.
FFDC	27 03		BEQ	DONE2		
FFDE	7E FF DB		JMP	DELAY2		
FFE1	4D	DONE2	TSTA			If at zero output,
FFE2	27 03		BEQ	LOOP		run up.
FFE4	7E FF D4		JMP	DOWN		If not, run down.
FFE7	7E FF C0	LOOP	JMP	UP		
FFFE	FF C0					Reset vector

"Burn" an EPROM with this program and observe the voltage output. You may wish to experiment with different rise and fall times by changing the values loaded into X at addresses FFC4, FFC5 and FFD9, FFDA. If you are ambitious, you may write your own program for a trapezoidal or other more exotic waveform.

4.3 THIRTEEN/NINETEEN: A NUMBER GAME

This game is great for helping you (or your school-age kids) sharpen your arithmetic skills. It also gives you a better feeling for what real-world microcomputer programs are like, because the program is about three times longer than any you have seen so far.

If you have looked ahead at the program listing, you may be feeling intimidated right now. You should; programs of this size are not comprehensible, even to the writer, by scanning the complete listing. The flow chart and a program explanation give the big picture with the help of the listing and comments.

The rules of the game. Upon RESET, the computer will light a seven-segment LED display with a series of random numbers from 2 to 9, holding each one on for about 1 second. You are to add these numbers mentally as they appear, and hit the reset button if the total equals 13 or 19. (This will happen slightly less than half of the time.) You will be rewarded with a happy "beep" tone.

If the total runs over 19, you should immediately press the RESET button. The computer will respond with a less enthusiastic "boop" tone. If you panic and hit the button when the total is not 13, nor 19, nor in excess of 19, you will get a low-pitched "blatt" tone. And if you fail to push the button within one second of a 13, 19, or over-19 total, you will be reprimanded with an even lower-pitched buzz.

The system schematic is shown in Fig. 4-4. The 4-bit latch at address $4000 drives a 7447 IC which decodes the binary numbers representing counts 0 through 9 to light the appropriate segments of a common-anode LED display. The D0 output bit also drives a small speaker to produce audio tones if switched at an audio rate.

The program flowchart is given in Fig. 4-5. This flowchart is more general than the ones we have seen previously. The entire chart of Fig. 3-6, for example, was devoted to generating two tones. Here, tone generation is disposed of with a single box. This is what we meant about flowcharts giving the big picture. We could expand the *tone* box to a half-dozen boxes and diamonds to show the details of how the tones are generated, but this would obscure the big picture of how the tone routine and the other routines fit together in the overall program function.

Good flowcharts generalize as far as necessary to get the total number of boxes and diamonds down to 20 or 30. If any of these boxes are so complicated that they cannot be understood directly from the program listing, a separate sub-flowchart should be used to dissect the inner workings of that "box."

The tone to be produced is determined during program execution and stored as a "number of delay loops" value in the 6802 RAM. This value is not lost by RESETTING, and the first thing the program does upon release of the RESET button is fetch the tone value and generate the tone. The number of delay loops is obtained by counting from the TONE value up to 256 (which is one more than $FF, and rolls an 8-bit register back to $00). The number of audio cycles to be made is determined by counting TONE down one after each half cycle. High tones, which have short periods, receive more cycles than do low tones.

The tones are produced by feeding the half-cycle counter to the output latch. This counter is decremented each half cycle, and binary decrement always changes the value of bit 0.

The random numbers are generated by the following routine:

```
     ADR    01      02      03
             A       B       C     D = A + B + C + 1
           ↙       ↙       ↙     ↙
    Lost  ↙   X_H ↙   X_L ↙  AccA
                ↙       ↙       ↙
                 A       B       C
```

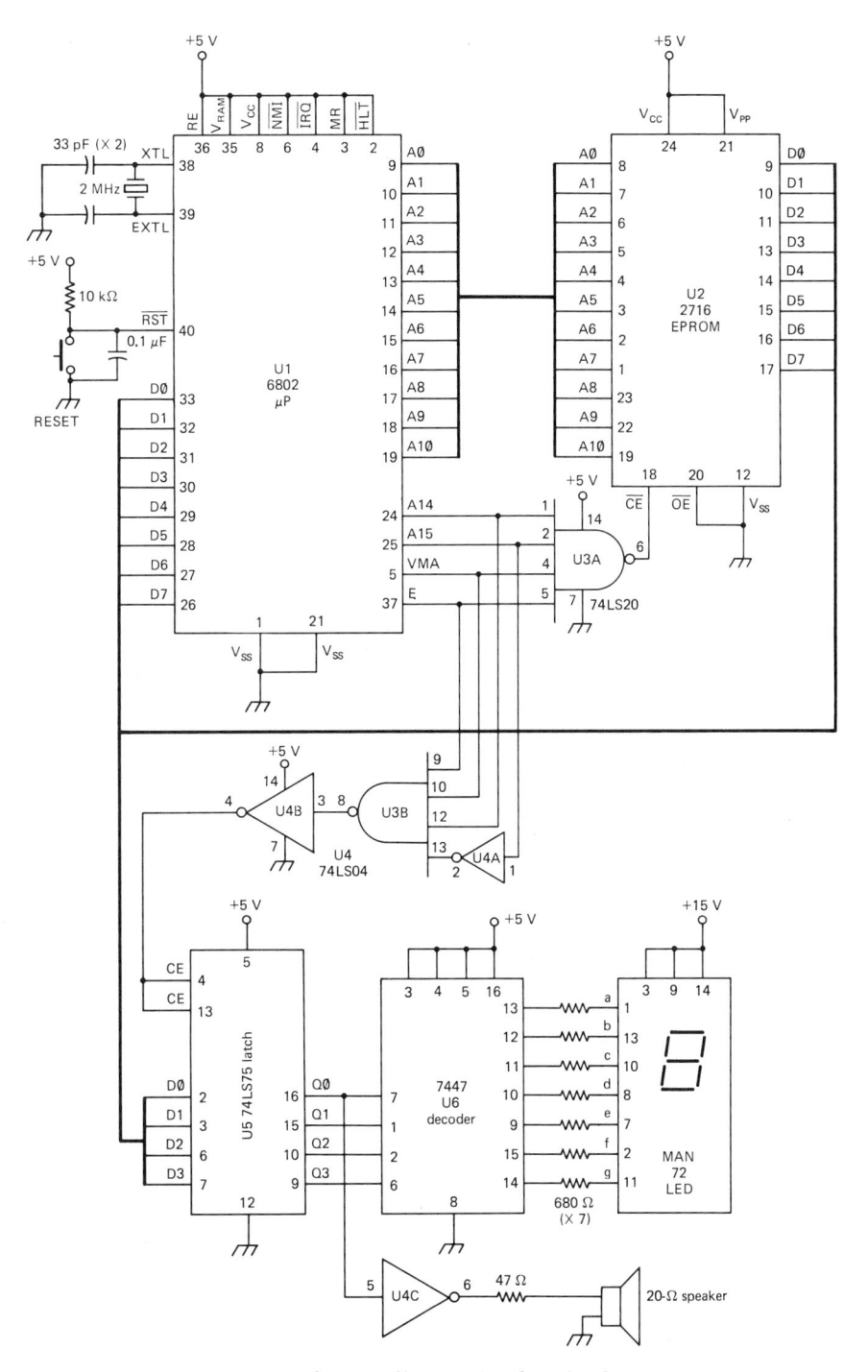

Figure 4-4 System diagram for the 13-19 game.

[Flow chart]

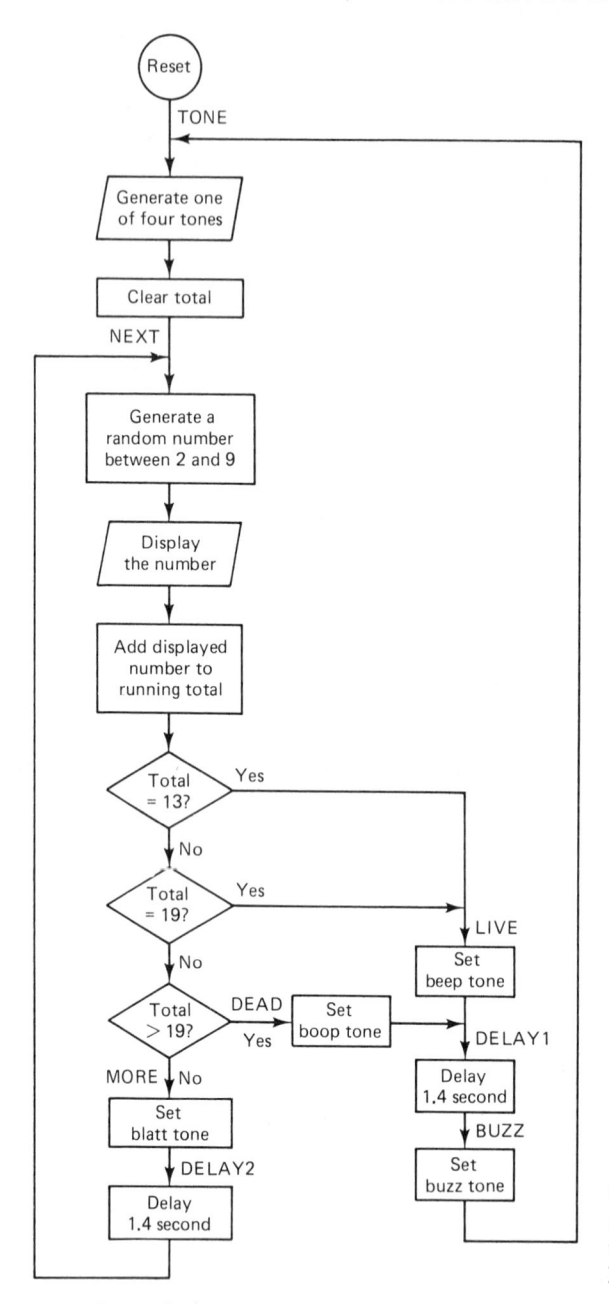

Figure 4-5 Program flow chart for the 13-19 game. Tone set in previous run is generated as soon as RESET is released.

A, B, and C are three 8-bit numbers contained in memory locations 0001, 0002, and 0003, respectively. A new "random" number D is formed from $A + B + C + 1$. The numbers B and C are then transferred to the A and B locations, respectively, via the X register, and location C is filled with the new number D, in preparation for the next random-number generation.

Sec. 4.3 Thirteen/Nineteen: A Number Game

The numbers D are not truly random, but they will not "hang up" on all zeros, all evens, all odds, or any simple series. We are counting on the RAM locations B and C to assume random nonzero values at power-up to produce a *different* number series each time the game is turned on.

The 8-bit number D is ANDed with $07 (binary 0000 0111) to zero out the high 5 bits, producing a range 0 through 7. Two increments then give a range 2 through 9 for D. This number is displayed and added to the running total stored at address 0004.

The total is compared to 13 and then to 19, and the TONE/DELAY byte (address 0000) is set for highest tone if an equal-to-zero results. The CMPA instruction is a kind of "fake" subtract. The contents of accumulator A are not changed, but a subsequent *branch* instruction works as though the operand word had actually been subtracted from the accumulator.

A final branch test is made to see if the fake subtraction instruction ($AccumA - 19$) caused a borrow, indicating a total less than 19. If so, TONE is set to the second lowest pitch, so a premature RESET will cause a "blatt" tone. If not (no borrow, indicating a total over 19) the second highest tone is set, so a RESET catching on overrun will be rewarded.

The BCS (Branch on Carry or borrow Set) instruction responds to a borrow from a previous command.

A delay of 1.4 seconds is entered in all cases to give the player time to react to the display. An appropriate RESET during the delay (right-hand loop, total = 13, 19, or >19) avoids the lowest tone setup, which occurs if the delay is allowed to run out. A RESET when not appropriate (total < 19) causes the second-lowest tone, but if this left-hand loop (DELAY2 in Fig. 4-5) is allowed to run out, no tone is produced and another number is displayed.

Here is the complete program listing for the 13-19 addition-drill game.

Address	Object Code	Label	Mnemonic	Operand	Cycles	Comments
						*Thirteen/Nineteen
FF00	B6 00 00	SOUND	LDAA	TONE		Generate various tones
FF03	F6 00 00	CYCLE	LDAB	TONE		by toggling bit 0 of
FF06	5C	LOOP1	INCB			output latch. Num-
FF07	27 03		BEQ	OUT1		ber of half-cycles =
FF09	7E FF 06		JMP	LOOP1		(TONE).
FF0C	4A	OUT1	DECA			Number of delay loops
FF0D	B7 40 00		STAA	OUTPUT		per half-cycle = 256 −
FF10	27 03		BEQ	START		(TONE).
FF12	7E FF 03		JMP	CYCLE		
FF15	7F 00 04	START	CLR	TOTAL		Start with zero total.
FF18	FE 00 02	NEXT	LDX	NUMB		Generate a "random"
FF1B	BB 00 01		ADDA	NUMA		number, D =
FF1E	BB 00 02		ADDA	NUMB		$A + B + C + 1$;
FF21	BB 00 03		ADDA	NUMC		Note that Accum A
FF24	4C		INCA			leaves SOUND rou-
FF25	FF 00 01		STX	NUMA		tine with 00.

62   Output Interfaces: Waveform Generators and Number Games   Chap. 4

Address	Object Code	Label	Mnemonic	Operand	Cycle	Comments
FF28	B7 00 03		STAA	NUMC		Replace $B \to A$, $C \to B$,
FF2B	84 07		ANDA	#$07		and $D \to C$.
FF2D	4C		INCA			Mask to range 0–7 and
FF2E	4C		INCA			increment to range
FF2F	B7 40 00		STAA	OUTPUT		2–9.
FF32	BB 00 04		ADDA	TOTAL		Display digit 2–9 and
FF35	B7 00 04		STAA	TOTAL		add to running total.
FF38	81 0D		CMPA	#$0D		Live to score if total =
FF3A	27 0E		BEQ	LIVE		decimal 13 or 19.
FF3C	81 13		CMPA	#$13		
FF3B	27 0A		BEQ	LIVE		
FF40	25 1E		BCS	MORE		If total < 19, add more.
FF42	C6 90		LDAB	#$90		Set for second-highest
FF44	F7 00 00		STAB	TONE		tone if total > 19.
FF47	7E FF 4F		JMP	DEAD		
FF4A	C6 D0	LIVE	LDAB	#$D0		Set for highest tone if
FF4C	F7 00 00		STAB	TONE		total = 13 or 19.
FF4F	CE FF 00	DEAD	LDX	#$FF00		Total = 13, = 19, or
FF52	09	DELAY1	DEX			> 19; delay approx.
FF53	27 03		BEQ	BUZZ		1.4. seconds.
FF55	7E FF 52		JMP	DELAY1		If RESET during delay,
FF58	C6 50	BUZZ	LDAB	#$50		second highest tone.
FF5A	F7 00 00		STAB	TONE		If delay runs out on live
FF5D	7E FF 00		JMP	SOUND		or dead, get lowest
FF60	C6 70	MORE	LDAB	#$70		tone.
FF62	F7 00 00		STAB	TONE		Set for second lowest
FF65	CE FF 00		LDX	#$FF00		tone if RESET
FF68	09	DELAY2	DEX		4	wrongly when more
FF69	27 03		BEQ	CONTIN	4	needs to be added
FF6B	7E FF 68		JMP	DELAY2	3	(delay 1.4 sec.)
FF6E	7E FF 18	CONTIN	JMP	NEXT		Get next number
FFFE	FF 00					after delay.

Reset vector
TONE = 0000
NUMA = 0001
NUMB = 0002
NUMC = 0003
TOTAL = 0004
OUTPUT = 4000

Modifications to the game are easy to make and keep it from "going stale" for you. The immediate values loaded into X at $FF4F and $FF65 can be reduced to speed up the game. The operands of the CMPA instructions at $FF38 and $FF3C can be changed to make the game 17/23, 54/40, or any pair of numbers up to 255. More *Compare* and *Branch* commands can be inserted after address $FF3B to increase the number of "live" answers (but all subsequent addresses will have to be resequenced).

If you are feeling pretty confident about programming, you may want to try inserting a routine at about $FF2F which compares the new digit

Sec. 4.4   An Eight-Bit Waveform Generator and Data Generation with Basic   **63**

just generated to the previous digit (which you must store in a new RAM location). If they are the same, the new digit should not be displayed, but the program should jump back to NEXT to get a different digit. This will avoid the uncertainty that accompanies the display of the same digit for 2.8 seconds.

4.4 AN EIGHT-BIT WAVEFORM GENERATOR AND DATA GENERATION WITH BASIC

Figure 4-6 shows a waveform generator using a 74LS373 eight-bit latch and a 1408 eight-bit digital-to-analog converter. Notice that a separate -15-V supply is required for the 1408. The output is capable of assuming 256 different levels, so a nearly continuous waveform can be produced. Programs similar to those in Section 4.2 can be written to generate fairly smooth ramp and triangle waves. Just change the operand of the CMPA instruction that ends the ramp from $10 to $FF. These simple programs can also serve as diagnostic tools to check out the hardware system.

More complex waveforms can be produced with this system if we use a *data-lookup table* rather than a simple increment and decrement scheme to set the binary value of the output data word. Thus, the processor will read a series of data words from successive memory locations, latching the data to the output as it goes. When it reaches the end of this data file, it will start back at the beginning and run through again. The output waveform produced is determined entirely by the data which the programmer stores in the file.

For a sample program we will load the data file to produce an output wave proportional to a sine wave of frequency f, plus a one-half value cosine wave of frequency $2f$. This "fundamental plus second harmonic" waveshape approaches a half-wave-rectified waveform, and is of some significance in electronic circuit analysis. If you're not deep enough into circuit analysis to appreciate this, don't let it bother you. Just concentrate on the programming techniques involved.

A BASIC-language program will be used to generate the 128 data words which will comprise our data file. This program can be run on any of the popular "home" computers, since they all run BASIC. Our objective is to demonstrate on a small scale how a general-purpose computer (called a *number cruncher*) can be used to help generate the program for a small special-purpose (called a *dedicated*) computer.

Here is a BASIC program to print $\sin \theta + 0.5 \cos 2\theta$, scaled to fill values from 0 to 255 vertically and to break one cycle ($\theta = 0$ to $\theta = 2\pi$ radians) into 128 increments.

```
10    PI = 3.141593
20    FOR N = 0 TO 127
30    Y = SIN (N * PI/64) + COS (N * PI/32) * 0.5
40    Y = INT (Y * 256/3 + 0.5) + 128
```

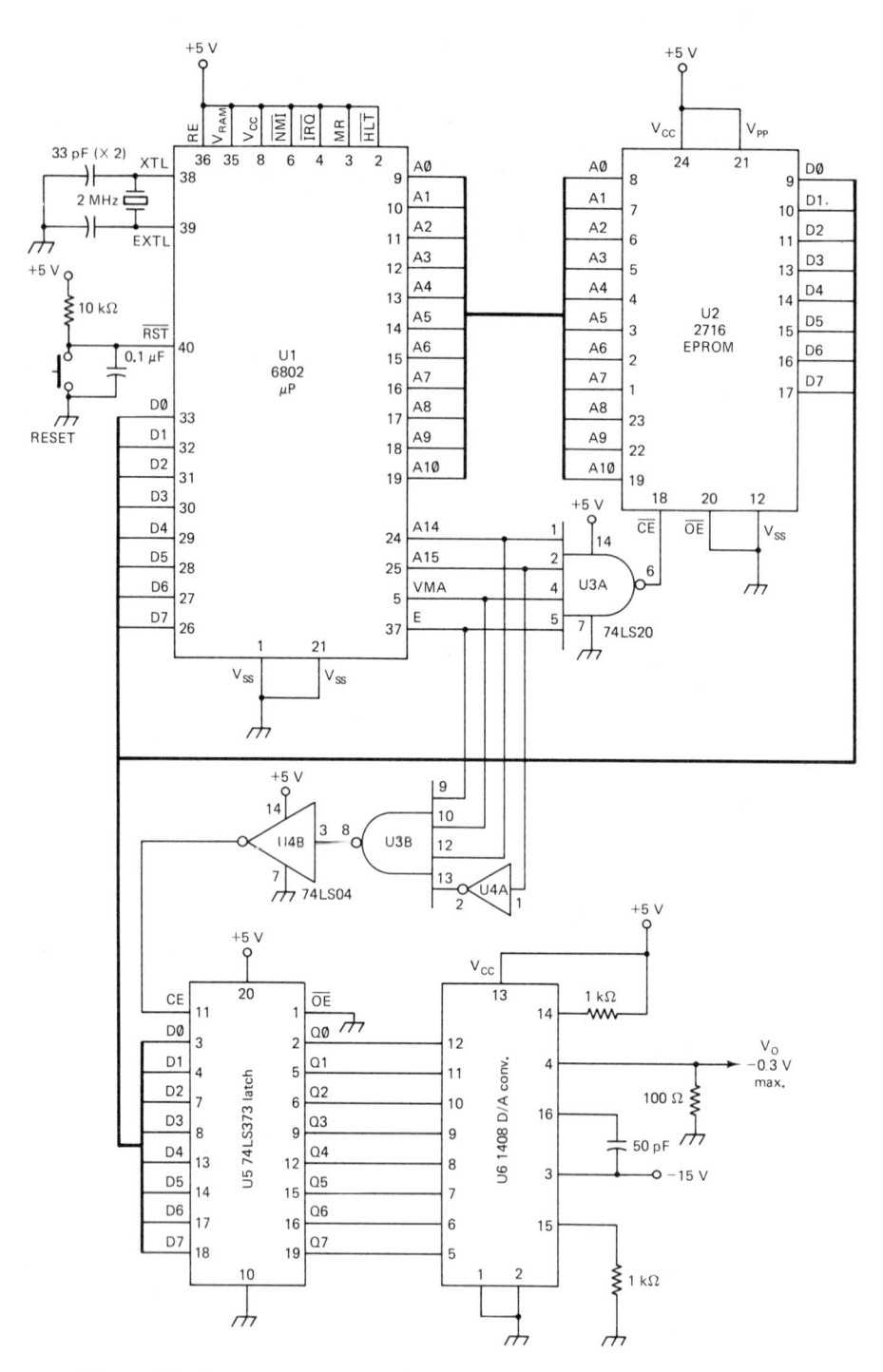

Figure 4-6 Microcomputer waveform generator. An 8-bit D/A converter is used to provide 256 different output levels.

Sec. 4.5   Indexed Addressing for the Waveform Generation   65

```
50    MS = INT (Y/16)
60    LS = INT ((Y/16 – MS) * 16 + 0.01)
70    PRINT N; SPC (3); MS; SPC (1); LS,
80    NEXT N
90    END
```

The values of sin θ may range over ±1, and 0.5 cos θ may range over ±0.5, so the total range generated in line 30 cannot exceed ±1.5 or a span of 3.0. In line 40 we therefore divide by 3 and multiply by 256 to scale the range to 256 (±128) maximum. Adding 128 makes all the values positive. The INT (integer) operation simply lops off the decimal part of a number, so 0.5 is added in line 40 to convert it to a true rounding to the nearest whole number.

MS and LS are the most- and least-significant nibbles of the data word, which are printed as two decimal numbers from 0 to 15. The data-word number is printed (in decimal) preceding this.

If you don't have access to a computer that runs BASIC, you *can* calculate all 128 data words on a hand calculator. It will help you to appreciate the convenience of computer data generation.

4.5 INDEXED ADDRESSING FOR THE WAVEFORM GENERATOR

Now that we have 128 words for our data file, how do we get the processor to store them successively in the output latch? It would be unreasonable to write the routine LOAD, STORE, and BRANCH IF END for each address in the file (128 times). There should be a way to write the routine once and have the program loop through it 128 times, accessing a successive file location each time. There is, indeed, a way to do this. It makes use of indexed addressing.

Indexed-mode instructions pick up the address of the operand data from the current value of the 16-bit X register. The starting address of the file is loaded into X before the first pass through the LOAD-STORE loop, and X is incremented at the end of the loop so that the next pass will pick up the next piece of data in the file. Figure 4-7 illustrates loading from a file using the X register and indexed addressing.

Indexed-mode instructions are two bytes long. The base operand address is the current value of X. The second byte of the instruction gives the *offset* (if any) of the operand address from the value in X. Thus, if X = $FE02 and the second (offset) byte were $03, the address accessed would be $FE05. For the time being we will not use the offset feature, and the second byte of all indexed instructions will be 00.

Figure 4-8 shows a flowchart for fetching 128 data bytes from a file and returning to the start when the end of file is reached. Following is a program listing for the waveform generator using the hardware of Fig. 4-6 and the data generated by the BASIC program.

66   Output Interfaces: Waveform Generators and Number Games   Chap. 4

Address						
FE00	DATA 1					
FE01	DATA 2					
FE02	DATA 3					
FE03	DATA 4					
FE04	DATA 5					
FE05	DATA 5					

X register: 11111110 00000000

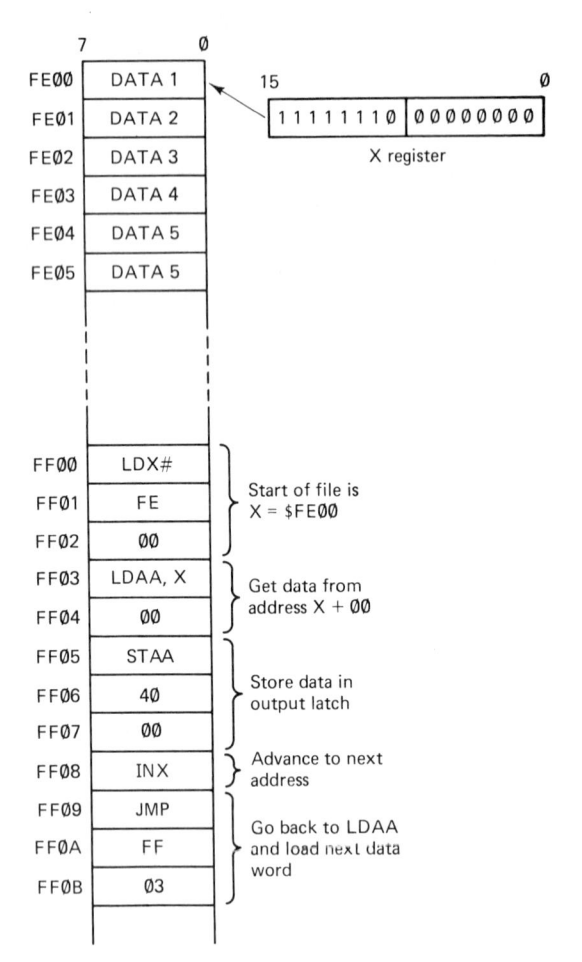

```
FF00  LDX#    ⎫
FF01  FE      ⎬  Start of file is X = $FE00
FF02  00      ⎭
FF03  LDAA,X  ⎫  Get data from
FF04  00      ⎭  address X + 00
FF05  STAA    ⎫
FF06  40      ⎬  Store data in output latch
FF07  00      ⎭
FF08  INX     }  Advance to next address
FF09  JMP     ⎫
FF0A  FF      ⎬  Go back to LDAA and load next data word
FF0B  03      ⎭
```

Figure 4-7 Indexed addressing permits a single routine to access an extensive file of data by incrementing X to point to the next address and looping back through the routine.

Address	Object Code	Label	Mnemonic	Operand	Cycles	Comments
						*256-Level Waveform
FE00	XX					Data File from
FE7F	XX					BASIC Program
FF00	CE FE 00	START	LDX	#$FE00		Start of file.
FF03	A6 00	LOOP	LDAA	00,X	5	Pick up next data word.
FF05	B7 40 00		STAA	OUTPUT	5	Put in output latch.
FF08	08		INX		4	Advance to next file
FF09	8C FE 80		CPX	#$FE80	3	word; if off end of
FF0C	27 03		BEQ	GOSTRT	4	file, start over.
FF0E	7E FF 03		JMP	LOOP	3	Otherwise, go to next
FF11	7E FF 00	GOSTRT	JMP	START		word.
FFFE	FF 00					Reset vector

Sec. 4.6 Hex Drill: A Computer Tutor   67

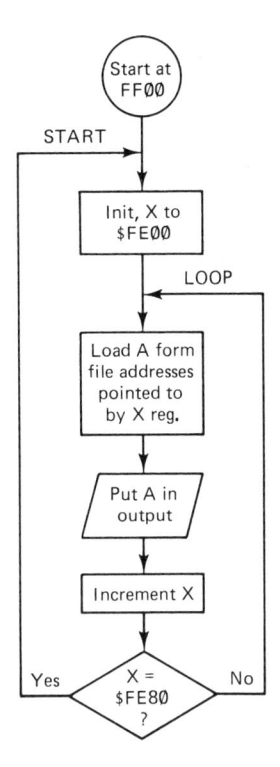

Figure 4-8 Flowchart to generate a waveform from a file of 128 data words.

Project procedure. Program an EPROM, storing the 128 data bytes from the BASIC program at $FE00 through $FE7F. Data printed as 10 15, for example, must be encoded as hex AF. An address listed as 0 is machine address $FE00 and EPROM address $600. Similarly, listed address 99 (in hex, 63) is $FE63 to the 6802 and $663 when programming the 2716.

Burn the program and reset vectors into the EPROM, and run the system. Check the output of the 1408 D/A converter on the 'scope. Measure the period of the output waveform and compare with the calculated period for 128 passes through the loop of 24 machine cycles.

4.6 HEX DRILL: A COMPUTER TUTOR

By now you must be aware that microcomputer programming requires quite a facility with hexadecimal arithmetic. Here is a relatively simple microcomputer project that will help you to learn your hex addition tables. It will also introduce you to a new use for indexed addressing.

The program runs continuously without user input. A short "beep" tone announces the start of each problem. A random hex digit from 0 to F is then displayed for 1 second on a seven-segment LED display. (The letters

68 Output Interfaces: Waveform Generators and Number Games Chap. 4

A, C, E, and F are capitals; b and d are lowercase. The numeral 6 and the letter b are distinuished by having the top bar lit for the 6.) This is followed immediately by a 1-second display of a second random hex digit. The display then goes dark for 1 second, during which time you are to give verbally the hex sum of the two digits. At the end of this time the display lights with the correct sum to either confirm or correct your answer. The decimal point lights to indicate a 1 carried to the 16s column of the hex answer. After 1 second of answer display, the program repeats with a *beep* and two new random numbers.

Software decoding is used to convert the binary-digit patterns into the appropriate segment-display patterns. This is quite a contrast to the 7447 hardware decoder that was used in the 13/19 game of Section 4.3. Here is how it works.

Each output data word contains 8 bits, and each bit is devoted to lighting one of the LED segments (or decimal point). By encoding selected patterns of binary 1s and 0s and outputting them as data words, we can light any selection of segments, leaving the others off. In fact, we encode 32 such data words, corresponding to the hex numbers 00 through 1F, and store them in memory locations $FF00 through $FF1F, respectively.

The segment-identification letters for the LED display are given with Fig. 4-9. Here is the data file for displaying digits 00 through 1F as generated in binary, and then converted to hex for entry into the memory. A low level (binary 0) is used to light a segment by pulling the cathode to ground.

Value	Address	Binary Code dp g f e d c b a	Hex	Value	Address	Binary Code dp g f e d c b a	Hex
00	FF00	1 1 0 0 0 0 0 0	C0	10	FF10	0 1 0 0 0 0 0 0	40
01	FF01	1 1 1 1 1 0 0 1	F9	11	FF11	0 1 1 1 1 0 0 1	79
02	FF02	1 0 1 0 0 1 0 0	A4	12	FF12	0 0 1 0 0 1 0 0	24
03	FF03	1 0 1 1 0 0 0 0	B0	13	FF13	0 0 1 1 0 0 0 0	30
04	FF04	1 0 0 1 1 0 0 1	99	14	FF14	0 0 0 1 1 0 0 1	19
05	FF05	1 0 0 1 0 0 1 0	92	15	FF15	0 0 0 1 0 0 1 0	12
06	FF06	1 0 0 0 0 0 1 0	82	16	FF16	0 0 0 0 0 0 1 0	02
07	FF07	1 1 1 1 1 0 0 0	F8	17	FF17	0 1 1 1 1 0 0 0	78
08	FF08	1 0 0 0 0 0 0 0	80	18	FF18	0 0 0 0 0 0 0 0	00
09	FF09	1 0 0 1 1 0 0 0	98	19	FF19	0 0 0 1 1 0 0 0	18
0A	FF0A	1 0 0 0 1 0 0 0	88	1A	FF1A	0 0 0 0 1 0 0 0	08
0B	FF0B	1 0 0 0 0 0 1 1	83	1B	FF1B	0 0 0 0 0 0 1 1	03
0C	FF0C	1 1 0 0 0 1 1 0	C6	1C	FF1C	0 1 0 0 0 1 1 0	46
0D	FF0D	1 0 1 0 0 0 0 1	A1	1D	FF1D	0 0 1 0 0 0 0 1	21
0E	FF0E	1 0 0 0 0 1 1 0	86	1E	FF1E	0 0 0 0 0 1 1 0	06
0F	FF0F	1 0 0 0 1 1 1 0	8E	1F	FF1F	0 0 0 0 1 1 1 0	0E

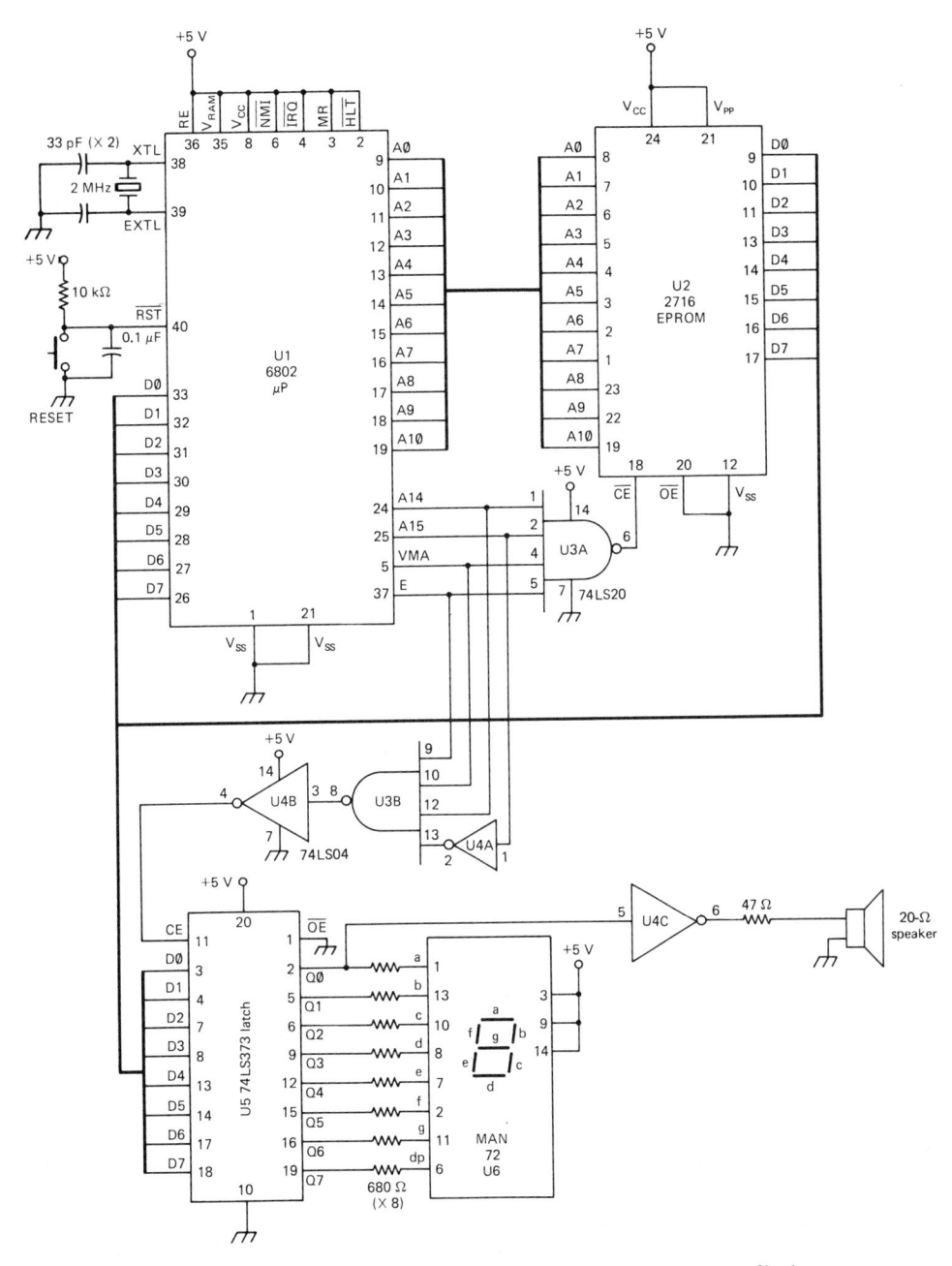

Figure 4-9 The *Hex Drill* system uses software decoding to eliminate the 7447 LED decoder.

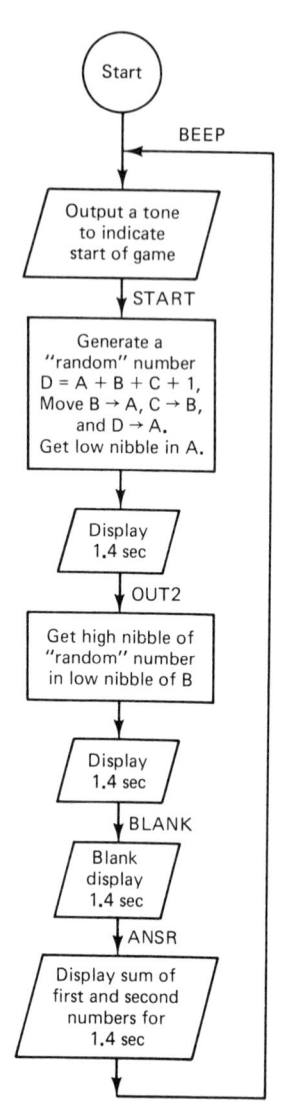

```
                    Start
                      │
                      │◄──────── BEEP
                      ▼
             ┌──────────────────┐
             │  Output a tone   │
             │   to indicate    │
             │  start of game   │
             └──────────────────┘
                      │ START
                      ▼
             ┌──────────────────┐
             │   Generate a     │
             │ "random" number  │
             │ D = A + B + C + 1,│
             │  Move B → A, C → B,│
             │   and D → A.     │
             │Get low nibble in A.│
             └──────────────────┘
                      │
                      ▼
             ┌──────────────────┐
             │     Display      │
             │     1.4 sec      │
             └──────────────────┘
                      │ OUT2
                      ▼
             ┌──────────────────┐
             │ Get high nibble of│
             │ "random" number  │
             │ in low nibble of B│
             └──────────────────┘
                      │
                      ▼
             ┌──────────────────┐
             │     Display      │
             │     1.4 sec      │
             └──────────────────┘
                      │ BLANK
                      ▼
             ┌──────────────────┐
             │      Blank       │
             │     display      │
             │     1.4 sec      │
             └──────────────────┘
                      │ ANSR
                      ▼
             ┌──────────────────┐
             │  Display sum of  │
             │  first and second│
             │   numbers for    │
             │     1.4 sec      │
             └──────────────────┘
                      │
                      └──────────┘
```

Figure 4-10 Program flow for the *Hex Drill*. The function blocks are quite generalized, and could apply to any computer.

The hardware for the hex drill is similar to that for the waveform generator, except that the eight outputs of the data-latch drive the seven segments and decimal point of the LED, instead of a D/A converter. Figure 4-9 shows the system diagram.

A flowchart for the program is given in Fig. 4-10. It is quite generalized because most of the routines have been used before and should be familiar to you. The tone and random-number generators were described in Section 4.3, and the delay loops are similar to those used in Section 3.5.

Sec. 4.6 Hex Drill: A Computer Tutor

Indirect addressing. The program will produce the binary values of the digits to be displayed in one of the accumulators. The segment-decoding file is conveniently located so that the bits for displaying 00 are in the first address ($FF00), those for displaying 1A are at address $FF1A, and so on. How, then, can we use the binary value to access the corresponding segment code?

Since the program is in ROM, we are not able to change the operand of a LOAD, EXTENDED command (ROM cannot be written to by the program). The indexed-addressing mode can be used to access different addresses, but how can we get the appropriate addresses ($FF00 through $FF1F) into the X register? There is no single instruction that will transfer the contents of an accumulator (say, 1A) to the low-order byte of the X register (making it, say, FF1A), but this can be accomplished through RAM memory.

Thus, we will define two consecutive bytes of RAM ($0004 and $0005 in our program) as holding bytes intended for XHI and XLO, respectively. We will load RAM XHI with $FF and leave it at that. RAM XLO we will load with the current binary value ($1A, in the example we have been using). We will then LDX from RAM XHI (realizing that the low byte of X will be automatically loaded from the next address RAM XLO). Finally, we will use an LDAA, INDEXED command to pick up the appropriate segment code from the file and output it to the latch. All of this is illustrated in Fig. 4-11.

The LDAA instruction that fetches the operand data refers to the X register for the address of the operand, but the X register in turn refers to RAM locations XHI and XLO for its contents. XHI and XLO are thus called the indirect address, and this technique of hopping about in a file by changing an address stored in RAM is called indirect addressing. Many processors, such as the 6502 and the 6809, have an indirect addressing mode which permits this process to be implemented in a single instruction without tying up the X register.

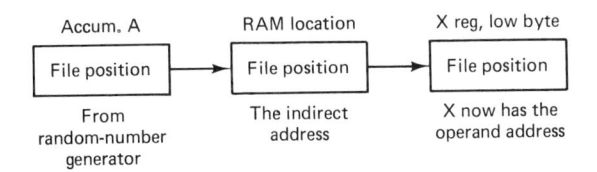

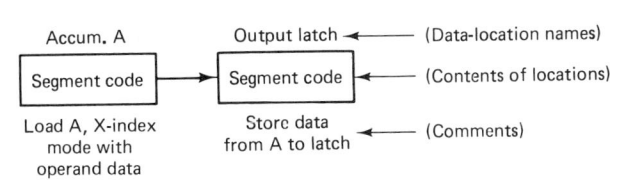

Figure 4-11 Indirect addressing allows file data to be accessed randomly, rather than sequentially. In this example, a number in accumulator A is used to access the corresponding LED segment code in a file.

Direct addressing is the only 6802 mode left to be explained, and it is so simple that we may as well take care of it right now. Direct addressing is like extended addressing except that there is only one operand byte following the instruction, and it gives the low-order byte of the operand address. The high-order byte is assumed to be 00. This mode saves a byte of program memory and a cycle of execution time per instruction, but other than that it doesn't do anything that extended addressing can't do.

The high-order byte of a two-byte address is often referred to as the *page* number, with the low-order byte specifying one of 256 *words* on that page. Direct addressing always refers to words on page 00, and this mode is sometimes called *zero-page* addressing.

The complete program listing for the *Hex Drill* project is given below. You should set up the hardware system of Fig. 4-9 and burn an EPROM with the data file and program object code. After you have used the program for a while, you may want to speed it up. This will require inserting LDX IMMEDIATE commands before LOOP2, LOOP3, LOOP4, and/or LOOP5 to keep the delays from looping 65 536 times. The addresses will have to be reshuffled. Don't forget that some of the *operands* (LOOP2, LOOP3, LOOP4, LOOP5) will have to be changed to refer to the new addresses.

Hex Drill: Program Listing

```
                    1000  *-----------------------------------------------
                    1010  *       *****  HEX DRILL - A COMPUTER TUTOR  *****
                    1020  *
                    1030         .OR   $FF80    ORIGIN (START) OF PROGRAM IN EPROM.
                    1040         .TA   $4780    TARGET ADDRESS IN APPLE FOR ASEMBLER.
0000-               1050  FIRST  .EQ   $0000    FIRST NUMBER (0 - $F) AT ADR 0000.
0001-               1060  NUMA   .EQ   $0001    NUMBER A KEPT IN RAM ADR 0001.
0002-               1070  NUMB   .EQ   $0002    NUMBER B
0003-               1080  NUMC   .EQ   $0003    NUMBER C
0004-               1090  XHI    .EQ   $0004    STORES X REGISTER, HI BYTE,
0005-               1100  XLO    .EQ   $0005       AND LO BYTE.
4000-               1110  OUTPUT .EQ   $4000    ADR OF OUTPUT LATCH.
                    1120  *
FF80- 86 D0         1130  BEEP   LDAA  #$D0     GENERATE A TONE
FF82- C6 D0         1140  CYCLE  LDAB  #$D0     WITH $D0 HALF CYCLES AND
FF84- 5C            1150  LOOP1  INCB           (FF - D0) LOOPS
FF85- 27 03         1160         BEQ   OUT1     PER AUDIO HALF-CYCLE.
FF87- 7E FF 84      1170         JMP   LOOP1
FF8A- 4A            1180  OUT1   DECA
FF8B- B7 40 00      1190         STAA  OUTPUT
FF8E- 27 03         1200         BEQ   START
FF90- 7E FF 82      1210         JMP   CYCLE
                    1220  *
FF93- 86 FF         1230  START  LDAA  #$FF     SEGMENT FILE IS AT $FFXX.
FF95- 97 04         1240         STAA  XHI      SET UP HI BYTE.
FF97- DE 02         1250         LDX   NUMB     GENERATE A RANDOM NUMBER:
FF99- 9B 01         1260         ADDA  NUMA
FF9B- 9B 02         1270         ADDA  NUMB     D = A + B + C + 1
FF9D- 9B 03         1280         ADDA  NUMC
FF9F- 4C            1290         INCA
FFA0- DF 01         1300         STX   NUMA     MOVE B INTO A, C TO B, D TO C,
FFA2- 97 03         1310         STAA  NUMC        IN PREP FOR NEXT RAND NUMBR.
FFA4- 16            1320         TAB
```

Sec. 4.6   Hex Drill: A Computer Tutor   73

```
FFA5- 84 0F      1330           ANDA #$0F      SAVE 2 NIBBLES, MASK OFF HI NIBBLE
FFA7- 97 00      1340           STAA FIRST     AND SAVE FIRST NUMBR (0 - F).
FFA9- 97 05      1350           STAA XLO       SET LO BYTE OF X-INDEX TO FIRST
FFAB- DE 04      1360           LDX  XHI       RANDOM NUMBER.
FFAD- A6 00      1370           LDAA 00,X      FETCH SEGMENT CODE FROM FILE
FFAF- B7 40 00   1380           STAA OUTPUT    AND LIGHT SEGMENTS.
                 1390 *
FFB2- 09         1400 LOOP2     DEX            DELAY FOR 1.4 SEC BY COUNTING X
FFB3- 27 03      1410           BEQ  OUT2      FROM $FF0X TO ZERO.
FFB5- 7E FF B2   1420           JMP  LOOP2
FFB8- 54         1430 OUT2      LSRB           MOVE HIGH NIBBLE SAVED IN
FFB9- 54         1440           LSRB           ACCUM B DOWN TO LOW NIBBLE.
FFBA- 54         1450           LSRB           HIGH NIBBLE FILLS IN
FFBB- 54         1460           LSRB           WITH 0000.
FFBC- D7 05      1470           STAB XLO       SET INDEX REGISTER TO POINT TO
FFBE- DE 04      1480           LDX  XHI       SEGMENT CODE OF 2ND RAND NUMB.
FFC0- DB 00      1490           ADDB FIRST     GET TOTAL OF FIRST AND 2ND RAND
FFC2- A6 00      1500           LDAA 00,X      NUMBERS IN ACCUM B.
FFC4- B7 40 00   1510           STAA OUTPUT    LIGHT SEGMENTS FOR 2ND DIGIT
FFC7- 09         1520 LOOP3     DEX            AND DELAY 1.4 SEC.
FFC8- 27 03      1530           BEQ  BLANK
FFCA- 7E FF C7   1540           JMP  LOOP3
FCD-  86 FF      1550 BLANK     LDAA #$FF      BLANK ALL SEGMENTS;
FFCF- B7 40 00   1560           STAA OUTPUT
FFD2- 09         1570 LOOP4     DEX            DELAY FOR 1.4 SEC.
FFD3- 27 03      1580           BEQ  ANSR
FFD5- 7E FF D2   1590           JMP  LOOP4
FFD8- D7 05      1600 ANSR      STAB XLO       SET INDEX REGISTER TO POINT TO
FFDA- DE 04      1610           LDX  XHI       SEGMENT CODE FOR ANSR DIGIT(S).
FFDC- A6 00      1620           LDAA 00,X
FFDE- B7 40 00   1630           STAA OUTPUT    LIGHT SEGMENTS WITH ANSWER AND
FFE1- 09         1640 LOOP5     DEX            DELAY FOR 1.4 SEC.
FFE2- 27 03      1650           BEQ  DONE
FFE4- 7E FF E1   1660           JMP  LOOP5
FFE7- 7E FF 80   1670 DONE      JMP  BEEP      DO IT ALL AGAIN.
                 1680 *
                 1690 * END OF PROGRAM *
                 1700 *
                 1710           .OR  $FF00     HEX DIGIT FILE STARTS AT ADR $FF00.
                 1720           .TA  $4700     APPLE RAM STORES FILE AT $4700.
                 1730 * HEX STRING OF 2 DIGITS PER NUMERAL FOLLOWS:
FF00- C0 F9 A4
FF03- B0 99 92
FF06- 82 F8 80
FF09- 98 88 83
FF0C- C6 A1 86
FF0F- 8E 40 79
FF12- 24 30      1740           .HS  C0F9A4B0999282F880988883C6A1868E40792430
FF14- 19 12 02
FF17- 78 00 18
FF1A- 08 03 46
FF1D- 21 06 0E   1750           .HS  191202780018080834621060E
                 1760 *
                 1770           .OR  $FFFE     RESET VECTOR AT $FFFE, FFFF POINTS TO
                 1780           .TA  $47FE     START OF PROGRAM AT $FF80.
FFFE- FF 80      1790           .HS  FF80
                 1800           .EN            END OF LISTING.
```

You may want to exercise your programming skill by trapping out successive displays of the same number or trapping out digits 0 through 3 as too trivial. For a real challenge you may want to program a Morse code trainer, which beeps code letters and, after a programmable delay, flashes the corresponding letter. The letters A, b, C, d, E, F, g, H, I, J, L, n, O, P, r, S, t, U, and y can be displayed reasonably on seven segments. You will have to come up with creative new symbols for K, M, Q, V, W, X, and Z.

CHAPTER SUMMARY

1. An output latch holds the data that was present on the data bus during the last cycle in which its memory address was accessed. The 74LS373 is an 8-bit output latch.
2. VMA, R/$\overline{\text{W}}$ (inverted), E, and several high-order address lines are ANDed to select the latch. The low-order address lines can be anything (mirroring), but we choose to set them all to ∅.
3. A D/A converter outputs an analog voltage proportional to the binary value of its digital inputs. The 1408 is an 8-bit D/A converter.
4. In the indexed-addressing mode, the address of the operand is stored in the X register. This register can be incremented at the end of a "Load Accumulator" loop, so the *Load* accesses sequential locations in a file on each pass through the loop.
5. Larger general-purpose computers, running high-level languages such as BASIC, are often used to generate data tables for smaller dedicated (fixed-program) computers.
6. Software decoding uses a memory lookup table to output desired bit patterns in response to different input data. It performs the function of a hardware decoder (such as a 7447 LED decoder for digits 0-9), but can be programmed for any desired patterns (such as digits ∅-F).
7. Indirect addressing stores operand addresses in RAM, where they can be changed by the program.
8. The high byte of a two-byte address is referred to as the *page* number. There are a possible 256 words on each of 256 pages, a total of 65 536 words. Direct or zero-page addressing assumes that the operand address is on page ∅∅, and specifies only the low-order byte.

5

Troubleshooting: Single-Step and Bus-Display Hardware

Like most electronic projects, microcomputer systems seldom work the first time they are turned on. But the worst part is that there is usually no trail to follow to lead you to the trouble. In an audio amplifier you can trace the signal from preamp to driver to output stage and see where it is getting lost. In a microcomputer system, one error—in hardware or software—is usually enough to render the whole system nonfunctional, and oscilloscope signal-tracing techniques will be almost useless. This chapter acquaints you with some tools and techniques that are useful in microcomputer troubleshooting.

5.1 HALT AND DISPLAY ADDRESS!

One of the most common problems is that the microcomputer gets stuck somewhere in an endless loop. Maybe you want to branch out of the loop when $X = \emptyset$, but through a programming error, X never does reach zero. Or maybe instead of branching out of the loop, you branch right back into it. If you could just read the address where the processor is getting stuck, you would know what part of your program to examine closely for such an error.

Address checks can be made with the very simple system alteration shown in Fig. 5-1. With S2 open, the system will run normally. When S2 is closed, the processor will complete its current instruction and halt, and the LEDs will display the address of the next instruction. By opening and closing S2 several times and reading the hex equivalent of the binary address

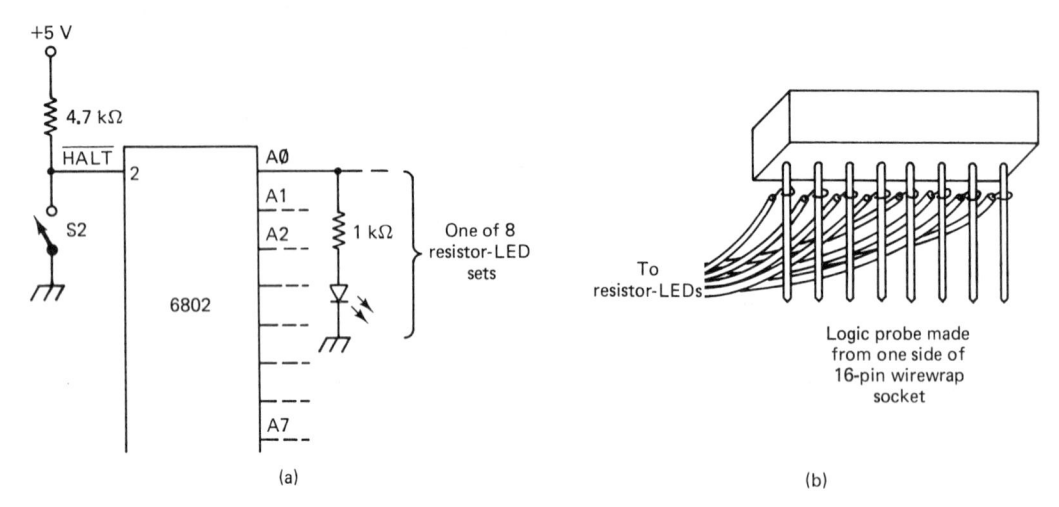

Figure 5-1 A simple LED address readout and HALT switch (a) can locate many hardware and software problems. A probe for the address readout (b).

display, you can determine whether the processor is getting hung up, and if so, where.

You can connect LEDs to all 16 address lines if you like, but our elementary programs are not longer than one page (256 words), so 8-bit display is usually adequate to trace them. If the machine is getting stuck, a second run with the LEDs plugged into A8 through A15 will check the high address byte. A probe for making this change quickly can be made from an old 16-pin IC socket, as shown in Fig. 5-1 (b).

You should be aware that this halt-and-display technique will not work on most other microprocessors. The 6802 is unusual in that its address bus is not tri-state and remains active during the *halt*. Most processors place both buses in a high-Z state upon being halted. The 6802 *data* bus cannot be read out in this way because it goes into a high-Z state during *halt*.

Dynamic display. The LEDs can be useful with S2 open and the processor running. Let us say that we observe no light at all on the A3 LED, yet the program is supposed to spend considerable time in a loop from addresses $FF17 to FF29, many of which addresses would bring A3 *high* and light the LED. Perhaps line A3 is shorted to ground, or it could be that the processor is stuck in another loop in which A3 is always *low*.

5.2 A SINGLE-STEP CIRCUIT

The circuit of Fig. 5-2 allows the 6802 to execute one instruction at a time. It uses only two TTL ICs, and can be added to any of the 6802 systems in this book. A single instruction, of however many machine cycles, will be

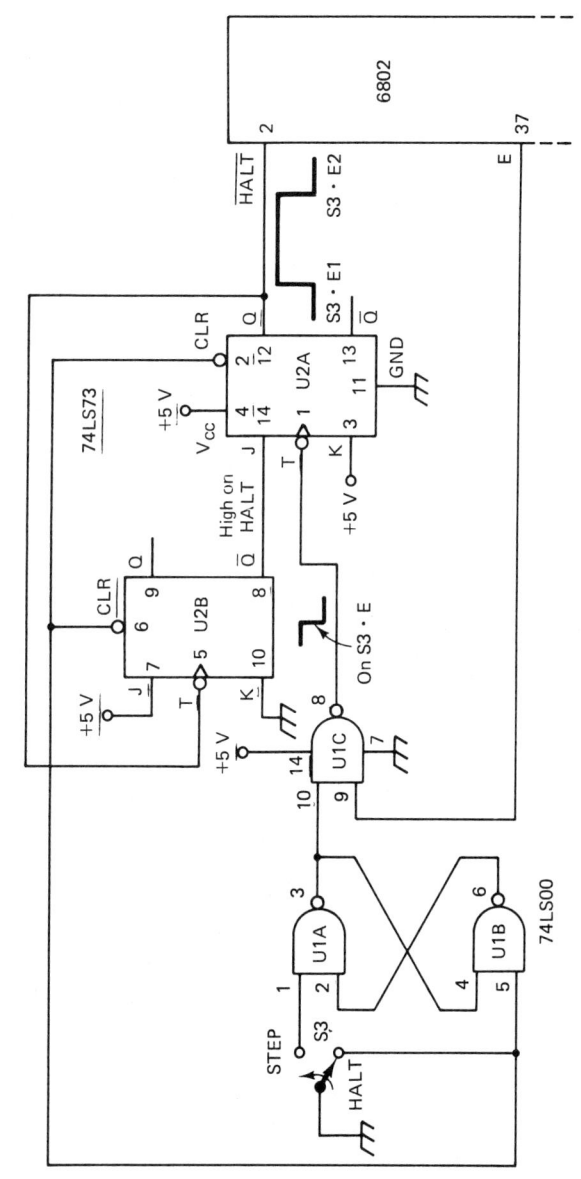

Figure 5-2 Two ICs and a pushbutton switch can make the 6802 step through a program one instruction at a time.

executed each time S3 is pushed. The address bus will then display the address of the next instruction. The processor can thus be stepped through a program and the source of any jump to an unknown address can be located.

The operation of the circuit is as follows. When S3 is pressed, U1A and U1B debounce the switch and pin 10 of U1C is held *high*. The E clock, which continues to run while $\overline{\text{HALT}}$ is low, is then passed, inverted, to the trigger input of U2A. Since J and K are both *high*, U2A toggles (changes states) at each negative edge at pin 1 (positive edge of E). Recall that a JK flip-flop toggles on trigger if J and K are 1, holds state if J and K are $\emptyset$, sets ($Q = 1$, $\overline{Q} = \emptyset$) if $J = 1$ and $K = \emptyset$, and resets or clears if $J = \emptyset$ and $K = 1$.

The first rise of E thus *sets* the Q output, driving the $\overline{\text{HALT}}$ line of the processor *high*. The second rise of E switches this line *low* again, one machine cycle later. This fall of the U2A output (pin 12) triggers U2B to *set*, and its $\overline{Q}$ output (pin 8) goes *low*. The J input of U2A is now *low* while K is *high*, so subsequent E pulses (after the first two) only hold U2A in the *reset* state, which it is already in. With $\overline{\text{HALT}}$ *low* the processor completes its current instruction and halts with the address of the next instruction asserted on the address bus, and the data bus floating.

Doing the one-step. In troubleshooting with single step you should have the address-bus LEDs connected as shown in Fig. 5-1. Check the program listing and decide what address the processor should halt at if it executes the first instruction. Press the STEP button and see if the address displayed confirms your expectation. Continue with expectation and confirmation until you find an address jump that you did not anticipate. Then check the program in that area very thoroughly.

5.3 DATA-BUS DISPLAY

As we mentioned earlier, the 6802 data bus is tri-state and will not drive a display when the processor is halted, but the data on the bus just before the halt can be latched (stored in a set of eight flip-flops) for display. There exists a very convenient (but rather expensive) IC package that will not only latch 4 bits of data, but decode the data to a hex digit $\emptyset$ through F and display it on a 5 × 7 dot-matrix LED. It is called a *TIL 311*, and a pair of them for data-bus display will cost you about $22. Figure 5-3 shows how they can be connected to a 6802 system to display the last byte on the data bus during the execution of the last instruction. This circuit should be used in conjunction with the address display LEDs of Fig. 5-1 and the single-step circuit of Fig. 5-2. Fortunately, the NAND gate required for the latch is available in the 74LS00 pack from the single-step circuit, so the entire bus-display and single-step system requires only four 14-pin IC packs and eight discrete LEDs.

Sec. 5.3 Data-Bus Display

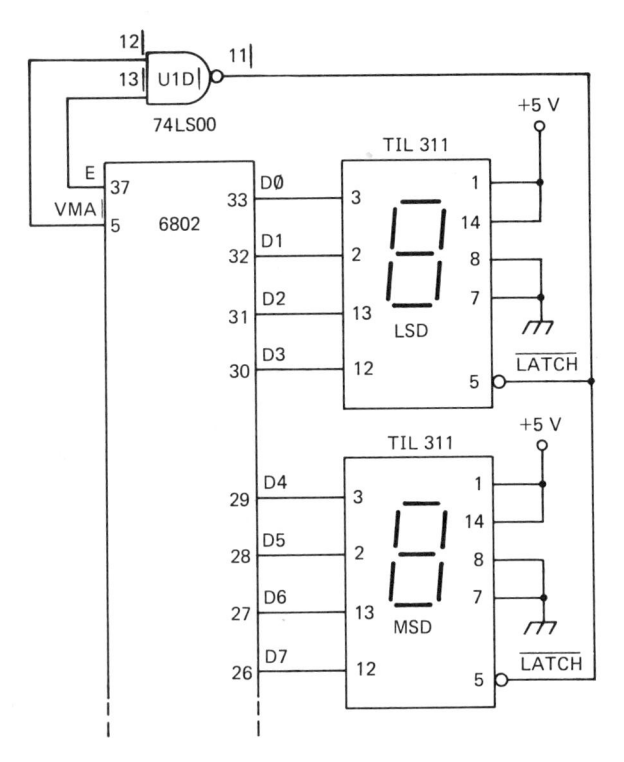

Figure 5-3 Two TIL-311 ICs latch the last word on the data bus and display it in hex while the processor is halted.

The data-bus display when the processor is halted requires some interpretation:

- For most 8-bit data operations the display will be the final data as loaded, stored, summed, rotated, and so on, by the last instruction executed.
- For 16-bit operations the display will be the low-order byte of the final data from the last instruction.
- For Branch operations the data display will be the displacement (number of bytes to be skipped if the branch is taken). Again, the branch is the *last* instruction executed.
- For inherent-mode (single-byte) instructions the display will be the op code of the *next* instruction to be executed.

Remember that the *address* bus, when halted, always displays the address of the next instruction to be executed. Appendix C contains complete details on the data appearing on the address and data buses for each cycle.

If you have money you can display the address bus on *TIL 311s*, too. Just connect them as you did for the data bus, but omit the NAND gate and connect the LATCH inputs (pin 5) directly to ground.

5.4 ADDRESS RECOGNITION

Single stepping through an entire program can become a little tedious if the first thing you run into happens to be a delay loop that decrements X from $FFFF to ∅ in 200 000 easy pushes of the button. Figure 5-4 shows a circuit that will allow the processor to run at full speed until a preselected section of the program is reached, whereupon it will halt and wait for single-step commands.

Skip-two-my-loops. Let's say that we are running the *Hex Drill* program listed on page 72. Upon reset, the tone is heard and the first hex digit appears, but then the processor gets lost. The first digit just stays there and nothing else happens.

Using the circuit of Fig. 5-4, we set the address switches to 1∅1∅ 1111, (or $AF), which is the low-byte address where the processor outputs the first hex digit. We now push the GO switch S4 and the program runs through the instruction at address $FFAF, passing through the BEEP loop in a fraction of a second. We now single step six times or so. Let us assume that reading the address and data displays convinces us that we are following LOOP2 properly. We don't want to follow it 65 000 times, however, so we reset the address switches to 1∅11 1∅∅1 (or $B9), which is the first address after LOOP2. We push the GO button again, thus running through LOOP2. Now we single-step through the second-digit routine (addresses $FFB9–$FFC7. Undoubtedly, we will find that the processor does not follow the program as expected in this area, and it should be a fairly simple matter to check the object code to determine why.

If, after pressing GO, the displays never come to rest, the address we have selected is never being reached. Pressing HALT (S5) will allow us to see where the processor is getting hung up. If this happens, it would be a good idea to set the address recognizer for an earlier point in the program, and then step through subsequent instructions to see where the departure from the listed program occurred.

Circuit operation. Figure 5-4 shows the single-step circuit and the address-recognition circuit together so that their interrelationship can be seen. The address- and data-bus displays should be used with these circuits.

U5A and B comprise a *set-reset* flip-flop. With S4 open a momentary *low* at pin 1 of U5A (from S5 closure or address recognition via U6) will reset output pin 3 high. This delivers a *false* input to negative-true OR gate U5C, and $\overline{\text{HALT}}$ is held low to keep the processor in the WAIT state (although a low pulse at $\bar{Q}$ can *step* the processor in this state).

Pushing the GO button causes a momentary *low* at pin 5 of U5B, setting pin 6 *high* and pin 3 *low*. This permits the processor to run until U6 or S5 resets the flip-flop.

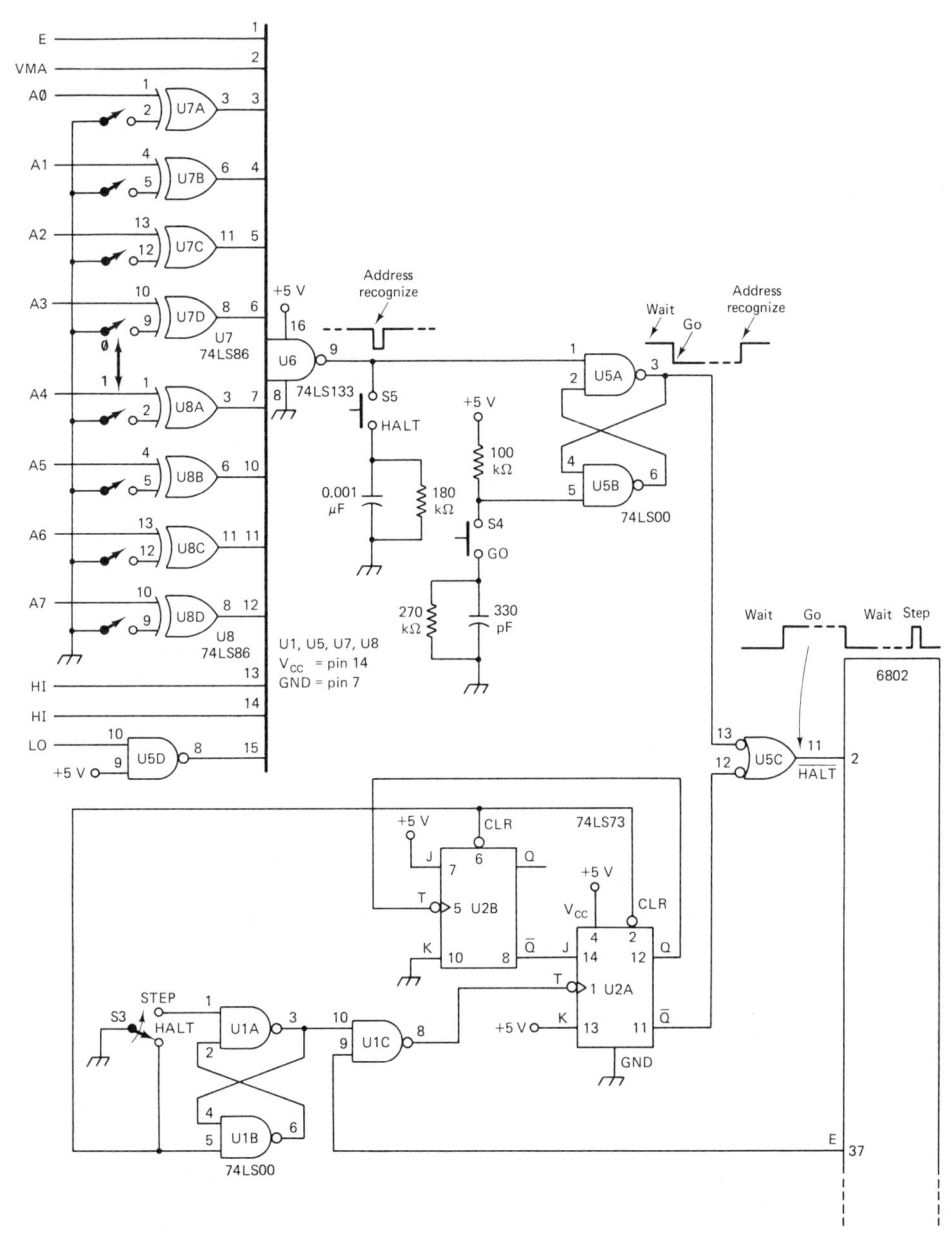

Figure 5-4 This circuit lets the processor run to a predetermined address, set by the eight switches at the upper left. The program can then be traced from that point by single-stepping.

Eight exclusive-or gates are used to select the address to be recognized. The output of an exclusive-or gate goes *high* when one input OR the other is *high*, but *not* when both inputs are *high* together. Setting the switched input *low* will make the output high only when the address input is *high*, and vice versa. A 13-input NAND gate is used to produce an active-low output only when all eight address lines are at the selected binary values.

The *E*-clock and Valid Memory Address lines must also be *high* to enable the halt-on-address function. Three more inputs, two active *high* and one active *low*, are provided to further specify the *halt* location. If the program accesses different addresses with identical low-order bytes, one or more of these lines may be connected to selected address lines to differentiate among them. For example, the systems that we have been building might access the following four addresses, which are identical in the low-order byte but unique in the bit (or bit combination) indicated:

$0000   (RAM)   A14 = 0
$4000   (LATCH)   A14 = 1 and A15 = 0
$FE00   (ROM)   A8 = 0 and A9 = 1
$FF00   (ROM)   A8 = 1

These extra three inputs can be used to halt on a data write ($R/\overline{W}$ line) or on a data output (latch output) if desired. If not used, these HI and LO lines should be connected to V_{CC} and ground, respectively.

5.5 MICROCOMPUTER TROUBLESHOOTING TIPS

Malfunctions in a microcomputer system can be caused by either hardware or software problems. Although there is usually no simple way to determine whether the trouble is caused by hardware or software, there are some probabilities to be considered.

- A new system, just breadboarded, wirewrapped, or soldered up is likely to contain hardware and software errors, but the hardware errors must be eliminated before we can make much of a start looking for software errors.
- A system which had been functioning, but suddenly malfunctions for no apparent reason, undoubtedly has good software. Suspect hardware problems, such as a bad chip or shorted or broken wiring.
- If a system worked with one program but malfunctions when a new or modified program is installed, suspect software errors.

Hardware errors are extremely difficult to find. The best defense is not to make the error in the first place. This is very obvious, and everyone nods in agreement when you say it, but it is discouraging to see how many people will, nevertheless, rush through a wiring job with a scribbled half-finished system diagram, using odd lengths of wire and slipshod techniques. Here are some pointers for avoiding and locating hardware errors.

1. Make a copy of the system diagram just for construction notes, and brite-line each pin number and component as the connections are completed.
2. Don't settle for poor connections. If a breadboard spring feels weak, if a socket pin seems about to break off, if a wirewrap termination seems to have overstressed the wire—don't just hope for good luck. Get rid of the faulty material and do it over so it's solid.
3. Check *all* the pins that are supposed to be tied to V_{CC} for +5.0 V. If any of the voltages are below 4.9 V, use heavier wire for V_{CC} and ground. If the 'scope shows noise pulses larger than 0.1 V p-p, place a 0.1-μF capacitor from V_{CC} to ground at that point.
4. Check the E clock for square waves. A 2-MHz crystal should give a 2-μs period at E. Check the crystal and associated capacitors if the clock signal is faulty.
5. Observe the address lines on the 'scope. Are there any that seem stuck *high* or *low*? *"Low"* should be several tens of millivolts, and *"high"* should fall considerably short of V_{CC}. Do any seem to be shorted to V_{CC} or ground?
6. Sometimes a line switches so infrequently and for such a short period to its other state that it cannot be seen on the 'scope trace. Set the 'scope to 5 ms/division, driven (not auto) sweep. If a trace appears repetitively on the screen at any fixed position of the trigger level control, there is obviously a triggering signal present, even if it is too short to be observed.
7. Write a simple diagnostic program that switches all address and data lines and observe them on the 'scope (see Section 3.3).
8. As you single-step through the program, keep notes of all misinterpreted instructions, and convert them to binary. For example, if an op code loaded as $86 (LDAA, binary 1000 0110) is being interpreted as $8A (ORAA, binary 1000 1010), it may be that data lines D2 and D3 have been crossed. Other instances of data or address bytes having bits 2 and 3 interchanged will confirm this.

Software errors are of two kinds: slip-ups and fudge mistakes. Slip-ups are easy to fix once you spot them with the single-step circuit or a logic analyzer (Chapter 7). They consist of miscopied digits, miscounted branch displacements, a BCC where you wanted a BCS, and the like.

Fudge mistakes are hard to spot and harder to fix, because they arise from lack of a clear understanding of the program you are writing in the first place. The basis of troubleshooting is checking out your expectations of what should be happening against what is actually happening in the hardware. It follows that if you don't have clear expectations about what should be happening, you can't troubleshoot. Here are some notes on software trouble location.

1. Halt the processor at random several times and read the address display. Is it landing at addresses outside the listed program?
2. Use the circuit of Fig. 5-4 (or the logic analyzer of Chapter 7) to follow the program, step by step, skipping the delay loops. Investigate any unexpected branches.
3. Examine the instruction-set specifications (last two pages), paying particular attention to the boolean/arithmetic operation description and the effects of the instruction on the condition-code register flags. Program errors often result from misunderstanding of the details of an instruction's function.
4. If the problem is not corrected by this stage, it is probable that there is a flaw in the program logic.

Checking program logic. Get out your flowchart and make sure that you understand clearly every operation on it. Label the flowchart using the same names that you have on the program listing. If some parts of the chart are too general to make the machine functions clear, make a sub-flowchart in more detail for these sections.

Follow the chart mentally. Think like a 6802. Take each loop twice, on the first pass and on the last pass. Jot down the resulting register and RAM data for some sample starting data. Make sure that you have it clearly in mind what conditions are necessary to get into and out of each loop. Make notations on the flowchart.

Now follow the program source-code listing in the same way. Read the labels and comments, and make sure that they reflect the plan presented in the flowchart. Modify them and make notes where appropriate. Put example data in the comments to lend some concreteness to your thinking. Follow that data through a few loops to see how it is affected by the program.

Check the object code against the source code. Do the op codes given match the stated instructions for addressing mode as well as function? Are the branches counted correctly?

5.6 CORRECTING SOFTWARE ERRORS

Changing program errors requires an exorbitant amount of work. One misprogrammed byte, one missing instruction, and you have to go back and load the whole thing into another EPROM, byte by byte. There must be a way

Sec. 5.6 Correcting Software Errors

around all this. In fact, there are three. The easiest to implement is also the least satisfactory. We will list them in order.

Leave holes in your program every five or ten instructions. A "hole" is simply a group of three unprogrammed bytes in the EPROM. These will read as $FF, $FF, $FF, which the 6802 will interpret as "Store the contents of the X register at addresses $FFFF and $0000." The former address is ROM, so the processor's efforts to write to it will be in vain. We can make it a practice to avoid using the latter, which is an internal RAM byte. You can go back later and insert new instructions in these unprogrammed bytes, and if you are lucky, patch up your program. If you need to add a long routine, just insert a JMP to a free portion of the EPROM and then JMP back to pick up your original program flow. Remember these precautions if you leave holes in your EPROM.

1. You must leave multiples of three bytes, or the processor will get out of step and confuse data types. Three or six bytes every 10 instructions is a good bet.
2. The STX changes the Z, N, and V flags, so be sure not to place your hole between an instruction that sets these flags and one that senses them. The next chapter explains flags in detail.
3. Each STX instruction takes six machine cycles. This could throw off your timing, especially if the "hole" is in a loop.
4. When filling the holes with new instructions, fill any unused bytes with NOP instructions ($01). If you leave $FFs in anything other than multiples of three, you'll crash the program (see 1 above).

Build the development system described in Chapter 9. This will allow you to key your programs into RAM, change the RAM bytes at will (not just binary 1s to binary 0s, as with the EPROM), and store the programs in EPROM or on cassette tape. You still have to leave holes in your program, or else, if you have to insert a routine in the middle of it, you'll have to re-enter the whole second half.

Buy a cross-assembler. This is a program for a desktop micro or larger computer, which translates source code into machine code and automatically keeps track of addresses and branches. Every instruction has a line number, and lines can be modified, copied, moved, inserted, or deleted at will. The machine code can then be fed directly to an EPROM burner. With an assembler and computer-driven programmer, you can change or add a few lines of source code in your program and have a new EPROM ready to try in about 3 minutes—even if the program is hundreds of bytes long. And you never have to worry about misreading the programming card, miscounting a branch, or forgetting to change an operand address.

The programs in this book, beginning with *Hex Drill*, were assembled on the S-C Macro 6800 Cross-Assembler from S-C Software (P.O. Box 280300, Dallas, TX 75228), and burned with the HMS3264 EPROM programmer from Hollister Microsystems (1455 Airport Blvd., San Jose, CA 95110).

Improving program logic. Sometimes program logic becomes such a tangled ball of yarn that no ordinary brain can hope to unravel it. You can tell when this is the case, because you keep losing track of the flow of the program. By the time you get to the third loop you have forgotten what happened in the first loop, but the two are interdependent, so you have to start over. In the next chapter, we reveal some techniques for straightening out tangled programs.

CHAPTER SUMMARY

1. Bringing the $\overline{\text{HALT}}$ line of the 6802 *low* stops the processor at the end of its current instruction. Bringing it *high* for one machine cycle, then *low* again, allows a single instruction to be executed at a time.
2. The 6802 address bus holds the address of the next instruction when the machine is halted. This can be displayed on discrete LEDs. The data bus is in a high-Z state during halt, but the last data on the bus can be latched and displayed in hex with a pair of *TIL 311* displays.
3. Address recognizers consist mainly of an AND gate with a large number of inputs, mostly connected to address lines, or inversions of them. They can be used to halt the processor at a selected address in a program.
4. Hardware troubles are more easily avoided than weeded out. Meticulous system diagrams and construction techniques are essential to avoid getting snowed under by hardware errors.
5. Software errors can be found by predicting the next address the machine will go to and single-stepping to see if it really goes there.
6. Software errors can sometimes be corrected without erasing the EPROM if you leave unprogrammed bytes ($FF) in multiples of three at intervals throughout your program.

6

Input Interfacing: Two Games of Skill

Up to now all our projects have operated with no data input, other than restarting the program. This chapter presents two interactive games using pushbutton inputs. We will find that this level of operator control invites us to make use of an internal processor register that we have not seen before, so we will spend some time on the various uses of the *stack pointer*. Finally, we will see how the second game, which is quite involved, requires a rather difficult program, and we will see how a technique called *top-down linear programming* makes it remarkably more simple.

6.1 MEM: A COMPUTER MEMORY GAME

This game involves inputting data to the computer data bus from four external pushbuttons. An interfacing problem arises because the data bus must also carry op codes, address bytes, and other program data. We cannot simply tie the switches to the data bus, because they would short out other essential data on the bus.

Input buffers are used to interface the data-input device to the microcomputer data bus. These are simply noninverting digital amplifiers with tristate outputs. The outputs are connected to the data bus and are left in the high-impedance (floating) state until the processor enables the outputs.

This enabling signal is a combination of high-order address bits, VMA, and the Read/Write-not line. Thus the input port (group of bits) is assigned an address by the logic that enables it. Figure 6-1 shows an input port selected by a read of address $2000. Only the low 4 bits (D0–D3) are shown, but there may be 8 if we use eight buffers.

The MEM game is a simple memory challenge. The board contains four pushbuttons, each with an associated LED. You can identify each pair with four numbers, colors, shapes, or whatever you like. The first player makes a series of button pushes—16 in all—in any order that he chooses. The second player then attempts to repeat that same series from memory. As soon as an error is made, the number of correct entries is displayed in binary on the four LEDs.

The hardware diagram for the MEM game is given in Fig. 6-2. To minimize the number of chips required, we have introduced the 74LS138 three-line to one-of-eight decoder. This chip contains all the AND gates and inverters to decode the high three address lines, A15–A13, and activate one of

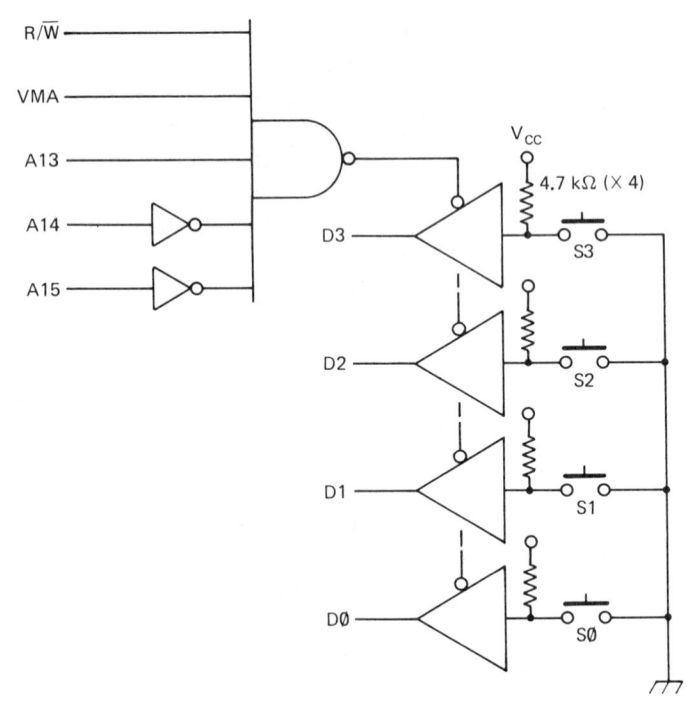

Figure 6-1 The input switches are connected to the data bus when the processor executes a *read* at any address from $2000 through $3FFF. A closed switch inputs a logic-0 bit.

Sec. 6.1   MEM: A Computer Memory Game

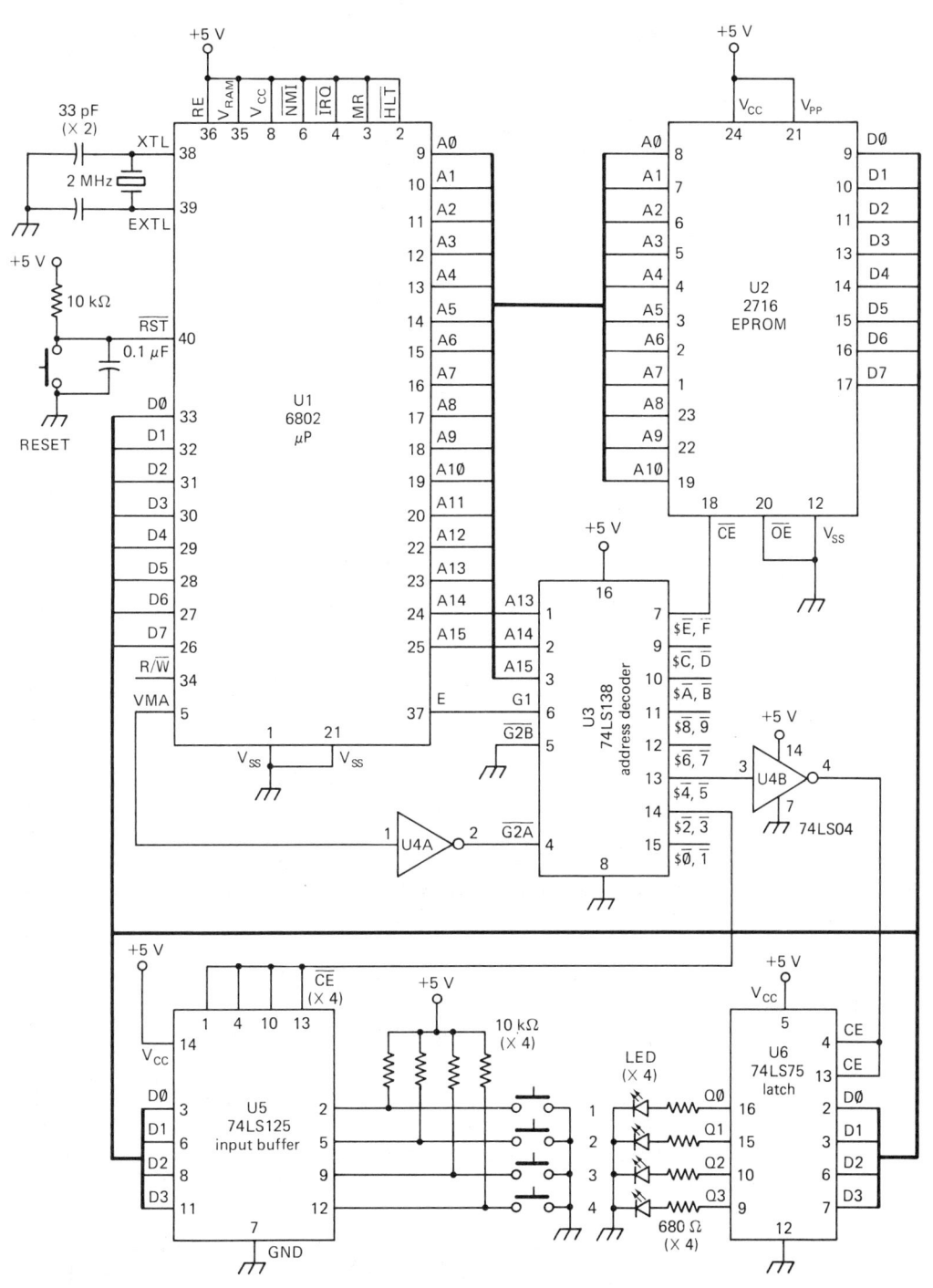

Figure 6-2 System diagram for the MEM game. A 74LS138 handles all address decoding.

eight devices according to the following schedule:

Address Lines			Base Address	Top Address
A15	A14	A13		
0	0	0	0000	1FFF
0	0	1	2000	3FFF
0	1	0	4000	5FFF
0	1	1	6000	7FFF
1	0	0	8000	9FFF
1	0	1	A000	BFFF
1	1	0	C000	DFFF
1	1	1	E000	FFFF

We have only the EPROM, the output port, and the input port to activate, so only three outputs will be used. The EPROM must use the highest output because it contains the reset vector (FFFE). The lowest output covers internal RAM addresses 0000-007F and thus cannot be used for external devices.

Normally-open pushbuttons are more readily available than the normally-closed type, so we use them even though they produce a logic 0 when selected. This is easily compensated for by the software COM (complement) instruction, which changes all 1s to 0s and all 0s to 1s. (Connecting the switch to V_{CC} and the resistor to ground would work as an alternative, but the inputs would be more vulnerable to noise pickup.)

The flowchart for the MEM game appears in Fig. 6-3. A file of data is built by incrementing the X register from 0000 through 000F and storing successive nonzero data from the input buffer. After complementing, the only data possibilities are $01, $02, $04, and $08. Any inputs from the high-order bits, D4-D7, are masked off by ANDing the complemented input with 0000 1111, or $0F.

A nested-loop delay runs accumulator B through 256 increments for each of 256 counts of a RAM location called COUNT ($0030), resulting in a 0.8-second delay after a key input is accepted. This is called a software debounce, and it prevents the processor from filling the whole file in less than a millisecond from one press of a button.

When 16 nonzero key inputs have been accepted and stored in the file, all LEDs flash to let the player know that it is time to repeat the sequence. The delay for this flash uses the X register, leaving it back at 0000 (the start of the file).

The program now accepts nonzero key inputs and compares them, successively, with those previously stored in the file. The X register contains the number of matching entries, which is the score. As soon as input data does not match corresponding file data, the score (low byte of X) is dis-

Sec. 6.1   MEM: A Computer Memory Game

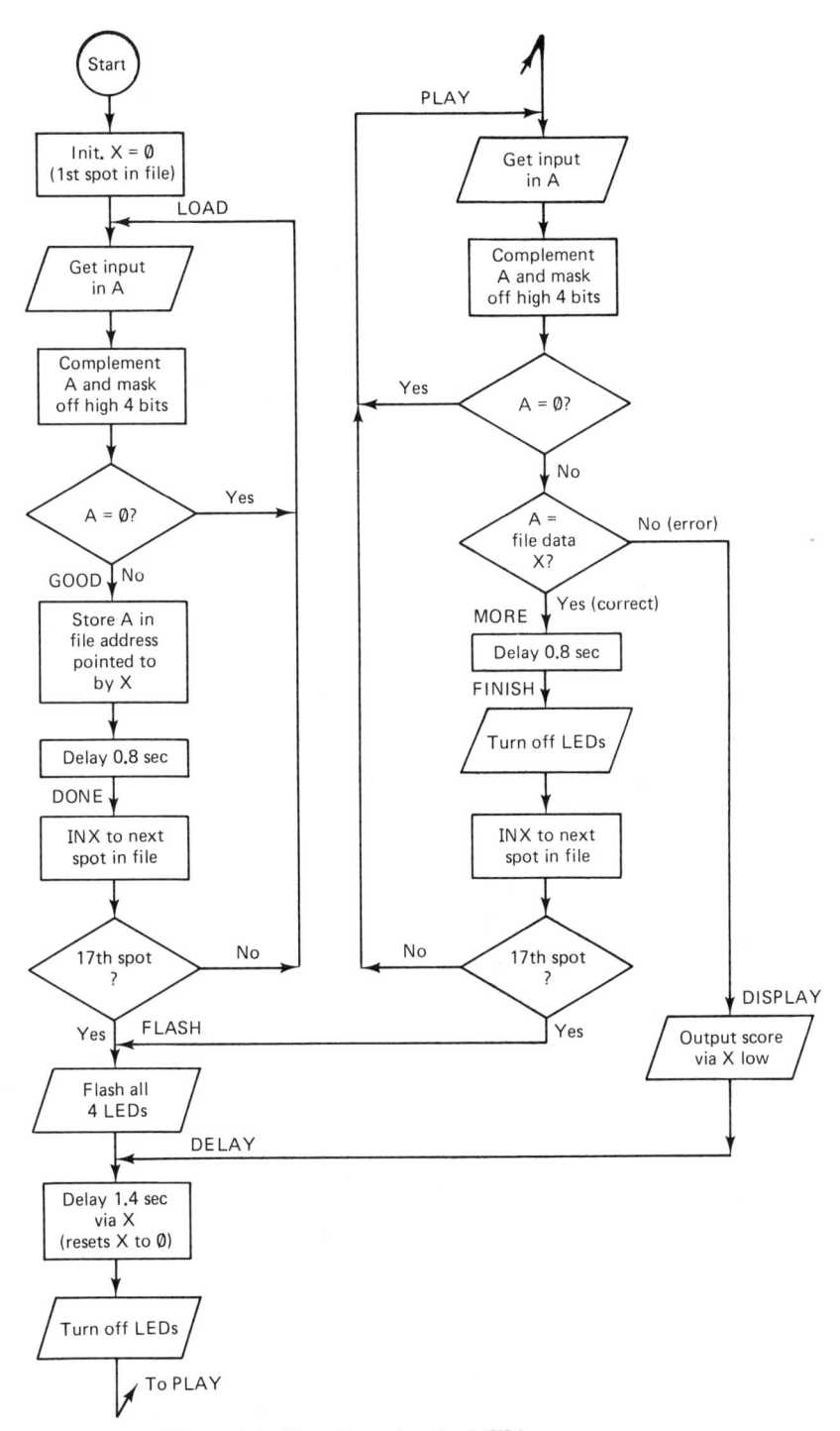

Figure 6-3 Flowchart for the MEM game program.

played. If all 16 data words match, all four LEDs flash. The first player is then given a chance to see if he can repeat his own series as well as his opponent did.

The complete program listing for the MEM game is given below.

MEM Game Version One: Program Listing

```
               1000 * ----------------------------------------------------------
               1010 ***********    MEM GAME -- VERSION ONE    ***********
               1020 *
               1030 * INPUT A SERIES OF 16 BUTTON PUSHES AND HAVE AN OPPONENT
               1040 *   TRY TO REPEAT THE SAME SERIES.  SCORE OF CORRECT MATCHES
               1050 *   IS DISPLAYED IN BINARY AFTER AN ERROR IS MADE.  YOU MAY
               1060 *   TRY AGAIN TO REPEAT THE SERIES AFTER AN ERROR OR CORRECT
               1070 *   RUN.  PUSH RESET TO LOAD A NEW SERIES.
               1080 *
               1090        .OR   $FF80       PROGRAM ORIGIN
               1100        .TA   $4780       ASSEMBLER WORKING RAM ADDRESS
0030-          1110 COUNT  .EQ   $30         DELAY-LOOP COUNTER
2000-          1120 INPUT  .EQ   $2000       BUFFER ADR (74125)
4000-          1130 OUTPUT .EQ   $4000       LATCH ADR (7475)
               1140 *
FF80- CE 00 00 1150        LDX   #0000       X REGISTER COUNTS 16 KEY INPUTS AND
               1160 *                          POINTS TO FILE SAVING KEY VALUES.
FF83- B6 20 00 1170 LOAD   LDAA  INPUT       GET KEY VALUE (1, 2, 4, OR 8).
FF86- 43       1180        COMA              INVERT SO "PRESSED" = LOGIC 1.
FF87- B7 40 00 1190        STAA  OUTPUT      LIGHT LED BY PRESSED KEY.
FF8A- 84 0F    1200        ANDA  #$0F        MASK OFF HI NIBBLE.
FF8C- 26 03    1210        BNE   GOOD        SCAN FOR KEY IN AGAIN IF
FF8E- 7E FF 83 1220        JMP   LOAD          NO KEY IN SENSED.
FF91- A7 00    1230 GOOD   STAA  00,X        STORE KEY VALUE IN FILE.
FF93- 5F       1240        CLRB              DELAY 1.2 SEC  WITH
FF94- 7F 00 30 1250        CLR   COUNT        NESTED LOOPS; ACC B GOES
FF97- 5C       1260 INNER  INCB                00 TO $FF IN INNER LOOP.
FF98- 27 03    1270        BEQ   OUTER
FF9A- 7E FF 97 1280        JMP   INNER
FF9D- 7C 00 30 1290 OUTER  INC   COUNT       RAM "COUNT" GOES 00 TO $FF
FFA0- 27 03    1300        BEQ   DONE          IN OUTER LOOP.
FFA2- 7E FF 97 1310        JMP   INNER
FFA5- 08       1320 DONE   INX               ADVANCE TO NEXT FILE SLOT.
FFA6- 8C 00 10 1330        CPX   #$0010      LAST FILE SLOT?
FFA9- 27 03    1340        BEQ   FLASH
FFAB- 7E FF 83 1350        JMP   LOAD        NO: GET ANOTHER KEY IN.
FFAE- 86 0F    1360 FLASH  LDAA  #$0F        YES: LIGHT ALL 4 LEDS.
FFB0- B7 40 00 1370        STAA  OUTPUT
FFB3- 08       1380 DELAY  INX               DELAY 1.4 SEC BY
FFB4- 27 03    1390        BEQ   DARK          COUNTING X TO $FFFF.
FFB6- 7E FF B3 1400        JMP   DELAY
FFB9- 7F 40 00 1410 DARK   CLR   OUTPUT      DARKEN ALL LEDS.
               1420 *
FFBC- B6 20 00 1430 PLAY   LDAA  INPUT       GET KEY IN.
FFBF- 43       1440        COMA
FFC0- 84 0F    1450        ANDA  #$0F        MASK OFF HI NIBBLE.
FFC2- 26 03    1460        BNE   VALID       IF NO KEY IN THEN
FFC4- 7E FF BC 1470        JMP   PLAY          LOOK AGAIN.
FFC7- B7 40 00 1480 VALID  STAA  OUTPUT      LIGHT LED BY KEY PRESSED.
FFCA- A1 00    1490        CMPA  00,X        IS KEY VALUE SAME AS STORED
FFCC- 27 03    1500        BEQ   MORE          IN FILE BY "LOAD" ROUTINE?
FFCE- 7E FF F2 1510        JMP   DISPLY      NO: DISPLAY SCORE
FFD1- 5F       1520 MORE   CLRB              YES: DELAY 1.2 SEC WITH
FFD2- 7F 00 30 1530        CLR   COUNT         NESTED LOOPS WHILE
FFD5- 5C       1540 INNR   INCB                DISPLAYING KEY LED.
```

Sec. 6.2 Subroutines and the Stack

```
FFD6- 27 03        1550          BEQ   OUTR
FFD8- 7E FF D5     1560          JMP   INNR
FFDB- 7C 00 30     1570  OUTR    INC   COUNT
FFDE- 27 03        1580          BEQ   FINISH
FFE0- 7E FF D5     1590          JMP   INNR
FFE3- 7F 40 00     1600  FINISH  CLR   OUTPUT
FFE6- 08           1610          INX         ADVANCE TO NEXT FILE ADR.
FFE7- 8C 00 10     1620          CPX   #$0010 LAST FILE LOCATION (16TH)?
FFEA- 27 03        1630          BEQ   PERFCT
FFEC- 7E FF BC     1640          JMP   PLAY   NO: GET NEXT KEY.
FFEF- 7E FF AE     1650  PERFCT  JMP   FLASH  YES: ALL 16 RIGHT; FLASH & PLAY.
FFF2- FF 40 00     1660  DISPLY  STX   OUTPUT SCORE IN LO BYTE OF X STORED LAST AT
FFF5- 08           1670  DELY    INX         ADR $4001 (STILL LATCH ADR).
FFF6- 27 03        1680          BEQ   AGAIN  DISPLAY SCORE FOR 1.4 SEC
FFF8- 7E FF F5     1690          JMP   DELY
FFFB- 7E FF BC     1700  AGAIN   JMP   PLAY   AND PLAY AGAIN.
                   1710  *
                   1720          .OR   $FFFE  RESET VECTOR AT $FFFE, FFFF
                   1730          .TA   $47FE  POINTS TO PROGRAM START
FFFE- FF 80        1740          .HS   FF80   ADR $FF80.
                   1750  * 6802 ADR $FF80= APPLE TA $4780 & 2716 ADR $0780
                   1760          .EN          END LISTING
```

6.2 SUBROUTINES AND THE STACK

If you look closely at the MEM flowchart you will notice that several routines from the LOAD section are repeated in the PLAY section of the program. Would't it be more efficient if we could use the same routines over, instead of writing them out twice? This is made possible by the instruction JSR (Jump to SubRoutine).

A **subroutine** is a program section that is stored in a sequence of memory locations separate from the sequence of the main program. It would not normally be accessed by the program counter. The JSR instruction has a two-byte operand which is the starting address of the subroutine, and the program counter jumps to this address on meeting a JSR.

The subroutine operates on the same accumulators, X register, RAM, and I/O data as used by the main program. The last instruction in the subroutine must normally be RTS (ReTurn from Subroutine). This command sets the program counter back to the address of the next instruction following the JSR in the main program. Figure 6-4 illustrates an example *jump to* and *return from* subroutine. Only one *call* of the subroutine is shown, but of course the advantage is that the subroutine can be called from several points in the main program, while the code need be written only once.

The stack and the stack pointer. How does the processor remember the address in the main program to which it must return when the subroutine is finished? This address is stored in a specially designated area of RAM called the *stack*. The JSR command automatically stores the low- and high-order bytes of the return address in the highest and second-highest locations of the stack area. (This is in addition to its function of jumping the program counter to the subroutine. Note that the JSR instruction takes nine machine cycles.) The RTS instruction then automatically re-

94   Input Interfacing: Two Games of Skill   Chap. 6

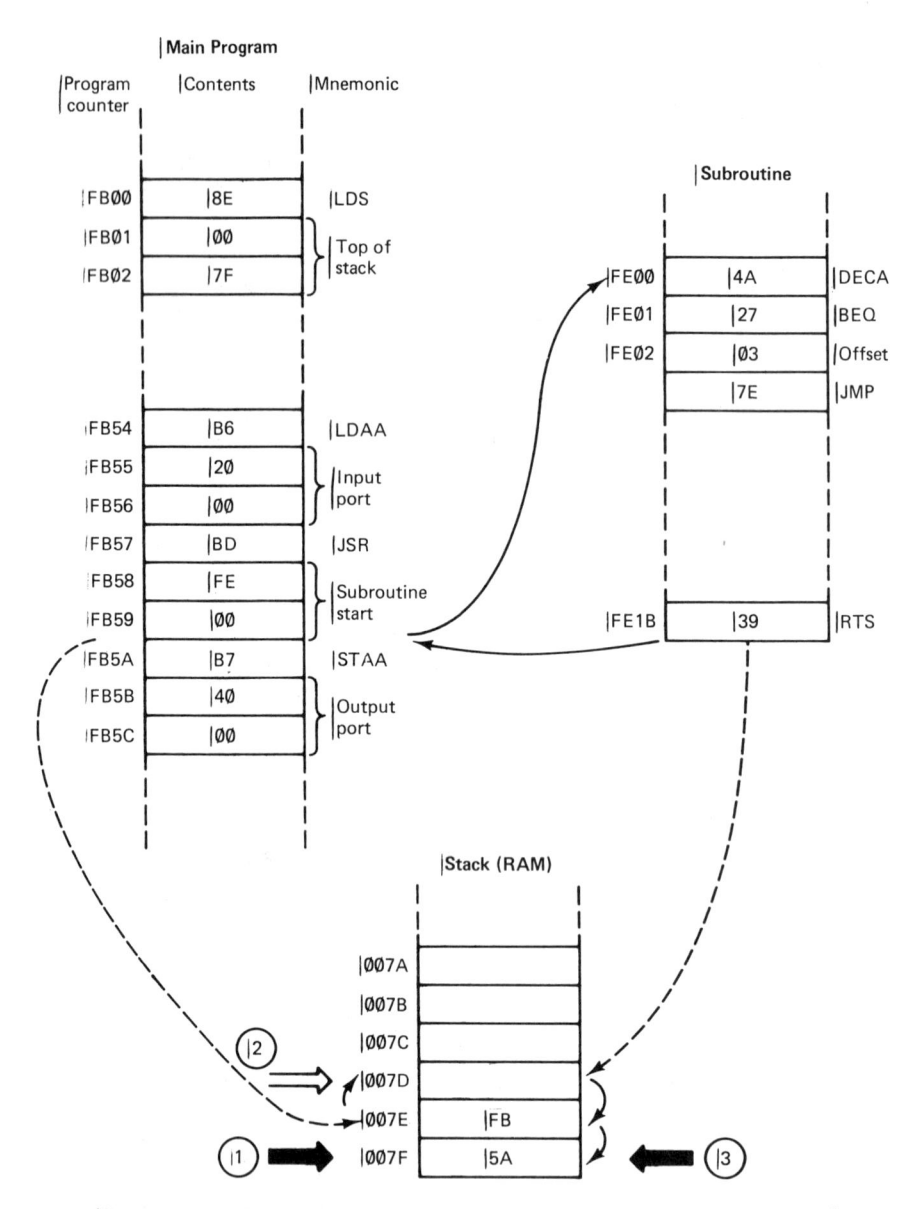

Program counter	Contents (Main Program)	Mnemonic
FB00	8E	LDS
FB01	00	Top of stack
FB02	7F	
FB54	B6	LDAA
FB55	20	Input port
FB56	00	
FB57	BD	JSR
FB58	FE	Subroutine start
FB59	00	
FB5A	B7	STAA
FB5B	40	Output port
FB5C	00	

Program counter	Contents (Subroutine)	Mnemonic
FE00	4A	DECA
FE01	27	BEQ
FE02	03	Offset
	7E	JMP
FE1B	39	RTS

Stack (RAM)	
007A	
007B	
007C	
007D	
007E	FB
007F	5A

Figure 6-4 A JSR causes the processor to leave the main program and execute a subroutine, after which it returns to the main program. The stack (a part of RAM) stores the return address. The stack pointer is at 1 before the subroutine, 2 during the subroutine, and 3 after the subroutine.

trieves these bytes from the stack and places them in the program counter. This is also illustrated in Fig. 6-4.

What, then, is this "stack area" of RAM? How do we know where it is, so that we don't inadvertently use those RAM bytes for something else? The answer is that there is an internal 16-bit machine register (this is the last one—I promise), called the *stack pointer*, which contains the address of the next RAM location available for stacking data. The programmer sets the stack pointer to the highest address in the desired stack area as part of the program initialization. (This is unnecessary if the program will not use subroutines, interrupts, or data stacking.)

Each time a word is stored in the stack, the stack-pointer register is automatically decremented, so it then points to the next lower RAM address. Each time a word is to be retrieved from the stack, the stack-pointer register is automatically incremented first, so the next higher location is actually read. To get the idea, visualize a deck of cards laid down one at a time on a stack, and then picked up one at a time. This is called a last-in, first-out stack or LIFO.

The stack provides a very convenient place to store data if you intend to retrieve it in inverse order of its stacking. Two instructions facilitate this: PSHA (push A data onto stack and decrement stack pointer) and PULA (increment stack pointer and pull data from stack into A). PSHB and PULB are also available.

More uses for the stack pointer. The stack-pointer register (SP) was designed for the uses just described and named accordingly, but don't let that limit your conception of its usefulness. It is a 16-bit register capable of being loaded, stored, incremented, and decremented. If you need to transfer double bytes of data between memory locations and SP isn't being used, by all means use it to move data.

The data in the X register can be transferred to SP, and vice versa, with the TXS and TSX commands, so the index register can be saved and retrieved with single-byte instructions.

The stack pointer can be used like an index register to read data forward through a file (autoincrement) or store data backward through a file (autodecrement). For example, here is a routine that will transfer 256 bytes from page $FA (ROM) to page $02 (RAM).

```
         START   LDS     #$F9FF
                 LDX     #$0200
         LOOP    PULA
                 STAA    00, X
                 INX
                 CPX     #$0300
                 BEQ     OUT
                 JMP     LOOP
         OUT
```

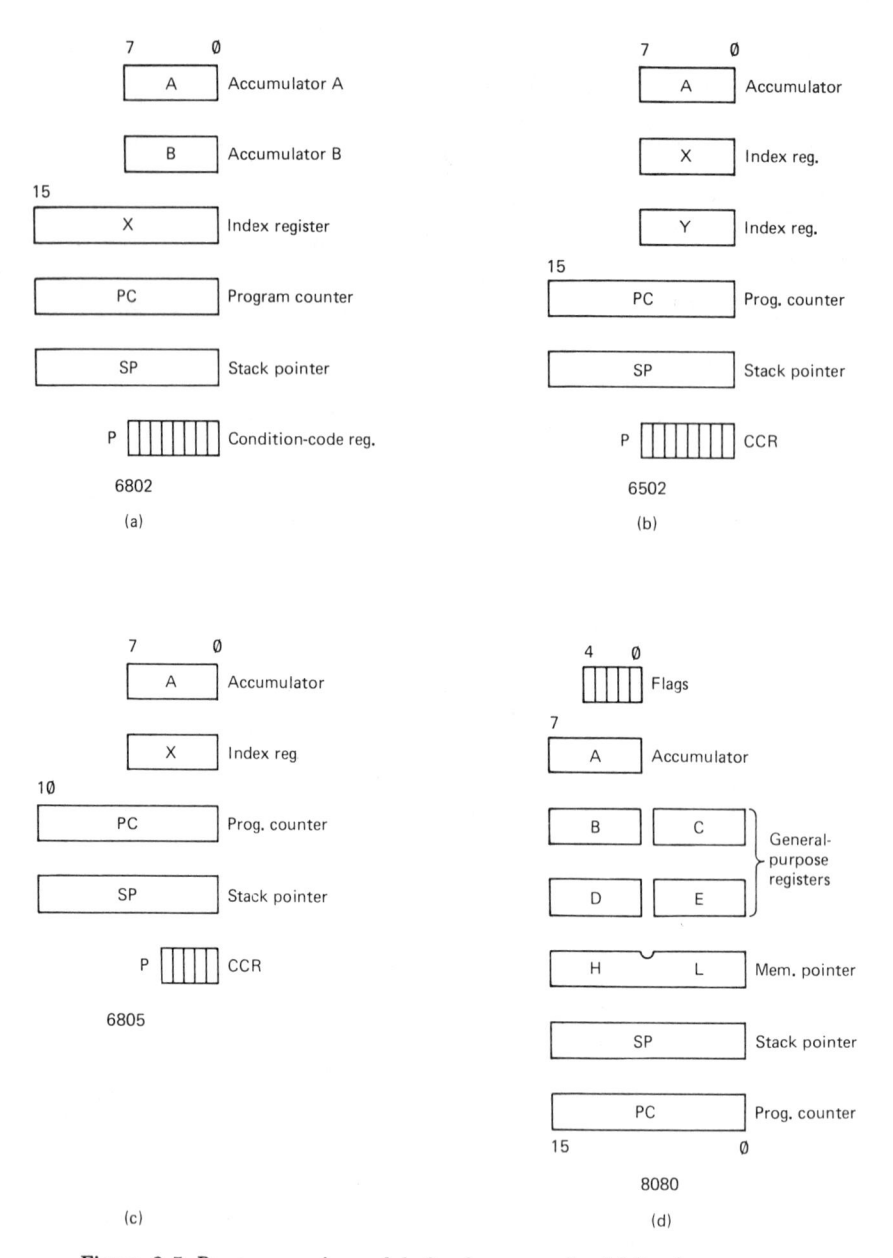

Figure 6-5 Programmer's models for four popular 8-bit microprocessors.

6.3 THE PROGRAMMER'S MODEL

Now that we have been introduced to all of the internal 6802 registers, we can draw a representation of them called a programmer's model. This model helps us keep the various registers in mind so that we are less likely to miss some of the possibilities when we are designing a program. It also provides a means for comparing different microprocessors. As an example, Fig. 6-5(a), (b), (c), and (d) show, respectively, the models for the 6802; the 6502, which was developed later by a group of 6800 veterans; the 6805, which is a simplified single-chip microcomputer with RAM, ROM, and I/O ports on one chip; and the 8080, which was one of the first microprocessors on the scene.

It can be seen that the 6802 and 6502 are very similar, except that the latter has one accumulator instead of two, and two 8-bit index registers.

The 6805 also has only a 256-word (8-bit) indexing range, and one accumulator; and it can access only 2^{11} or 2048 words of memory. None of these differences is difficult to understand if you understand the 6802.

The 8080, however, is apparently quite a bit different from the first three processors. In particular, we would want to delve into the uses of the four "general-purpose" registers and the H-L register if learning the 8080 were important to us. We would also want to find out how data files are handled, since nothing is specifically designated as an index register.

6.4 INTERRUPTS AND THE STACK

It is a frequent requirement to change some parameter of a program while the program is running, without resetting and starting it over. This is possible by using the interrupt pins on the 6802 processor. There are two: $\overline{\text{IRQ}}$ (Interrupt ReQuest, low-active) and $\overline{\text{NMI}}$ (Non-Maskable Interrupt, negative-transition active).

The Interrupt Request is recognized if $\overline{\text{IRQ}}$ pin 4 is held at a low level while the interrupt-mask flag (bit 4 of the condition-code register) is low. This flag is automatically set high at RESET, so a CLI (CLear Interrupt mask) must be placed in the main program to allow the $\overline{\text{IRQ}}$ to be seen. The interrupt service will not start until the current instruction is completed.

Upon recognizing the $\overline{\text{IRQ}}$, the processor will store all machine registers (except the stack pointer) on the stack. Figure 6-6(a) shows the stacking order for an example where the stack was initialized to $007F.

The program counter is then loaded with the starting address of the interrupt routine, which the programmer has stored at $FFF8 (high byte) and $FFF9 (low byte). These are called the IRQ *vectors* because they direct (vector) the processor to the interrupt routine. The IRQ internal routine also automatically sets the interrupt-mask flag bit (I) of the condition-code register. This prevents switch bounces from sending the processor back to the IRQ vector on each bounce.

The interrupt routine may then make free use of all machine registers, knowing that they will be restored to their original status once the interrupt routine is finished and the processor returns to the main program. The only

98 Input Interfacing: Two Games of Skill   Chap. 6

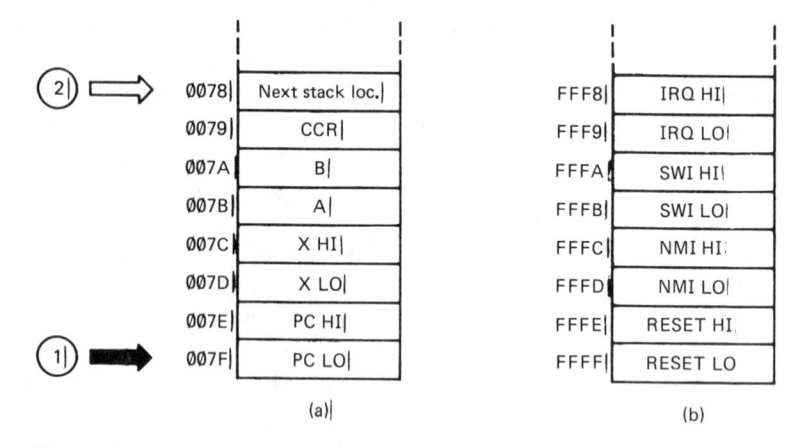

② ⇒ 0078		Next stack loc.		FFF8		IRQ HI
0079|	CCR		FFF9|	IRQ LO
007A		B		FFFA		SWI HI
007B		A		FFFB		SWI LO
007C		X HI		FFFC		NMI HI
007D		X LO		FFFD		NMI LO
007E		PC HI		FFFE		RESET HI
① ➡ 007F|	PC LO		FFFF|	RESET LO
	(a)			(b)

Figure 6-6 (a) Stacking order for interrupts with stack pointer initialized at $007F (point 1). Point 2 shows stack pointer after interrupt. RTI reads $79 through $7F, returning stack pointer to 1. (b) Interrupt and Reset vector locations.

exceptions are:

1. If the interrupt routine stores anything on the stack, it must retrieve it before returning to the main program.
2. If any timing operations were going on in the main program, they will be thrown off by the interrupt routine.
3. Any RAM locations altered by the interrupt routine and read by the main program will, of course, affect the main program.

The last instruction in the interrupt routine should normally be an RTI (ReTurn from Interrupt). This command will restore the machine registers from the stack, and the procesor will pick up the main program exactly as it left it.

If the $\overline{\text{IRQ}}$ is to be recognized more than once some provisions must be made for clearing the interrupt-mask bit with a CLI instruction that will be encountered after every interrupt. This instruction should normally be placed in the main program rather than in the interrupt routine, so it will be encountered *after* the RTI is serviced. You can see that a second recognition of $\overline{\text{IRQ}}$ before an RTI would drive the stack pointer another seven bytes down the RAM. If continued, this could overwrite the whole RAM down to 0000.

Care must also be taken to ensure that the $\overline{\text{IRQ}}$ is not recognized a second time just because the button is held down for a half a second. Remem-

Sec. 6.5   More about Branch Commands   99

ber that the computer can execute about 100 000 instructions in 0.5 second. To ensure that the $\overline{\text{IRQ}}$ signal is gone before the CLI instruction is encountered, we might:

- Insert a delay of 0.5 to 1.0 second between RTI and CLI.
- Drive the $\overline{\text{IRQ}}$ line from a one-shot which delivers one 10-μs *low* pulse for each button push.
- Include a program routine which checks for a *high* on the $\overline{\text{IRQ}}$ line (via an input buffer) before executing CLI.

The **Non-Maskable Interrupt** is similar to the $\overline{\text{IRQ}}$, with these three exceptions:

1. The vector address is $FFFC (high byte) and $FFFD (low byte).
2. The interrupt cannot be masked by the I flag or any other software device.
3. The $\overline{\text{NMI}}$ input (pin 6) responds to a high-to-low *transition*, rather than to a low level.

These last two considerations make it impossible to software-debounce the $\overline{\text{NMI}}$ input. A switch tied to $\overline{\text{NMI}}$ will cause seven bytes to be stored on the stack for each bounce, driving the stack down through your working RAM and back past address ØØØØ. If $\overline{\text{NMI}}$ is used, it should be driven by a hardware-debounce circuit, such as that shown by U1A and U1B in Fig. 5-2. The $\overline{\text{NMI}}$ input is quite sensitive to noise pickup, so lines to it should be kept short, and if not used, it should be tied directly to V_{CC}.

The SWI (software interrupt) responds to a program instruction, rather than to a hardware input. Figure 6-6(b) shows the vector address for the three interrupts and reset of the 6802.

6.5 MORE ABOUT BRANCH COMMANDS

Thus far we have made much use of the BEQ and BNE branch tests, but there are many other branch tests and features available with the 6802. This section will sort them out for you.

Back-branching or *negative* branching is possible by simply selecting a branch operand greater than $7F. Here is a table of forward and back branches:

$HI Digit ↓						Backward Relative (Decimal)								
8 -	128	127	126	125	124	123	122	121	120	119	118	117	116	115	114	113
9 -	112	111	110	109	108	107	106	105	104	103	102	101	100	99	98	97
A -	96	95	94	93	92	91	90	89	88	87	86	85	84	83	82	81
B -	80	79	78	77	76	75	74	73	72	71	70	69	68	67	66	65
C -	64	63	62	61	60	59	58	57	56	55	54	53	52	51	50	49
D -	48	47	46	45	44	43	42	41	40	39	38	37	36	35	34	33
E -	32	31	30	29	28	27	26	25	24	23	22	21	20	19	18	17
F -	16	15	14	13	12	11	10	9	8	7	6	5	4	3	2	1
$LO →	0	1	2	3	4	5	6	7	8	9	A	B	C	D	E	F
0 -	0	1	2	3	4	5	6	7	8	9	10	11	12	13	14	15
1 -	16	17	18	19	20	21	22	23	24	25	26	27	28	29	30	31
2 -	32	33	34	35	36	37	38	39	40	41	42	43	44	45	46	47
3 -	48	49	50	51	52	53	54	55	56	57	58	59	60	61	62	63
4 -	64	65	66	67	68	69	70	71	72	73	74	75	76	77	78	79
5 -	80	81	82	83	84	85	86	87	88	89	90	91	92	93	94	95
6 -	96	97	98	99	100	101	102	103	104	105	106	107	108	109	110	111
7 -	112	113	114	115	116	117	118	119	120	121	122	123	124	125	126	127

Forward Relative (Decimal)

To understand back branching, consider the odometer on a new car fresh off the assembly line. If we drove it backward for 3 miles, the odometer would run from 00000 to 99997. Thus -3 is indicated by 99997. Similarly, a branch operand of $FD indicates three counts back from $00, or -3.

So far we have always branched forward, and used the JMP instruction to return to earlier parts of the program. Now we can branch back directly and eliminate the JMP instruction. Remember that if the Branch is *not* taken, the program counter will be at the instruction following the Branch instruction. If the Branch *is* taken, the program counter will be displaced from this point, forward or backward, by the number of bytes given in the table above.

The BEQ and BNE instructions actually test a bit in the condition-code register (CCR) called the Z flag. This bit is set or cleared by an instruction preceding the Branch instruction. The Z flag is set when an operation involves an 8- or 16-bit word, all bits of which are zero. If any bits are non-zero the Z flag is cleared. Branch and Jump operations, operations involving the stack pointer, and operations on the condition-code register do not affect the Z flag. All other instructions do affect it.

The carry flag, C, is bit 0 of the condition-code register. In general, this flag is set when an operation involving an 8-bit data word causes the binary

Sec. 6.5 More about Branch Commands

value of that word to go from less than 256 (hex 1∅∅) to 256 or more. It is reset or cleared when an operation that could cause a carry set fails to do so. BCS and BCC test for carry set and carry clear, respectively.

The various subtract instructions cause C to be set if the subtraction causes a borrow (memory data greater than data in A for SUBA; B greater than A in SBA). The C flag is actually a B (borrow) flag for subtract operations.

The ADCA and ADCB instructions add the current value of the carry (1 or ∅) to the accumulator before performing the indicated addition. Similarly, SBCA and SBCB first subtract the borrow bit before performing the indicated subtraction. This allows multiple-precision arithmetic. The processor first adds the low-order byte and adds any carry generated into the addition of the high-order byte. ADDA, SUBB, and similar operations affect the C flag but do not take it into account in performing their operations.

Logic operations (AND, OR, EOR) and data-transfer operations (LDA, STA, TAB) cannot possibly cause a carry and do not affect the C flag. Nor do Branch, Jump, or 16-bit operations affect it.

The negative flag, N, is bit 3 of the CCR. The name was given because if a programmer is dealing with signed-number arithmetic, he uses the most-significant bit of the data words as a sign bit. A "1" in the highest bit indicates a negative byte. The value of the number is then interpreted "odometer style" as explained under the *back-branching* paragraph above ($FF = -1, $FE = -2, etc.).

Actually, the N flag simply takes on the status of the most-significant bit of the last 8- or 16-bit word handled, so this instruction can be used to check whether the word is above or below half of its maximum value, if unsigned or straight-binary arithmetic is being used.

Exceptions are Branch and Jump instructions; PUL and PSH stack operations; and Decrement, Increment, and Transfer operations on the X register and stack, none of which affect the N flag. BMI branches if N is set (minus result) and BPL branches if N is clear (plus result).

The overflow flag, V, is bit 1 of the CCR. It is like the carry flag but it is set when an overflow occurs from bit 6 to bit 7 (C is set by an overflow from bit 7). It is intended for use as a carry when signed-number arithmetic makes bit 6 the highest numeric bit. Decrement, Shift, Negate, and CPX instructions have varying effects on the V flag. Check the programming card (last two pages) for details. BVS and BVC branch on *set* and *clear* overflow flags, respectively.

Combination branch tests BGE, BGT, BLE, and BLT are meant to be used with signed-number arithmetic. Combinational test BHI is used after a SUB or CMP instruction in unsigned arithmetic. The branch is taken if the minuend (accumulator) is larger (higher) than the subtrahend (memory byte). BLS (Branch if Lower or Same) is the complement of BHI; if BHI would be taken, then BLS would *not* be taken, and vice versa.

The **half-carry flag**, H, is bit 5 of the CCR. It is similar to C, but is set by an overflow from bit 3 to bit 4. Its use is in programming for decimal addition rather than binary addition. It is sensed only by the Decimal Adjust A (DAA) instruction and not by any Branch commands.

The **interrupt-mask flag**, I, is bit 4 of the CCR. It is not sensed by any branch commands.

6.6 MEM GAME WITH SUBROUTINES AND INTERRUPT

Here is a new version of the MEM game, originally presented in Section 6.1. It uses subroutines for the *delay* and *key-input* portions of the programs, and back-branching is employed in several places in lieu of branch-forward and jump. The coding is therefore more compact than the original version.

An interrupt vector is included which changes the number of times a button needs to be entered from 16 to the current value. This permits the *play* sequence to begin before 16 inputs have been loaded, so you can start with a less challenging game.

An interrupt is accepted only during the KEYIN subroutine. The stack will thus contain the program counter address for Return from Subroutine, *and* the machine registers to be restored on Return from Interrupt. This poses no problem as long as we RTI before we RTS. Such "nesting" of interrupts and subroutines is diagrammed in Fig. 6-7(a). To avoid pulling the wrong data from the stack, every subroutine should end with an RTS and every interrupt should vector to a routine that terminates with RTI.

The interrupt routine puts $06 (2 bits high) in accumulator A to get out of the KEYIN routine and flag the LOAD routine not to store the data. The hardware system is the same as for the original MEM game (Figure 6-2), except for the addition of a pushbutton on $\overline{\text{IRQ}}$ as shown in Fig. 6-7(c). The flowchart is given in Fig. 6-7(b) and the program listing follows.

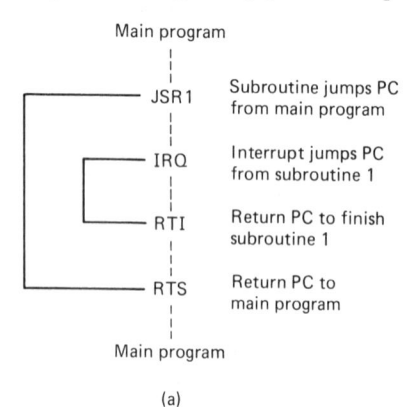

Figure 6-7 (a) Nested subroutines and interrupts.

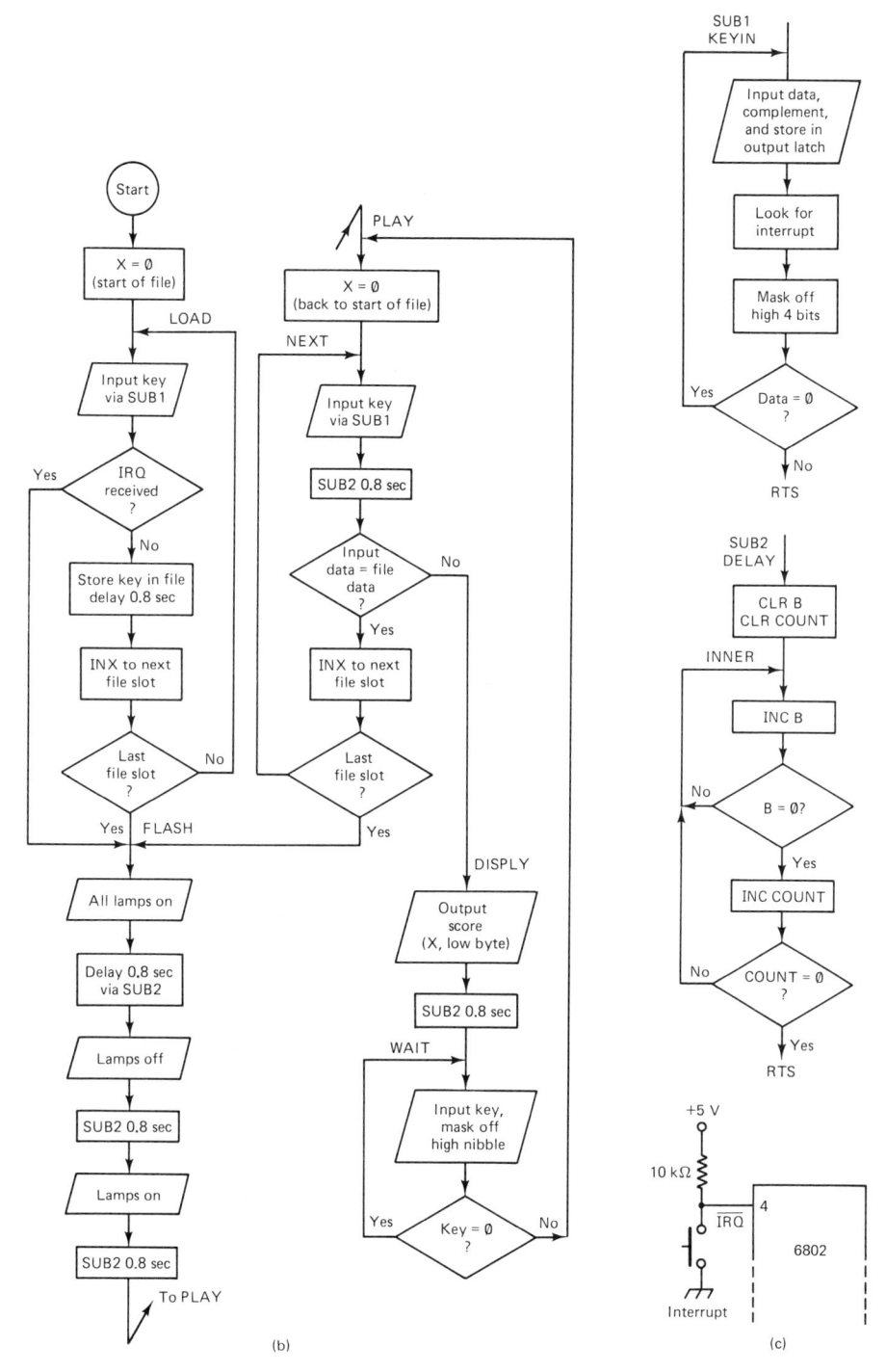

Figure 6-7 (*Cont.*) (b) Flowchart for MEM game using subroutines and interrupt. (c) Hardware modification to implement interrupt.

MEM Game, Version Two: Program Listing

```
              1000 * ------------------------------------------------------------
              1010 ********       MEM GAME  --  VERSION TWO       **********
              1020 *
              1030 * PROGRAM DEMONSTRATES SUBROUTINES AND INTERRUPT FUNCTION.
              1040 *
              1050 * RULES:
              1060 * 1. PUSH RESET TO START.
              1070 * 2. PUSH ANY OF THE 4 BUTTONS IN A SEQUENCE TO BE
              1080 *       REMEMBERED. (OVER .8 SEC GIVES A DOUBLE STROKE)
              1090 * 3. AFTER 16 ENTRIES ALL LAMPS WILL FLASH TWICE, AND IT
              1100 *       IS NOW YOUR TURN TO REPEAT THE SEQUENCE.
              1110 * 4. YOU CAN INTERRUPT THE LOADING SEQUENCE AT LESS THAN
              1120 *       16 ENTRIES BY PUSHING THE IRQ BUTTON.
              1130 * 5. THE MACHINE WILL FOLLOW YOUR ENTRIES UNTIL YOU MAKE A
              1140 *       MISTAKE, THEN DISPLAY YOUR SCORE IN BINARY.
              1150 * 6. AFTER THE SCORE IS DISPLAYED YOU MAY TRY AGAIN
              1160 *       TO REPEAT THE SAME SEQUENCE.
              1170 * 7. IF ANYONE REACHES 16 RIGHT ALL 4 LAMPS FLASH TWICE.
              1180 *
              1190        .OR    $FF80     PROGRAM ORIGIN
              1200        .TA    $4780     ASSEMBLER TARGET ADDRESS
0030-         1210 COUNT  .EQ    $0030     DELAY COUNTER
0031-         1220 TIMES  .EQ    $0031     NUMBER OF MOVES TO REPEAT
2000-         1230 INPUT  .EQ    $2000     INPUT BUFFER ADR
4000-         1240 OUTPUT .EQ    $4000     OUTPUT LATCH ADR
              1250 *
FF80- CE 00 10 1260       LDX    #$0010    START WITH A 16-MOVE GAME.
FF83- DF 31    1270       STX    TIMES
FF85- CE 00 00 1280       LDX    #$0000    START KEY FILE AT BEGIN OF RAM.
FF88- 8E 00 7F 1290       LDS    #$007F    STACK (FOR IRQ & JSR) AT END OF RAM.
FF8B- BD FF D6 1300 LOAD  JSR    KEYIN     GET KEY VALUE IN ACC A.
FF8E- 81 06    1310       CMPA   #06       CODE 06 MEANS IRQ WAS RECEIVED;
FF90- 27 0A    1320       BEQ    FLASH     END INPUTS & FLASH 4 LEDS.
FF92- A7 00    1330       STAA   00,X      PUT KEY VALUE IN FILE.
FF94- BD FF E5 1340       JSR    DELAY     DISPLAY KEY LED 0.8 SEC.
FF97- 08       1350       INX              NEXT FILE SLOT:
FF98- 9C 31    1360       CPX    TIMES     LAST SLOT?
FF9A- 26 EF    1370       BNE    LOAD        NO: LOAD NEXT KEY.
FF9C- 86 0F    1380 FLASH LDAA   #$0F      YES: LIGHT 4 LEDS
FF9E- B7 40 00 1390       STAA   OUTPUT         VIA OUTPUT LATCH
FFA1- BD FF E5 1400       JSR    DELAY         FOR 0.8 SEC.
FFA4- 7F 40 00 1410       CLR    OUTPUT    THEN DIM ALL LEDS
FFA7- BD FF E5 1420       JSR    DELAY         FOR 0.8 SEC.
FFAA- B7 40 00 1430       STAA   OUTPUT    THEN LIGHT ALL 4 AGAIN
FFAD- BD FF E5 1440       JSR    DELAY         FOR 0.8 SEC.
              1450 *
FFB0- CE 00 00 1460 PLAY  LDX    #$0000    BACK TO START OF KEY FILE
FFB3- BD FF D6 1470 NEXT  JSR    KEYIN     GET KEY VALUE IN ACC A.
FFB6- BD FF E5 1480       JSR    DELAY     DISPLAY KEY LED FOR 0.8 SEC.
FFB9- A1 00    1490       CMPA   00,X      SAME VALUE AS STORED IN FILE?
FFBB- 26 08    1500       BNE    DISPLY      NO: DISPLAY SCORE
FFBD- 08       1510       INX              YES: GO TO NEXT FILE SLOT.
FFBE- 9C 31    1520       CPX    TIMES     LAST FILE SLOT?
FFC0- 26 F1    1530       BNE    NEXT        NO: GET NEXT KEY.
FFC2- 7E FF 9C 1540       JMP    FLASH     YES: FLASH ALL - YOU WON!
FFC5- FF 40 00 1550 DISPLY STX   OUTPUT    SCORE IS IN X, LO BYTE.
FFC8- BD FF E5 1560       JSR    DELAY     DISPLAY IT 0.8 SEC MIN.
              1570 *
FFCB- B6 20 00 1580 WAIT  LDAA   INPUT     WAIT FOR KEY INPUT;
FFCE- 43       1590       COMA
FFCF- 84 0F    1600       ANDA   #$0F
FFD1- 27 F8    1610       BEQ    WAIT      PLAY AGAIN IF KEY
FFD3- 7E FF B0 1620       JMP    PLAY          INPUT IS FOUND.
              1630 *
```

Sec. 6.7 Air Raid: An Action Game

```
                    1640 *SUBROUTINE 1 ** GET KEY VALUE IN ACCUM A **
                    1650 *
FFD6- B6 20 00      1660 KEYIN  LDAA  INPUT    GET KEY;
FFD9- 43            1670        COMA           INVERT SO "PRESSED" = 1.
FFDA- 0E            1680        CLI            LOOK FOR INTERRUPT
FFDB- 01            1690        NOP            FOR A FEW MICROSECS.
FFDC- 0F            1700        SEI            MASK (DISABLE) INTERRUPTS.
FFDD- B7 40 00      1710        STAA  OUTPUT   LIGHT LED BY KEY.
FFE0- 84 0F         1720        ANDA  #$0F     MASK OFF HI 4 BITS.
FFE2- 27 F2         1730        BEQ   KEYIN    WAIT FOR A VALID KEY.
FFE4- 39            1740        RTS
                    1750 *
                    1760 *SUBROUTINE 2 ** DELAY FOR 0.8 SECONDS **
                    1770 *
FFE5- 5F            1780 DELAY  CLRB           DELAY 0.8 SEC
FFE6- 7F 00 30      1790        CLR   COUNT    VIA NESTED LOOPS
FFE9- 5C            1800 INNER  INCB           COUNTING ACC B AND
FFEA- 26 FD         1810        BNE   INNER    RAM "COUNT" FROM 00
FFEC- 7C 00 30      1820 OUTER  INC   COUNT    THRU $FF, AND BACK
FFEF- 26 F8         1830        BNE   INNER    TO 00.
FFF1- 39            1840        RTS
                    1850 *
                    1860 **** INTERRUPT (IRQ) ROUTINE **** STOP LOADING
                    1870 *
FFF2- DF 31         1880 ENUFF  STX   TIMES    PUT CURRENT NUMBER OF INPUTS IN "TIMES",
FFF4- 86 06         1890        LDAA  #06      REPLACING VALUE 16. LOAD ACC A WITH
FFF6- 3B            1900        RTI            FLAG 06 WHICH MAIN PROG INTERPRETS AS
                    1910 *                     "STOP INPUTTING".
                    1920 *
                    1930        .OR   $FFF8    ROM ADR $FFF8, FFF9 CONTAINS IRQ VECTOR
                    1940        .TA   $47F8        (THIS ADR FOR BENEFIT OF ASSEMBLER)
FFF8- FF F2         1950        .DA   ENUFF    WHICH IS ADR OF IRQ ROUTINE "ENUFF"
                    1960        .OR   $FFFE    RESET VECTOR
                    1970        .TA   $47FE        (ASSEMBLER TARGET ADR)
FFFE- FF 80         1980        .HS   FF80     START ADR OF PROGRAM.
                    1990 *
                    2000 *                     6802 ADR FF80 = TA 4780 = EPROM 0780
                    2010 *                     6802 ADR FFF8 = TA 47F8 = EPROM 07F8
                    2020 *
                    2030        .EN            END
```

6.7 AIR RAID: AN ACTION GAME

Air Raid simulates a duel between four ground-based antiaircraft batteries (represented by four pushbuttons) and planes flying overhead (represented by a left-to-right shifting light in a row of eight LEDs above the buttons). The hardware is very similar to that for the MEM game. The only difference is the 74LS373 output latch, which drives eight LEDs, whereas the 74LS75 drove four LEDs. Figure 6-8 shows the system diagram.

The rules for *Air Raid* become obvious to the player after a few minutes of experimentation, but we will define them precisely here as a first step in developing the program.

1. The "plane" LED shifts from left (position 7) to right (position 0) through the Carry bit (no light) and then back to bit 7. It dwells in each position for about 0.8 second at first, and speeds up after each shift, reaching 0.4 second after 14 passes.

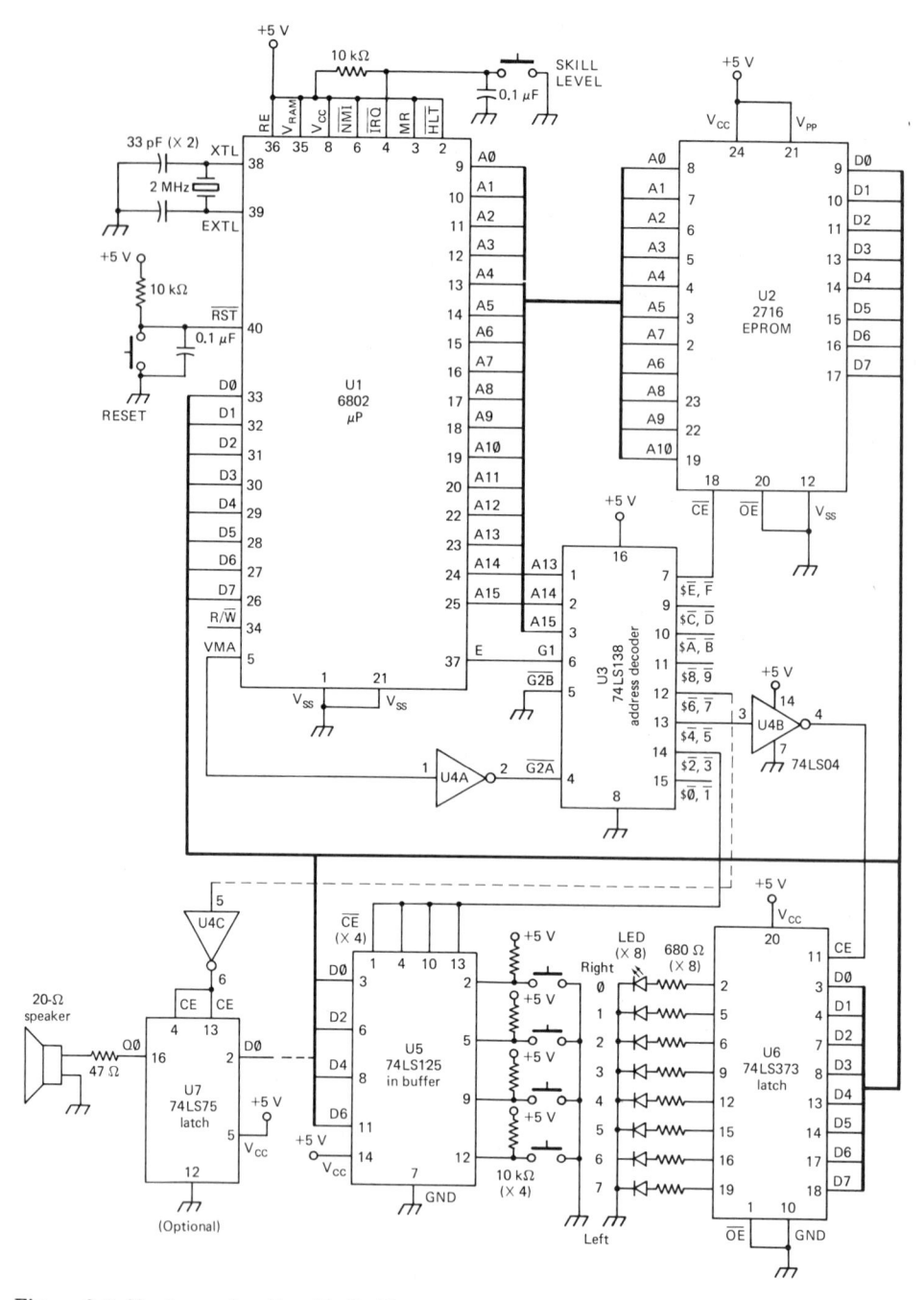

Figure 6-8 Hardware for the *Air Raid* game. U7 and the speaker may be omitted if the program for sound is not implemented.

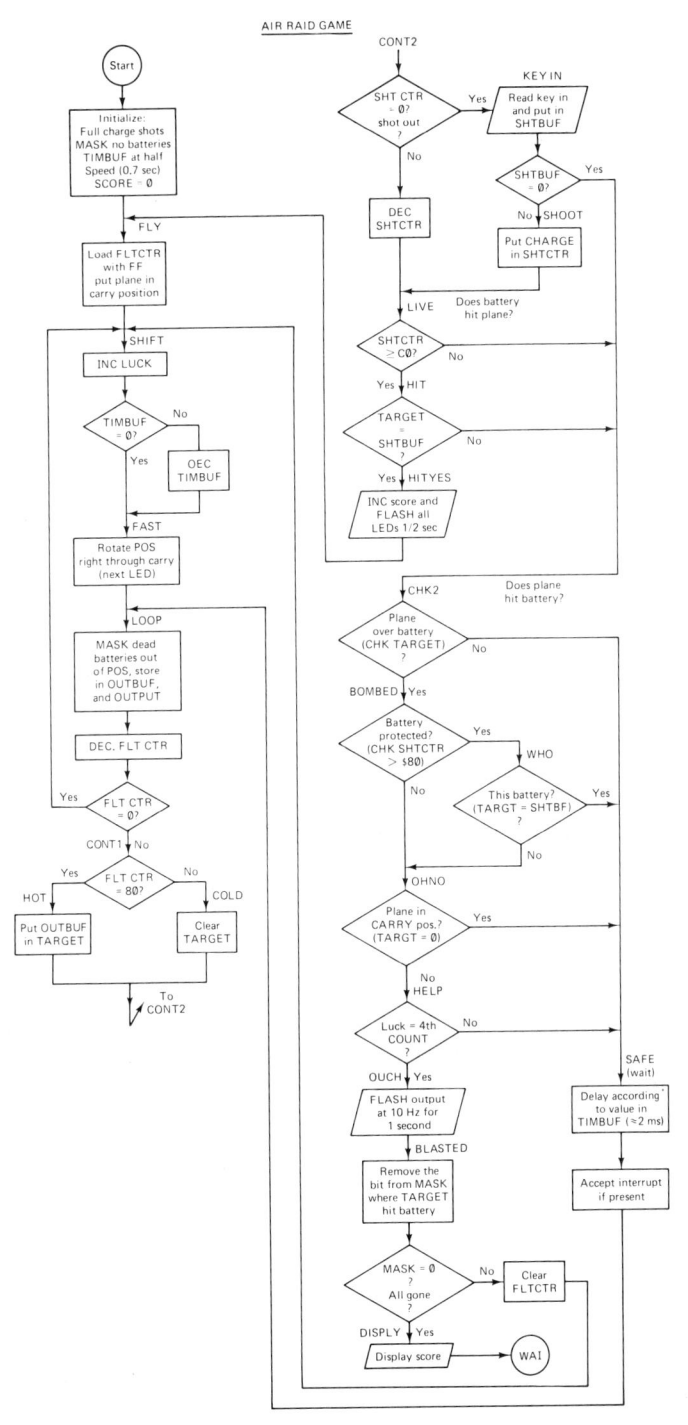

Figure 6-9 Flowchart for the "rat's nest" version of the *Air Raid* game.

107

2. A "Battery" button is located under LEDs 6, 4, 2, and 0. Touching a button during the third quarter of the plane's dwell over that button will hit the plane, lighting the whole sky (all eight LEDs) red as the plane explodes, and raising your score by 2.

3. The plane will attempt to shoot the battery at a point three-fourths of the way through its dwell. It will be able to make a hit only one-fourth of the time. If the battery is hit, the LED above it will flicker for about 1 second. That LED will then remain dark for all subsequent fly-overs, indicating a dead battery.

4. The battery is protected from being shot if the button is pushed during the second or third quarter of the plane's dwell. (The plane is too busy evading your shot.)

5. You cannot make another shot until one complete dwell time has elapsed from the previous shot.

6. You can make a harder game by pressing the IRQ button (but not during a "hit" flash). This will make each hit count 3 points instead of 2, but the plane will be vulnerable to your shot for only four-fifths as long a period. You can press IRQ up to four times, for hits that count up to 6 points each and a live time (near the $\frac{3}{4}$ dwell point) only $\frac{1}{20}$ of a dwell.

7. The game ends when all of your batteries have been shot out. Your score is then displayed in binary.

The flowchart for the *Air Raid* program is given in Fig. 6-9. If you are a bit intimidated by this chart, things are as they should be. It is meant to be a horrible example of an incomprehensible program. Actually, I wrote this program in perfectly good faith a few years ago, before I had learned much about programming philosophy. The detractors of this type of programming use the term "rat's nest" to describe it, and I have accepted the term. To give the program due credit, it *does* work and it *is* understandable, albeit with some difficulty. The labels on the flowchart match those on the source code, and the program is a fair representative of its type.

It will be a profitable exercise for you to go through this flowchart and the source code and comments that follow until you understand them. A good place to start is with the variable names at the start of the program listing. These will help you to interpret the flowchart. You can then see how the flowchart is implemented in source code, taking it piece by piece.

Air Raid "Rat's Nest": Program Listing

```
1000 * ------------------------------------------------------------
1010 *                         -- AIR RAID GAME --
1020 *            ILLUSTRATING "RAT'S NEST" PROGRAM STYLE
1030 *       COPYRIGHT 1984                      BY D. L. METZGER
1040 *------------------------------------------------------------
1050 *
1060         .OR  $FD00    PROGRAM ORIGIN
1070         .TA  $4000    ASSEMBLER TARGET ADR
```

Sec. 6.7 Air Raid: An Action Game

```
0000-              1080 MASK   .EQ  0         DARKENS LEDS OVER SHOT-OUT BATTERIES
0001-              1090 TIMBUF .EQ  1         DECR EACH FLIGHT TO SPEED GAME
0002-              1100 CHARGE .EQ  2         HOLDS TIME OF VALID SHOT. DECR BY IRQ
0003-              1110 SCORE  .EQ  3         INCREASED BY BATT HITTING PLANE
0004-              1120 SHTCTR .EQ  4         PICKED UP FROM CHARGE; COUNTED DOWN
0005-              1130 POS    .EQ  5         HOLDS POSITION OF PLANE; BIT 7 = LEFT
0006-              1140 PBUF   .EQ  6         HOLDS CARRY BIT DURING ROTATE INSTR
0007-              1150 OUTBUF .EQ  7         HOLDS CURRENT PLANE POS; 0 IF BATT OUT
0008-              1160 TARGET .EQ  8         PICKED UP FROM OUTBUF; IS BATT HIT?
0009-              1170 SHTBUF .EQ  9         HOLDS POS OF SHOT; COMPARE TO TARGET
000A-              1180 LUCK   .EQ 10         PLANE HITS BATT EVERY 4TH CHANCE
000B-              1190 FLASHR .EQ 11         COUNTS OUT 10 FLASHES WHEN BATT HIT
                   1200 *                     FLIGHT COUNTER IS ACCUM B
2000-              1210 INPUT  .EQ $2000      QUAD SWITCH BUFFER
4000-              1220 OUTPUT .EQ $4000      OCTAL LATCH
                   1230 *
FD00- 86 FF        1240        LDAA #$FF      INITIALIZE TIME OF
FD02- 97 02        1250        STAA CHARGE    VALID SHOT.
FD04- 97 00        1260        STAA MASK      MASK NO POSITIONS TO START.
FD06- 86 80        1270        LDAA #$80      INIT TIME DELAY 0.7 SEC
FD08- 97 01        1280        STAA TIMBUF    PER SHIFT.
FD0A- 7F 00 03     1290        CLR  SCORE     ZERO SCORE TO START.
                   1300 *
FD0D- C6 FF        1310 FLY    LDAB #$FF      START OUTER LOOP;
FD0F- 7F 00 04     1320        CLR  SHTCTR    FLIGHT COUNTER = 255,
FD12- 7F 00 05     1330        CLR  POS       NO SHOT TAKEN,
FD15- 86 01        1340        LDAA #01       PLANE IS IN
FD17- 97 06        1350        STAA PBUF      CARRY POSITION.
FD19- 7C 00 0A     1360 SHIFT  INC  LUCK      MIDDLE LOOP: PLANE'S LUCK
FD1C- 7D 00 01     1370        TST  TIMBUF    CHANGES.
FD1F- 27 03        1380        BEQ  FAST      SPEED UP SHIFTS UNLESS
FD21- 7A 00 01     1390        DEC  TIMBUF    ALREADY AT FASTEST.
FD24- 96 06        1400 FAST   LDAA PBUF      ROTATE THRU CARRY,
FD26- 06           1410        TAP            USING CARRY FLAG
FD27- 76 00 05     1420        ROR  POS       SAVED IN RAM PBUF.
FD2A- 07           1430        TPA
FD2B- 97 06        1440        STAA PBUF
                   1450 *
FD2D- 96 05        1460 LOOP   LDAA POS       MASK OUT DISPLAY OF
FD2F- 94 00        1470        ANDA MASK       PLANE LED OVER
FD31- 97 07        1480        STAA OUTBUF    DEAD BATTERY.
FD33- 5A           1490        DECB           DECR FLIGHT COUNTER;
FD34- 26 03        1500        BNE  CONT1     IF = 0, SHIFT PLANE
FD36- 7E FD 19     1510        JMP  SHIFT     RIGHT.
FD39- C1 80        1520 CONT1  CMPB #$80      IF FLIGHT COUNTER > $80
FD3B- 26 07        1530        BNE  COLD      PLANE IS NOT VULNERABLE.
FD3D- 96 07        1540 HOT    LDAA OUTBUF    IF FLT CTR = $80, PLANE IS
FD3F- 97 08        1550        STAA TARGET    VULNERABLE; PUT PLANE POS
FD41- 7E FD 47     1560        JMP  CONT2     IN TARGET, & BATTERY FIRES!
FD44- 7F 00 08     1570 COLD   CLR  TARGET    (NO TARGET IN THIS CASE)
FD47- 7D 00 04     1580 CONT2  TST  SHTCTR    IF SHOT TIME HAS RUN OUT,
FD4A- 27 06        1590        BEQ  KEYIN     LOOK FOR NEW SHOT.
FD4C- 7A 00 04     1600        DEC  SHTCTR    OTHERWISE RUN SHOT COUNTER
FD4F- 7E FD 63     1610        JMP  LIVE      DOWN & TEST IF STILL LIVE.
                   1620 *
FD52- B6 20 00     1630 KEYIN  LDAA INPUT     PICK UP KEY AND INVERT
FD55- 43           1640        COMA           SO "PRESSED" = LOGIC 1.
FD56- 84 55        1650        ANDA #$55      MASK OUT BITS NOT OVER KEY.
FD58- 97 09        1660        STAA SHTBUF    STORE BINARY 1 WHERE BATT SHOOTS.
FD5A- 26 03        1670        BNE  SHOOT     IF NOT ZERO, BATT IS SHOOTING.
FD5C- 7E FD 86     1680        JMP  CHK2      IF ZERO PLANE TRIES TO BOMB YOU.
FD5F- 96 02        1690 SHOOT  LDAA CHARGE    START SHOT COUNTER.
FD61- 97 04        1700        STAA SHTCTR    WITH VALUE $FF.
FD63- 96 04        1710 LIVE   LDAA SHTCTR    SHOT IS LIVE AS LONG AS SHT CTR
FD65- 81 C0        1720        CMPA #$C0      IS > OR = $C0.
FD67- 24 03        1730        BCC  HIT       IF LIVE CHECK BATT HIT PLANE?
```

```
FD69- 7E FD 86  1740           JMP  CHK2     IF NOT, CHECK PLANE HIT BATT?
FD6C- 96 08     1750 HIT       LDAA TARGET
FD6E- 91 09     1760           CMPA SHTBUF     IF PLANE IS OVER
FD70- 27 03     1770           BEQ  HITYES      SHOOTING BATTERY,
FD72- 7E FD 86  1780           JMP  CHK2       (IF NOT, ARE YOU HIT?)
FD75- 7C 00 03  1790 HITYES    INC  SCORE    YOU HIT HIM; SCORE!
FD78- 86 FF     1800           LDAA #$FF     FLASH ALL 8 LEDS FOR
FD7A- B7 40 00  1810           STAA OUTPUT    0.8 SEC, DELAY VIA X.
FD7D- CE 60 00  1820           LDX  #$6000   (GOSH, THE WHOLE
FD80- 09        1830 BACK1     DEX              SKY WENT RED WHEN
FD81- 26 FD     1840           BNE  BACK1       I HIT HIM)
FD83- 7E FD 0D  1850           JMP  FLY      FLY A NEW PLANE.
                1860 *
FD86- 96 08     1870 CHK2      LDAA TARGET   IF PLANE IS OUTSIDE
FD88- 84 55     1880           ANDA #$55       TARGET ZONE, YOU'RE SAFE.
FD8A- 26 03     1890           BNE  BOMBED
FD8C- 7E FD E0  1900           JMP  SAFE
FD8F- 7D 00 04  1910 BOMBED    TST  SHTCTR   PLANE BOMBS BATTERY.
FD92- 2A 09     1920           BPL  OHNO     IS SHTCTR > OR = $80?
FD94- 96 08     1930 WHO       LDAA TARGET    YES: SOMETHING IS PROTECTED.
FD96- 91 09     1940           CMPA SHTBUF   IF PLANE NOT OVER SHOT, THEN
FD98- 26 03     1950           BNE  OHNO      BATT IS VULNERABLE.
FD9A- 7E FD E0  1960           JMP  SAFE     SAFE IF TARGET IS OVER SHOT.
FD9D- 7D 00 08  1970 OHNO      TST  TARGET   IF TARGET & SHOT BOTH = 0, WE'RE
FDA0- 26 03     1980           BNE  HELP      SAFE, OF COURSE (PLANE IN CARRY)
FDA2- 7E FD E0  1990           JMP  SAFE
FDA5- 96 0A     2000 HELP      LDAA LUCK     CHECK LAST 2 BITS OF LUCK COUNTER.
FDA7- 84 03     2010           ANDA #03       IF THEY = 00, YOU'RE BOMBED.
FDA9- 27 03     2020           BEQ  OUCH         (SORRY)
FDAB- 7E FD E0  2030           JMP  SAFE
FDAE- 97 0B     2040 OUCH      STAA FLASHR   SET FLASHER TO COUNT 10 FLICKERS.
FDB0- 96 08     2050 CYCLE     LDAA TARGET   PUT PLANE POSITION IN ACC A.
FDB2- 7F 40 00  2060           CLR  OUTPUT   TURN OFF LED.
FDB5- CE 0D 00  2070           LDX  #$0D00
FDB8- 09        2080 BACK2     DEX           DELAY 50 MILLISEC.
FDB9- 26 FD     2090           BNE  BACK2
FDBB- B7 40 00  2100           STAA OUTPUT   LIGHT LED OVER BOMBED BATTERY.
FDBE- CE 0D 00  2110           LDX  #$0D00
FDC1- 09        2120 BACK3     DEX           DELAY 50 MS.
FDC2- 26 FD     2130           BNE  BACK3
FDC4- 7A 00 0B  2140           DEC  FLASHR   AFTER 10 FLASHES, YOU'RE
FDC7- 27 03     2150           BEQ  BLASTD    BLASTED AWAY.
FDC9- 7E FD B0  2160           JMP  CYCLE
FDCC- 96 00     2170 BLASTD    LDAA MASK     REMOVE THE BLASTED BATTERY
FDCE- 90 08     2180           SUBA TARGET    FROM THE MASK.
FDD0- 97 00     2190           STAA MASK
FDD2- 84 55     2200           ANDA #$55     NOT COUNTING BITS WHERE NO BATTS,
FDD4- 27 04     2210           BEQ  DISPLY   IF ALL BATTERIES OUT, END GAME.
FDD6- 5F        2220           CLRB          IF NOT, START FLIGHT COUNTER AT 00
FDD7- 7E FD 19  2230           JMP  SHIFT     AND SHIFT PLANE TO NEXT POSN.
                2240 *
FDDA- 96 03     2250 DISPLY    LDAA SCORE    SHOW SCORE IN BINARY ON
FDDC- B7 40 00  2260           STAA OUTPUT    8 LEDS,
FDDF- 3E        2270           WAI            AND HALT.
                2280 *
FDE0- 96 01     2290 SAFE      LDAA TIMBUF   PICK UP DELAY TIME
FDE2- 27 04     2300 WAIT      BEQ  FINISH    DELAY 18 US PER LOOP.
FDE4- 4A        2310           DECA           TIMES "A" LOOPS.
FDE5- 7E FD E2  2320           JMP  WAIT
FDE8- 0E        2330 FINISH    CLI           LOOK FOR INTERRUPT
FDE9- 01        2340           NOP
FDEA- 0F        2350           SEI           NO MORE INTERRUPTS.
FDEB- 7E FD 2D  2360           JMP  LOOP     CHECK FOR HITS AGAIN.
                2370 *
                2380 *                       INTERRUPT ROUTINE (IRQ):
```

Sec. 6.8 Programming Philosophy and a Second Air Raid   111

```
FDEE- 0F          2390 BOOST  SEI              ACCEPT NO MORE INTERRUPTS.
FDEF- 96 02       2400        LDAA CHARGE
FDF1- 80 0A       2410        SUBA #10         REDUCE CHARGE (LIVE-SHOT)
FDF3- 97 02       2420        STAA CHARGE        TIME BY TEN (DECIMAL).
FDF5- 96 03       2430        LDAA SCORE
FDF7- 8B 05       2440        ADDA #5          ADD FIVE TO SCORE.
FDF9- 97 03       2450        STAA SCORE
FDFB- 0E          2460        CLI              READY FOR ANOTHER INTERRUPT.
FDFC- 3B          2470        RTI
                  2480        .OR  $FFF8       IRQ VECTOR
                  2490        .TA  $42F8         POINTS TO
FFF8- FD EE       2500        .DA  BOOST         BOOST ROUTINE.
                  2510        .OR  $FFFE       RESET VECTOR
                  2520        .TA  $42FE         POINTS TO
FFFE- FD 00       2530        .HS  FD00          START OF PROGRAM.
                  2540        .EN              END
```

6.8 PROGRAMMING PHILOSOPHY AND A SECOND AIR RAID

In this section we present three concepts that will make programs easier for you to write and easier for others to interpret. Then we will have a look at a new version of the *Air Raid* program using the new programming techniques.

Top-down program building. Rat's-nest programmers start from the beginning and work to the end. Top-down programmers start from the top and work down.

You have seen that flowcharts can be detailed or more generalized. A top-down programmer starts with a flowchart that is generalized in the extreme. Figure 6-10(a) shows what we mean. It's a single box which is assumed to contain all the routines necessary to solve the problem.

The programmer now splits this box into a series of boxes representing parts of the total program. This is done in Fig. 6-10(b). Each box must have only one entry point and one exit point. The boxes may be connected in a loop. For extensive programs some of the parts of diagram (b) may have to be broken, in turn, into several boxes. Still, each box may have only one entry point and one exit.

Notice that we now have a series of *modules*, each relatively independent of the rest. The top-down approach thus lends itself to the task of writing very large programs. Each member of a team is assigned a module. Also, one or more of the modules may be standard. We may have already written it for a project completed three months ago. If every module has only one entry and one exit, transplanting modules from an old program to a new one presents no problem.

Now the function of each box is stated as clearly and completely as possible. These statements are given for the *Air Raid* program in Fig. 6-10(c). At this point a list of variables that the program is going to deal with is developed. Some of these will be used by only one module and some may be used by several. It is a good idea to try to minimize the number of variables that are accessed by more than one module.

(a)

Run AIR RAID

(b)

| 0 Initialize | 1 Check position of plane and time | 2 Check shot status | 3 Check battery hit plane? (flash all 8) | 4 Check plane hit battery? (flicker 1) | 5 Check all batteries out? (show score) |

(c)

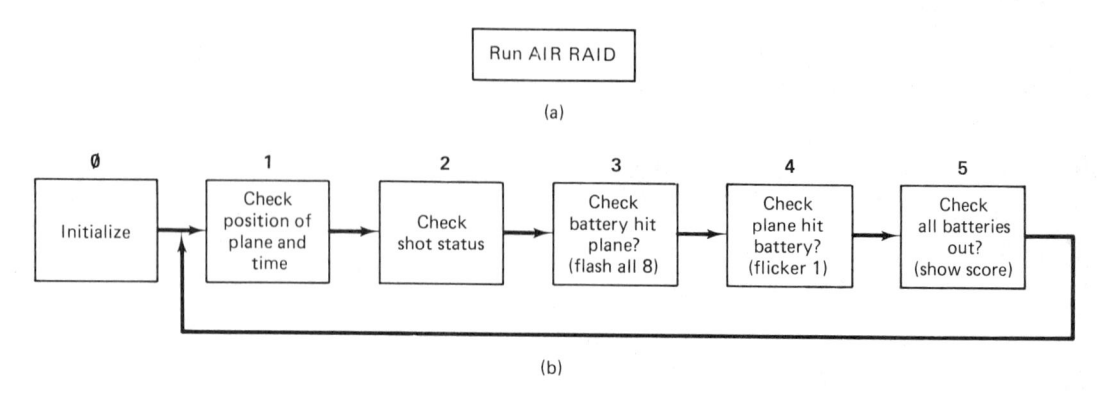

0 Score = 0, Luck = 0, Mask = FF, Delay = FF, Position = Carry, Shot position = 0, Shot Count = 0, Dwell Count = 0, Charge = FF, Points = 02.

1 (a) If dwell count is over, shift right and restart dwell count.
   (b) Light output LED unless battery under that LED is shot out.
   (c) Delay and speed up for next dwell.

2 (a) If shot count is over, read shot input. Decrement shot count unless it's already zero.
   (b) Store shot position and store charge in shot count.

3 If plane is over battery, and battery is not shot out, and shot count $\geq$ C0, and dwell count = 40, then plane is hit.
   (a) Flash all LEDs twice.
   (b) Increase score.

4 If plane is over battery, and battery is not shot out, and shot count $>$ 7F, and luck count is a multiple of 4, then battery is hit.
   (a) Flash one LED 10 times.
   (b) Mask out display of this LED.

5 If Mask = 1010 1010, then display score and halt. Otherwise, accept interrupts.

Figure 6-10 Top-down programming starts with the complete task (a), and breaks it into a linear series of subtasks (b). Each subtask is specified as completely as possible (c).

Finally, a flowchart is made for each module. Figure 6-11 shows the flowcharts for the four main modules of *Air Raid*. The following paragraphs give some guidelines for these charts.

Structured programming. Rat's-nest programs are produced by indiscriminate use of Branches and Jumps. By limiting the program components to the three structures shown in Fig. 6-12, we avoid the growth of rat's nests and limit the program flow to single entry and exit points. In a common variation of Structure (c), operation B is a nullity (straight-through line), resulting in a "bypass if true" branch.

It has been demonstrated that these three basic structures, in combination, are sufficient to handle any solvable programming problem. Structured computer languages have been developed that allow the programmer to use

Sec. 6.8   Programming Philosophy and a Second Air Raid   113

Module 1

↓ PLAY
- Decrement dwell counter
- Dwell counter = ∅? — No → WAIT
- Yes ↓
- Retrieve carry bit in CCR
- Rotate plane position right through carry
- Mask out LED if over dead battery
- Light plane LED
- Change luck counter
- Speed game by decrementing DELAY
- → WAIT
- Delay max. 3 ms via RAM DELAY

(a)

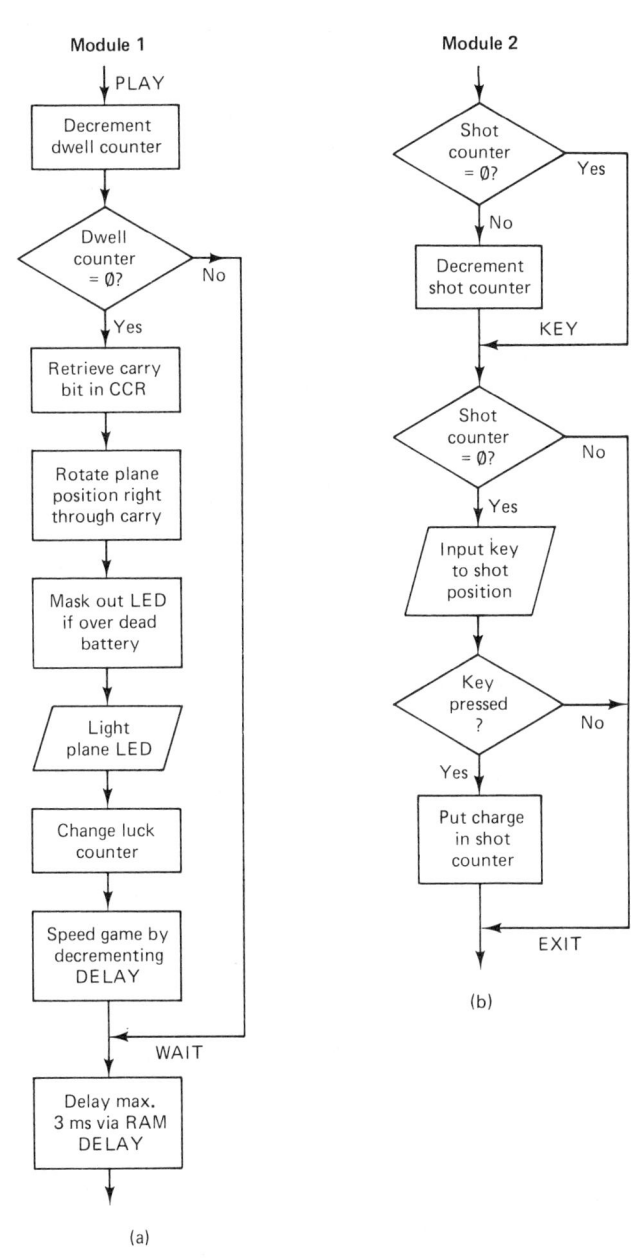

Module 2

↓
- Shot counter = ∅? — Yes →
- No ↓
- Decrement shot counter
- ← KEY
- Shot counter = ∅? — No →
- Yes ↓
- Input key to shot position
- Key pressed? — No →
- Yes ↓
- Put charge in shot counter
- → EXIT

(b)

Figure 6-11 Divide and conquer: the subtasks specified in Fig. 6-10 are flowcharted individually. Modules ∅ and 5 are comparatively trivial.

Module 3
Does battery hit plane?

- Dwell = $40 ?
  - No →
  - Yes ↓
- Is battery already dead?
  - Yes →
  - No ↓
- Shot counter > $C0 ?
  - No →
  - Yes ↓

ONE
TWO
THREE
/ Flash all 8 LEDs twice /

Increment score

NOHIT

(c)

Module 4
Does plane hit battery?

- Dwell = $41 ?
  - No →
  - Yes ↓
- Plane pos over batt ?
  - No →
  - Yes ↓
- Is battery already dead?
  - Yes →
  - No ↓
- Plane pos. = shot pos.?
  - No →
  - Yes ↓
- Shot counter > $7F ?
  - Yes →
  - No ↓

LUCKY

- LUCK AND #$03 = 0?
  - No →
  - Yes ↓

CYCLE / Flash one LED 10 times /

Subtract plane pos. bit from mask

SAFE

(d)

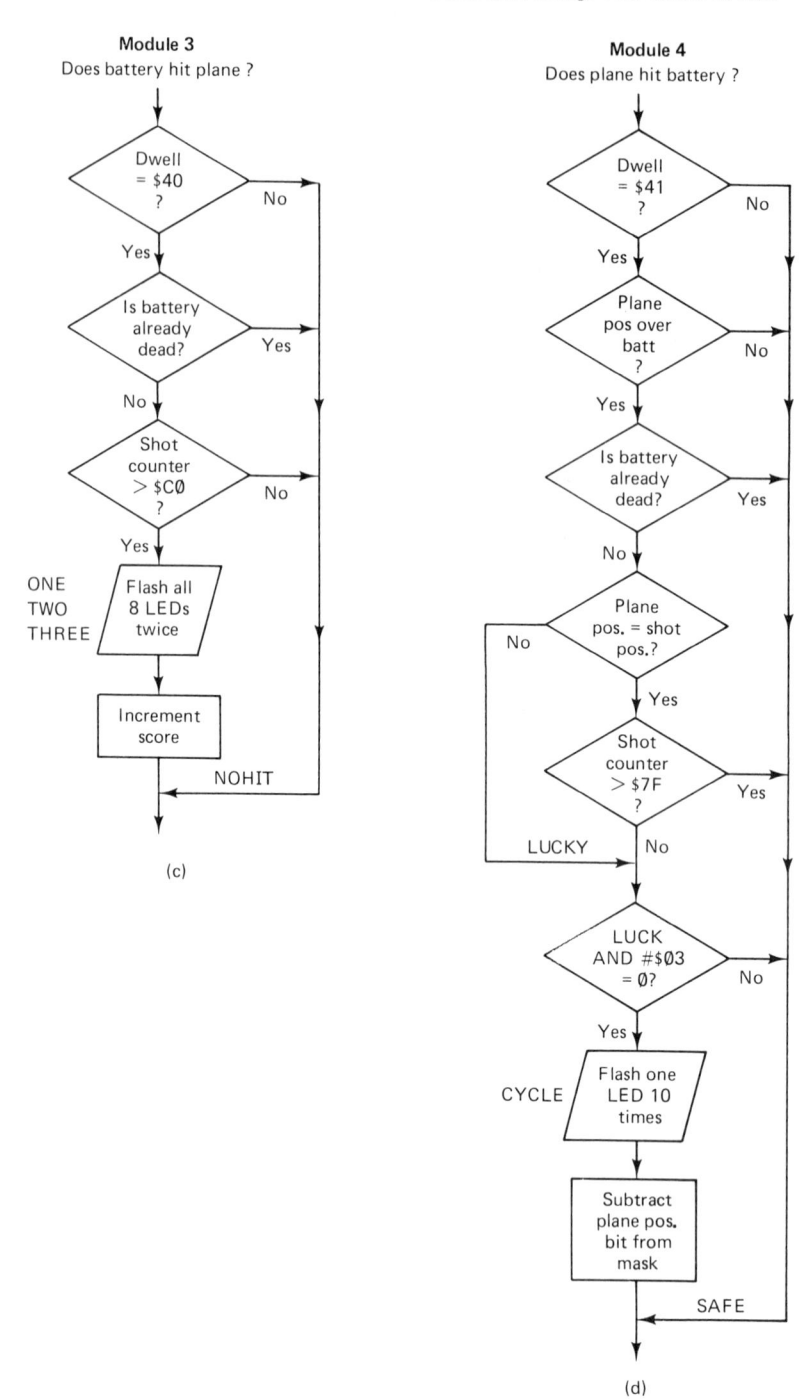

Figure 6-11 (*cont.*)

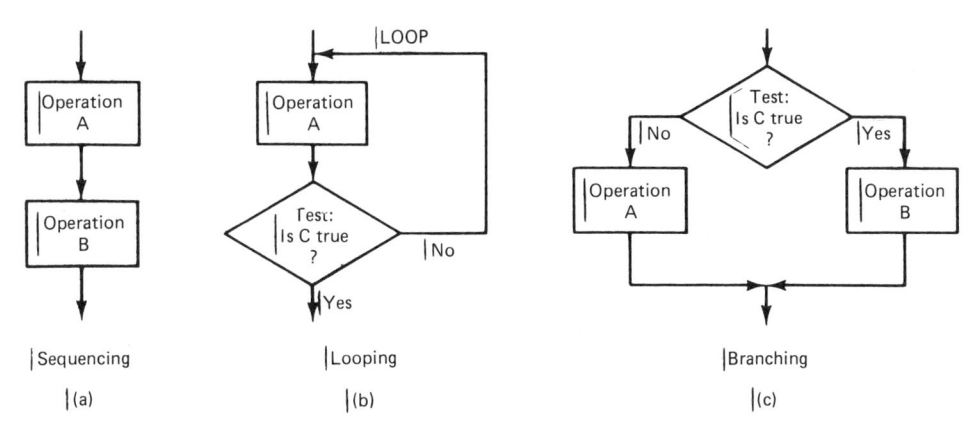

Sec. 6.8 Programming Philosophy and a Second Air Raid   115

```
    |                          |LOOP
    ▼                          ▼
┌─────────┐              ┌─────────┐
|Operation|              |Operation|
|    A    |              |    A    |
└─────────┘              └─────────┘
    │                        │
    ▼                        ▼
┌─────────┐              ╱ Test: ╲                    ╱ Test:  ╲
|Operation|             ╱ Is C true╲──|No      |No  ╱ Is C true ╲ |Yes
|    B    |             ╲     ?    ╱      ◄────────╲      ?     ╱────►
└─────────┘              ╲       ╱                   ╲         ╱
    │                     │Yes                        │
    ▼                     ▼                    ┌─────────┐       ┌─────────┐
                                               |Operation|       |Operation|
                                               |    A    |       |    B    |
                                               └─────────┘       └─────────┘
|Sequencing          |Looping                     |Branching
   |(a)                 |(b)                         |(c)
```

Figure 6-12 Three basic program structures are sufficient to handle all programming problems.

only a predefined set of structures, thus forcing a disciplined approach to problem solving.

Linear programming structure avoids branches that split the program flow into multiple paths. The program flow follows a single path, and the only decisions that the computer makes are "Shall I exit this loop?" and "Shall I bypass this operation?."

Figure 6-13 shows the program flow for the *Air Raid* game to determine if the battery hits the plane and if the plane hits the battery. In the first version of the program at (a), the flow is nonlinear. If the battery hits the plane, the plane cannot possibly hit the battery, so the second test is bypassed. In the second version at (b), the flow is linear. If the result of the first test is true, the second test will certainly be false, but we make the test anyway, just to preserve the linear program structure. Notice that the linear program can be broken into two modules with single entry and exit points, whereas the nonlinear program cannot.

Some rules for better programming are listed below. You can break a rule occasionally if it seems advisable, but the more you follow them, the more orderly, understandable, and fixable your program will tend to be.

1. Use the JMP instruction only for joining the end to the beginning of a continuous-loop program, and for halting the program (HALT JMP HALT). Other uses of JMP are almost certainly indicative of a nonlinear, unstructured program style. (Don't use BRA or complementary pairs such as BEQ and BNE to sneak around this rule.)

2. Branch forward to bypass a routine, in preference to placing a routine in the "Branch around" route. This keeps the program linear. Notice in Fig. 6-13(b) that the FLASH and FLICKER routines are in the main program flow, with branches bypassing them. The DEC TIMBUF block near the start of Fig. 6-9 shows an example of a routine in the branch-around.

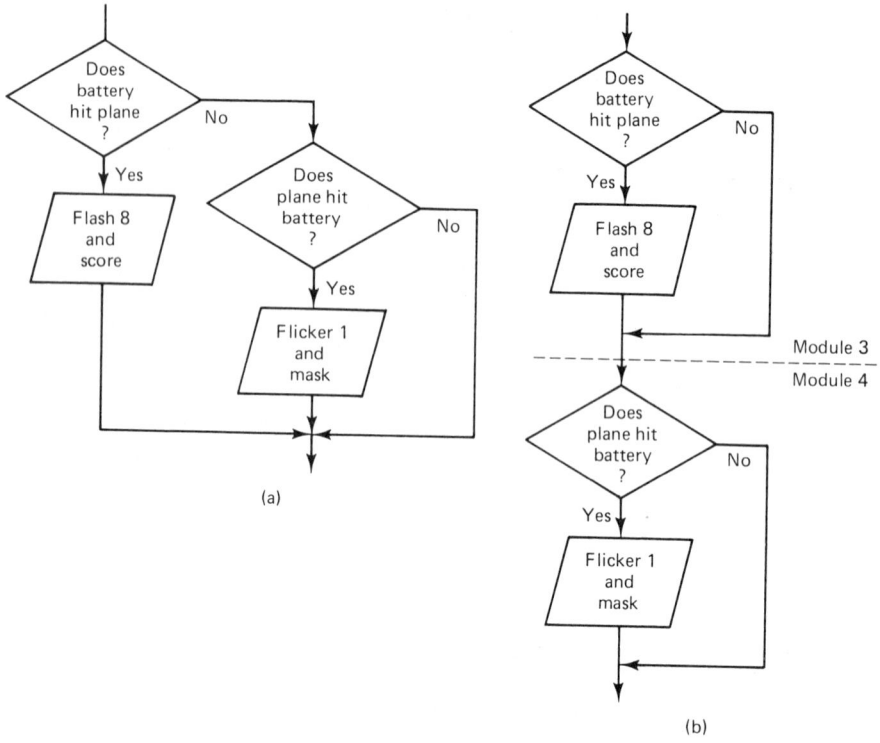

Figure 6-13 Nonlinear (a) and linear (b) versions of the same program segment. The linear version can be split into two modules with single entry and exit points.

3. Branch backward only to make repetitive passes through a routine (as in the familiar delay loop).
4. Use labels sparingly. START should be the only label that is distant from its source. All other labels should be quite near their branch-forward or branch-back sources. Overuse of labels and labels distant from sources defeat linear-program and modular-program advantages.
5. If different parts of a program require the use of the same routine, put that routine in a subroutine and access it as often as needed. Do not attempt to combine the different parts of the program.

In defense of rats it must be said that clever programmers can write rat's-nest programs that require less memory space and execute faster than their top-down counterparts. In mass-produced items, such as home appliances and automotive engine controllers, saving one ROM chip per item might produce a total savings of a million dollars. Rat's nests suddenly seem very desirable.

However, for novice programmers, for low-volume production, and for prototypes, top-down design and linear structured programming will un-

Sec. 6.8 Programming Philosophy and a Second Air Raid

doubtedly save development and troubleshooting time worth many times the extra memory chips required.

The program listing for the top-down, linear-structured *Air Raid* is given below. Notice that comments are given module by module, rather than as a running commentary. This is intended to help you visualize the program as a series of modules, rather than as a long string of machine instructions. Compare the number of labels in the first and second versions of the program. Labels indicate jumps and branches, and that involves non-linear programming.

Air Raid Linear Structure: Program Listing

```
                    1000 *-----------------------------------------------------------
                    1010 *     AIR RAID GAME     COPYRIGHT 1984 BY D. L. METZGER
                    1020 *
                    1030 * ILLUSTRATING TOP-DOWN LINEAR PROGRAM STRUCTURE.
                    1040 * FOUR ANTIAIRCRAFT BATTERIES SHOOT DOWN  WAVES OF
                    1050 *   ATTACKING PLANES. HOW MANY HITS CAN YOU SCORE BEFORE
                    1060 *   THEY WIPE OUT ALL OF YOUR BATTERIES?
                    1070 *-----------------------------------------------------------
                    1080 *              -- RULES OF THE GAME --
                    1090 * PLANE FLYING ACROSS INDICATED BY ROW OF 8 LIGHTS.
                    1100 * PLANE DWELLS ON EACH LIGHT ABOUT 0.8 SEC TO START,
                    1110 *   SPEEDING UP ON   EACH PASS.
                    1120 * PLANE IS VULNERABLE TO BE SHOT DOWN DURING THE THIRD
                    1130 *   QUARTER OF EACH DWELL PERIOD. TWO POINTS PER HIT.
                    1140 * PLANE SHOOTS AT BATTERY AT 3/4 THROUGH
                    1150 *   DWELL PERIOD.  BATTERY (BUTTON) PROTECTED
                    1160 *   FROM BEING SHOT BY PLANE FOR 1/2 A
                    1170 *    DWELL PERIOD AFTER SHOT. IRQ BUTTON REDUCES PLANE-
                    1180 *   VULNERABLE AND BATTERY-PROTECTED TIMES BUT ADDS
                    1190 *   1 POINT PER HIT TO SCORING.
                    1200 * USE 4 TIMES MAX OR SHOTS BECOME DUDS. LED DARKENS
                    1210 *   OVER BATTERY AFTER IT IS SHOT OUT. PLANE IS LUCKY
                    1220 *   ENOUGH TO HIT BATTERY ONLY EVERY 4TH CHANCE.
                    1230 *   SCORE DISPLAYED IN BINARY WHEN ALL BATTERIES   SHOT
                    1240 *   OUT.  ******   MODULE 0 -- INITIALIZATION
                    1250 *-----------------------------------------------------------
2000-               1260 INPUT   .EQ  $2000
4000-               1270 OUTPUT  .EQ  $4000
0000-               1280 SCORE   .EQ  00
0001-               1290 LUCK    .EQ  01
0002-               1300 DELAY   .EQ  02
0003-               1310 MASK    .EQ  03
0004-               1320 DWLCT   .EQ  04
0005-               1330 CHARGE  .EQ  05
0006-               1340 SHPOS   .EQ  06
0007-               1350 SHCT    .EQ  07
0008-               1360 POINTS  .EQ  08
                    1370         .OR  $FD00
                    1380         .TA  $4500
                    1390 *-----------------------------------------------------------
                    1400 * ACCUM B = PLANE POSITION. MASK DARKENS   LEDS OVER
                    1410 * SHOT-OUT BATTERIES. DELAY OF   $FF STARTS WITH ABOUT
                    1420 *  0.8 SEC PER SHIFT.   CARRY SAVED ON STACK
                    1430 *  FOR ROTATING PLANE POSITION THROUGH CARRY BIT.
                    1440 *-----------------------------------------------------------
FD00- 5F            1450         CLRB
FD01- 7F 00 00 1460                 CLR  SCORE
FD04- 7F 00 01 1470                 CLR  LUCK
FD07- 7F 00 04 1480                 CLR  DWLCT
```

```
FD0A- 7F 00 06   1490         CLR    SHPOS
FD0D- 7F 00 07   1500         CLR    SHCT
FD10- 86 FF      1510         LDAA   #$FF
FD12- 97 03      1520         STAA   MASK
FD14- 97 05      1530         STAA   CHARGE
FD16- 97 02      1540         STAA   DELAY
FD18- 86 02      1550         LDAA   #$02
FD1A- 97 08      1560         STAA   POINTS
FD1C- 8E 00 7F   1570         LDS    #$007F
FD1F- 0D         1580         SEC
FD20- 07         1590         TPA
FD21- 36         1600         PSHA
                 1610  *------------------------------------------------------------
                 1620  * MODULE 1 -- CHECK PLANE STATUS, OUTPUT  PLANE POSITION,
                 1630  *   AND DELAY.
                 1640  * IF DWELL COUNT = 0, ROTATE PLANE RIGHT   THRU CARRY,
                 1650  *   MASK IF OVER DEAD BATTERY.  DISPLAY POSITION, CHANGE
                 1660  *   LUCK COUNTER FOR MODULE 4,
                 1670  *------------------------------------------------------------
FD22- 7A 00 04   1680  PLAY   DEC    DWLCT
FD25- 26 12      1690         BNE    WAIT
FD27- 32         1700         PULA
FD28- 06         1710         TAP
FD29- 56         1720         RORB
FD2A- 07         1730         TPA
FD2B- 36         1740         PSHA
FD2C- 37         1750         PSHB
FD2D- D4 03      1760         ANDB   MASK
FD2F- F7 40 00   1770         STAB   OUTPUT
FD32- 33         1780         PULB
FD33- 7C 00 01   1790         INC    LUCK
FD36- 7A 00 02   1800         DEC    DELAY
FD39- 96 02      1810  WAIT   LDAA   DELAY
FD3B- 4A         1820  LOOP   DECA
FD3C- 26 FD      1830         BNE    LOOP
                 1840  *------------------------------------------------------------
                 1850  * MODULE 2 -- CHECK SHOT STATUS AND INPUT SHOT IF TIMED OUT
                 1860  *------------------------------------------------------------
                 1870  * IF SHOT COUNTER NOT = 0, DECREMENT IT.  IF = 0, PLACE
                 1880  *   KEY INPUT IN SHOT POSITION MASKING OUT NO-BATTERY
                 1890  *   AND DEAD-BATTERY BITS.  IF THERE IS A VALID INPUT,
                 1900  *   RECHARGE SHOT COUNTER.
                 1910  *------------------------------------------------------------
FD3E- 7D 00 07   1920         TST    SHCT
FD41- 27 03      1930         BEQ    KEY
FD43- 7A 00 07   1940         DEC    SHCT
FD46- 26 10      1950  KEY    BNE    EXIT
FD48- B6 20 00   1960         LDAA   INPUT
FD4B- 43         1970         COMA
FD4C- 84 55      1980         ANDA   #$55
FD4E- 94 03      1990         ANDA   MASK
FD50- 97 06      2000         STAA   SHPOS
FD52- 27 04      2010         BEQ    EXIT
FD54- 96 05      2020         LDAA   CHARGE
FD56- 97 07      2030         STAA   SHCT
FD58- 01         2040  EXIT   NOP
                 2050  *------------------------------------------------------------
                 2060  * MODULE 3 -- FLASH ALL LEDS IF BATTERY   HITS PLANE.
                 2070  *------------------------------------------------------------
                 2080  * IF PLANE IS 3/4 WAY THROUGH ITS DWELL, AND SHOT POSITION
                 2090  *   = PLANE POSITION, AND MASK SHOWS BATTERY NOT
                 2100  *   SHOT OUT, AND SHOT COUNT >= $C0,
                 2110  *   THEN FLASH ALL 8 LEDS TWICE (1-SEC DELAYS)
                 2120  *   AND ADD TO SCORE.
                 2130  *------------------------------------------------------------
                 2140  *
```

Sec. 6.8   Programming Philosophy and a Second Air Raid   119

```
FD59- 96 04       2150          LDAA  DWLCT
FD5B- 81 40       2160          CMPA  #$40
FD5D- 26 2D       2170          BNE   NOHIT
FD5F- D1 06       2180          CMPB  SHPOS
FD61- 26 29       2190          BNE   NOHIT
FD63- D5 03       2200          BITB  MASK
FD65- 27 25       2210          BEQ   NOHIT
FD67- 96 07       2220          LDAA  SHCT
FD69- 81 C0       2230          CMPA  #$C0
FD6B- 25 1F       2240          BCS   NOHIT
FD6D- 86 FF       2250          LDAA  #$FF
FD6F- B7 40 00    2260          STAA  OUTPUT
FD72- CE FF FF    2270          LDX   #$FFFF
FD75- 09          2280  ONE     DEX
FD76- 26 FD       2290          BNE   ONE
FD78- 7F 40 00    2300          CLR   OUTPUT
FD7B- 09          2310  TWO     DEX
FD7C- 26 FD       2320          BNE   TWO
FD7E- 86 FF       2330          LDAA  #$FF
FD80- B7 40 00    2340          STAA  OUTPUT
FD83- 09          2350  THREE   DEX
FD84- 26 FD       2360          BNE   THREE
FD86- 96 00       2370          LDAA  SCORE
FD88- 9B 08       2380          ADDA  POINTS
FD8A- 97 00       2390          STAA  SCORE
FD8C- 01          2400  NOHIT   NOP
                  2410  *-------------------------------------------------------
                  2420  * MODULE 4 -- IF PLANE HITS BATTERY FLASH ONE LED TEN TIMES.
                  2430  *-------------------------------------------------------
                  2440  * IF PLANE IS 3/4 THROUGH DWELL, AND PLANE IS OVER ANY
                  2450  *   BATTERY, AND MASK SHOWS BATTERY IS LIVE, AND IF
                  2460  *   THERE IS NO SHOT AT THE PLANE OR SHOT COUNTER
                  2470  *   <80, AND LUCK COUNTER LOW TWO BITS ARE ZERO,
                  2480  *   THEN FLICKER PLANE LED 10 TIMES AT 8 HZ AND
                  2490  *   REMOVE BATTERY BIT FORM MASK.
                  2500  *-------------------------------------------------------
                  2510  *
FD8D- 96 04       2520          LDAA  DWLCT
FD8F- 81 41       2530          CMPA  #$41
FD91- 26 33       2540          BNE   SAFE
FD93- C5 55       2550          BITB  #$55
FD95- 27 2F       2560          BEQ   SAFE
FD97- D5 03       2570          BITB  MASK
FD99- 27 2B       2580          BEQ   SAFE
FD9B- D1 06       2590          CMPB  SHPOS
FD9D- 26 05       2600          BNE   LUCKY
FD9F- 7D 00 07    2610          TST   SHCT
FDA2- 2B 22       2620          BMI   SAFE
FDA4- 96 01       2630  LUCKY   LDAA  LUCK
FDA6- 84 03       2640          ANDA  #$03
FDA8- 26 1C       2650          BNE   SAFE
                  2660  *
                  2670  * ACCUM A IS USED TO COUNT OFF TEN FLICKERS OF PLANE LED
                  2680  *
FDAA- 86 0A       2690          LDAA  #$0A
FDAC- F7 40 00    2700  CYCLE   STAB  OUTPUT
FDAF- CE 0D 00    2710          LDX   #$0D00
FDB2- 09          2720  BACK1   DEX
FDB3- 26 FD       2730          BNE   BACK1
FDB5- 7F 40 00    2740          CLR   OUTPUT
FDB8- CE 0D 00    2750          LDX   #$0D00
FDBB- 09          2760  BACK2   DEX
FDBC- 26 FD       2770          BNE   BACK2
FDBE- 4A          2780          DECA
FDBF- 26 EB       2790          BNE   CYCLE
FDC1- 96 03       2800          LDAA  MASK
```

```
FDC3- 10           2810              SBA
FDC4- 97 03        2820              STAA  MASK
FDC6- 01           2830  SAFE        NOP
                   2840  *
                   2850  *----------------------------------------------------
                   2860  * MODULE 5 --   ACCEPT INTERRUPT AND DISPLAY SCORE.
                   2870  *----------------------------------------------------
                   2880  *
FDC7- 0E           2890              CLI
FDC8- 96 03        2900              LDAA  MASK
FDCA- 81 AA        2910              CMPA  #$AA
FDCC- 26 08        2920              BNE   GO
FDCE- 96 00        2930              LDAA  SCORE
FDD0- B7 40 00     2940              STAA  OUTPUT
FDD3- 7E FD D3     2950  HALT        JMP   HALT
FDD6- 0F           2960  GO          SEI
FDD7- 7E FD 22     2970              JMP   PLAY
                   2980  *
                   2990  *----------------------------------------------------
                   3000  * INTERRUPT ROUTINE (IRQ) - REDUCES CHARGE MAKING TIMING
                   3010  *   MORE CRITICAL AND PLANE HARDER TO HIT. INCREMENTS
                   3020  *   POINTS PER HIT. IMPOSSIBLE TO HIT PLANE IF USED MORE
                   3030  *   THAN 4 TIMES.
                   3040  *----------------------------------------------------
                   3050  *
FDDA- 0F           3060  BOOST       SEI
FDDB- 96 05        3070              LDAA  CHARGE
FDDD- 80 0D        3080              SUBA  #$0D
FDDF- 97 05        3090              STAA  CHARGE
FDE1- 7C 00 08     3100              INC   POINTS
FDE4- CE C0 00     3110              LDX   #$C000
FDE7- 09           3120  HOLD        DEX
FDE8- 26 FD        3130              BNE   HOLD
                   3140
FDEA- 0E           3150              CLI
FDEB- 3B           3160              RTI
                   3170  *
                   3180  *----------------------------------------------------
                   3190  *   INTERRUPT REQUEST AND RESET VECTORS.
                   3200  *----------------------------------------------------
                   3210  *
                   3220              .OR   $FFF8
                   3230              .TA   $47F8
FFF8- FD DA        3240              .DA   BOOST
                   3250              .OR   $FFFE
                   3260              .TA   $47FE
FFFE- FD 00        3270              .HS   FD00
                   3280  *
                   3290  * 6802 SYSTEM ADR         FD00    FFF8
                   3300  * APPLE TARGET ADR        4500    47F8
                   3310  * WORKSPACE & 2716 ADR    0500    07F8
                   3320  *
                   3330              .EN
```

6.9 SOUND EFFECTS AND OTHER GAME MODIFICATIONS

Certainly you will want to breadboard the MEM and *Air Raid* games. You may even want to hard-wire a permanent version. But don't stop there. Try your hand at adding improvements to the game programs. Remember that when you add a routine to the middle of a program, all of the subsequent addresses will have to be shuffled back to make room for it. Any jumps to points in the shuffled section will have to be changed to point to the new

Sec. 6.9 Sound Effects and other Game Modifications 121

address. This is another reason for avoiding JMPs and using linear modular programming.

Sound effects for MEM will add greatly to the appeal of the game. A scale of tones should be generated for the four buttons; perhaps 350, 400, 450, and 500 Hz, respectively for buttons 1, 2, 3, and 4. A win (all 16 right) should produce a 700-Hz beep, and a mistake should produce a 200-Hz blat. These tones can be generated by a subroutine such as this:

```
SOUND   LDAA   #$FF
TOGL    STAA   OUTSND
        STAB   TONE
WAIT    DEC    TONE
        BNE    WAIT
        DECA
        BNE    TOGL
        RTS
```

Accumulator B has been previously loaded with a delay count which fixes the tone. TONE is a page-zero RAM location loaded for accumulator B and decremented to count the delay time for each half-cycle of the tone. A value of $80 in TONE will produce 200 Hz for about 0.7 second. A value of $24 will produce 700 Hz for about 0.2 second.

LDAB and JSR SOUND commands inserted before the DISPLAY and FLASH routines, respectively, will sound the *error* and *win* tones. Intermediate values should be stored in TONE during the KEYIN subroutine, depending on the value input by the key:

```
KEYIN   LDAA   INPUT     Get key.
        COMA             Pressed = 1, 2, 4, or 8.
        STAA   OUTPUT    Light LED.
        ANDA   #$0F      Mask high nibble.
        BEQ    KEYIN     No key? Keep looking.
        LDAB   #$48      Set f = 350 Hz.
        CMPA   #$01      Key = 1?
        BEQ    FOUND     Take it.
        LDAB   #$40      Set f = 400 Hz.
        CMPA   #$02      Key = 2?
        BEQ    FOUND     Take it.
        LDAB   #$38      Set f = 450 Hz.
THREE   CMPA   #$04      Key = 4?
          .      .         .
          .      .         .
          .      .         .
FOUND   JSR    SOUND     Make tone per B.
        RTS              To main program.
```

Notice that the SOUND subroutine is called from within the KEYIN subroutine. This "nesting" of subroutines causes no problems, thanks to the "stack-in-RAM" system of saving the return addresses.

The output location OUTSND should be one-fourth of a 74LS75 latch on data line D0. The latch may be decoded for address $6000.

Sound effects for Air Raid should include an airplane motor drone which increases in pitch as the game speeds up, a high-to-low pitched whine (say, 400 Hz to 250 Hz over 2 seconds) as the planes crash, and a stuttering machine gun sound as the plane shoots a battery.

The first is easy to generate because the main loop, starting at PLAY in the top-down version, has a period of about 300 Hz. Toggling the D0 output by incrementing the contents of $6000 will produce a 150-Hz buzz which rises in pitch as the game progresses. Simply insert an INC $6000 instruction at PLAY.

The 400-Hz to 250-Hz "crash" sound may be generated with the routine flowcharted in Fig. 6-14 inserted just before the NOP at the end of module 3. The constants given are for a system with a 0.5-MHz clock. FREQ holds the number of delay loops per half-cycle, and is incremented to lower the pitch. SNBUF is a buffer decremented from the value in FREQ to zero to count the delay. REPS counts the number of repetitions at each frequency; about 12 cycles each are needed to slow the rate of frequency decrease. All three of these variables are stored in RAM locations of your choice. Be sure not to change accumulator B with this routine, since *Air Raid* uses it for plane position. You may wish to remove the dark period and second flash (lines labeled TWO and THREE and the two lines preceding and following each) to reduce the time taken to dispose of the unfortunate airplane and get back to the game.

The stuttering-gun sound can be produced by replacing the delay routine which holds the LED on with a routine which generates a 140-Hz rasp for the same period. The delay to be removed is the line labeled BACK1 in module 4, and the single lines preceeding and following it. The routine to be inserted is as follows:

```
         LDAA   #$FF      256 loops per half
         STAA   GUNDLY      audio cycle
         LDAA   #$18      24 half cycles per
BANG     DEC    GUNDLY      burst
         BNE    BANG      7 machine cycles/loop
         DECA                X 2 µs X 256 loops
         STAA   OUTSND      X 2 half-cycles/cycle
         BNE    BANG      → 140-Hz tone
```

More improvements for the games will probably occur to you as you use them. Here are a few additional ideas.

1. The hardware for MEM and *Air Raid* are so similar that they could both be played on one system. Store both programs in ROM (move the MEM game; it's shorter). You will have to write a routine to translate the key inputs at bits 6, 4, 2, and 0 (as used by *Air Raid*) over to bits 3, 2, 1, and 0 (as used by MEM). Let the reset vector point to

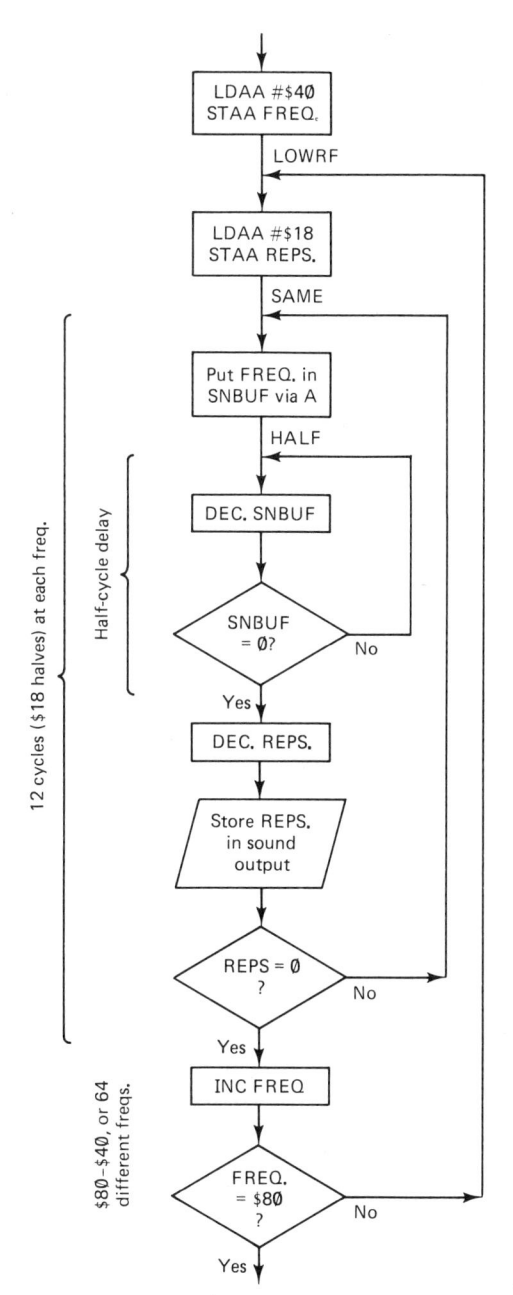

Sec. 6.9 Sound Effects and other Game Modifications   123

Figure 6-14 Flowchart for a "whine" sound, simulating a crashing plane in *Air Raid*.

the start of MEM and the NMI vector ($FFFC and FFFD) point to the start of *Air Raid*. Don't forget to hardware-debounce the $\overline{\text{NMI}}$ input.
2. Have MEM display the correct sequence after a player makes an error.
3. The LUCK counter in module 1 of *Air Raid* increments on every shift of the LEDs through nine plane positions. The battery is vulnerable on every fourth count of LUCK. This creates a regular pattern of vulnerability. Try replacing "INC LUCK" with the "random"-number generator from the *Hex Drill* program of Section 4.6.
4. Use the random-number generator to have the MEM game load its own series of numbers into the file, so you can play against the computer.
5. Add a short sound or single flicker to *Air Raid* to indicate when the plane shot at you but missed because of LUCK (indicating that your shot timing did not have you protected).
6. Write a routine to change the *Air Raid* score from binary to decimal, and light a pair of seven-segment displays with the decimal score.

CHAPTER SUMMARY

1. Data is input to the microcomputer by buffers with tristate outputs to the data bus. The buffers are activated by microprocessor read of an address decoded to drive their enable line(s).
2. Subroutines can be accessed many times at various points in the main program, but they need only be written once.
3. The *stack* is an area of RAM which saves the program-counter address so that the main program can be returned to after a subroutine. The 16-bit *stack-pointer* register holds the address of the next free RAM location, as the stack is filled from high to low addresses.
4. When the Interrupt Request ($\overline{\text{IRQ}}$) line is brought low, the processor stores seven bytes on the stack (program counter HI and LO, XHI, XLO, A, B, and condition-code register), and goes to the interrupt routine whose address is stored at $FFF8 (HI) and $FFF9 (LO). An RTI at the end of the interrupt routine restores the registers from the stack and returns the processor to the main program.
5. The *I* bit of the CCR masks (prevents) an IRQ from operating when set (SEI). A system *reset* or a response to an interrupt will set the *I* bit. The CLI instruction clears it. Software interrupt SWI can be masked, but hardware interrupt $\overline{\text{NMI}}$ cannot.
6. Branch operands $8∅ through $FF are negative or back-branches. $FF = -1, $FE = -2, and so on, up to $8∅ = -128.

7. The N flag of the CCR takes on the state of bit 7 (the sign bit) of an 8-bit result. BMI (minus) is taken if bit 7 = 1; BPL (plus) is taken if bit 7 = $\emptyset$.
8. Top-down linear programming is a technique for splitting a program into modules, each with a single entry and single exit point. Modular programs tend to be a little longer and a little slower than their unstructured counterparts, but they are generally a great deal easier to write, troubleshoot, and modify.

7

A Logic Analyzer to Build

7.1 INTRODUCTION TO LOGIC ANALYZERS

Voltmeters and oscilloscopes are of limited usefulness in troubleshooting microcomputer systems. Oscilloscopes display one or two channels of repetitive information. To analyze microcomputer operation we need to display the information on eight data lines and 16 address lines, and usually this information is not repetitive. The task is simplified somewhat by the fact that the analog voltage levels on these lines are not important. Only the logic levels (∅ or 1) need to be displayed.

A **hardware logic analyzer** presents an oscilloscope-like display of eight to 32 lines of a computer system. Commonly displayed are A∅ through A15, D∅ through D7, and four additional control or peripheral lines. This display is obtained by reading out a memory within the instrument which has stored the levels as they appeared in the microcomputer system. A single-shot routine can thus be displayed by repetitively reading out the logic analyzer's memory.

Each microcomputer clock cycle is typically broken into 10 or 20 time slots for storage in the analyzer memory. The analyzer memory must therefore be very fast, and relatively few computer cycles can be stored. The advantage of multiple stores per computer cycle is that timing differences between transitions of the various lines can be observed.

A **software logic analyzer** (or logic-state analyzer) stores in its memory only one bit per computer cycle for each input line. Thus its memory can be slower and it can store more extensive routines, but it cannot display

126

timing differences between lines. The display can be presented in the "multi-trace oscilloscope" format, as it is with the hardware analyzer, but no information is lost, and it is easier to compare the readout with the object code if it is presented as groups of hex digits, each digit representing four input lines during one clock cycle.

Sophisticated (and expensive) logic analyzers will translate the object code into source-code mnemonics for the processor you are using and display this on a 'scope screen. "Personality" plug-in modules or programs adapt the analyzer to different processors. Binary (1 and $\emptyset$) and decimal display options are also available.

7.2 TRIGGERING AND USING A LOGIC ANALYZER

Triggering options on a logic analyzer determine when it starts and stops storing data. Most software analyzers store a few hundred machine cycles. Consider that an *Air Raid* game run may last a few hundred seconds, with the processor executing 500 000 cycles per second, and it becomes obvious that we must be selective in deciding what to store.

The simplest option is to begin storing when a preselected memory address is accessed by the computer and stop storing when the analyzer memory is full. This requires that we set a *word recognizer* to the desired trigger address. Some other options are listed below.

1. Trigger randomly. This will allow you to see if the processor is stuck in a loop, or is spending most of its time on one routine.
2. Trigger when data is written to a specified memory location. This requires that the $R/\overline{W}$ line be inverted and ANDed with the address word recognizer.
3. Trigger when a specified data word is written to the specified address. This requires that a second word recognizer, set to sense the specified data value, be ANDed with the address word recognizer and inverted $R/\overline{W}$ line.
4. Trigger (for example) on the 264th pass through a loop beginning at address $F893. This requires a counter in addition to the word recognizer. It will allow you to see the exit from a delay loop.

Data-storage qualification is often used to conserve memory space in the analyzer. Thus only accesses of certain "qualified" addresses are stored, or storage may be switched on or off by word recognizers set to qualify storage in (or outside of) certain critical addresses. This technique is used to screen out useless storing of repetitive delay loops.

Compared to **single-step display,** logic-analyzer display has the following advantages:

1. It displays the data from every machine cycle. Single-step displays only the address of the next instruction and the last data-bus exchange.
2. The analyzer can be temporarily tapped into any system using the processor for which it is designed. No system modifications are necessary.
3. The processor can be running at full speed while the data is recorded. Transient effects and self-oscillations might not appear when single stepping.

Troubleshooting with a logic analyzer is much like troubleshooting by single-stepping the system (see the discussion of software errors in Section 5.5. The key is to think the program through and anticipate where the program will jump to after each instruction. Only then should you check to see where it did jump to. Don't just read through the analyzer's memory without forming expectations; you will be sure to miss the logic errors unless you think through each instruction before you observe it. You will want to make extensive use of Appendix C (Cycle-by-Cycle Operation of 6802 Instructions), comparing the addresses and data actually stored in the analyzer with what is listed for each instruction.

7.3 CIRCUIT DESCRIPTION

The circuit diagram for the logic analyzer project is given in Figure 7-1. It may look rather extensive, but much of the circuitry is repetitive, so there really is not that much to understand.

Input and word recognizer. U13 is an eight-line buffer which connects the address bus of the system to a Read/writable memory chip U10 while the analyzer is storing data from a program run. The memory is a type 6810 (8-bit × 128-word RAM). The outputs of U13 are in the floating state while the analyzer memory contents are being displayed.

U3 is a word recognizer which starts loading the RAM when all its inputs are *high*. The eight address lines are fed through exclusive-OR gates (U1 and U2) to the U3 inputs. The output of an exclusive-OR is *high* when one or the other input is *high*, but *not* when they are both *high*. Grounding one input thus makes the output respond (with a *high* level) when the other input is *high*. Letting the first input float *high* makes the gate respond to a *low* on the other input. Extra inputs are provided to the word recognizer, three active *high* and two active *low*, to permit other input requirements to be added to the trigger decision. These may be taken from the R/$\overline{\text{W}}$ line, higher-order address lines or selected data lines. If not used, these lines should be held *high* or *low* as required to enable the NAND gate.

Sec. 7.3 Circuit Description

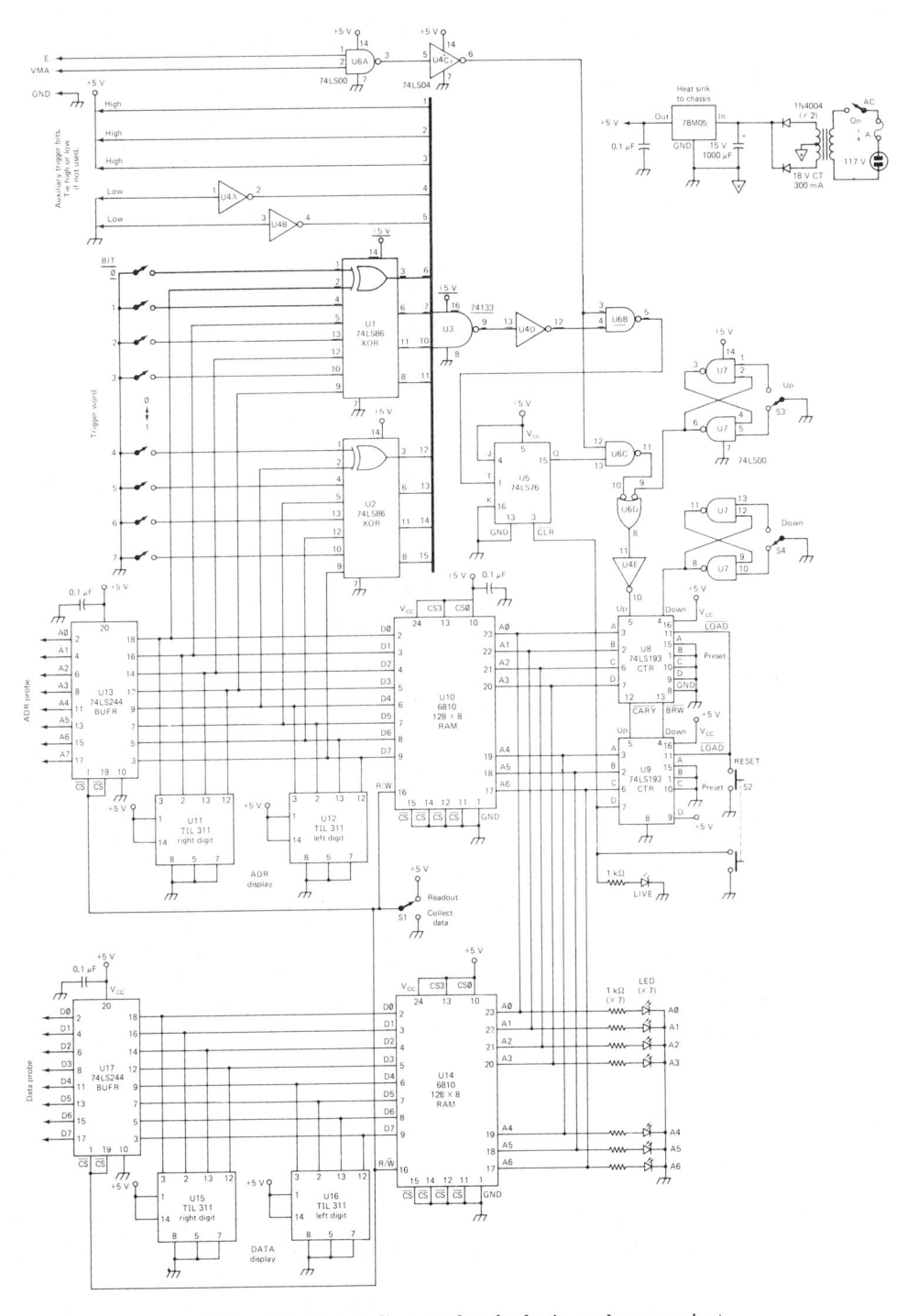

Figure 7-1 Wiring diagram for the logic-analyzer project.

Trigger and count circuits. Flip-flop U5 is set when the word recognizer is satisfied *and* the E clock *and* VMA are *high*. (U6B implements the first AND; U6A implements the second.) Once the flip-flop is set, E clocks that occur during a VMA-true cycle are passed, inverted, to the UP-count input of binary counter U8. At the end of each machine cycle E goes *low*, the count input transitions high, and the counter increments to the next address. The data that was on the bus at the end of the cycle is thus saved at the previous RAM address.

U9 continues the binary count sequence started by U8 through $7F, the highest RAM address. The next count brings the D output of U9 *low*, clearing the flip-flop and stopping data storage.

The flip-flop was cleared and the counters were set to zero (except U9D, which was set *high*) by throwing the RESET switch before the beginning of the LOAD. When the memory is full, the LIVE light will go out. S1 is now set to READOUT and the counters are again RESET to zero. The stored data can now be reviewed by using the UP and/or DOWN pushbuttons to increment or decrement the analyzer memory address being displayed.

Display and application A pair of TIL-311 hexadecimal displays are used for each 8-bit bus. The analyzer shown handles two 8-bit buses. This was thought to be a fair compromise with cost, complexity, and performance factors. Normally, U10 stores the low byte of the address bus, U14 stores the data bus, and the trigger is primarily based on the address. If desired, the probes from U13 and U17 can be exchanged so that the trigger can be based on a selected data word. (No discrimination as to data *type* is possible, however. See Sections 1.3 and 1.4.) Another option, useful for longer programs, is to have U13 input A4 through A11, so triggering can be set only to the nearest multiple-of-16 address, and the middle two hex digits of the full four-digit address will be displayed.

If you feel confident about adding to the already large amount of circuitry, there is no reason why a third input buffer, RAM, and pair of displays could not be added to display the high address byte. More switches, exclusive-or gates, and NAND logic could also be added to extend the word recognizer, and a word recognizer could be ANDed in at the U6C position to qualify the data, that is, store data only on cycles for which the word recognizer is true. For starters, however, it would be best to stick with the diagram given.

7.4 CONSTRUCTION DETAILS

The prototype logic analyzer is shown in Figs. 7-2 and 7-3. The total cost of the project should be under $75. This is not cheap, but consider that commercial logic analyzers start at about $2000 for bare-bones units.

Component selection. Wirewrap and perfboard is the only way to go

Sec. 7.4   Construction Details

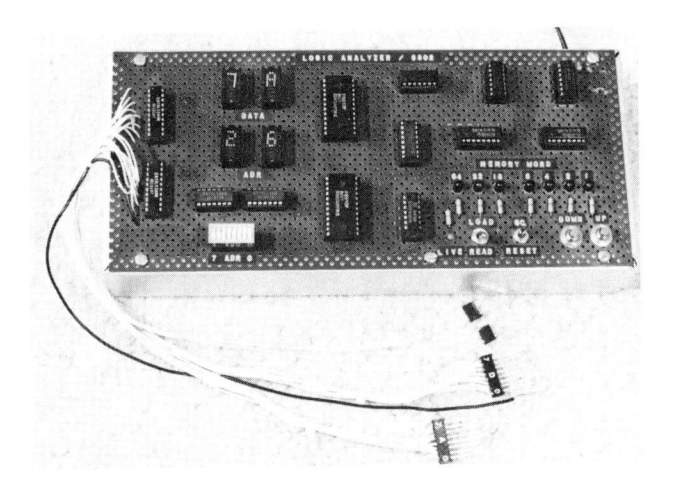

Figure 7-2 The prototype logic analyzer.

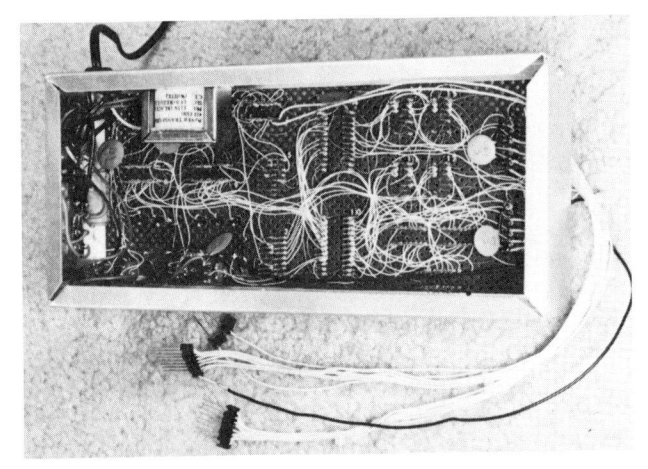

Figure 7-3 Inside the logic analyzer.

for a project like this, so be sure to get wirewrap IC sockets. The perfboard *must* be glass epoxy. Phenolic-and-paper board has a habit of shattering somewhere during the last five connections, making you wish that you had taken up tree surgery instead of electronics. Get a $4\frac{1}{2}$-inch × 10-inch piece with holes on a 0.1-inch-square grid pattern.

The ICs should all be of the 74LS family. This thing draws enough current without using full-power ICs. If you are poverty stricken, you can substitute 16 discrete LEDs in series with sixteen 680-Ω resistors for the four TIL-311 displays, for a savings of about $40. Reading the data out in binary is most inconvenient, but maybe with practice you'll get good at it.

Wiring hints.   Heat-sink the 7805 regulator directly to the chassis. Take the power wires to the circuit from the regulator *out* and *ground* pins, *not* from the transformer center tap or chassis ground connection. The 74LS244s make nasty spikes on the supply line. Wire a 0.1-μF bypass dir-

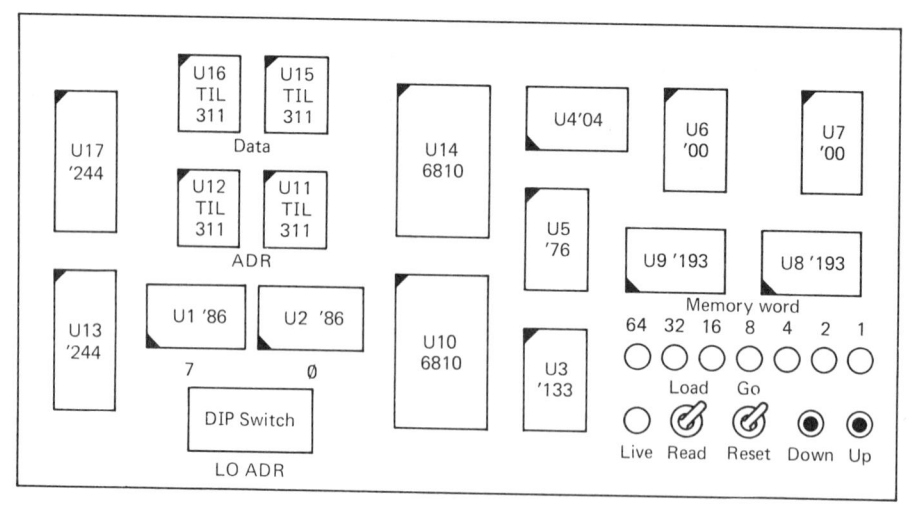

Figure 7-4 Suggested parts placement for the logic analyzer, top view.

rectly from pin 20 to pin 10 on each of them, and spot three more 0.1-μF bypasses elsewhere around the board.

Figure 7-4 shows a recommended parts placement. Try to get several colors of wirewrap wire. Use one for ground, one for V_{CC}, one for even-numbered bus lines (A0, D6, etc.), one for odd-numbered bus lines (D1, A5, etc.), and one for miscellaneous.

Make a copy of the wiring diagram and brite-line each pin number as the termination to that pin is made. Make each wire about 1 inch longer than it needs to be to get where it is going. Wirewrap wire is delicate and if you overstress it or have to change a connection, you will want enough length for a retermination. The capacitors, resistors, and LEDs will have to be soldered, in some cases to the IC-socket pins, so wire them last.

Troubleshooting. There is little chance that a project this extensive will work the first time you turn it on. Here is a step-by-step troubleshooting procedure.

1. Check V_{CC}, first at the regulator output, and then at each IC.
2. Check that pin 6 of U7 goes *low* when S3 is pressed, and pin 8 goes *low* when S4 is pressed.
3. First be sure that pin 3 of U6 is *high*. (Ground *E* and VMA inputs if not.) Then check that pins 5 and 4 of U8 are *high* and go *low* when S3 and S4, respectively, are pressed.
4. Check that U8 pin 3 changes state every time S3 or S4 is pressed.
5. Switch S1 to COLLECT DATA and jumper the A0 through A7 inputs to V_{CC} and ground, in turn, checking that the D0 through D7 pins of

U10 follow suit. Repeat this for the D0 through D7 inputs and the corresponding pins of U14.

6. Close all the word-recognizer switches and connect the A0–A7 inputs to V_{CC}. Tie the auxiliary inputs to V_{CC} or ground as indicated. Check for a *low* level at the U3 output and a *high* at U5 pin 15. With the VMA input *high*, check that pin 5 of U8 goes *high* when the *E* input is brought from *high* to *low*.

8

An IC Tester: Introducing the 6821 Programmable I/O Chip

8.1 TESTER OPERATION AND OVERVIEW

This chapter presents construction details and programming for a microcomputer-based tester for digital ICs. The ICs must be in 14-pin packages with the ground and +5-V supply at pins 7 and 14, respectively, or in 16-pin packages with ground and V_{CC} at pins 8 and 16, respectively. These pinouts are standard and cover all but a few of the popular digital ICs (notably the 7473, 7475, and 7476).

5400- and 7400-series TTL chips of the standard, low-power (L), Schottky (S), and low-power Schottky (LS) families and the pin-compatible CMOS (74C series) can be tested, but not differentiated; that is, a 74LS04 will test the same as a 7404.[1]

TTL chips with open-collector outputs can be distinguished from those with totem-pole outputs. Thus a 7404 (hex inverter) and a 7405 (hex inverter, open collector) can be differentiated, but a 7406 (hex inverting buffer with high-voltage open-collector outputs) will test the same as a 7405.

The CD4000 series of CMOS ICs and the older DTL logic ICs can be tested. The tester will not work for 74H00 series TTL, ECL, or RTL chips In the form presented it will not handle chips in packages with more than 16 pins, although it could be extended using the same principles to larger

---

[1] Note that in the 7400 series the "L" pinouts differ from the standard pinouts for types 85, 86, 93, and 95. The "L" and "LS" pinouts differ from standard for types 51, 54, and 91. Special program data must be supplied to test these chips.

packages. The tester will not check linear ICs such as op amps, nor hybrids such as the 555 timer or 565 phase-locked loop.

Only the basic logic functions of the chip are tested. Propagation delay, rise and fall times, and marginal logic levels are not checked. For example, a 7400 could have an output *low* level of 0.6 V (spec. 0.4 V) and delay time of 200 ns (spec. 22 ns) and still test as being good.

Chip sorting. The tester operates by applying a succession of library data sets for a number of chip types to the chip under test. If the chip passes the test for one of these types, the program halts and displays the type number on three seven-segment LEDs. If the chip does not pass any of the tests in the library, the letters "bAd" are displayed.

Thus unmarked ICs may be tested and sorted if the library (in EPROM) contains data for the types encountered. A bAd indication really means "not one of the library types." The chip could be good, but of a type not in the library. A single 2716 will hold the program plus data for about 90 different ICs. All these tests are completed in less than 0.1 second. Data for 12 ICs (mostly those used in projects presented in this book) is given with the program. Data for additional types can be developed using spec sheets for the types desired and the data-development form which is included later in this chapter.

8.2 THE 6821 PROGRAMMABLE I/O CHIP: BASIC FUNCTION

To illustrate the need for a new type of I/O device, consider that our library of IC types to be tested will certainly include the 7400 quad NAND and the 7404 hex inverter. But pin 2 of the 7400 is an input, which must be fed by an output latch from the microprocessor, whereas pin 2 of the 7404 is an output, which the microprocessor must read via an input buffer. Apparently, the latches and buffers we have been using for I/O will not do for the IC tester, where each line must be able to change, in microseconds, from input to output as library data for each IC type is applied.

Bitwise programmability of each of 16 lines for input or output function is the key feature of the 6821 chip, which Motorola calls a PIA (Peripheral Interface Adapter). The PIA comes in a 40-pin DIP, shown in Figure 8-1.

Pin functions. Eight of these pins are bidirectional tri-state lines which are connected directly to the system data bus. They place data on the bus (processor read) or pick up data from the bus (processor write). There are two 8-bit input–output ports, and 16 pins are devoted to these. Two pins are taken for the mandatory V_{CC} (+5 V) and V_{SS} (ground) connections. That's 26 pins—only 14 left.

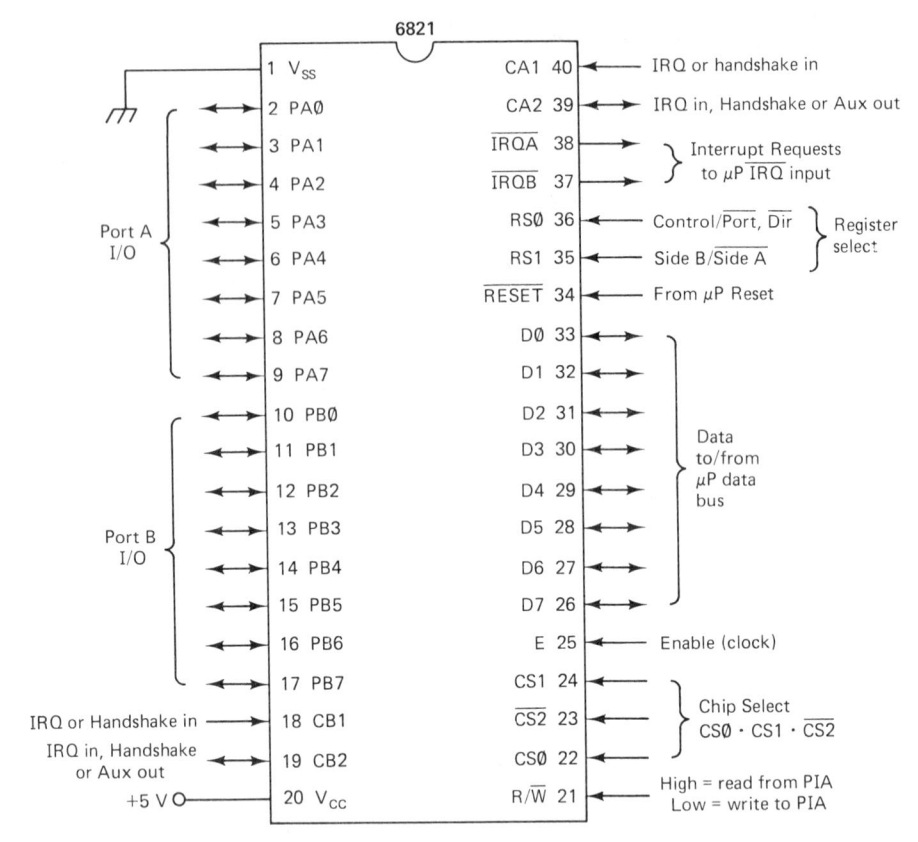

```
                        6821
                1  V_SS        CA1  40  ←—— IRQ or handshake in
       ←→  2  PA0             CA2  39  ——→ IRQ in, Handshake or Aux out
       ←→  3  PA1            IRQA  38  ——→  ⎞ Interrupt Requests
       ←→  4  PA2            IRQB  37  ——→  ⎠ to μP IRQ input
Port A ←→  5  PA3             RS0  36  ←——  Control/Port, Dir  ⎞ Register
 I/O   ←→  6  PA4             RS1  35  ←——  Side B/Side A      ⎠ select
       ←→  7  PA5           RESET  34  ←——  From μP Reset
       ←→  8  PA6              D0  33  ←→
       ←→  9  PA7              D1  32  ←→
       ←→ 10  PB0              D2  31  ←→  ⎞
       ←→ 11  PB1              D3  30  ←→  ⎟ Data
       ←→ 12  PB2              D4  29  ←→  ⎬ to/from
Port B ←→ 13  PB3              D5  28  ←→  ⎟ μP data
 I/O   ←→ 14  PB4              D6  27  ←→  ⎟ bus
       ←→ 15  PB5              D7  26  ←→  ⎠
       ←→ 16  PB6               E  25  ←——  Enable (clock)
       ←→ 17  PB7             CS1  24  ←——  ⎞
IRQ or Handshake in —→ 18  CB1  CS2  23  ←——  ⎬ Chip Select
IRQ in, Handshake                              ⎠ CS0 · CS1 · CS2
  or Aux out      —→ 19  CB2    CS0  22  ←——
       +5 V ——→   20  V_CC     R/W  21  ←——  High = read from PIA
                                               Low = write to PIA
```

Figure 8-1 Pin functions for the 6821 Peripheral Interface Adapter. Output-latch and input-buffer functions are provided for two 8-bit ports.

Three pins are tied directly to the corresponding pins on the 6802 processor. These are $\overline{\text{RESET}}$ (reset, low-active), R/$\overline{\text{W}}$ (Read/Write-not), and E (enable, clock). Three others are chip-select lines: CS0, CS1, and $\overline{\text{CS2}}$. These could be fed directly from high-order address lines to decode the address to which the PIA responds, but we have elected to use the 74LS138 for device selection. Thus we will tie CS0 and CS1 high and connect $\overline{\text{CS2}}$ to the low-active output $2XXX of the 74LS138.

Six pins ($\overline{\text{IRQA}}$, $\overline{\text{IRQB}}$, CA1, CB1, CA2, and CB2) are interrupt and control lines, which we will not use in this project. (For the sake of completeness, their functions are covered in Section 8-3.) This leaves only two pins, RS0 and RS1, to explain at this time.

Register select pin RS1 causes port A to be accessed when it is low and port B to be accessed when it is high. RS1 is usually tied to address line A1. Thus, if the base address for chip select is $2000, the base address for port A is $2000 (line A1 = 0) and the base address for port B is $2002 (line A1 =

Sec. 8.2   The 6821 Programmable I/O Chip: Basic Function   137

1). Since the 11 lines from A2 through A12, inclusive, are not used for chip select or register select, the PIA registers are accessible identically at 2^{11} or 2048 different addresses. However, we have agreed in such cases to use the lowest address, to avoid confusion.

Peripheral Register and Data-Direction Register. Each port (A and B) has two registers associated with its output: the peripheral registers (PAD and PBD) and the data-direction registers (DDRA and DDRB). These are illustrated in Fig. 8-2 with example data contents.

The DDR is loaded first with a bit pattern that determines which lines will be outputs and which will be inputs. A binary 1 in a DDR bit sets that port line as an output, whereas a binary 0 sets the line as an input. In the figure, DDRA is loaded with binary 1111 0000 (hex F0), setting the low four lines as inputs and the high four lines as outputs.

The PAD register is then loaded with a bit pattern (in the figure, binary 0101 0101 or hex 55). Only the high nibble is passed to the output. Bits PAD0 through PAD3 are disconnected from the output by the 0 bits in DDRA.

A read of port A (LDAA $2000) will pick up the high nibble as loaded into PAD and the low nibble as input into the port from the peripheral device. In Fig. 8-2 this read data is binary 0101 0011, or hex 53. The low nibble stored in PAD is ignored in the read operation.

Accessing the PAD and DDRA registers is more complicated than it might seem because *they are both located at the same address*, $2000. The one that is accessed at a given time is determined by a bit set into a third register, the *control register* for port A (CRA). Bit 2 of the control register

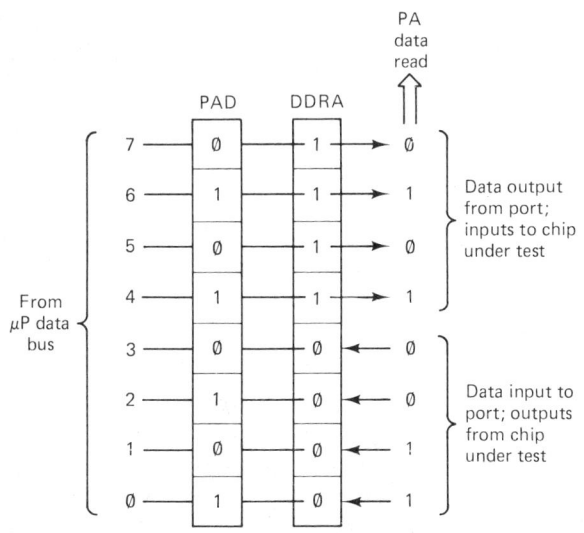

Figure 8-2 The data-direction register determines which the bits of the port data register will be output to the port.

is cleared to 0 to access the data-direction register and set to 1 to access the port itself.

The control register is selected by bringing Register Select line RS0 (pin 36) high. (RS0 is low to access PAD and DDRA). RS0 is usually tied to address line A0, so port A is accessed by these addresses:

$2000	DDRA	(direction, CRA2 = 0)
	PAD	(port, CRA2 = 1)
$2001	CRA	(control)

Port B has a similar control register, CRB, and is accessed at these addresses:

$2002	DDRB	(direction, CRB2 = 0)
	PBD	(port, CRB2 = 1)
$2003	CRB	(control)

The other 7 bits of the control registers will not be used in this project, so for the time being we can access DDRA at $2000 by first clearing CRA at $2001, and then access PAD at $2000 by first storing $04 into CRA at $2001. This initialization procedure is illustrated for ports A and B in Figure 8-3.

Why do we have to go through the control registers to change from accessing the data-direction register to accessing the port itself? Why didn't Motorola just assign a different address for each function when they designed the chip? The answer lies in those six control/interrupt lines which we have deferred discussing. The remaining 7 bits of the control registers are used to program the function of those lines, as will be explained in Section 8.3. It was not considered practical to bring all 16 control-register

Port A
RS1 = 0

Clear $2001	Set direction bits into $2000.	Store $04 in address	Read or write data
RS0 = 1	Adr $2000 (RS0 = 0)	$2001.	at $2000.
CRA2 = 0	is DDRA, since CRA2 = 0.	RS0 = 1, CRA2 = 1	(PAD, since CRA2 = 1)

Port B
RS1 = 1

Clear $2003	Set direction bits into $2002.	Store $04 in address	Read or write data
RS0 = 1	Adr $2002 (RS0 = 0)	$2003.	at $2002.
CRB2 = 0	is DDRB, since CRB2 = 0	RS0 = 1, CRB2 = 1	(PBD, since CRB2 = 1)

Set Control Register to access Data-Direction Register

Load Direction Register bits
1 = output
0 = input

Set Control Register to access Port Data Register

Input or output via Port Data register

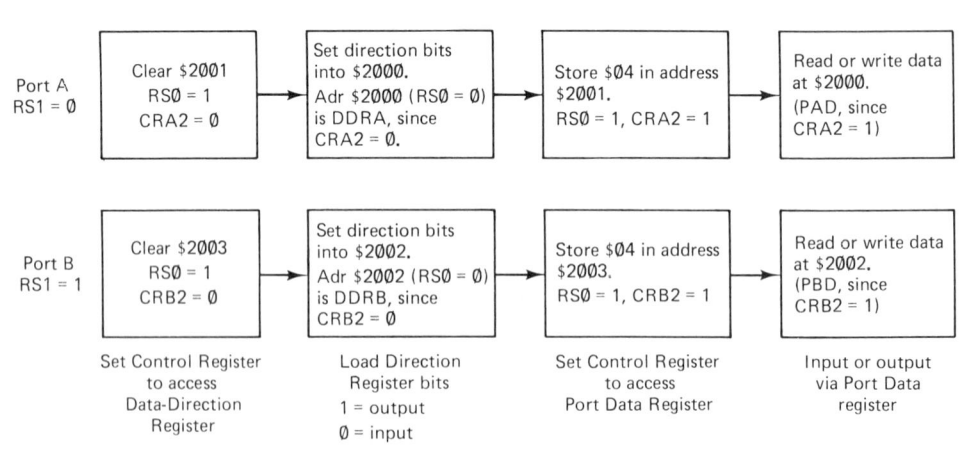

Figure 8-3 Programming steps for initializing PIA ports for input/output. Chip select is presumed to be decoded for base address $2000. RS0 and RS1 are driven, respectively, by address lines A0 and A1.

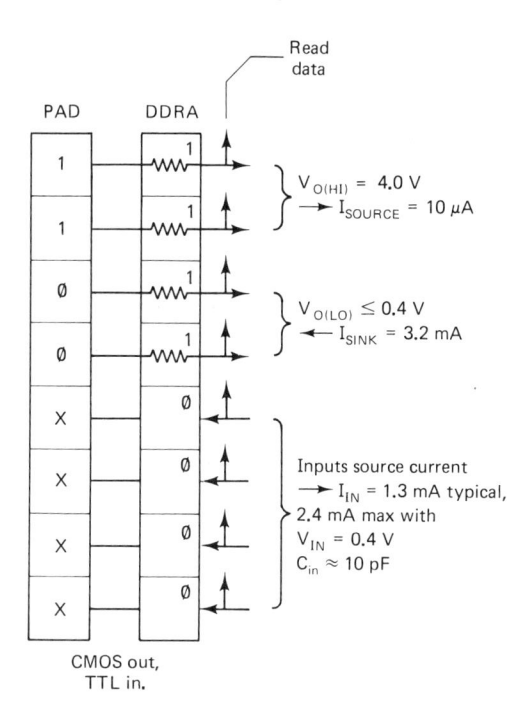

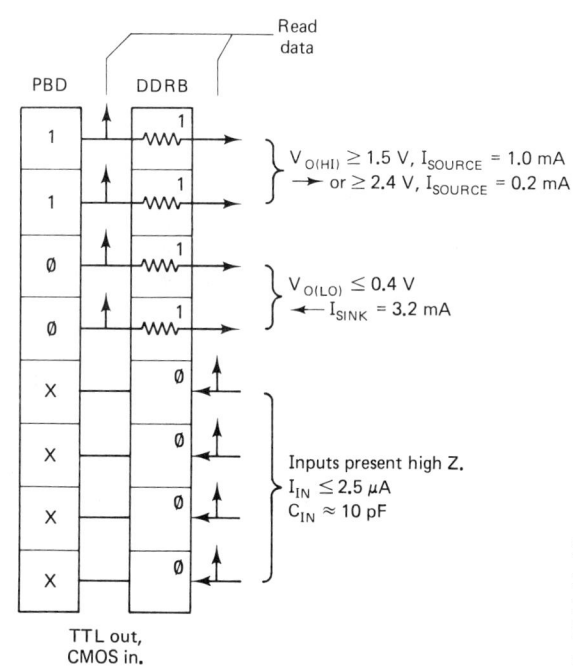

Sec. 8.2 The 6821 Programmable I/O Chip: Basic Function   139

Figure 8-4 Port A outputs pull to higher voltage, but port B outputs provide more drive current. Port A inputs will source current like TTL inputs, while port B inputs present a high impedance like CMOS.

bits out to PIA-package pins, and no special preference was given to the two bits which control data/data-direction register selection.

Differences between port A and port B should be noted.

1. **Port A drives CMOS logic** as well as TTL. It pulls high to about +4.0 V if negligible load current is drawn. However, it can deliver only a few tens of microamperes to a load at high output.
   Port B feeds relay- and lamp-driver transistors nicely, since it can deliver 1 mA to a load at high output. However, it pulls high to only +2.4 V, which is not enough to ensure a logic-1 input to CMOS chips. External pull-up resistors are required from port B outputs to +5 V to drive CMOS.

2. **Port A is read right at the output pins** when DDRA is loaded with 1s for outputs. Thus if port A output lines are forced high or low by a "stiff" output, they will be read as forced.
   Port B is read from an output buffer register in the output mode, so data bits written to the output lines will be picked up intact by a read operation, even though a stiff load may be forcing the pin voltages to the opposite states.

3. **When programmed for inputs** by ∅s in DDRA, port-A inputs source current and tend to pull high like TTL inputs. Port B lines present a high impedance like CMOS when programmed for inputs.

These differences are illustrated in Figure 8-4.

8.3 INTERRUPTS AND HANDSHAKING WITH THE PIA

This section explains the functions of the 6821 control lines CA1, CB1, $\overline{IRQA}$, $\overline{IRQB}$, CA2, and CB2, and their relationships to the other 7 bits of the control registers CRA and CRB. These functions are covered here for the sake of completeness, but they are not used in the projects presented in this book. You may wish to skip directly to Section 8.4 and return to this section at a later time.

Input lines CA1 and CB1 function identically to control the low-active output lines $\overline{IRQA}$, and $\overline{IRQB}$, respectively. These interrupt outputs are normally tied together and to the $\overline{IRQ}$ input of the 6802 processor. Three of the corresponding control-register bits are associated with the CA1 and CB1 functions:

- Bit 7 is set (logic 1) and latched when an interrupt is sensed at the CA1 (or CB1) input. Even if the processor is not programmed to respond to the interrupt quickly, it can still read the control register later (masking out all but bit 7) to see if an interrupt has occurred. Bit 7 of CRA (or

Sec. 8.3 Interrupts and Handshaking with the PIA 141

CRB) will be cleared by a processor read of port A (or port B). A hardware reset or a write of a byte having bit 7 = $\emptyset$ to CRA (or CRB) will also clear it.

- Bit 1 is used to program the type of input at CA1 (or CB1) that will set the interrupt flag, bit 7. If CRA1 is *cleared* (logic $\emptyset$), a negative transition (high to low) on input CA1 will set the interrupt flag. If CRA1 is *set* (logic 1), a positive transition on CA1 will *set* bit 7. The "B" side behaves identically.

- Bit $\emptyset$ is used to disable the $\overline{IRQ}$ output lines. If CRA$\emptyset$ is *cleared* (logic $\emptyset$, then $\overline{IRQA}$ stays *high*, regardless of the CA1 input or flag bit 7. If CRA$\emptyset$ is *set*, the $\overline{IRQA}$ line goes *low* whenever the interrupt flag bit CRA7 goes *high*. Side "B" behaves identically.

Control lines CA2 and CB2 are used as inputs *if the corresponding control-register bit 5 is cleared* (logic $\emptyset$). In this case, the lines simply provide additional interrupt inputs for external devices. *Which* device caused the interrupt must then be determined by reading the control registers and examining the flag bits.

- Bit 6: interrupt flag *set* by valid input to CA2 (or CB2). Cleared by *read* of corresponding port.
- Bit 5: must be *cleared* ($\emptyset$) to use line CA2 (or CB2) as an input.
- Bit 4: *cleared* ($\emptyset$) to make negative transition of CA2 (or CB2) the valid input; *set* (1) to make positive transition the valid input.
- Bit 3: *cleared* ($\emptyset$) is disable $\overline{IRQA}$ output response to flag bit 6. *Set* (1) to bring $\overline{IRQA}$ low when CRA6 goes *high*.

Figure 8-5 illustrates the control functions for input modes only.

		CRA bit	
	CA1 flag	7	Set 1 by valid CA1 input; cleared $\emptyset$ by read of Port A.
	CA2 flag	6	Set 1 by valid CA2 input; cleared $\emptyset$ by read of Port A.
	CA2 input control	5	$\emptyset$ to establish CA2 as input; see Fig. 8-6 for output.
		4	$\emptyset$ = CA2 input ↓ valid; 1 = input ↑ valid.
		3	$\emptyset$ = $\overline{IRQA}$ output by CA2 disabled; 1 = enabled.
	DDRA/PAD	2	$\emptyset$ = select Data Direction Register; 1 = Port Data.
	CA1 input control	1	$\emptyset$ = CA1 input ↓ valid; 1 = input ↑ valid.
		0	$\emptyset$ = $\overline{IRQA}$ output by CA1 disabled; 1 = enabled.

↓ = high-to-low transition.
↑ = low-to-high transition.

Figure 8-5 Bit functions for control register A of the 6821 PIA with CA2 programmed as an input. Bit functions for CRB are identical in this mode. See Fig. 8-6 for CA2 and CB2 output functions.

Control lines CA2 and CB2 are used as outputs if the corresponding control-register bit 5 is *set* (logic 1). Bits 4 and 3 of the control registers then determine the mode of operation of the respective outputs (CA2 or (CB2). There are five distinct modes, summarized in Fig. 8-6.

1. **Auxiliary outputs.** Bit 4 is *set* (logic 1) and the CA2 output follows the state of bit 3 of the control register. (CRA3 = 1, CA2 high; CRA3 = ∅, CA2 low). Side B is identical.

2. **Fast inputs, A side.** Bit 4 is *cleared* (∅) and bit 3 is *set* (1). Output CA2 goes *low* when the processor reads data from port A and returns high when the PIA is deselected. In operation, a peripheral device is inputting data to port A and line CA2 goes low for a few machine cycles to tell the peripheral, "I have read that byte, so now put a new byte on port A."

3. **Fast outputs, B side.** Bit 4 is *cleared* (∅) and bit 3 is *set* (1). Output CB2 goes *low* when the processor writes data to port B and returns high when the PIA is deselected. In operation, a peripheral device is receiving data from port B and line CB2 pulses *low* to tell the peripheral, "Here is a new byte of data; read it."

4. **Handshaking inputs, A side.** Bit 4 and bit 3 are both *cleared* (∅). Output CA2 goes *low* when the processor reads data from port A and goes high when a valid input is received on input line CA1. (CRA1 = ∅ specifies negative-transition valid, CRA1 = 1 specifies positive-transition valid.) In operation, the peripheral will signal the processor that it has data ready via an input to CA1. This will *set* CRA7 (flag bit) and may initiate an interrupt request. It will also cause output CA2 to go *high*, which the peripheral must interpret to mean "Don't send more data yet." When the processor reads the data sent to port A, output CA2 goes low, telling the peripheral, "I'm ready for more data any time you are."

5. **Handshaking outputs, B side.** Bit 4 and bit 3 are both *cleared* (∅). Output CB2 goes *low* when the processor writes data to port B and goes *high* when a valid input is received via input line CB1. In operation, the processor will signal the peripheral that it has applied new data at the output with a *low* on the CB2 line. It may take some time for the peripheral to process this data. When it has finished and is ready to accept more data, the peripheral signals the processor via the $\overline{CB1}$ line. This *sets* flag bit CRB7 and may cause an interrupt via the $\overline{IRQB}$ line. It also brings CB2 high again.

Figure 8-7 illustrates the various peripheral-control modes. Mode 1 is simply a convenience for driving external devices. Modes 2 and 3 are "blind." The processor takes complete control of the timing, and assumes that the peripheral can supply input data (or accept output data) as fast as

Sec. 8.3 Interrupts and Handshaking with the PIA 143

CA2 flag	6	Not affected with CA2 established as an output.
CA2 output control	5	1 to establish CA2 as output; see Fig. 8-5 for input.
	4	0 = data control [Fig. 8-6 (b) and (c)] ; 1 = CA2 follows bit 3.
	3	0: (CA2 output = 0) 1: (CA2 output = 1) [if bit 4 = 1].

(a)

CRA bits only — | 4 | 0 |, | 3 | 1 | — Fast data input. CA2 output pulled low by read of port A; pulled high on next cycle which does not address PIA.

CRA bits only — | 4 | 0 |, | 3 | 0 | — Handshake data input. CA2 output pulled low by read of port A; pulled high by valid input at CA1.

(b)

CRB bits only — | 4 | 0 |, | 3 | 1 | — Fast data output. CB2 output pulled low by write to port B; pulled high on next cycle which does not address PIA.

CRB bits only — | 4 | 0 |, | 3 | 0 | — Handshake data output. CB2 output pulled low by write to port B; pulled high by valid input at CB1. Note: CRB7 must first be cleared by a read of port B.

(c)

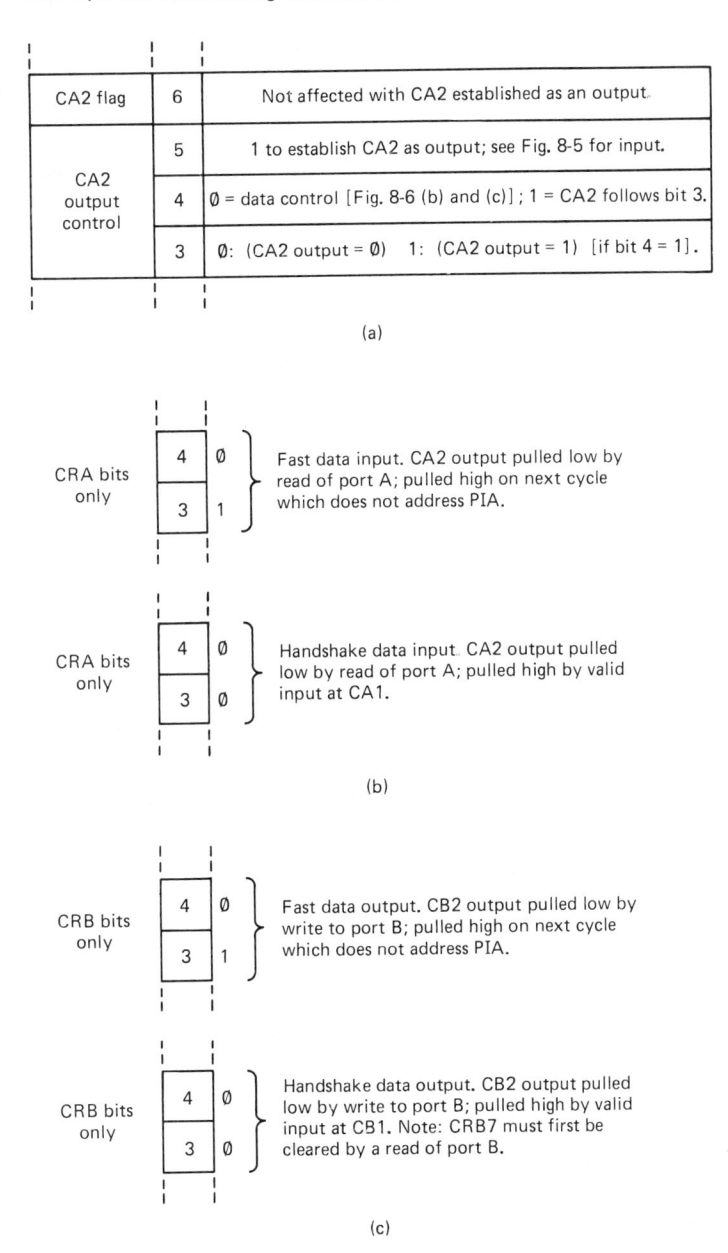

Figure 8-6 PIA bit functions for CA1 and CB2 programmed as outputs; (a) auxiliary-output mode, both sides; (b) port A side, and (c) port B side, in *fast* and *handshake* modes.

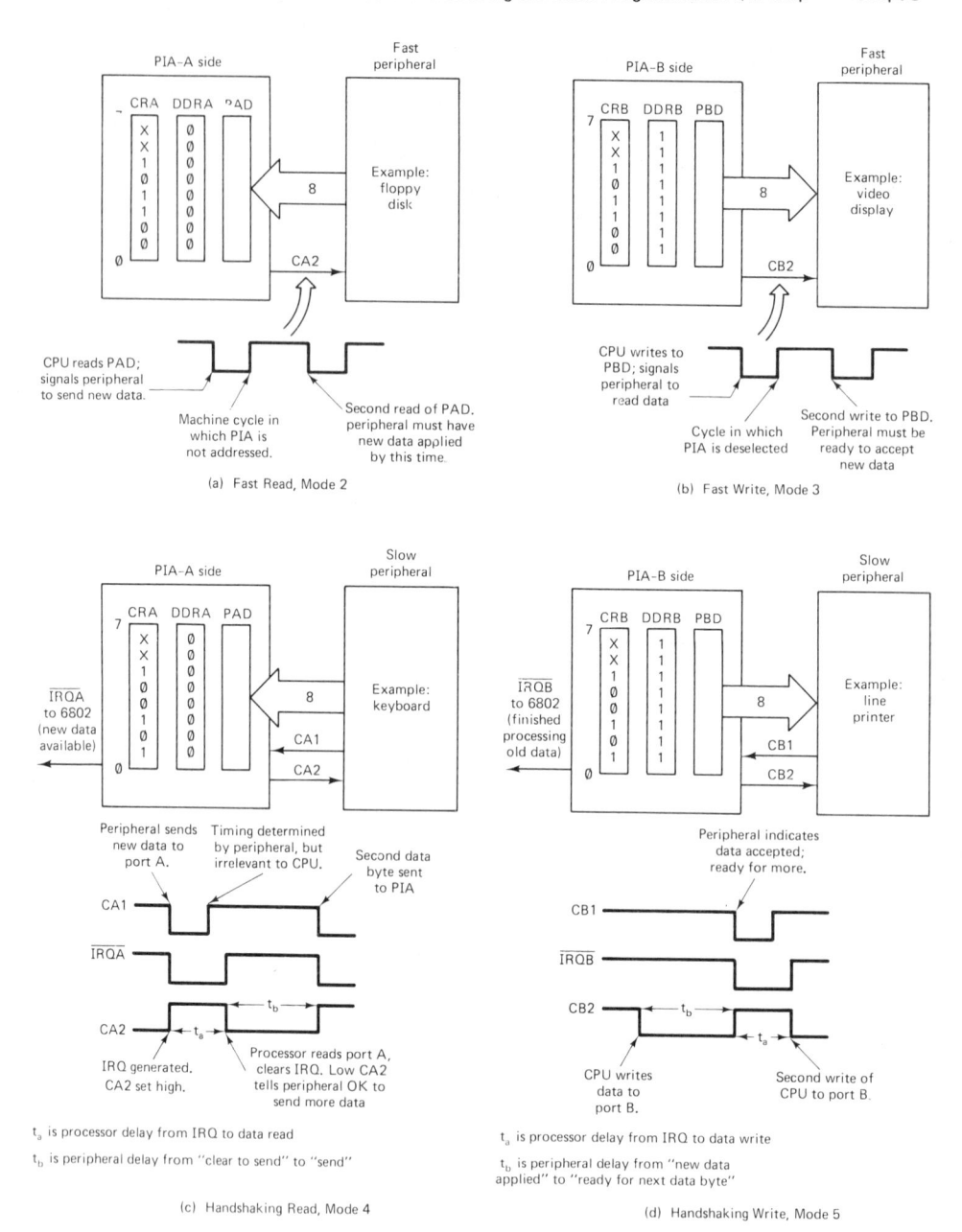

144   An IC Tester: Introducing the 6821 Programmable I/O Chip   Chap. 8

Figure 8-7 Examples of peripheral control with the PIA.

Sec. 8.4   IC-Tester Hardware   145

the program can request it to. This is often unrealistic. Motors, relays, photoresistive cells, and humans may take many milliseconds to respond. In such cases it is absurd to have the processor spitting out new commands every 10 μs.

Mode 4 permits the peripheral and the processor to signal, via lines CA1 and CA2, when they have finished their respective parts of the read-peripheral operation. Mode 5 permits the same control via lines CB1 and CB2 on a write-to-peripheral operation. Thus, there may be an indefinitely long delay by the peripheral (as when a keyboard operator can't decide which key to push) or by the processor (as when the program masks out the $\overline{IRQ}$ or enters a long $\overline{NMI}$ routine), but still nobody reads the same data over and over, and nobody sends new data until the other party is ready to receive it. This two-way ready/acknowledge in data transfer is called *handshaking*. The details of a procedure for transferring data are called *protocol*, and may include handshaking, parity checking (even or odd number of 1 bits in each byte), checksums (binary total of a string of bytes), or echoing (receiving device sends a copy of data received back to be compared with data sent).

8.4 IC-TESTER HARDWARE

The system hardware for the IC tester is diagrammed in Fig. 8-8(a). The base address for the EPROM (U3) is $F8∅∅, and for the PIA it is $2∅∅∅. PIA pins PA∅ through PA6 and PB∅ through PB6 (14 in all) are used as inputs and outputs for the chip under test. Since two pins of this chip must be tied directly to V_{CC} and ground, these 14 are sufficient to test a 16-pin chip. Lines PA7 and PB7 are reserved for special control functions to be described later. The "7" bits were chosen because their status can be tested easily with the BMI (bit 7 = 1) and BPL (bit 7 = ∅) instructions.

Passive pull-up of all pins on the chip under test is provided by the fourteen 10-kΩ resistors for most logic tests. These resistors are pulled high by Q5, which is turned *on* when a logic 1 at PA7 turns Q4 *on*. This pullup allows open-collector chips to present high outputs, and pulls the port-B outputs (normally only +2.4 V) up high enough to drive CMOS chips with logic-1 inputs.

For special tests PA7 is programmed for a low output, which turns Q6 *on* and pulls the 10-kΩ resistors *low*. This causes floating or open-collector outputs to remain *low* even when not actively pulled *low*, and provides a means to distinguish open-output chips from active-output types.

The display mode is entered when the chip-test mode is done. An 8-bit output latch U5 appears at base address $4∅∅∅, and is used to pull selected cathodes of the three seven-segment displays low through 150-Ω resistors. All three corresponding cathodes are pulled *low* together, but the anodes of only one display at a time are pulled *high*.

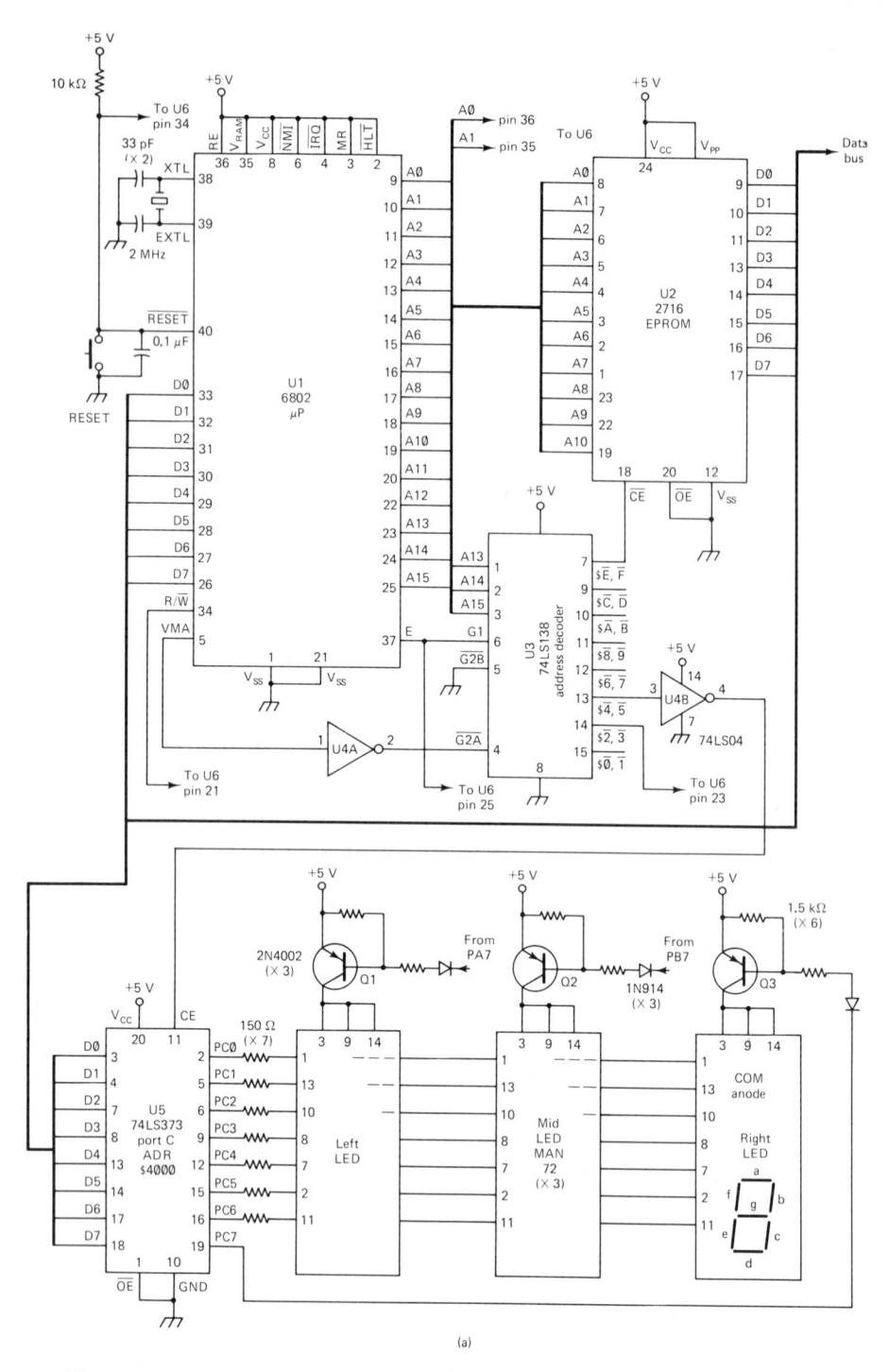

Figure 8-8 Hardware diagram for the IC tester (a), with photographs of a breadboard version (b), and a permanent version (c).

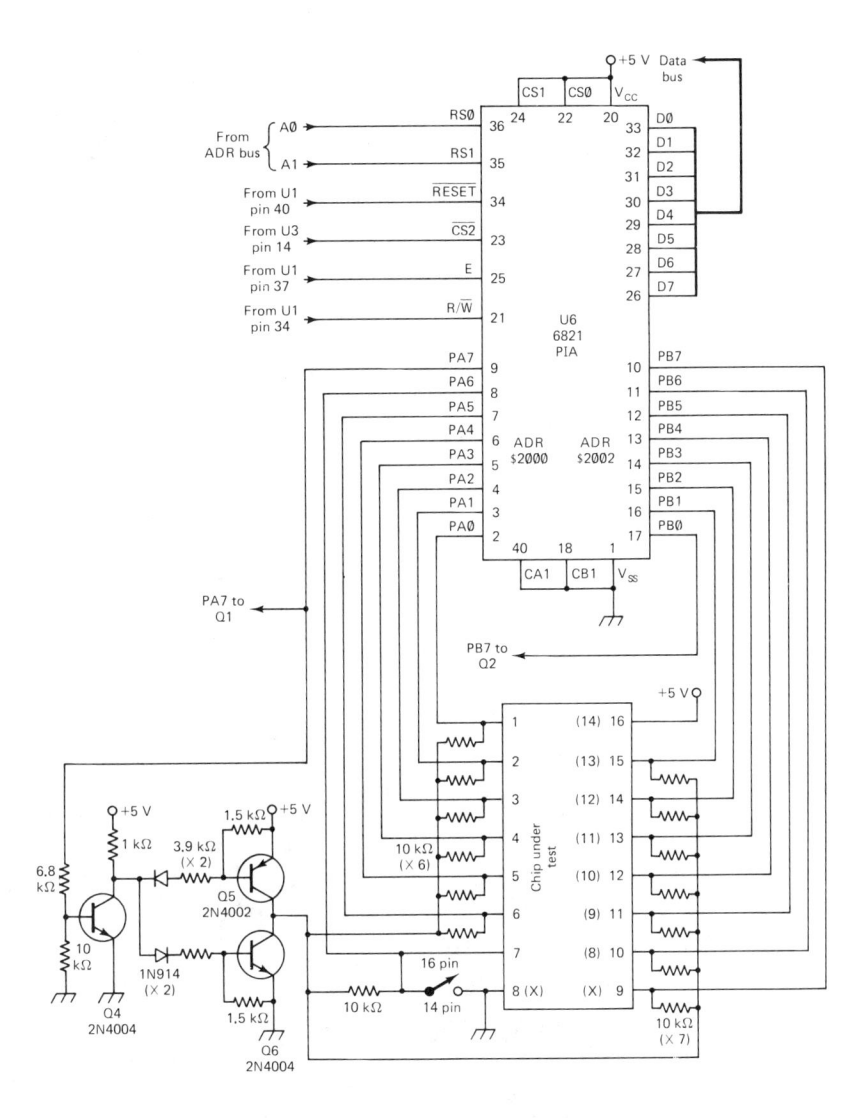

Figure 8-8a (*cont.*)

(b)

(c)

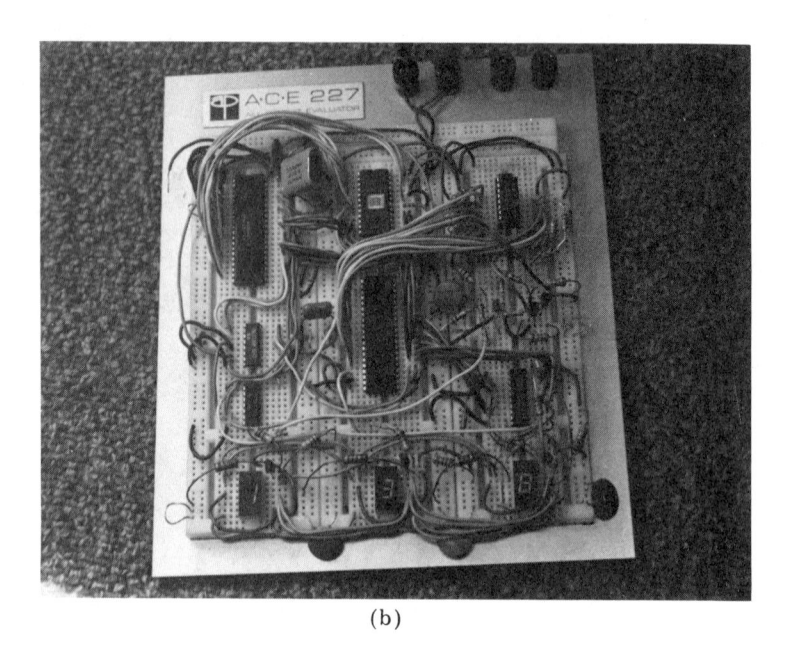

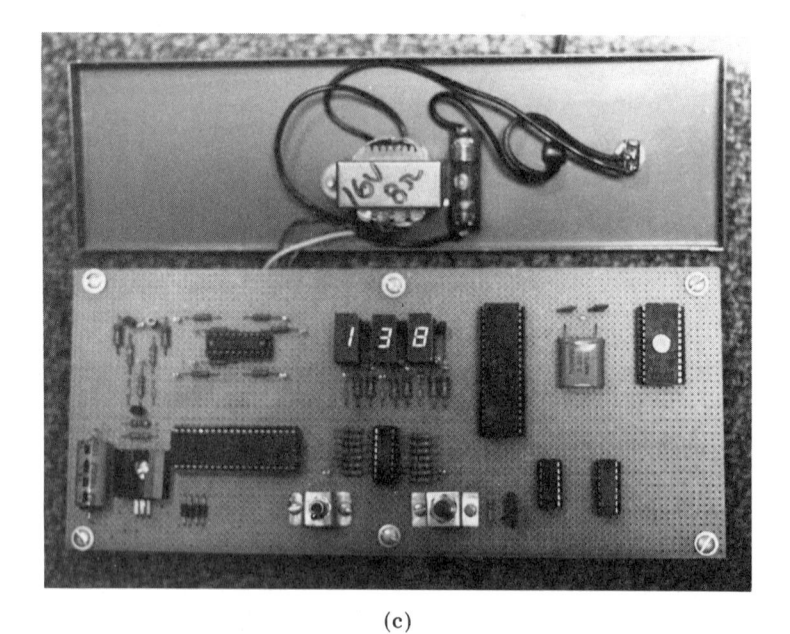

Figure 8-8 (*cont.*)

Bits 7 of port A, port B, and port C (latch U5) are used for turning on the selected display (high, middle, and low digit) via Q1, Q2, and Q3, respectively. A *low* bit-7 output turns the selected transistor *on*, lighting the selected display. Thus (7 + 3) or 10 output lines can control three seven-segment displays (21 lines) by lighting each one for one-third of the time. This process is called *strobing* the display. Each digit is *on* for about 5 ms, giving a flicker frequency of about 70 Hz—too fast for the eye to perceive. Note that the 150-Ω current-limiting resistors are lower in value than normal to compensate for the display being *on* for only one-third of the time. Breadboard and wirewrap versions of the completed IC tester are shown in Figures 8-8(b) and 8-8(c), respectively.

8.5 IC-TESTER SOFTWARE

The test and display portions of the program occupy memory locations $F800 through $F8AE. At $F8AF begin the data files containing the bit patterns to be applied for testing various types of ICs. Test data is picked up in pairs of bytes, one destined for port A and the other for port B. Within the *test* portion of the program there are four options. These are specified by the reserved bits A7 and B7 of the test data.

A7	B7	Test Option
1	1	**Normal test.** Apply data and check outputs. Pull *high* with 10-kΩ resistors.
1	0	**Setup only.** Flip-flops are being set up for trigger on next test. Skip check of outputs.
0	1	**Open-collector test.** Pull *low* with 10-kΩ. Apply data and check outputs.
0	0	**Type-number data.** Exit test mode. Enter display mode.

Data format. Since the test program exists only to handle the data files, we will examine the data-file format first. Here are the functions of the data-file bytes, in ascending-address sequence.

DIR A } Data-direction bits. A7 and B7 = 1 to output LED strobes during display. For 14-pin types A6 = 0 to avoid tying to ground pin, and B0 = 1 to avoid a floating voltage
DIR B } on this pin.

DATA A1	Normal test or setup: A7 = 1.
DATA B1	Normal test: B7 = 1; Setup only: B7 = 0.
DATA A2	For 14-pin types, A6 = 0 since ground will be read as 0.
DATA B2	For 14-pin types let B0 = 1, just to be consistent.

⋮ } Any number of normal or setup data pairs.

DATA An	Optional open-collector test. If used, A7 = 0, B7 = 1, and
DATA Bn	six display bytes must follow.
TYPE HI	Type number for active-output chip.
TYPE MID	All bits 7 must = 0. TYPE *HI* = blank for two-digit TTL,
TYPE LO	$C for CD4000 series.
O.C. HI	Optional open-collector type number. Use if and only if
O.C. MID	DATA An and Bn are included.
O.C. LO	Displayed if O.C. test *fails*.
END TYPE	Constant $F0 marks end of data for this type.

⋮ } Any number of additional *type* files containing at a minimum two DIR bytes, two DATA bytes, three TYPE bytes, and one END byte, $F0.

END FILE	Two consecutive constant $FF bytes mark end of data
END FILE	file.

There are two restrictions on the data bytes that may be included in the file.

1. Hex F0 may appear only in the following positions:

   DIR A   DIR B
   DATA A1   END TYPE

   Any other use will cause an error. Fortunately, the display produced by the code $F0 is not useful, and any need to use $F0 as a DATA byte can be avoided by a slight alteration in the sequence of tests.

2. Hex FF must not appear as the direction byte for both DIR A and DIR B. This all-inputs-to-chip condition may be desired if the tester is used to exercise a device with no electrical outputs, such as an LED display. However, at least one bit must be programmed as a chip output (PIA input) to avoid a false end-of-file flag. The "output" pin will be pulled high during test by Q5 through 10-kΩ.

Sec. 8.5   IC-Tester Software   151

The open-collector (O.C.) test is optional, but if used it must consist of a single pair of bytes following the active-output data, and three O.C. type-number bytes must appear after the three active-output type-number bytes. The open-collector test is simply a repeat of one of the previous tests with the 10-kΩ resistors pulling the outputs low. It is meant to be failed by O.C. devices and, if failed, the O.C. type numbers will be displayed.

The end-of-file flag was chosen as $FF because this is the logic state of an unprogrammed EPROM byte. Thus data for new types can be appended to the file at any time. The EPROM need not be erased, and a new end-of-file flag will automatically be present after the last programmed byte.

The program flowchart is given in Fig. 8-9. Notice that the labels on the various return points are the same as those used in the program listing, which appears on the following pages.

Module 1 reads the DIR A and DIR B bytes for a specific type and sets port A and port B appropriately for inputs and outputs. It also checks for end-of-file (two consecutive $FF bytes).

Module 2 reads a pair of data bytes and checks flag bit A7. If A7 = $\emptyset$ (end of type—all tests successful) a jump to module 4 is made to determine whether the chip is active-output or open-collector. If A7 = 1, the DATA A and DATA B bits in "PIA output" positions are applied to the chip under test. If bit B7 = $\emptyset$, the program loops back immediately to apply a second set of bits to the chip. If B7 = 1, the "PIA input" (chip output) bits are compared to the corresponding bits from the data file. If they are identical, another pair of data bytes is fetched to perform the next test for the current IC type. If not, module 3 is entered.

Module 3 indexes through the data file until the end-of-type flag (F\emptyset$) is found, then advances one more byte (to the DIR A byte of the next type) and jumps to the beginning of the test routine (NXTYP).

Module 4 is entered only if the chip has already passed all the tests for the current type with the 10-kΩ resistors pulling *up* and a DATA A byte is encountered with bit A7 = $\emptyset$ (the BPL tests for this). It then remains to be determined whether the chip is simply an OK active-output type, or whether it is an open-collector type (OK or OC). If DATA B, bit B7 = $\emptyset$ (another BPL test), there is no open-collector test, and the program proceeds directly to DISPLAY the type number coded in the last three bytes of data for that type of number.

If B7 = 1, all pins of the chip under test are pulled *low* through 10-kΩ resistors. The *low* on output line A7 does this through Q4 and Q6. The output lines of the PIA easily override this light pulldown and apply the desired logic levels to the inputs of the chip under test. If the outputs of the chip under test are active (such as the TTL "totem-pole" output), they also override the 10-kΩ pulldown, and the final O.C. test is passed (BEQ TOTEM). The program thus advances two steps, so the X register points to the Type-Number-High data.

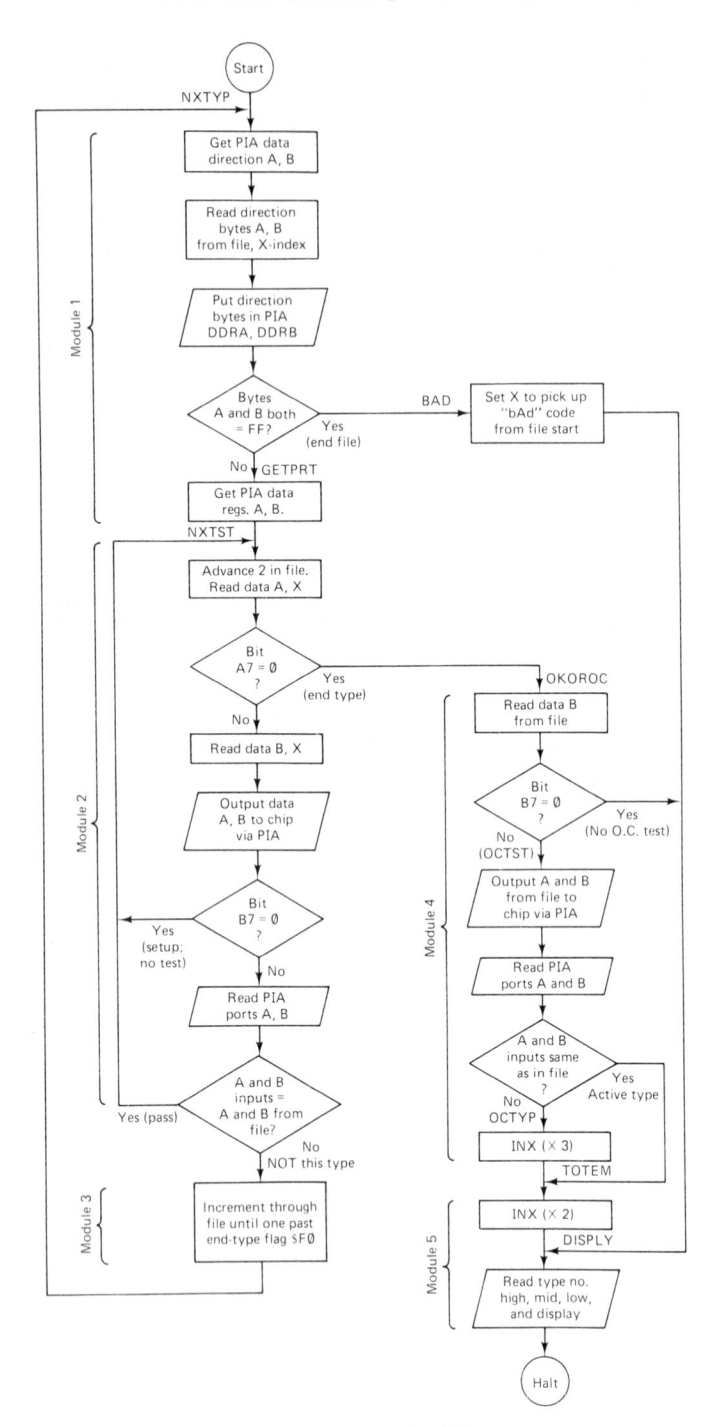

Figure 8-9 Flowchart for IC-tester program.

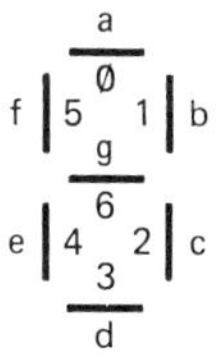

Sec. 8.5   IC-Tester Software   **153**

Display	Binary 7654	(Low = lit) 3210	Hex
0	0100	0000	40
1	0111	1001	79
2	0010	0100	24
3	0011	0000	30
4	0001	1001	19
5	0001	0010	12
6	0000	0010	02
7	0111	1000	78
8	0000	0000	00
9	0001	1000	18
A	0000	1000	08
b	0000	0011	03
C	0100	0110	46
d	0010	0001	21
blank	0111	1111	7F

Segment-to-bit assignment diagram:
```
    a
  ┌─0─┐
f │ 5 │ b
  │ g │
  ├─6─┤
e │ 4 2│ c
  │ 3 │
  └─d─┘
```

Figure 8-10 Hex codes for seven-segment display, showing development from binary, and LED segment-to-bit assignments.

However, if the outputs are open-collector, the final test will sense low outputs from the chip under test (inputs to the PIA), where the test is structured to produce high outputs. The final test will thus be failed, and the program will advance three additional bytes, skipping the normal type number to display the open-collector type number.

Unfortunately, the port-A inputs of the PIA pull up through approximately 3.6 kΩ and cannot reasonably be pulled down to a logic-0 level by external resistors. (See Fig. 8-4 for review of port-A versus port-B characteristics.) Thus any outputs on the left side of the chip under test will not be pulled *low* in the test of module 4. We must rely on outputs from the right half of the chip, which feed the high-impedance port-B inputs, to force the open-collector ICs to fail the module-4 test. This limitation could be overcome by using the port-B sides of two different PIAs, but the single-PIA design shown in Fig. 8-8 was chosen for simplicity.

The display routine is module 5 of the program. It loads port C output latch U6 with three successive display words using X-register offsets of 00, 01, and 02. Bits 0 through 6 of this latch are used to pull selected cathodes of the seven-segment displays *low* according to the segment codes given in Fig. 8-10. Bits 7 of ports A, B, and C are set to 0, successively, to pull the anodes of one digit at a time *high* via Q1, Q2, and Q3, respectively. A RAM location DLY is decremented through 256 counts at each digit to hold each display on for about 5 ms. If the chip under test passes none of the library tests in the file, X is pointed to three default bytes which display the message bAd.

Here is a listing of the IC-tester source code, comments, and object code, as prepared by the SC6800 Assembler on an Apple II computer.

IC Tester: Program Listing

```
          1000 * ------------------------------------------------------------
          1010 *        **********    I C   T E S T E R    ************
          1020 *        COPYRIGHT 1984       ------------------ BY D. L. METZGER
          1030 *------------------------------------------------------------
          1040 *
          1050 * THIS PROGRAM WILL TEST DIGITAL IC'S WITH +5-V SUPPLIES
          1060 *   AND 14- OR 16-PIN PACKS.
          1070 * VCC AND GND MUST BE IN THE STANDARD 14/7 OR 16/8
          1080 *   POSITIONS UNLESS A SPECIAL SOCKET IS PROVIDED
          1090 *   FOR THE ODD CONFIGURATION.
          1100 * THE PROGRAM TESTS FOR LOGIC AND MEMORY FUNCTIONS ONLY
          1110 *   LOGIC-LEVEL AND TIMING LIMITS ARE NOT CHECKED.
          1120 * 5400/7400, C,  S, LS, AND STANDARD SERIES CAN BE
          1130 *   TESTED BUT NOT DIFFERENTIATED.
          1140 * CD4000 SERIES CHIPS CAN BE TESTED. OPEN-COLLECTOR
          1150 *   AND ACTIVE OUTPUT CHIPS CAN BE DIFFERENTIATED BY
          1160 *   A LOGIC TEST WHICH AUTOMATICALLY PULLS ALL OUTPUTS
          1170 *   LOW THROUGH A 10-K RESISTOR.
          1180 *
          1190 *------------------------------------------------------------
          1200 *
          1210            .OR   $F800   PROGRAM ORIGIN
          1220            .TA   $4000   ASSEMBLER TARGET ADR
0000-     1230 DLY        .EQ   $0000   DELAY COUNTER STROBES LEDS 3 MS EACH
```

Sec. 8.5   IC-Tester Software   **155**

```
2001-                1240  CRA    .EQ   $2001   PIA CONTROL REGISTERS
2003-                1250  CRB    .EQ   $2003
2000-                1260  DRA    .EQ   $2000   PIA DATA / DATA-DIRECTION REGISTERS
2002-                1270  DRB    .EQ   $2002
4000-                1280  SEGS   .EQ   $4000   ADR OF DISPLAY LED SEGMENT DRIVER
                     1290  *
                     1300  * -----------------------------------------------------------
                     1310  * MODULE 1 -- SET UP I/O PORTS FOR INPUTS AND OUTPUTS.
                     1320  *   CHECK FOR END OF FILE FLAG ($FF).
                     1330  * -----------------------------------------------------------
                     1340  *
F800- CE F8 AF       1350         LDX    #T7400  DATA FILE STARTS WITH TTL TYPE 7400.
F803- 7F 20 01       1360  NXTYP  CLR    CRA
F806- 7F 20 03       1370         CLR    CRB
F809- A6 00          1380         LDAA   00,X
F80B- E6 01          1390         LDAB   01,X
F80D- B7 20 00       1400         STAA   DRA
F810- F7 20 02       1410         STAB   DRB
F813- 81 FF          1420         CMPA   #$FF
F815- 01             1430         NOP
F816- 01             1435         NOP
F817- 26 07          1440         BNE    GETPRT
F819- C1 FF          1450         CMPB   #$FF
F81B- 26 03          1460         BNE    GETPRT
F81D- 7E F8 71       1470         JMP    BAD
F820- 86 04          1480  GETPRT LDAA   #04
F822- B7 20 01       1490         STAA   CRA
F825- B7 20 03       1500         STAA   CRB
                     1510  *
                     1520  * -----------------------------------------------------------
                     1530  * MODULE 2 -- CHECK FOR END OF TYPE FLAG  (A7 & B7 LO) AND
                     1540  *   DISPLAY TYPE NO. IF SO. OTHERWISE OUTPUT 2 BYTES TO
                     1550  *   CHIP.   IF A7 = 1 & B7 = 0, A F-FLOP OR COUNTER IS BEING
                     1560  *   SET UP.  SKIP TEST AND LOOP BACK FOR 2 MORE BYTES.
                     1570  *   OTHERWISE TEST CHIP OUTPUTS AGAINST FILE DATA.
                     1580  * -----------------------------------------------------------
                     1590  *
F828- 08             1600  NXTST  INX
F829- 08             1610         INX
F82A- A6 00          1620         LDAA   00,X
F82C- 2A 23          1630         BPL    OKOROC
F82E- E6 01          1640         LDAB   01,X
F830- B7 20 00       1650         STAA   DRA
F833- F7 20 02       1660         STAB   DRB
F836- 2A F0          1670         BPL    NXTST
F838- B6 20 00       1680         LDAA   DRA
F83B- A1 00          1690         CMPA   00,X
F83D- 26 07          1700         BNE    NOT
F83F- F6 20 02       1710         LDAB   DRB
F842- E1 01          1720         CMPB   01,X
F844- 27 E2          1730         BEQ    NXTST
                     1740  * ------------------   MODULE 3   ------------------------
                     1750  * IF COMPARISON FAILS SHUFFLE THRU FILE UNTIL END-OF-TYPE
                     1760  *   FLAG (F0) IS FOUND. THEN ADVANCE 1 MORE TO NEXT TYPE.
                     1770  * -----------------------------------------------------------
F846- 08             1780  NOT    INX
F847- A6 00          1790         LDAA   00,X
F849- 81 F0          1800         CMPA   #$F0
F84B- 26 F9          1810         BNE    NOT
F84D- 08             1820         INX
F84E- 7E F8 03       1830         JMP    NXTYP
                     1840  *
                     1850  * ------------------   MODULE 4   ------------------------
                     1860  * IF A7 = 0 AND B7 = 0 THEN DISPLAY TYPE, BUT IF A7 = 0
                     1870  *   AND B7 = 1 THEN PULL ALL IC PINS LOW THRU 10 KOHMS AND
                     1880  *   DO A LAST LOGIC TEST. IF TEST IS PASSED CHIP IS ACTIVE
```

```
                        1890 *  OUTPUT; DISPLAY FIRST SET OF 3 TYPE-NO. DIGITS. IF TEST
                        1900 *  FAILED, CHIP IS O.C.; DISPLAY 2ND SET OF 3 DIGITS.
                        1910 * ------------------------------------------------------------
                        1920 *
F851- E6 01             1930 OKOROC LDAB 01,X
F853- 2A 1F             1940        BPL  DISPLY
F855- B7 20 00          1950        STAA DRA
F858- F7 20 02          1960        STAB DRB
F85B- B6 20 00          1970        LDAA DRA
F85E- A1 00             1980        CMPA 00,X
F860- 26 07             1990        BNE  OCTYP
F862- F6 20 02          2000        LDAB DRB
F865- E1 01             2010        CMPB 01,X
F867- 27 03             2020        BEQ  TOTEM
F869- 08                2030 OCTYP  INX
F86A- 08                2040        INX
F86B- 08                2050        INX
F86C- 08                2060 TOTEM  INX
F86D- 08                2070        INX
F86E- 7E F8 74          2080        JMP  DISPLY
                        2090 * ------------------------------------------------------------
                        2100 * MODULE 5 -- DISPLAY OUTPUT TYPE NUMBER. PORT C BITS 0 - 6
                        2110 *  PULL CATHODES OF THREE 7-SEG LED'S LOW ACCORDING TO TYPE
                        2120 *  NUMBR DATA FROM FILE.
                        2130 *  INVERT TO PULL ANODES OF HI, MID, & LO DIGITS HIGH
                        2140 *  SEQUENTIALLY TO STROBE DISPLAY.
                        2150 * ------------------------------------------------------------
                        2160 *
F871- CE F8 AC          2170 BAD    LDX  #DISBAD
                        2180 *
F874- C6 80             2190 DISPLY LDAB #$80
F876- A6 00             2200        LDAA 00,X
F878- 8A 80             2210        ORAA #$80
F87A- B7 40 00          2220        STAA SEGS
F87D- 7F 20 00          2230        CLR  DRA
F880- 7A 00 00          2240 DELAY1 DEC  DLY
F883- 26 FB             2250        BNE  DELAY1
F885- F7 20 00          2260        STAB DRA
                        2270 *
F888- A6 01             2280        LDAA 01,X
F88A- 8A 80             2290        ORAA #$80
F88C- B7 40 00          2300        STAA SEGS
F88F- 7F 20 02          2310        CLR  DRB
F892- 7A 00 00          2320 DELAY2 DEC  DLY
F895- 26 FB             2330        BNE  DELAY2
F897- F7 20 02          2340        STAB DRB
                        2350 *
F89A- A6 02             2360        LDAA 02,X
F89C- 84 7F             2370        ANDA #$7F
F89E- B7 40 00          2380        STAA SEGS
F8A1- 7A 00 00          2390 DELAY3 DEC  DLY
F8A4- 26 FB             2400        BNE  DELAY3
F8A6- F7 40 00          2410        STAB SEGS
F8A9- 7E F8 74          2420        JMP  DISPLY
                        2430 *
                        2440 * ------------------------------------------------------------
                        2450 * SEGMENT CODES TO DISPLAY MESSAGE "BAD":
F8AC- 03 08 21          2460 DISBAD .HS  030821
                        2470 *
                        2480 * ------------------------------------------------------------
                        2490 * TEST DATA FILES. LABELS GIVE IC TYPE. T = TTL, C = CMOS
                        2500 *
F8AF- 9B ED A4
F8B2- 92 B6 B6
F8B5- AD DA 9B
F8B8- EC 24 92
```

Sec. 8.5   IC-Tester Software   157

```
F8BB- 7F 40 40
F8BE- 7F 40 30
F8C1- F0           2510 T7400  .HS  9BEDA492B6B6ADDA9BEC24927F40407F4030F0
F8C2- 95 D5 AA
F8C5- AA 95 D4
F8C8- 2A AA 7F
F8CB- 40 19 7F
F8CE- 40 12 F0    2520 T7404  .HS  95D5AAAA95D42AAA7F40197F4012F0
F8D1- 9F FD 9B
F8D4- EC BA AE
F8D7- B9 CE B3
F8DA- E6 AB EA
F8DD- 20 82 7F
F8E0- 24 40 7F
F8E3- 24 24 F0    2530 T7420  .HS  9FFD9BECBAAEB9CEB3E6ABEA20827F24407F2424F0
F8E6- 9B ED 80
F8E9- 81 B6 B7
F8EC- AD DB 9B
F8EF- ED 2B DB
F8F2- 7F 00 02
F8F5- 79 30 02
F8F8- F0          2540 T7486  .HS  9BED8081B6B7ADDB9BED2BDB7F0002793002F0
F8F9- 9B ED 80
F8FC- 81 B6 B7
F8FF- AD DB BF
F902- FF 3F FF
F905- 7F 30 24
F908- 79 24 12
F90B- F0          2550 T74125 .HS  9BED8081B6B7ADDBBFFF3FFF7F3024792412F0
F90C- FF FE FF
F90F- FE FE FF
F912- FB FF EF
F915- FF BF FF
F918- FD FF F7
F91B- FF DF FF
F91E- 79 30 30
F921- F0          2560 T74133 .HS  FFFEFFFEFEFFFBFFEFFFBFFFFDFFF7FFDFFF793030F0
F922- BF 80 E0
F925- BF E1 DF
F928- E2 EF E3
F92B- F7 E4 FB
F92E- E5 FD E6
F931- FE A7 FF
F934- EF FF D7
F937- FF C7 FF
F93A- 79 30 00
F93D- F0          2570 T74138 .HS  BF80E0BFE1DFE2EFE3F7E4FBE5FDE6FEA7FFEFFFD7FFC7
                                   FF793000F0
F93E- 99 E7 99
F941- 6F 91 CF
F944- 98 5F EE
F947- 94 FE 1C
F94A- 9C 9C BC
F94D- 5A BC DE
F950- BD 9D 79
F953- 18 30 F0    2580 T74193 .HS  99E7996F91CF985FEE94FE1C9C9CBC5ABCDEBD9D791830F0
F956- B9 F3 B0
F959- E1 BF FF
F95C- 86 8D 10
F95F- D3 46 79
F962- 02 46 03
F965- 21 F0       2590 C4116  .HS  B9F3B0E1BFFF868D10D3467902460321F0
F967- FC 9F D1
F96A- C5 91 44
F96D- 96 B4 A2
F970- 22 A5 D2
F973- 8A A8 46
```

```
F976- 24 78 F0  2600  C4027  .HS  FC9FD1C5914496B4A222A5D28AA8462478F0
                2610   *
                2620   * --------------------------------------------------------------
                2630          .OR  $FFFE   PROGRAM ORIGIN IN RESET VECTOR
                2640          .TA  $47FE   ASSEMBLER TARGET
FFFE- F8 00     2650          .HS  F800    HEX STRING GIVES ORIGIN
                2660          .EN  END
```

8.6 DATA DEVELOPMENT

Test data for 10 IC types and their various buffer and open-collector versions are given with the program listing, but you will undoubtedly want to add other types to your tester's library. Some data-development sheets are included at the end of this section, and to make it easier for you, some of the sheets are filled out with data for the IC types listed. These types include 14- and 16-pin types, logic gates and counters, active-output and open-collector types, and CMOS as well as TTL. The best way to learn how to write new data files is to study the completed data-development sheets for types similar to those you are interested in. Here are some additional hints.

Start with the pin diagram for the chip you want to test. Choose a chip containing only logic gates (AND, OR, NAND, NOR) for your first efforts.

1. List the IC pin numbers under the port A0-B7 boxes. These will be the same as shown in the sample sheets, depending only on whether the chip is a 14-pin or 16-pin type. Note that V_{CC} and ground must be in the standard corner positions.
2. List binary "1s" on the first line under all input pins to the chip (PIA outputs) and "0s" under all outputs (PIA inputs). List "1" for A7 and B7 (code for normal test). For 14-pin types list B0 = 1 and A6 = 0 for the empty socket positions; and A6 = 0 for the ground position.

For logic gates you should make a truth table (input combination versus output states) and decide whether it is desirable or feasible to test the chip under all input combinations. For the 7400, with two inputs per gate (four combinations), this is easily done. For the 74133, with 13 inputs (8192 combinations), it is out of the question. In the latter case, choose a set of inputs such that each input line has at least one test in which, acting alone, it can alter the output state.

3. List one set of input conditions per line in binary, and include the anticipated binary outputs. List A7 = 1 and B7 = 1 (normal test, active output). For 14-pin types list A6 = 0 and B0 = 0 (unused pins).
4. If the chip has an open-collector version, include one open-collector test after the normal test data. Make the test identical to one of the

Sec. 8.6   Data Development   159

normal tests that brings the active output(s) *high*. Keep A6 and B0 = 0 for 14-pin types. Keep B7 = 1 but list A7 = 0 to pull the outputs *low* via PA7, Q4, and Q6 if the chip is open-collector. This test can also be used to identify tri-state (floating-output) devices.

5. Convert each byte of binary data to hex and record it in the right-hand columns. Notice the reversal of the left-to-right sequence in the hex columns.

Output type-number codes should be listed after the data. These consist of three bytes for the left, middle, and right digits of the standard IC type number, followed by three digits for the open-collector type number if an open-collector data set was included. Figure 8-10 shows codes for the characters normally used in the display. Any other letter or pattern can be produced by placing binary 0s in the bit positions corresponding to the segments to be lit.

6. List three bytes in hex corresponding to the type number to be displayed.
7. If open-collector data was supplied, list three more bytes for the open-collector type number.
8. Add an end-of-type flag $F0. You may now list data for the next type number, or $FF, FF for end-of-file.

Flip-flops and counters involve more complexity and judgment and should be attempted only after you have written a few data sets for logic gates. Usually, it is not practical to test every function and output state, so some selections must be made which will produce a high probability of catching a device with a defective function. A typical test sequence follows.

- Preclear
- Preset or Load
- Count up
- Count down
- Inhibit count

Flip-flops and counters are usually triggered by a high-to-low or low-to-high transition on the clock input. In developing data to test clock or trigger functions it is thus necessary to use a line of setup data in which the inputs are armed in readiness for the trigger, but the output states are not checked. This is accomplished by listing A7 = 1 and B7 = 0 in the data line. The next line of data will then cause the clock to transition, triggering the counter. All inputs except the clock will remain the same, but A7 and B7 are set to 1 on this line, so the output states will be checked.

IC Tester Data Development Sheet

	14-pin ~~16-pin~~ types	Binary Data																Hex	
		B7	B6	B5	B4	B3	B2	B1	BØ	A7	A6	A5	A4	A3	A2	A1	AØ	DTA A	DTA B
	IC pin numbers ⟶	X	13	12	11	10	9	8	X	X	Ø	6	5	4	3	2	1		
√	IC types/test notes																		
√	7400 Quad 2-In NAND	1	1	1	0	1	1	0	1	1	0	1	1	1	0	1	1	9B	ED
X	7403 O.C.	1	0	0	1	0	0	1	0	1	0	1	0	0	1	0	0	A4	92
√	7426 H.V.	1	0	1	1	0	1	1	0	1	0	1	1	0	1	1	0	B6	B6
√	7437 BUFR	1	1	0	1	1	0	1	0	1	0	1	0	1	1	0	1	AD	DA
X	7438 O.C.	1	1	1	0	1	1	0	0	1	0	0	1	1	0	1	1	9B	EC
√	74132 Schmitt Trig	1	0	0	1	0	0	1	0	0	0	1	0	0	1	0	0	24	92
											TYPE		74	00	→	7	F	4Ø	4Ø
											TYPE		74	03	→	7	F	4Ø	43
											End of Type					F	Ø		
√	7404 Hex Inverter	1	1	0	1	0	1	0	1	1	0	0	1	0	1	0	1	95	D5
X	7405 O.C.	1	0	1	0	1	0	1	0	1	0	1	0	1	0	1	0	AA	AA
X	7406 O.C.	1	1	0	1	0	1	0	0	1	0	0	1	0	1	0	1	95	D4
√	7414 Schmitt Trig	1	0	1	0	1	0	1	0	0	0	1	0	1	0	1	0	2A	AA
X	7416 O.C.										TYPE		74	04	→	7	F	4Ø	19
											TYPE		74	05	→	7	F	4Ø	12
											End of Type					F	Ø		
√	7420 Dual 4-In NAND	1	1	1	1	1	1	0	1	1	0	0	1	1	1	1	1	9F	FD
X	7422 O.C.	1	1	1	0	1	1	0	0	1	0	0	1	1	0	1	1	9B	EC
√	7440 BUFR	1	0	1	0	1	1	1	0	1	0	1	1	1	0	1	0	BA	AE
		1	1	0	0	1	1	1	0	1	0	1	1	1	0	0	1	B9	CE
		1	1	1	0	0	1	1	0	1	0	1	1	0	0	1	1	B3	E6
		1	1	1	0	1	0	1	0	1	0	1	0	1	0	1	1	AB	EA
		1	0	0	0	0	0	1	0	0	0	1	0	0	0	0	0	2Ø	82
											TYPE		74	20	→	7	F	24	4Ø
											TYPE		74	22	→	7	F	24	24
											End of Type					F	Ø		
√	7486 Quad EXOR	1	1	1	0	1	1	0	1	1	0	0	1	1	0	1	1	9B	ED
	(Not for 74L86)	1	0	0	0	0	0	0	1	1	0	0	0	0	0	0	0	8Ø	81
X	74136 O.C.	1	0	1	1	0	1	1	1	1	0	1	1	0	1	1	0	B6	B7
		1	1	0	1	1	0	1	1	1	0	1	0	1	1	0	1	AD	DB
		1	1	1	0	1	1	0	1	1	0	0	1	1	0	1	1	9B	ED
		1	1	0	1	1	0	1	1	0	0	1	0	1	1	0	1	2B	DB
											TYPE		74	86	→	7	F	ØØ	Ø2
											TYPE		74	136	→	7	9	3Ø	Ø2
											End of Type					F	Ø		

Figure 8-11 Data-development sheets for the IC tester.

IC Tester   Data Development Sheet

	14-pin, 16-pin types	\multicolumn{8}{c	}{Binary Data}								Hex	
		B7	B6	B5	B4	B3	B2	B1	B0	A7	A6	A5	A4	A3	A2	A1	A0	DTA A	DTA B
	14 pin IC pin numbers →	X	13	12	11	10	9	8	X	X	0	6	5	4	3	2	1		
✓	IC types/test notes																		
X	74125 Quad Tristate	1	1	1	0	1	1	0	1	1	0	0	1	1	0	1	1	9B	ED
	Buffer, Low Active	1	0	0	0	0	0	0	1	1	0	0	0	0	0	0	1	80	81
✓	7432 Quad 2-In OR	1	0	1	1	0	1	1	1	1	0	1	1	0	1	1	0	B6	B7
		1	1	0	1	1	0	1	1	1	0	1	0	1	1	0	1	AD	DB
		1	1	1	1	1	1	1	1	1	0	1	1	1	1	1	1	BF	FF
		1	1	1	1	1	1	1	1	0	0	1	1	1	1	1	1	3F	FF
										TYPE	7432 →			7F	30	24			
										TYPE	74125 →			79	24	12			
										End of Type				F0					
	16-pin type follows →	X	15	14	13	12	11	10	9	X	7	6	5	4	3	2	1		
✓	74133 13-In NAND	1	1	1	1	1	1	1	0	1	1	1	1	1	1	1	1	FF	FE
	Test every other input	1	1	1	1	1	1	1	0	1	1	1	1	1	1	1	1	FF	FE
		1	1	1	1	1	1	1	1	1	1	1	1	1	1	1	0	FE	FF
		1	1	1	1	1	1	1	1	1	1	1	1	1	0	1	1	FB	FF
		1	1	1	1	1	1	1	1	1	1	1	0	1	1	1	1	EF	FF
		1	1	1	1	1	1	1	1	1	0	1	1	1	1	1	1	BF	FF
		1	1	1	1	1	1	0	1	1	1	1	1	1	1	1	1	FF	FD
		1	1	1	1	0	1	1	1	1	1	1	1	1	1	1	1	FF	F7
		1	1	0	1	1	1	1	1	1	1	1	1	1	1	1	1	FF	DF
										TYPE	74133 →			79	30	30			
										End of Type				F0					
	14-pin type follows →	X	13	12	11	10	9	8	X	X	0	6	5	4	3	2	1		
✓	74138 3 to 8 decoder	1	0	0	0	0	0	0	0	1	0	1	1	1	1	1	1	BF	80
		1	0	1	1	1	1	1	1	1	1	1	0	0	0	0	0	E0	BF
		1	1	0	1	1	1	1	1	1	1	1	0	0	0	0	1	E1	DF
		1	1	1	0	1	1	1	1	1	1	1	0	0	0	1	0	E2	EF
		1	1	1	1	0	1	1	1	1	1	1	0	0	0	1	1	E3	F7
		1	1	1	1	1	0	1	1	1	1	1	0	0	1	0	0	E4	FB
		1	1	1	1	1	1	0	1	1	1	1	0	0	1	0	1	E5	FD
		1	1	1	1	1	1	1	0	1	1	1	0	0	1	1	0	E6	FE
		1	1	1	1	1	1	1	1	1	0	1	0	0	1	1	1	A7	FF
		1	1	1	1	1	1	1	1	1	1	1	0	1	1	1	1	EF	FF
		1	1	1	1	1	1	1	1	1	1	0	1	0	1	1	1	D7	FF
		1	1	1	1	1	1	1	1	1	1	0	0	0	1	1	1	C7	FF
										TYPE	74138 →			79	30	00			
										End of Type				F0					

Figure 8-11 (*cont.*)

IC Tester   Data Development Sheet

	14-pin, 16-pin types	B7	B6	B5	B4	B3	B2	B1	B0	A7	A6	A5	A4	A3	A2	A1	A0	Hex DTA A	Hex DTA B
	16 pin IC pin numbers →	X	15	14	13	12	11	10	9	X	7	6	5	4	3	2	1		
✓	IC types/test notes																		
✓	74193 Binary Counter	1	1	1	0	0	1	1	1	1	0	0	1	1	0	0	1	99	E7
	Clear to } setup	0	1	1	0	1	1	1	1	1	0	0	1	1	0	0	1	99	6F
	0000 } test	1	1	0	0	1	1	1	1	1	0	0	1	0	0	0	1	91	CF
	Count down } setup	0	1	0	1	1	1	1	1	1	0	0	1	1	0	0	0	98	5F
	to 1111 } test	1	0	0	1	0	1	0	0	1	1	1	0	1	1	1	0	EE	94
	Count up } setup	0	0	0	1	1	1	0	0	1	1	1	1	1	1	1	0	FE	1C
	to 0000 } test	1	0	0	1	1	1	0	0	1	0	0	1	1	1	0	0	9C	9C
	Set to ⎫	0	1	0	1	1	0	1	0	1	0	1	1	1	1	0	0	BC	5A
	0101, then ⎬	1	1	0	1	1	1	1	0	1	0	1	1	1	1	0	0	BC	DE
	change inputs ⎭	1	0	0	1	1	1	0	1	1	0	1	1	1	1	0	1	BD	9D
										TYPE 74193 →				7	9	18	3Ø		
										End of Type				F	Ø				
	14-pin type follows →	X	13	12	11	10	9	8	X	X	Ø	6	5	4	3	2	1		
✓	CD4116 Quad	1	1	1	0	0	1	1		1	0	1	1	0	0	1	89	F3	
	bilateral switch	1	1	1	0	0	0	1		1	0	1	1	0	0	0	BØ	E1	
✓	CD4066	1	1	1	1	1	1	1		1	0	1	1	1	1	1	BF	FF	
X	CD4016 can't pull	1	0	0	0	1	1	0		1	0	0	0	1	1	0	86	8D	
	TTL inputs low;	1	1	0	1	0	0	1		0	0	0	1	0	0	0	1Ø	D3	
	Reads as [bd]									TYPE CD4116 →	4	6	79	Ø2					
										TYPE CD4016 →	4	6	Ø3	21					
										End of Type			F	Ø					
	16-pin type follows →	X	15	14	13	12	11	10	9	X	7	6	5	4	3	2	1		
✓	CD4027 JK FF	1	0	0	1	1	1	1	1	1	1	1	1	1	0	0	FC	9F	
	Preset	1	1	0	0	0	1	0	1	1	1	0	1	0	0	0	1	D1	C5
	J=Ø, K=1 setup	0	1	0	0	0	1	0	0	1	0	0	1	0	0	0	1	91	44
	Clock & check Q=Ø	1	0	1	1	0	1	0	0	1	0	0	1	0	1	1	0	96	B4
	J=1, K=Ø setup	0	0	1	0	0	0	1	0	1	0	1	0	0	0	1	0	A2	22
	Clock & check Q=1	1	1	0	1	0	0	1	0	1	0	1	0	0	1	0	1	A5	D2
	Preclear	1	0	1	0	1	0	0	0	1	0	0	0	1	0	1	0	8A	A8
										TYPE CD4027 →	4	6	24	78					
										End of Type			F	Ø					
										End of File			F	F					
													F	F					

Figure 8-11 (cont.)

IC Tester   Data Development Sheet

	14-pin 16-pin types	\multicolumn{16}{c	}{Binary Data}	\multicolumn{2}{c	}{Hex}
		B7	B6	B5	B4	B3	B2	B1	B0	A7	A6	A5	A4	A3	A2	A1	A0	DTA A	DTA B
	IC pin numbers ⟶	X								X		6	5	4	3	2	1		
✓	IC types/test notes																		

Figure 8-11 (*cont.*)

Where applicable, it is a good idea to have counters count through an overflow or underflow so that *carry* and/or *borrow* outputs can be checked. Open-collector tests and associated second type-number sets are not generally applicable in testing flip-flops and counters.

The data-development sheets of Fig. 8-11 illustrate the procedures outlined above. Note the wide variety of types which read out as 7400 (active) or 7403 (open collector). Also interesting is the similarity of the logic tables for the 7432 two-input OR and 74125 tristate buffer, which allows the 74125 to be tested as an "open-collector" 7432. Finally, study how the last line of the CD4116 analog-switch test floats the outputs on the *right* side (port-B side) of the chip only, and displays "C16" only if the module-4 test is *passed*.

CHAPTER SUMMARY

1. The 6821 Peripheral Interface Adapter provides two 8-bit ports, A and B, whose lines are individually programmable as inputs or outputs.
2. Register Select pin RS1 = 0 selects port A. RS1 = 1 selects port B.
3. Register Select pin RS0 = 1 selects the control registers CRA or CRB. Normally, we write either data 00 or 04 to the control registers.
4. If CRA contains 00, setting RS0 = 0 accesses the data-direction register A. Storing a binary 1 bit in DDRA sets a line to be an output. Storing a 0 sets a line to be an input.
5. If CRA contains 04, setting RS0 = 0 accesses the Port A data register, also called PAD. Data can be output (store instruction) or input (load instruction) as selected by the bits in DDRA.
6. If the PIA is enabled at base address $2000 and A0 drives RS0 while A1 drives RS1, then

    ADR $2001 = CRA
    ADR $2000 = DDRA (CRA = 00) or PAD (CRA = 04)
    ADR $2003 = CRB
    ADR $2002 = DDRB (CRB = 00) or PBD (CRB = 04)

7. The PIA contains six control lines:

    CA1, CB1:   inputs for interrupts or handshaking.
    CA2, CB2:   interrupt inputs, auxiliary outputs, or handshake outputs.
    $\overline{\text{IRQA}}, \overline{\text{IRQB}}$: interrupt outputs to the processor.

9

Microchicken: A General-Purpose Computer with Monitor

9.1 COMPUTER OVERVIEW AND OPERATION

This chapter presents construction details and programs for a general-purpose user-programmable computer. Figure 9-1 is a photograph of the completed system. The system capabilities are as follows:

- Load machine-language programs and data into RAM via a 16-button keypad.
- Read memory data and addresses in hex on seven-segment displays, and modify RAM data.
- Run programs in ROM or RAM.
- Single-step through programs in RAM and read out the contents of all machine registers (A, B, X, CCR, and PC) after each step.
- Save RAM or ROM programs with a standard cassette recorder and reload them into RAM.
- Transfer programs or data from RAM to an external EPROM, or reload from EPROM to RAM.

Briefly, this will allow you to develop, test, and modify programs in RAM from a keypad, save them on tape while they are under development, and then burn them into EPROM once they are debugged. No more hand reloading of an entire program just to change one byte in an EPROM!

The system controls consist of a RESET (RS) pushbutton, a Single-Step

Figure 9-1 The basic Microchicken computer with keyboard.

switch (SST), and the 16 keys, ∅ through F. Upon receiving a RESET, the system displays the current address and simultaneously scans the keypad. Since the display consists of only two digits, the high address byte is displayed first, followed by the low address byte, and then a brief blanking of the display. The first key press following *RESET* is interpreted as a function-select code. The functions (∅ through F) are:

∅. **Change current address.** The first four keystrokes following a "∅" stroke are entered as the four digits (high to low) of the new address, which is then displayed. A subsequent keystroke is interpreted as a new function select.

1. **Display data** at current address. Subsequent presses of the 1 key **increment the current address** and display that data.

2. Display data at current address and await two key strokes to **input new data** to this location. Note that data can be stored only to RAM addresses. After the first keystroke the low digit of the current address is displayed as an aid to the programmer. Upon receiving the second keystroke the data at the next address is displayed and new data may be entered. To exit this function, press *RESET*.

3. Display data at current address. Subsequent "3" inputs **decrement the current address**.

4. **Run a program** whose first instruction is at the current address. This transfers control to the user's program, and subsequent key strokes will, in general, not be recognized. To regain keypad control, press *RS*.

5. **Jump to user program** at address ∅∅∅1. This is an "unassigned" key that can be used to transfer control to a user program.

6. **Burn EPROM with contents of RAM.** Start at RAM address stored at address $7A (HI), 7B (LO). Stop after RAM address stored at $7C, 7D.

Sec. 9.2 System Hardware   167

Start at EPROM address stored at $7E, 7F. Takes about 50 ms per byte; 13 seconds per page. Displays last RAM address upon completion of dump. Displays faulty ROM address upon failure to take data.

7. **Dump EPROM to RAM.** Same specifications as 6 above, except that time is about 50 μs per byte; 12 ms per page.

8. **Save RAM on tape.** Starting RAM address is stored at $7A, 7B; ending RAM address at $7C, 7D. Takes about 60 ms per byte; 15 seconds per page. Displays last RAM address upon completion.

9. **Load RAM from tape.** Same specifications as 8 above.

A. **Display accumulator A.**
B. **Display accumulator B.**
C. **Display condition-code register.** } Use after single-step.
D. **Display index Register.**
E. **Display program counter.**
F. **Single-step through program in RAM,** starting at current address. Display program counter (address of next instruction). Single-step switch must be ON. There must be at least one free RAM location before the start of the program.

Functions may be entered one after another by simply pressing the appropriate keys, except for function 2, in which all subsequent keys are interpreted as data, and functions 4 and 5, which transfer control from the keypad.

9.2 SYSTEM HARDWARE

The minimum system consists of a 6802 processor with 128 bytes of internal RAM, a 74LS138 address decoder, a 2716 EPROM which stores the operating program (monitor), a 74LS373 octal output latch which drives two seven-segment hex displays, and a 6821 PIA for input/output to external devices. This is shown in the wiring diagram of Fig. 9-2. This circuitry can be built on a double-sided circuit board using the master artwork given in Fig. 9-3(a) and (b). Only the +5-V power supply, hex keypad, and single-step switch need be connected externally at this stage. A 44-pin edge-card connector provides access for these and other interfaces which you may wish to add later.

The monitor program uses about 48 bytes of RAM, leaving only 80 bytes for user programs at this stage. Still, this is enough to allow you to become familiar with the system and begin trying some program ideas of your own. Several of the programs from Chapters 4 and 6 can be loaded and run in the system's RAM, and the first project in Chapter 10 is designed to run in the basic computer without expansions.

Construction hints. The double-sided circuit board, etched and drilled, is available from the author for $25, and a 2716 EPROM containing the

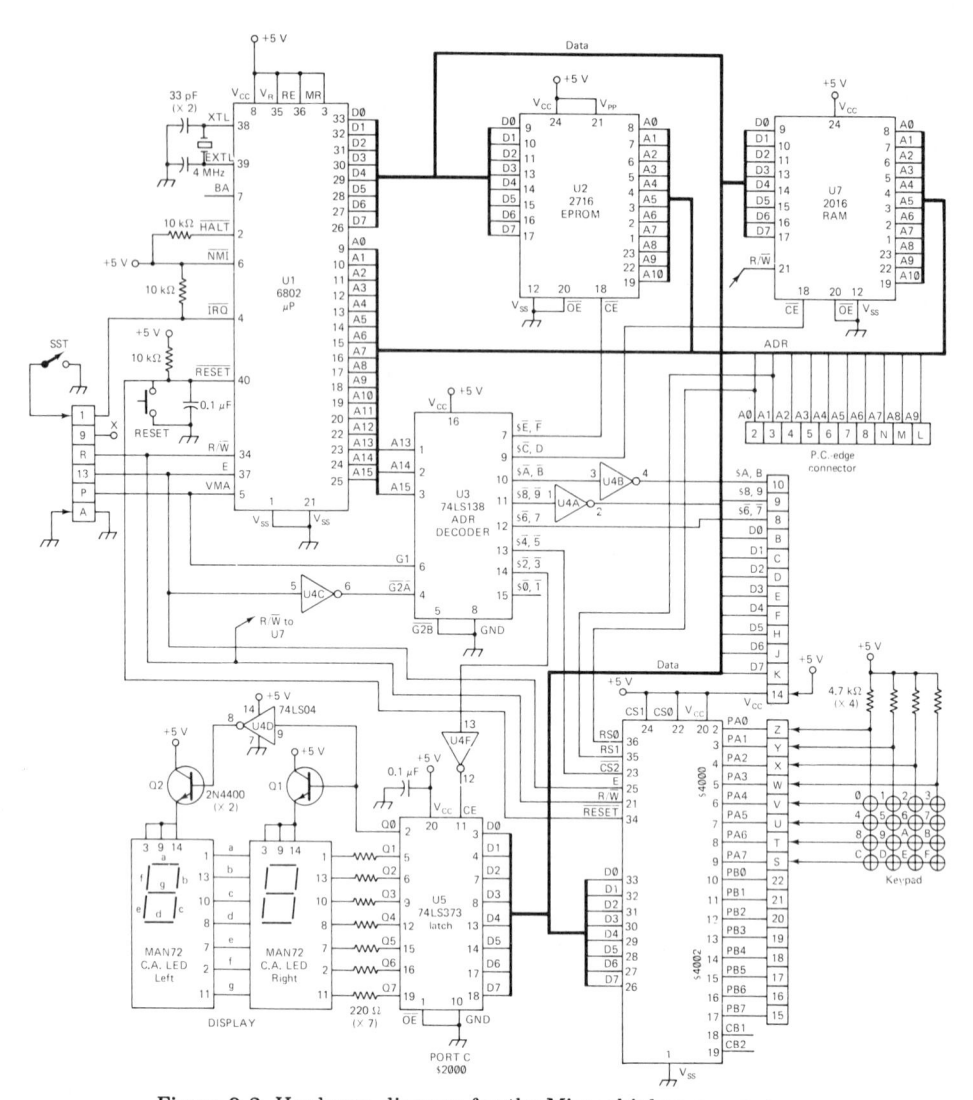

Figure 9-2 Hardware diagram for the Microchicken computer.

monitor program is available for $20. Write P.O. Box 466, Temperance, MI, 48182. If you etch your own circuit board, check any suspicious wire tracks with an ohmmeter; hairline cracks can leave an open circuit that a visual inspection may not catch. Scrub the photoresist off the contact fingers with steel wool.

Professionally made boards have plated-through holes to connect the tracks on one side with those on the other. You can make these "through the board" connections by using wirewrap IC sockets and soldering the pins on both sides. The sockets should be suspended about 2 mm (3/32 inch) off

Sec. 9.2 System Hardware   **169**

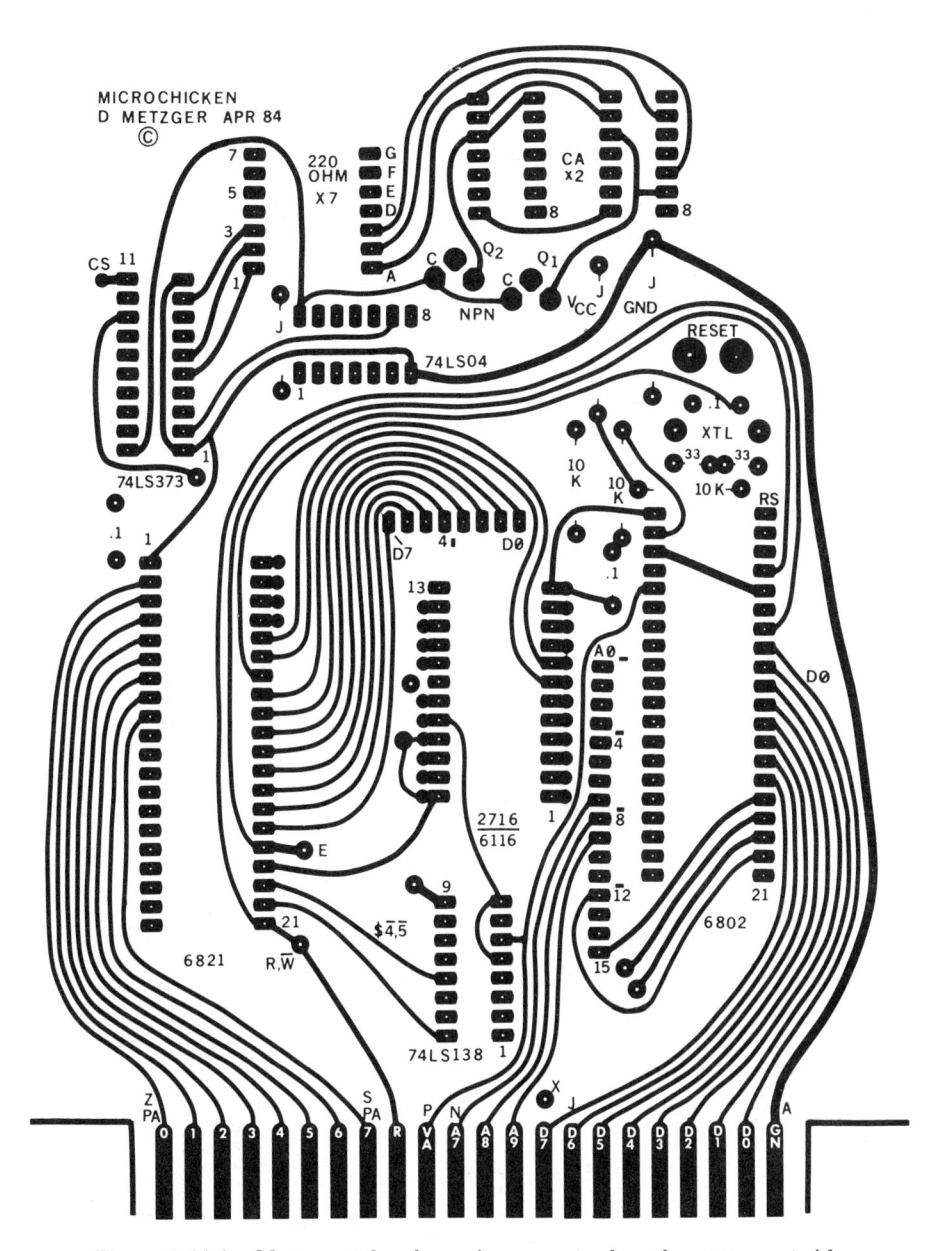

Figure 9-3(a)   Master art for the main computer board, component side.

the board to allow room to solder the pins to the pads on the top. The pins can be cut off flush with the bottom after soldering.

An alternative technique for making through-the-board connections is to pass a fine strand of bare wire through the hole, fold it flat, and solder it

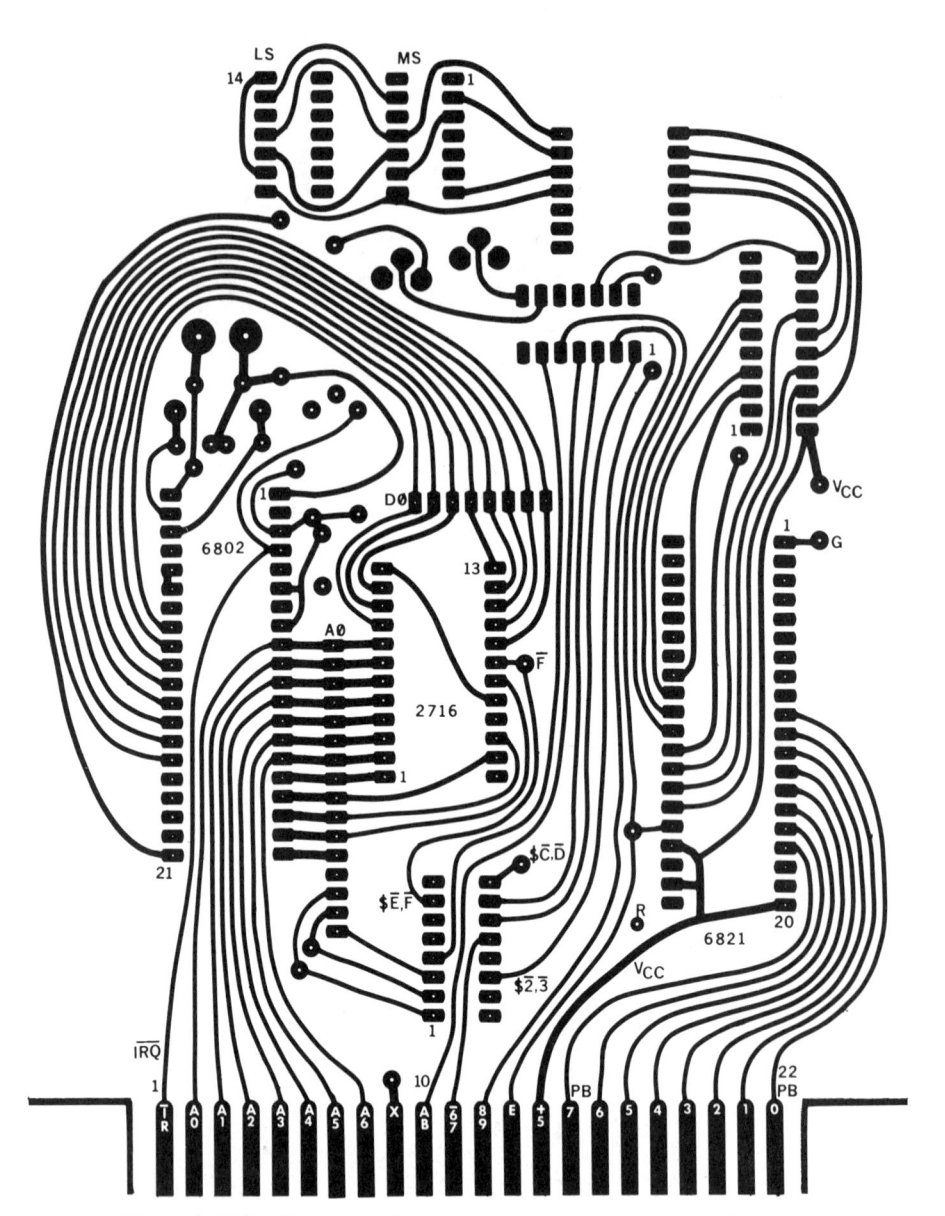

170 Microchicken: A General-Purpose Computer with Monitor Chap. 9

Figure 9-3(b) Master art for the main computer board, solder side.

top and bottom without letting solder fill the hole. Then the socket can be inserted and soldered on the bottom side only. The latter method should be used for the 2716 socket so that a **low-profile** socket can be used. This will be important in adding more RAM to the system later.

Adding the tape-record function. Port B, bit 6, (pin 16 of the 44-pin connector) outputs 3-V p-p 3600-Hz tones during function 8 (save RAM on

Sec. 9.2 System Hardware

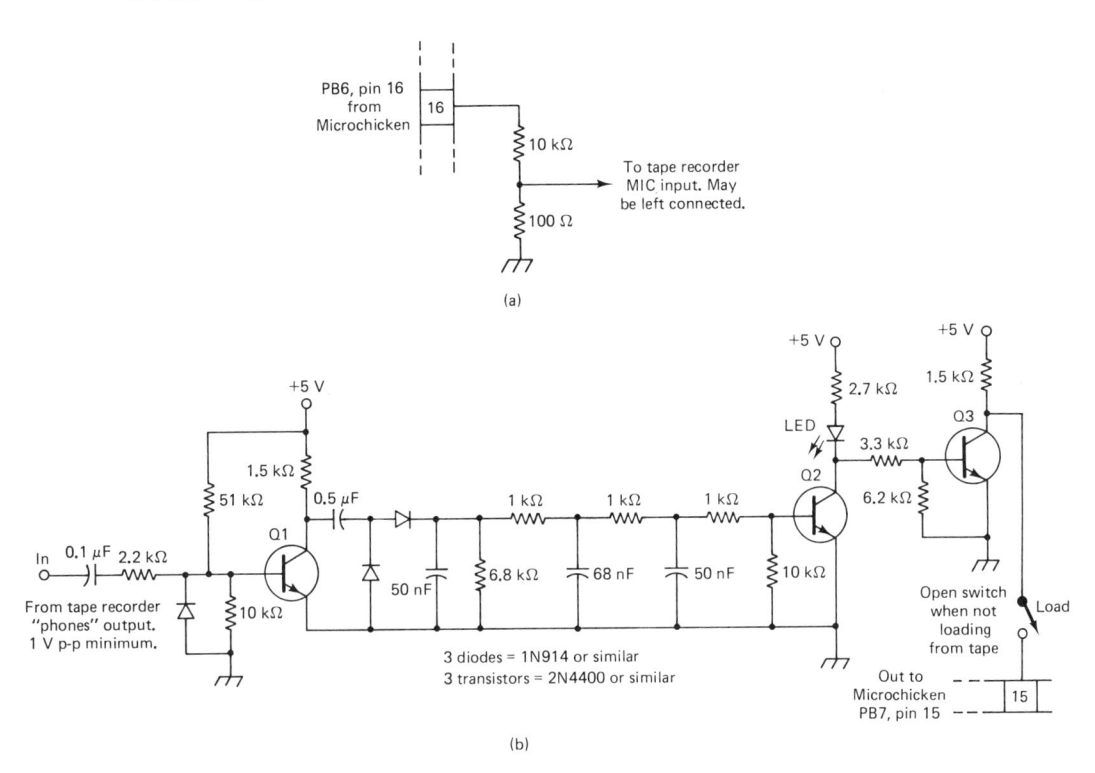

Figure 9-4 External circuitry for (a) Save-on tape and (b) Load-from-tape function.

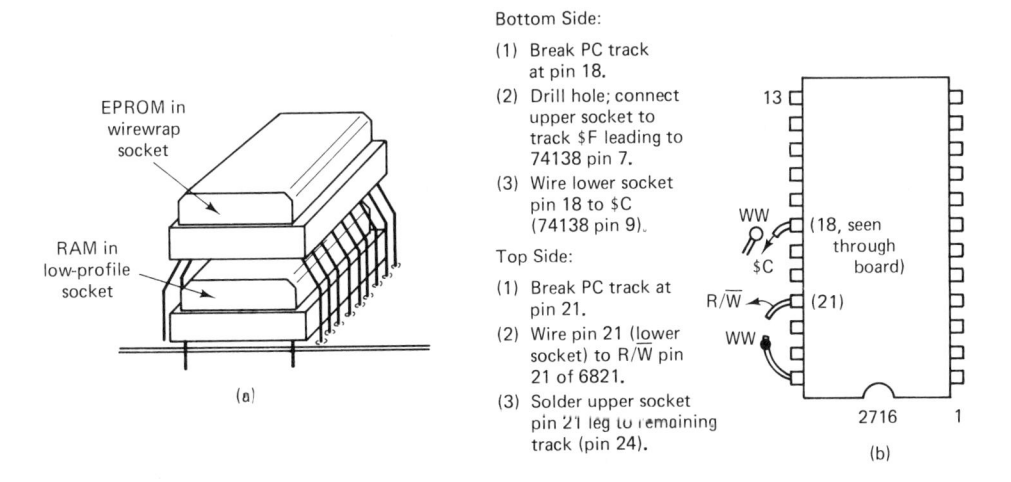

Figure 9-5 Physical details for adding 2 K of RAM to the Microchicken.

172   Microchicken: A General-Purpose Computer with Monitor   Chap. 9

tape). This should be voltage divided to about 30 mV before being applied to the recorder's microphone input. The voltage divider does not present a heavy load and may be left connected even when port B is being used for other functions. The voltage divider and connections are shown in Fig. 9-4(a).

Port B, pin 7 (pin 15 of the PC connector), is used to pick up data from the recorder and load it into RAM. The audio tones must first be converted to dc logic levels by the circuit of Fig. 9-4(b). Q_1 amplifies the 3600-Hz tones from the recorder's earphone output. The diodes rectify the ac to dc

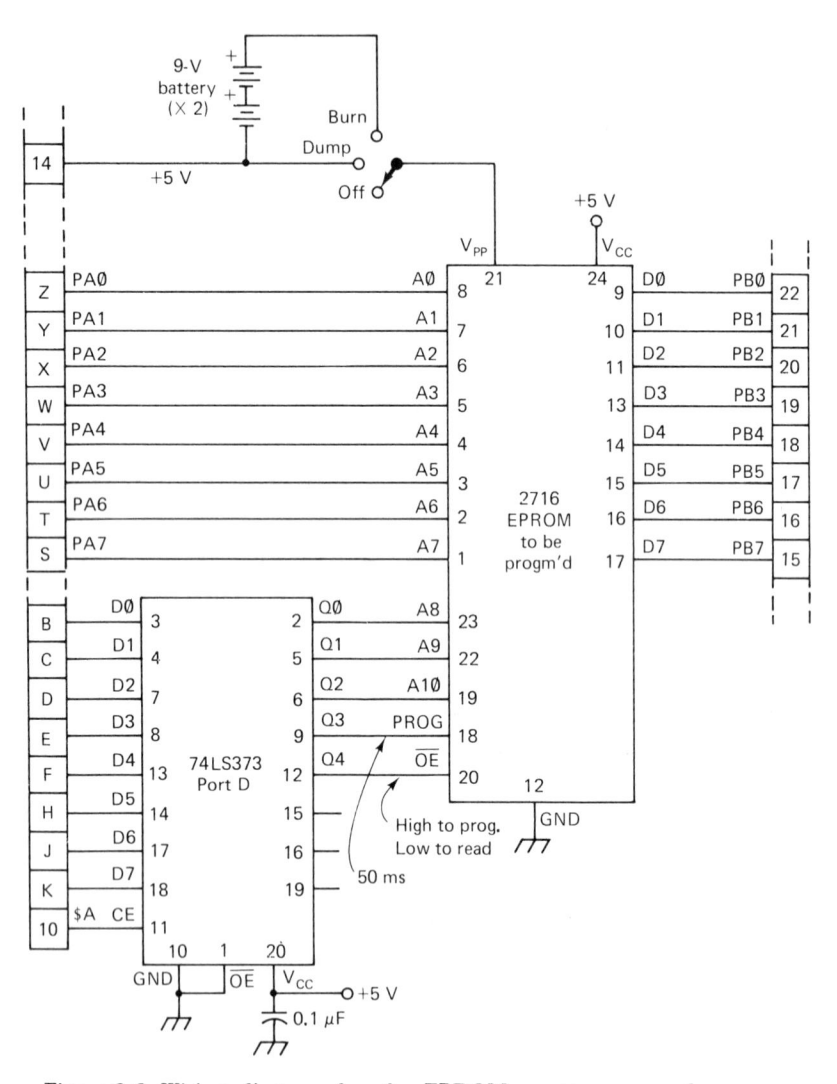

Figure 9-6 Wiring diagram for the EPROM programmer and connections to the Microchicken board. The Port A lines are already connected to the keyboard, but the lines to the EPROM can be added without interference between the two functions.

Sec. 9.2 System Hardware

and the three RC networks filter the 3600-Hz ripple without filtering out the timing of the tone-to-no-tone transition. Q_2 and Q_3 provide clean switching from logic *high* (tone) to logic *low* (no tone). The tape recorder output can be left connected, but the line to PB7 should be switched *off* if port B is used for other functions.

Adding 2 K of memory. Another 2048 bytes of RAM can be added to your computer by wiring a 2016 or 6116 RAM "piggyback" with the 2716 EPROM. All of the pins are connected to identical points except for pins 18 and 21, so a long-legged wirewrap socket is soldered over the original 2716 socket, as shown in Fig. 9-5(a). The RAM should never need changing, so it takes the lower bunk. The 2716 gets the top bunk so that it can be replaced easily if additions are made to the operating program. Figure 9-5(b) shows how cuts in the board tracks are made and jumpers used to rewire the bottom socket for the RAM at base address $C000.

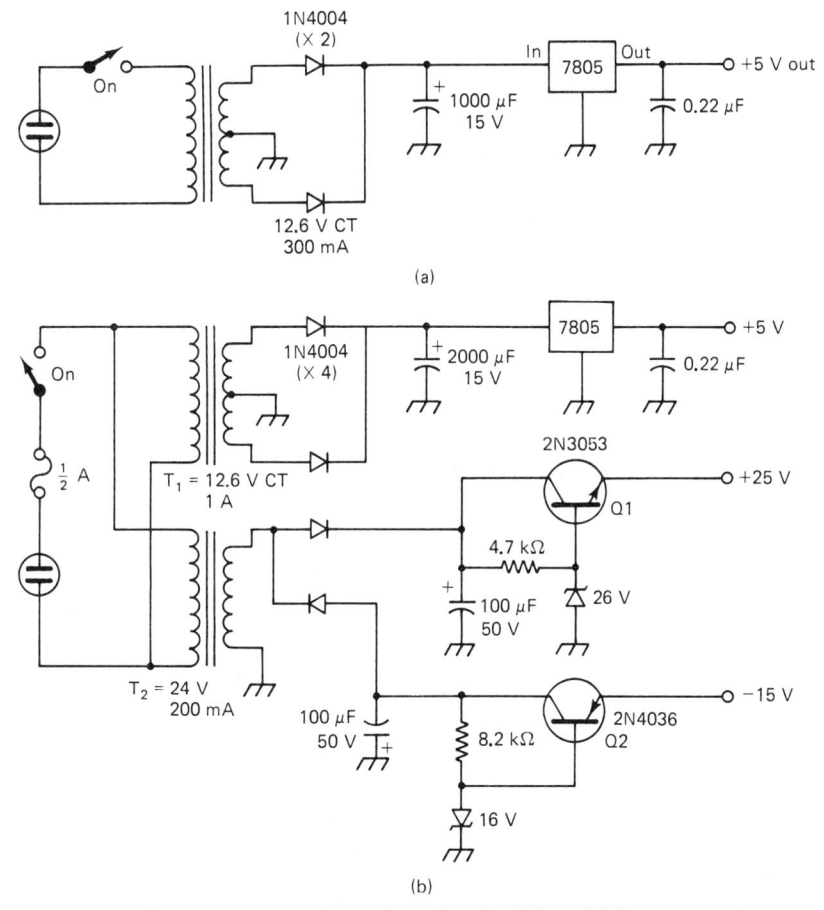

Figure 9-7 Two power-supply options for the Microchicken computer. Use option (b) if you intend to build the projects of Chapters 10 and 11.

Adding the EPROM Programmer. Figure 9-6 shows how a second 74LS373 output latch, a 24-pin socket, and a pair of 9-V batteries can be added external to the main board to implement the *Burn EPROM* and *Dump EPROM to RAM* features of the monitor program. Port A, which normally handles the keyboard, is freed from this duty once the *BURN EPROM* or *DUMP EPROM* routine is entered, so it is reprogrammed for all outputs and used to drive the low eight EPROM address lines. PB6 and PB7 are not needed for their *tape* functions during an EPROM routine, so port B is free to write or read EPROM data. There remain three address lines (A8–A10), a programming-pulse line (50-ms high to burn), and an output-enable line (HI to program, LO to read) on the 2716. These are driven by a 74LS373 latch decoded to appear at base address $A000.

Two power-supply options are shown in Fig. 9-7. The first provides +5 V for the computer system and +23 V for EPROM programming via two 9-V batteries. The second replaces the batteries with a regulated supply and provides −15 V for the A/D converter used in the following chapters.

9.3 MONITOR PROGRAM OVERVIEW

The Microchicken monitor program permits easy communication between the operator and the computer. It is about 1000 words long, and is listed at the end of this chapter.

Subroutines are used extensively by the monitor, because there are certain operations, notably with the keyboard and the LED displays, that are used repeatedly by several parts of the main program. These subroutines are available for you to use in your own programs. They have been designed so that all machine registers except CCR (status register) are restored to their original values before returning to the main program.

Subroutines Available in Monitor

KEY; $FC20; Typically 150 μs: Clears C if key press is sensed and puts key value in "COUNT" ($0078). Sets C if no key and leaves "COUNT" = 0.

KEYIN; $FC5E; 200 μs if no key, 25 ms if key sensed. Debounces key, puts value in COUNT and clears C if key pressed.

KEYUP; $FC7E; 200 μs if key up. Waits in loop until key is up.

BYTIN; $FCA0; Waits for two keystrokes. Puts first digit in high nibble, second digit in low nibble of BYTE ($0074). Displays lowest hex digit of current address between strokes.

DELAY; $FC8B; Delays according to value of CLOCK ($0076). $T = (C * C * 18) + (C * 14) + (16)$ microseconds. Minimum is 48 μs ($C = 1$); Maximum is 1.2 seconds ($C = 0$, treated as 256).

DISPLY; $FCD0; 6 ms. Flashes two digits from BYTE ($0074) on LEDs, 3 ms, once each. Leaves low digit *on*, high digit *off*.

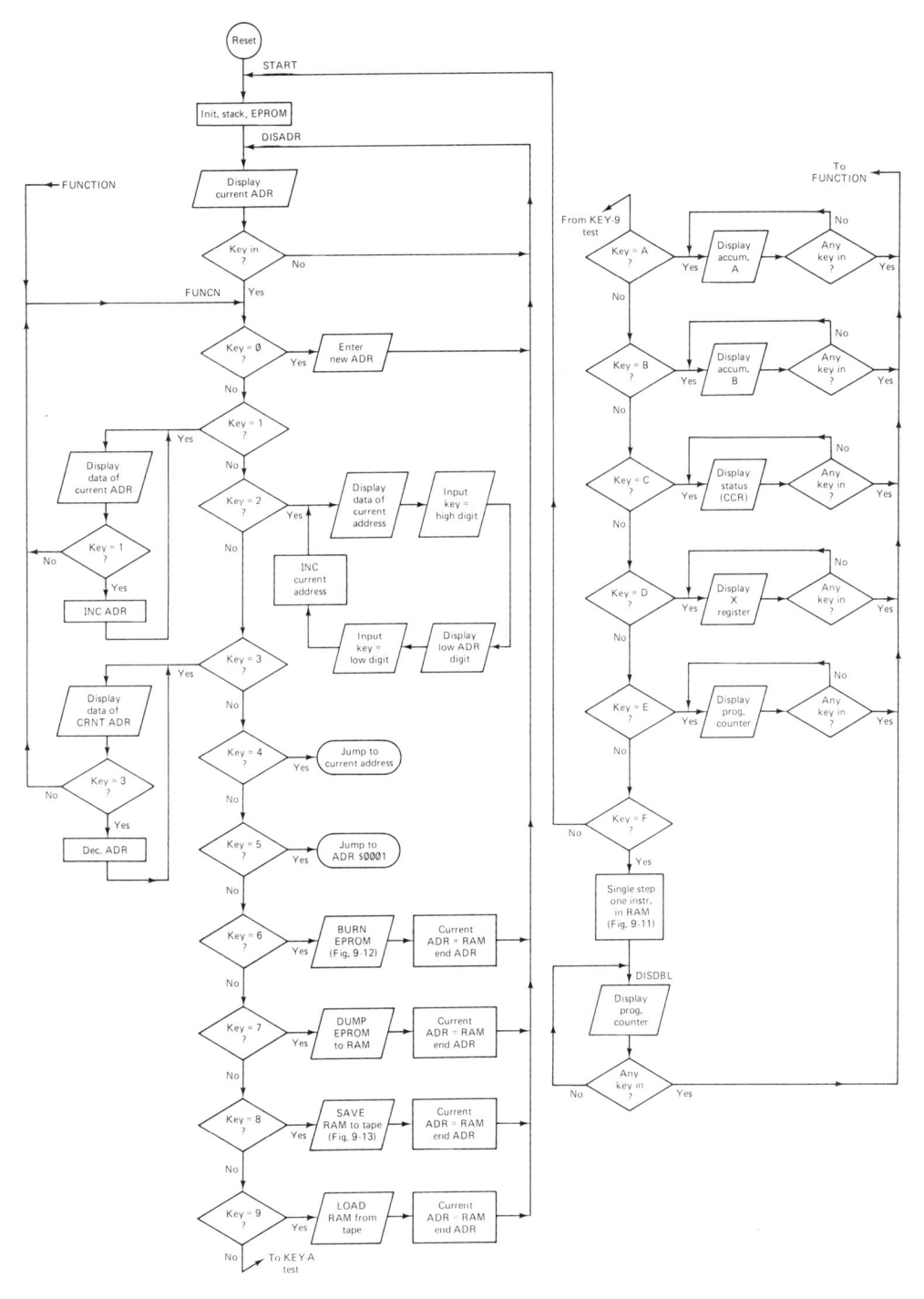

Figure 9-8 General flowchart for the Microchicken Monitor program. Single-step, EPROM, and Tape routines are detailed in Fig. 9-11 through 9-13.

175

DISDTA; $FD0A; Provides continous display of digits in current address until a key input is sensed.

DISFOR; $FD1F; Provides flashing display of four hex digits from HIDIS ($006F) and LODIS ($0070). Pattern is high byte, low byte, blank—until key input is sensed.

As an example of user application of Monitor subroutines, you may include the command JSR DISDTA (machine code BD FD 0A) in a program which you enter into RAM from the keyboard. Upon encountering this instruction, the machine will leave your program and devote itself to displaying the data of the "current address," which is pointed to by the contents of RAM locations $6D (HIADR) and $6E (LOADR). This will continue until a key input is sensed. It will then return to your program, with registers A, B, X, SP, and PC restored as if the subroutine had never happened. The first instruction it will execute will be the one following your JSR instruction.

The main-program flowchart appears in Fig. 9-8. It is extensive but quite simple because it is so linear. After a RESET the stack pointer is initialized at $0062 and the EPROM programmer is turned off. Then the *current address* is displayed until a key input is received. The rest of the flowchart is devoted to determining which key was pressed, and to implementing the function it calls for.

Most of these functions require only some exchanging of data with RAM buffers and calling on one or two of the subroutines. Exceptions are the EPROM, TAPE, and SINGLE-STEP functions. We will thus proceed to examine the subroutines in detail, and then the above-mentioned key functions.

9.4 KEYBOARD ROUTINES

The keypad consists of a 4 × 4 matrix of conductors forming 16 intersection points of horizontal and vertical conductors. Many keypads are constructed in this way, with only eight conductors leaving the assembly. Of course, 16 normally-open pushbutton switches can be wired in the same way. Figure 9-9(c) shows the connection.

KEY subroutine. In operation the vertical lines are connected to the four port-A input lines (0 through 3), which are pulled high by 4.7-kΩ resistors to V_{CC}. The horizontal lines are connected to the four port-A *output* lines (4 through 7), which are pulled *low* one at a time by the program. Pressing a key will cause one of the input columns to be pulled *low* when one of the rows is pulled *low*. The *9*-button, for example, pulls PA1 low when PA6 outputs a *low*. The flow chart of Fig. 9-9(a) shows how the KEY subroutine scans for a key press by pulling each of the four rows *low*, one at a time. Each time a row is pulled *low* the columns are examined. If none of the columns has been pulled *low* by a key press, the RAM location "COUNT" is incremented by four and the next row is pulled *low*.

When a low column is detected (PRESSD) the column bits are shifted

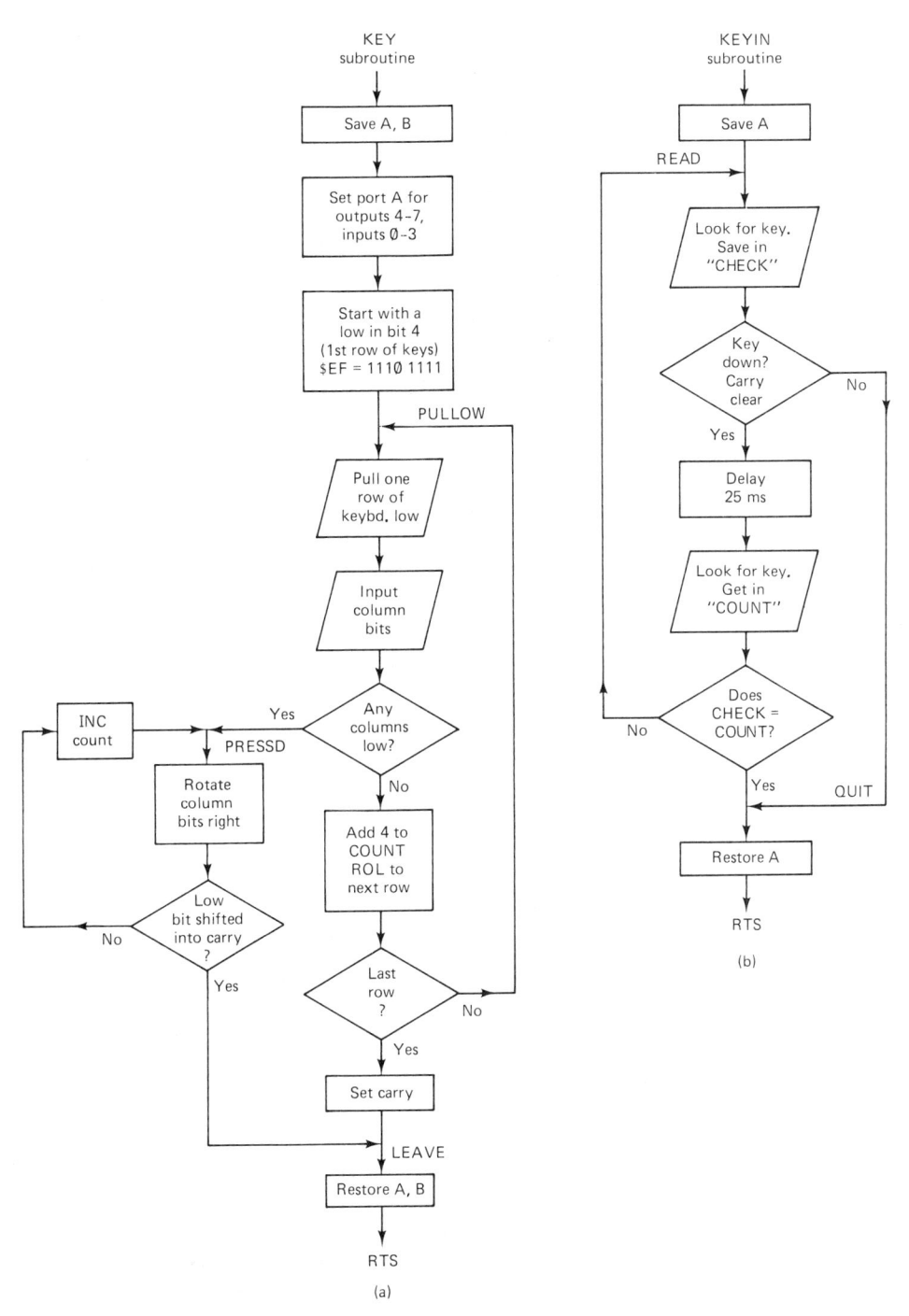

Figure 9-9 Keyboard subroutines. (a) KEY clears carry and puts value of key (∅∅–∅F) in COUNT. (b) KEYIN reads twice to screen out noise. (c) Keyboard wiring to PIA port A. (d) KEYUP holds processor in a loop until key is released. (e) BYTIN puts two keystrokes in RAM location BYTE.

177

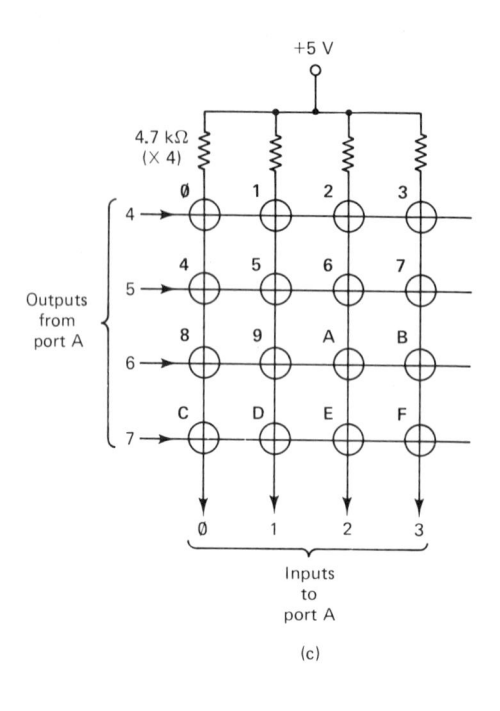

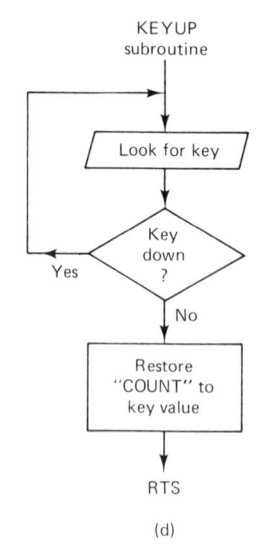

Figure 9-9 (*cont.*)

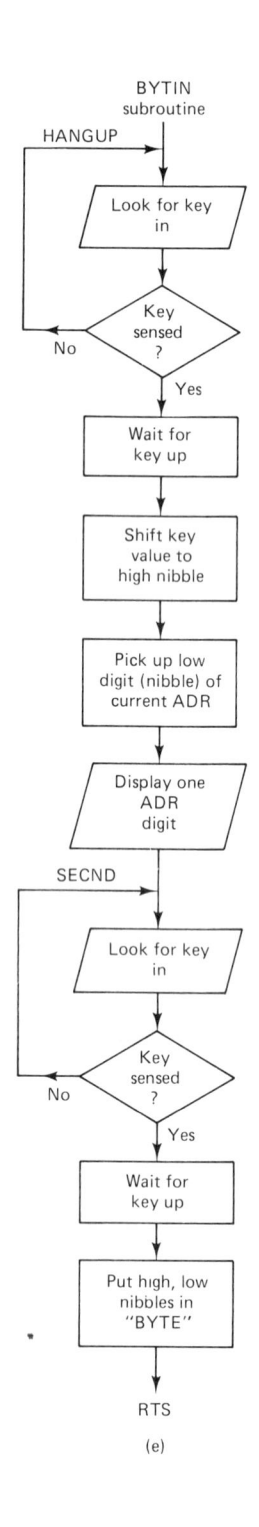

178

Sec. 9.4   Keyboard Routines   179

right into the carry, one at a time as COUNT is incremented. A *low* in the carry indicates that COUNT has reached the value of the key pressed. If no *low* column is detected, the carry flag is set to indicate "no key." The routine takes about 130 µs if no key is pressed.

KEYIN is a subroutine that calls the KEY routine and if a key is sensed, calls it again 25 ms later. If the two readings of the key are identical, the key value appears in COUNT and in CHECK, the carry flag is cleared, and the machine returns to the main program. If the readings are not identical, two more readings are taken via the KEY routine, until "no key" or "identical inputs" are sensed. Figure 9-9(b) shows the routine flowchart. This routine prevents random noise spikes from being interpreted as key inputs. It takes less than 200 µs if no key is pressed and no noise spikes are present, and about 25 ms if a key is pressed.

The KEYUP subroutine holds the processor in an endless loop of KEY checks until a "no key pressed" condition is sensed. This routine is needed because of the disparity between human and computer time scales. The computer can pick up the keystroke, process the data, store the result, and be back to the key for more data before the operator has time to get his finger off the key! The KEYUP routine simply forces the machine to wait until the key is released so that a single key input is not read as a few dozen identical inputs by the computer. Figure 9-9(d) shows the flowchart.

BYTIN is a subroutine which loads two keystrokes into the RAM location BYTE. The first stroke occupies the high nibble and the second stroke occupies the low nibble of BYTE. Once entered, this routine ties up the computer completely until two keystrokes are received. Figure 9-9(e) shows the routine flowchart.

Since BYTIN is most often used to load data from the keyboard to the system RAM, an address-check feature is included to help the programmer keep track of the RAM address being loaded. Between the first and second keystrokes a single hex digit is shown on the display—the other digit is dark. This is the least-significant digit of the current address.

It is interesting to contemplate the nesting of subroutines involved in using this subroutine. Assume that the stack pointer (SP) starts at address $62. As each subroutine is called, two bytes (PC Low and PC High) are saved on the stack, which counts down toward address 00. As each RTS is encountered, two bytes (PC High, PC Low) are retrieved from the stack, which counts back up.

- Main program running   SP = $62
- Main program calls BYTIN   SP ⟶ $60
- BYTIN calls KEYIN   SP ⟶ $5D
- KEYIN calls KEY   SP ⟶ $5A
- Return from KEY   SP ⟶ $5D
- KEYIN calls DELAY   SP ⟶ $5A
- Return from DELAY   SP ⟶ $5D

- KEYIN calls KEY   SP ⟶ $5A
- Return from KEY   SP ⟶ $5D
- Return from KEYIN   SP ⟶ $60
- BYTIN calls KEYUP   SP ⟶ $5E

⋮

(more calls of DISPLY, KEYIN, KEYUP)
- Return from KEYUP   SP ⟶ $60
- Return from BYTIN   SP ⟶ $62

9.5 DISPLAY ROUTINES

Display hardware. The system contains two seven-segment LED displays whose cathodes are tied together and pulled low selectively by bits 1 through 7 of a 74LS373 octal latch (port C, address $2000). Bit 0 of this latch determines which display is on at any instant by pulling up the anodes of the right-hand display (C0 = 1) or left-hand display (C0 = 0). Thus only one display is actually lit at a time; the software, however, switches between them so fast that they appear to be lit simultaneously.

The DISPLY subroutine picks up the value in RAM location BYTE and flashes the left LED with the hex digit corresponding to the high nibble of BYTE for 3 ms. It then flashes the right LED with the hex digit representing the low nibble of BYTE for 3 ms, and exits from the subroutine. Thus DISPLY must be called repeatedly to produce a continous display of both digits. However, since DISPLY is exited several hundred times per second, other routines, such as KEYIN and other data I/O functions, can be sandwiched between calls of DISPLY. The display will appear uninterrupted to the operator unless the added routines exceed several milliseconds in length.

The 4-bit nibble representing a hex digit is used to call up a 7-bit pattern which pulls selected cathodes *low* to form the character for that digit. A file containing the required bit patterns begins at ROM address $FC00. Figures 9-10(a) and (b) show the development of this file, as well as the flow-chart for the DISPLY routine. This file is entered by loading the X register from adjacent RAM locations PATHI and PATLO. PATHI has been preloaded with $FC, and PATLO contains the value of the nibble being displayed.

As an example, if BYTE contained data $81, the nibble $8 would first be placed in the low half of PATLO, with zeros filling in the high half. The X register would then be loaded from PATHI, PATLO, with $FC08. Indexed addressing would then be used to fetch data 00 from the bit-pattern file at address $FC08, and this data would be output to port C. All *lows* would light all seven segments of the left LED, producing the numeral 8.

Next, the nibble $1 would be loaded into PATLO and X would be used to fetch data $F2 from the file at $FC01. This value would be incremented to $F3 (bit 0 = 1 to turn on the right-hand LED) and output to port C. The

File address	Display	Binary 7654 3210	Hex
FC00	0	1000 0000	80
FC01	1	1111 0010	F2
FC02	2	0100 1000	48
FC03	3	0110 0000	60
FC04	4	0011 0010	32
FC05	5	0010 0100	24
FC06	6	0000 0100	04
FC07	7	1111 0000	F0
FC08	8	0000 0000	00
FC09	9	0011 0000	30
FC0A	A	0001 0000	10
FC0B	b	0000 0110	06
FC0C	C	1000 1100	8C
FC0D	d	0100 0010	42
FC0E	E	0000 1100	0C
FC0F	F	0001 1100	1C

Binary bit assignments ⟹

Bit 0:
0 = Left LED
1 = Right LED

Segment numbering:
1 (top), 6 (upper-left), 2 (upper-right), 7 (middle), 5 (lower-left), 3 (lower-right), 4 (bottom)

(a)

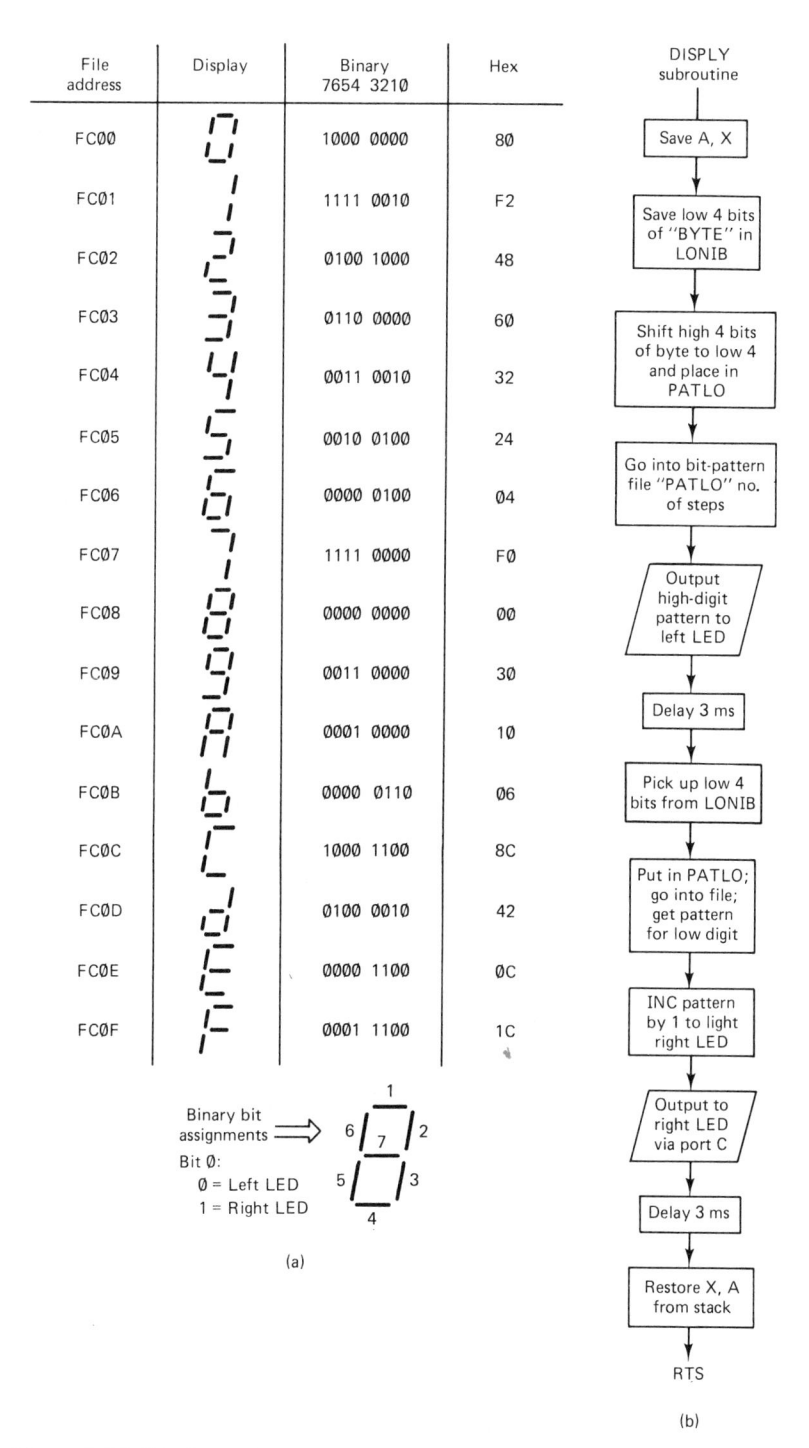

DISPLY subroutine

- Save A, X
- Save low 4 bits of "BYTE" in LONIB
- Shift high 4 bits of byte to low 4 and place in PATLO
- Go into bit-pattern file "PATLO" no. of steps
- Output high-digit pattern to left LED
- Delay 3 ms
- Pick up low 4 bits from LONIB
- Put in PATLO; go into file; get pattern for low digit
- INC pattern by 1 to light right LED
- Output to right LED via port C
- Delay 3 ms
- Restore X, A from stack
- RTS

(b)

Figure 9-10 Display subroutines for the Microchicken. (a) Data file for lighting LEDs by indirect addressing. (b) Routine for a single 3-ms flash of each LED. (c) Continuous display of two hex digits until key input is received. (d) Four-digit display—HI byte, LO byte, blank.

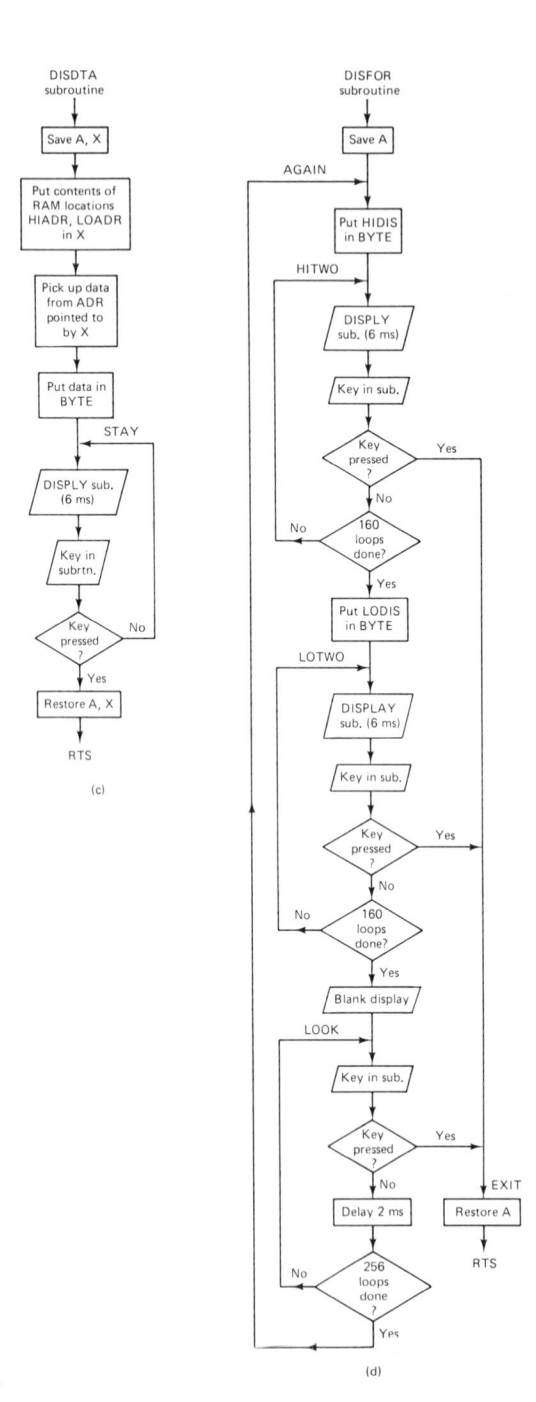

Figure 9-10 (*cont.*)

Sec. 9.6   The Monitor Single-Step Function   183

binary output (1111 0011) would pull segments 2 and 3 *low*, producing the numeral 1.

DISDTA is a subroutine that calls DISPLY repeatedly, checking for a key input every 6 ms. The routine is exited as soon as a keystroke is sensed. The data displayed is the byte contained at the "Current address"—that is, the address contained in RAM locations HIADR, LOADR. Figure 9-10(c) shows the flowchart.

Subroutine DISFOR displays four digits (two bytes) of data. These bytes are stored in RAM locations HIDIS and LODIS before calling the routine, and may represent a memory address or the contents of the *X* or *PC* register. The high-order byte is displayed first for about 1 second, followed by 1 second for the low-order byte. A $\frac{1}{2}$-second dark period precedes the next display of the high byte. During each of these periods the KEYIN subroutine is called every few milliseconds, and DISFOR is exited as soon as a keystroke is sensed. Figure 9-10(d) shows the DISFOR flowchart.

9.6 THE MONITOR SINGLE-STEP FUNCTION

One of the most useful features of the Monitor program is its ability to execute user programs one instruction at a time, and to permit examination of the machine registers (A, B, CCR, X, and PC) and RAM contents between steps. This is a powerful program-debugging tool, as will be shown at the end of this section.

The flowchart for the monitor single-step routine (SST) is given in Fig. 9-11. It makes use of the 6802's *interrupt* function because this automatically saves all the machine registers (except SP) on the stack. We need to get those registers out of the machine and into RAM because they cannot be examined with the machine halted and they will be altered by returning to the Monitor program.[1]

To use SST the 6802's IRQ line is switched permanently low. The resulting interrupt request is not acknowledged because the interrupt-mask bit *I* is set high when the processor is *reset*. Function key F (pressed after *reset* or completion of another function) selects the SST routine, which executes one step of the user program immediately. The routine accomplishes this by loading a CLI (clear interrupt mask) instruction, $0E, into the RAM location *preceding* the user instruction to be executed, and jumping to that location. The processor will execute the CLI and the instruction following it before responding to the interrup-line $\overline{\text{IRQ}}$, whereupon it will store the machine registers on the stack and jump to the address contained in IRQ vector locations $FFF8 and FFF9. The *I-mask* bit is set high again automatically when the IRQ is acknowledged. The interrupt routine RETURN pulls the machine registers off the stack and places them in RAM buffers with

---

[1] An exception is PC, which appears on the address bus of the 6802.

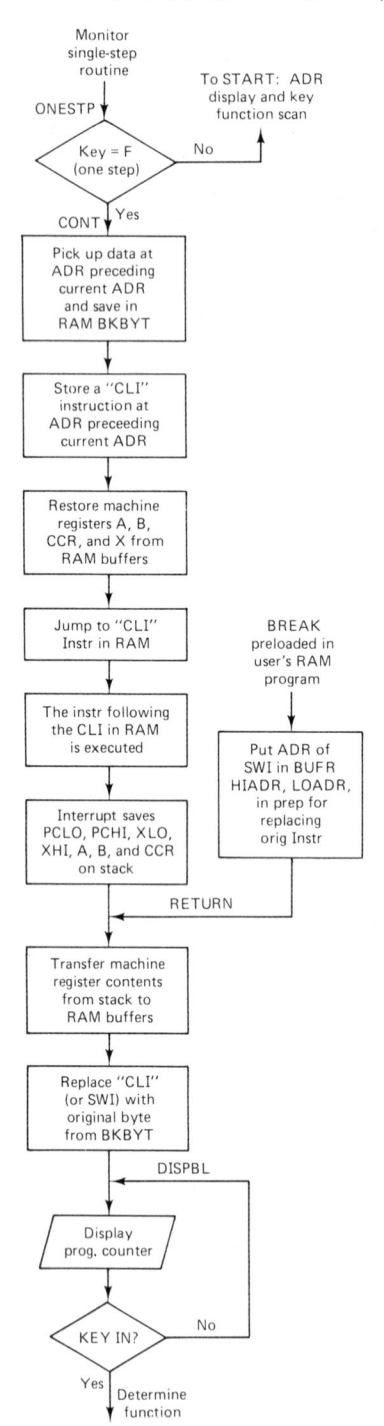

Figure 9-11 Single-step and break functions for the Microchicken Monitor.

Sec. 9.6   The Monitor Single-Step Function   185

fixed addresses. These *pulls* return the stack pointer to its original value, so the interrupt routine can be exited directly, rather than with an RTI command. Before exiting, the CLI byte that was poked into the user RAM is written over with the original byte (which we had thoughtfully saved in a buffer called BKBYT). The program counter value is also loaded into the *current address* buffer, so the DISFOR routine will display the address of the next instruction. The routine exits to DISDBL, which displays HIADR, LOADR, and scans for the next key input function.

In using SST you must keep several limitations in mind.
- SST works only for programs in RAM. The CLI cannot be poked into ROM-resident programs, so single-step will not work in ROM.
- A program to be single-stepped cannot begin at the first RAM address, since the first CLI is stored at the address before this. Get in the habit of *not* starting your programs at $0000 or $C000.
- The SST routine will double-step if the next instruction is TAP. (A NOP can be inserted to prevent skipping by an important instruction.)

To use SST, you must ground $\overline{IRQ}$ (SST switch *on*). Then:

1. Press RESET.
2. Press *function 0*—load current address.
3. Enter four-digit starting address of program.
4. Press *function F*—single-step.

The display will immediately show the address of the next instruction in the user's program. If a *branch* or *jump* was taken, the value will not be the next instruction in the program listing.

For a closer examination of the effect of the instruction just executed, you may wish to view the contents of one of the machine registers.

- Press *A* to view accumulator A.
- Press *B* to view accumulator B.
- Press *C* to view CCR (condition-code or status register).
- Press *D* to view *X* (index register).
- Press *E* to return to display of PC (program counter).

Viewing the data at a memory location or input port is a little more awkward. Here is the procedure:

1. Jot down the PC address displayed (next instruction).
2. Press *0* and enter the four-digit address desired.
3. Press *1* to switch to data display.
4. Press *0* and reenter the PC address (next instruction).
5. Press *F* to single step.

9.7 PROGRAM DEBUGGING WITH SST

Here are some tips for writing and debugging programs using the monitor and single-step functions.

1. **When writing the program** leave every tenth line of the coding form blank. When assembling, fill these lines in with three NOP bytes ($01). Then, if debugging shows that an instruction needs to be added in the middle of the program, a maximum of five lines (5 to 15 bytes) will have to be changed to add the new instruction and reshuffle the existing ones. When assembling, underline the operands of all *Branch* and *Jump* instructions, and check that they still point to the right places after making the program changes. If more than three bytes need to be inserted you may
   a) Reenter 10 or 20 lines of the program, replacing six or nine NOP bytes with new code.
   b) Make the added routine a subroutine and access it with a JSR inserted in the space made by removing three NOP bytes.
   c) Jump to a free area of RAM by inserting a JMP instruction, and jump back to the main program. Such "patch jobs" should be viewed as *temporary* structures, to be replaced with straight-line code once the routine is verified.
2. A first **check** of the program flow should be made by rather quickly stepping through it with the *F* (SST) button while observing the PC display. Checking this against the object-code listing should reveal such things as mistaken branch calculations and improper addressing-mode selections.
3. **Delay loops** are usually too extensive to step through by brute force. When single-stepping it is desirable to make one pass through the loop to check its integrity. Then you should exit the SST mode and load the counters from the keyboard with the values expected in the last pass through the loop. Reentering the SST mode, you may then observe how the loop is exited and continue through the main program. If a machine register, rather than a RAM location is used to count passes through the loop, the corresponding register buffer can be loaded with the desired value. SST will then pick up this altered value and load it into the machine before the next single-step. Here are the register-buffer addresses:

CCR	$79	XHI	$7C
ACCB	$7A	XLO	$7D
ACCA	$7B	PCHI	$7E
		PCLO	$7F

Sec. 9.7   Program Debugging with SST   187

4. **A breakpoint** can be inserted in a RAM program to allow the program to run full-speed to the selected point and then automatically enter the single-step mode. Here is the procedure:
   - Use Monitor *function 0* to select the address of the instruction following the last command to be executed. Use Monitor *function 2* to overwrite data $3F (the SWI instruction) into this address.
   - Use Monitor *functions 0* and *2* again to load the hex code of the instruction just overwritten into RAM buffer BKBYT at address $006B.
   - Use Monitor *function 0* to load the starting address of the program.
   - Turn the SST switch ON and invoke *function 4* (RUN).

The machine will run to the SWI instruction, replace the original program instruction, and display the address of that instruction. You may now examine the machine registers and continue through the program in the SST mode.

There are two restrictions on the use of breakpoints.

1. Breakpoints cannot be placed within a subroutine or interrupt routine, or after a push-on-stack. This is because the breakpoint routine picks up the program counter from the stack at fixed addresses $0061 and 0062.
2. A program under development in RAM often calls a subroutine in ROM. In debugging it is desirable to step through the RAM program, run through the ROM subroutine, and resume stepping after the RTS to RAM. This can be done, but the change from SST (*function F*) to RUN (*function 4*) must be made before the JSR instruction in RAM is executed. You cannot single-step into the ROM, and executing the JSR instruction would attempt to do this. The SWI breakpoint should be inserted in place of the instruction following the JSR in RAM.

A test program for SST and breakpoint functions is listed below. The program does nothing useful or impressive, but it does exercise all the machine registers (except the stack) and all the instruction modes. It should be loaded into RAM and the affected registers should be examined after each single-step. On the first pass the program will SKIP the JSR and JMP back to LOOP.

On the second pass the JSR will be encountered, as indicated by PC display 0014. At this point an SWI instruction $3F should be inserted at the return address $0017 and the instruction displaced (JMP, $7E) should be loaded into the RAM buffer at $006B. Address $0014 should now be reloaded and the RUN mode (*Function 4*) invoked. The computer will breeze through a 0.1-second DELAY subroutine and reenter SST mode at address $0017.

Monitor Signal-Step and Breakpoint Test

```
                   1000 *-----------------------------------------------------------------
                   1010 * TEST PROGRAM FOR MONITOR SINGLE-STEP AND BREAK FUNCTIONS *
                   1020 *
                   1030         .OR  $0002
FC8B-              1040 DELAY   .EQ  $FC8B
                   1050 *
0002- 86 47        1060 START   LDAA #$47       IMMEDIATE MODE; $47 -> A
0004- B7 C0 00     1070         STAA $C000      EXTENDED MODE; $47 -> $C000.
0007- 97 76        1080         STAA $76        LOAD CLOCK FOR 0.1-SEC DELY SUB.
0009- DE 0A        1090         LDX  $0A        DIRECT MODE; $0008 -> X
000B- E6 00        1100 LOOP    LDAB 00,X       INDEXED MODE; 0A ->B, THEN E6, 00, 08,..
000D- 08           1110         INX             INHERENT MODE; $000B -> X, THEN 000C,..
000E- 06           1120         TAP             SST DOUBLE STEPS ON TAP; $47 -> CCR,..
000F- 01           1130         NOP             (SKIPPED)
0010- 0C           1140         CLC             NOTE CCR = $46 AS BIT 0 CLEARED.
0011- 1B           1150         ABA             $51 -> A 1ST LOOP, $37 ->A 2ND LOOP,..
0012- 24 03        1160         BCC  SKIP       REL MODE; C CLR 1ST LOOP, SET 2ND LOOP.
0014- BD FC 8B     1170         JSR  DELAY      MONITOR SUB DELAYS 0.1 SEC ON 2ND LOOP.
0017- 7E 00 0B     1180 SKIP    JMP  LOOP       DELAY SKIPPED ON 1ST LOOP.
                   1190 *
                   1200         .EN

                   1210 *
                   1220 * TO RUN THROUGH DELAY AND RESUME STEPPING UPON RETURN:
                   1230 *   1. PUT $3F (BRK) AT ADR $0017.
                   1240 *   2. PUT $7E (DISPLACED INSTRUCTION) AT ADR $006B.
                   1250 *   3. LOAD ADR WHERE SINGLE STEPPING ENDED ($0014).
                   1260 *   4. SWITCH FROM SST TO RUN AND PRESS FUNCTION 4.
                   1270 *   5. DO NOT SST INTO ROM (BCC IS LAST SST INSTR).
```

9.8 THE EPROM ROUTINES

Programming a 2716 EPROM requires computer/EPROM interfacing over the following lines.

- **Port B:** Eight output lines drive the data bus of the 2716. To catch defective or unerased bits, this port must read and verify each byte after programming.
- **Port A:** Eight output lines drive EPROM address lines A0 through A7.
- **Port D:** Three output lines, PD0 through PD2, drive 2716 address lines A8 through A10. PD3 drives the Program Pulse input (50 ms) of the EPROM. PD4 selects *program* function (HI) or *read-and-verify* function (LO).

The basic program function is to transfer data from RAM addresses (counted upward and stored in RAM locations $7A, 7B) to EPROM addresses (counted upward and stored in RAM $7E, 7F), until the ending RAM address (fixed, stored in $7C, 7D) is reached. Figure 9-12(a) shows in detail how this is accomplished. The routine is entirely linear, and therefore quite easy to follow. The fact that the port-D lines are split between address and control functions may necessitate some comments. The ORAA #$10 (bi-

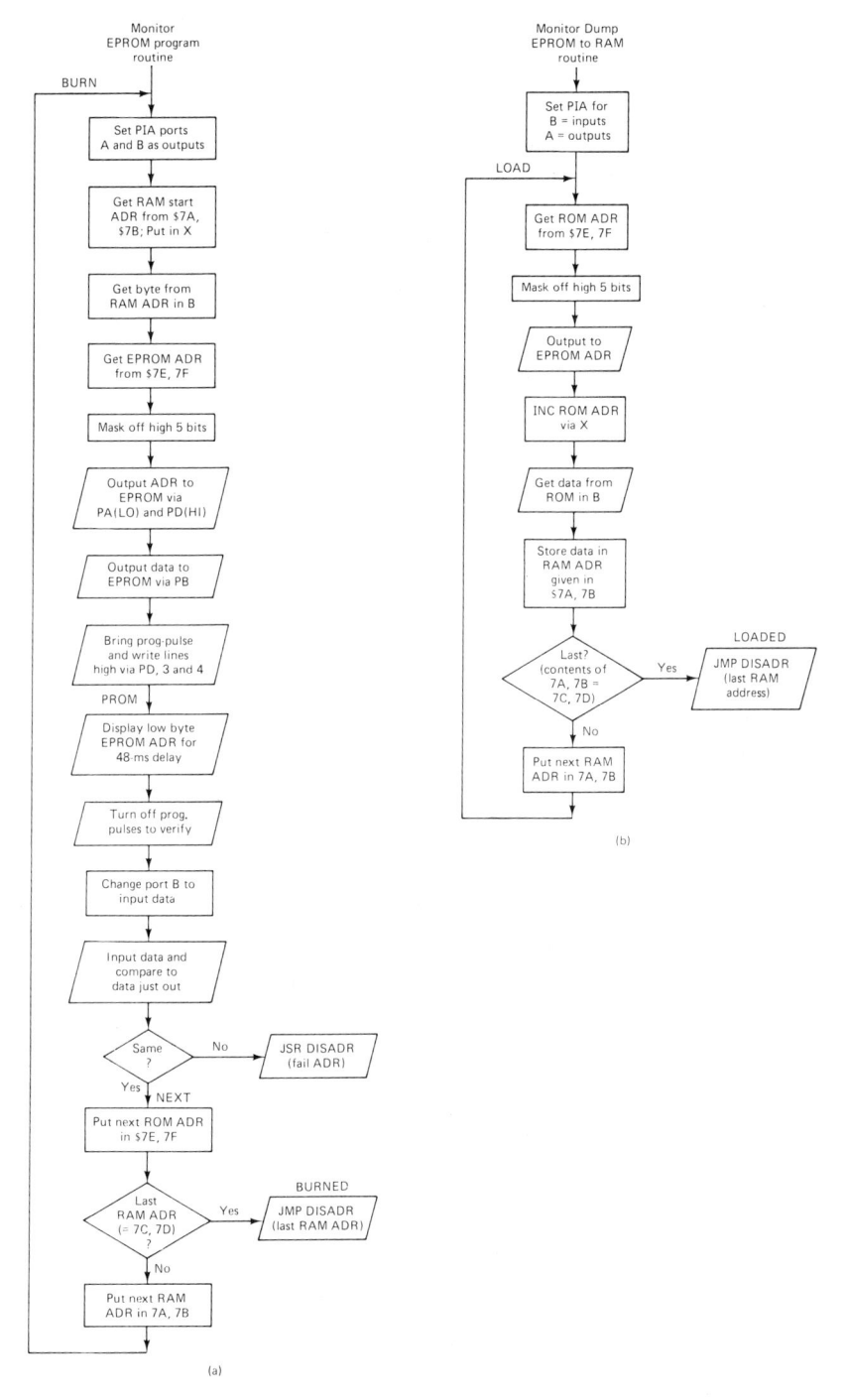

Figure 9-12 Monitor Burn-EPROM routine (a), and Dump-EPROM-to RAM routine (b).

nary 0001 0000) forces bit 4 ($\overline{\text{OE}}$/PROG) *high*, leaving bit 3 (PROG PULSE) *low* and the low three bits with their address values (see program address FE06). This places the EPROM data outputs in the HI-Z state. The ORAA #$18 (binary 0001 1000) forces bits 3 and 4 *high* (beginning the 50-ms BURN EPROM function) while leaving the other bits undisturbed (see program address FE10). Buffer RAM1 retains the port-D byte with bits 3 and 4 low for the read-and-verify function beginning at address FE25.

The 50-ms pulse required to "burn" the EPROM is obtained by eight repetitive calls of the DISPLY subroutine, with the current EPROM address, low byte, being displayed. The lower digit flashes at 20 Hz and is not legible, but the higher digit can be followed, and the active display assures the operator that programming is taking place. At 50 ms per byte the full 2 K of the 2716 requires 102 seconds for programming.

Dumping the EPROM into RAM is quite a bit faster; the entire 2 K can be dumped in about 0.1 second. There is no verification to be done, and there is no time for a display while the dump is in progress. A successful dump is assumed if the last RAM address being loaded appears on the display. Figure 9-12(b) shows the flowchart for the DUMP routine.

Programs developed in RAM are often transferred to EPROM for permanent storage. The Monitor program occupies the top 1 K of the Microchicken's EPROM, but the bottom 1 K ($F800 to FBFF) is free to hold permanent versions of programs you have developed. To use the bottom half of the on-board EPROM you must first copy the Monitor into an external EPROM by BURNing from address $FC00 to FFFF, starting at EPROM address $0400.

After testing this new "system ROM" by placing it in the on-board EPROM socket, you may proceed to burn your own programs from RAM into external EPROM addresses $0000 to 03FF. Before making the transfer you must check a few things.

- JMP and JSR commands specify addresses in absolute terms. In our system, RAM occupies $C000 through C7FF, but available EPROM extends from $F800 to FBFF. As an example, we may wish to transfer a program developed at $C001-C100 in RAM to $F901-FA00 in EPROM. The JMP command

    7E C0 53

    would have to be changed in RAM to

    7E F9 53

    before burning the EPROM.

- The computer can't write to an EPROM the way it can to a RAM. This sounds pretty elementary, but it's easy enough to develop a program in

Sec. 9.8 The EPROM Routines

RAM which contains buffers, counters, or tables of variables, and then try to transfer the whole thing to EPROM. A good practice is to put the program under development on pages C0 through C3, and keep buffers and counters on the page-00 RAM, from 0000 to 0050. The program can then be burned to EPROM pages F8 through FB, and the buffers and counters will not have to be moved.

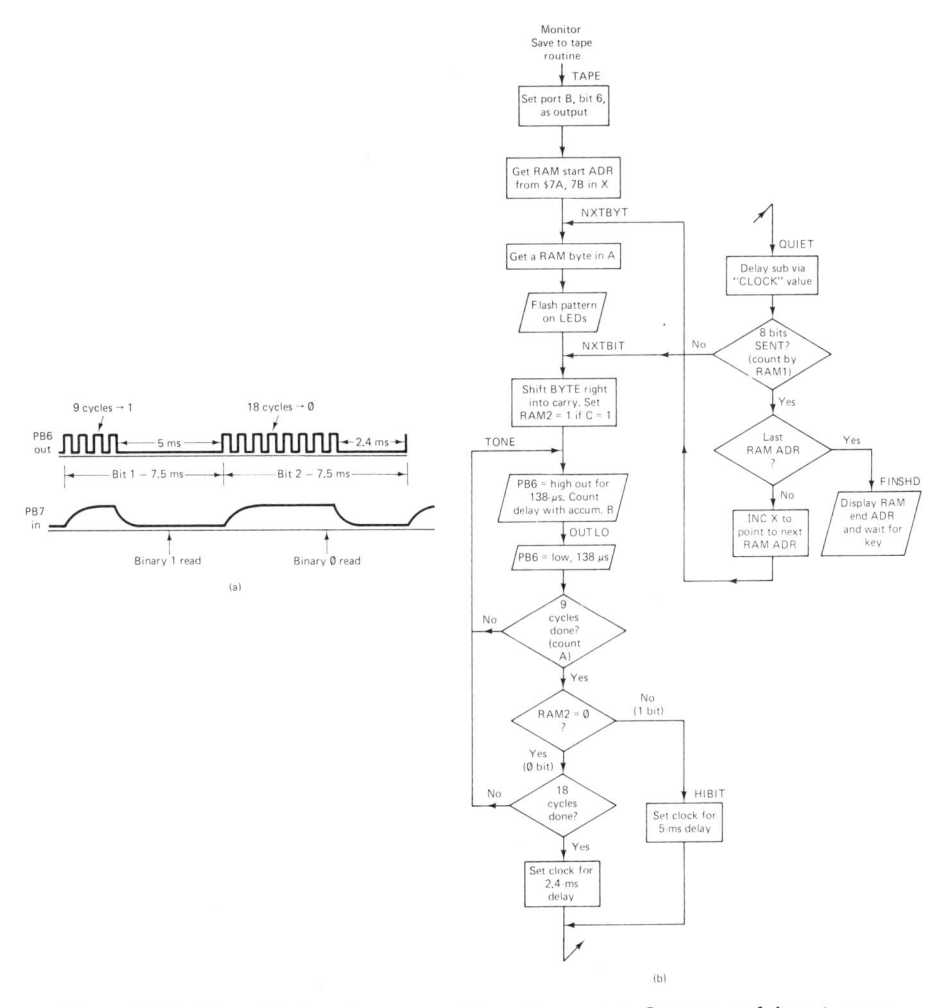

Figure 9-13 Microchicken tape-record functions. (a) Output and input waveforms for binary 1 and 0 bits, (b) program to output tones to recorder, and (c) program to input data from tape player via digitizer circuit of Fig. 9-4 (b).

192   Microchicken: A General-Purpose Computer with Monitor   Chap. 9

```
            Monitor
          Load from tape
             routine
               │
               ▼
        ┌──────────────┐
        │ Set port B,  │
        │ bit 7, as input │
        └──────────────┘
               │
               ▼
        ┌──────────────┐                          ┌──────────────┐
        │ Get RAM start│                          │ Store data   │
        │ ADR from $7A,│                          │ in RAM via X │
        │ $7B in X     │                          └──────────────┘
        └──────────────┘                                 │
               │                                         ▼
               │                                  ┌──────────────┐
               │             RDBYT                │ Flash pattern│
               │◄──────────────────────────       │  on LEDs     │
               ▼                                  └──────────────┘
        ┌──────────────┐                                 │
        │ "RAM1" counts bits. │                          ▼                       LAST
        │ "DATA" accumulates  │                       ╱ Last ╲                ┌──────────┐
        │ bits to form byte   │                     ╱  RAM ADR? ╲    Yes      │ Display  │
        └──────────────┘                           ╲  (7C, 7D)  ╱───────────► │ last ADR │
               │                 RDBIT              ╲         ╱               │ and wait │
               │◄──────────────────────              ╲       ╱                │ for key  │
               ▼                                      ╲  No ╱                 └──────────┘
        ┌──────────────┐                               ╲  ╱
        │ Read port B, bit 7 │                          ▼
        └──────────────┘                        ┌──────────────┐
               │                                │ INC X to     │
               ▼                                │ next RAM ADR │
           ╱ B7 = 0? ╲       No                 └──────────────┘
          ╱ (low level)╲──────────────────────────────►│
           ╲          ╱                                │
            ╲   Yes  ╱                                 │
 LOTOHI      ╲      ╱                                  │
    ┌──────────▼────┐                                  │
    │  ┌──────────────┐                                │
    │  │ Read port B, bit 7 │                          │
    │  └──────────────┘                                │
    │         │                                        │
    │         ▼                                        │
    │     ╱ B7 = 1? ╲       No                         │
    │    ╱(high level)╲──────┐                         │
    │     ╲          ╱        │                        │
    └──────╲  Yes   ╱─────────┘                        │
            ╲      ╱                                   │
             ▼                                         │
        ┌──────────────┐                               │
        │ Wait 4.5 ms  │                               │
        │ via delay    │                               │
        │ subrtn.      │                               │
        └──────────────┘                               │
               │                                       │
               ▼                                       │
        ┌──────────────┐                               │
        │ Read port B, bit 7 │                         │
        └──────────────┘                               │
               │                                       │
               ▼                                       │
        ┌──────────────────┐                           │
        │ If PB7 = 0, set C = 1 │                      │
        │ If PB7 = 1, set C = 0 │                      │
        └──────────────────┘                           │
               │  HIORLO                               │
               ▼                                       │
        ┌──────────────┐                               │
        │ Shift carry bit │                            │
        │ right into "DATA" │                          │
        └──────────────┘                               │
               │                                       │
               ▼                                       │
            ╱  8    ╲                                  │
           ╱ shifts  ╲      No                         │
          ╱ counted in ╲─────────────────────────────► │
           ╲ RAM1    ╱                                 │
            ╲   ?   ╱                                  │
             ╲    ╱                                    │
              Yes                                      │
               └───────────────────────────────────────┘
```

(c)

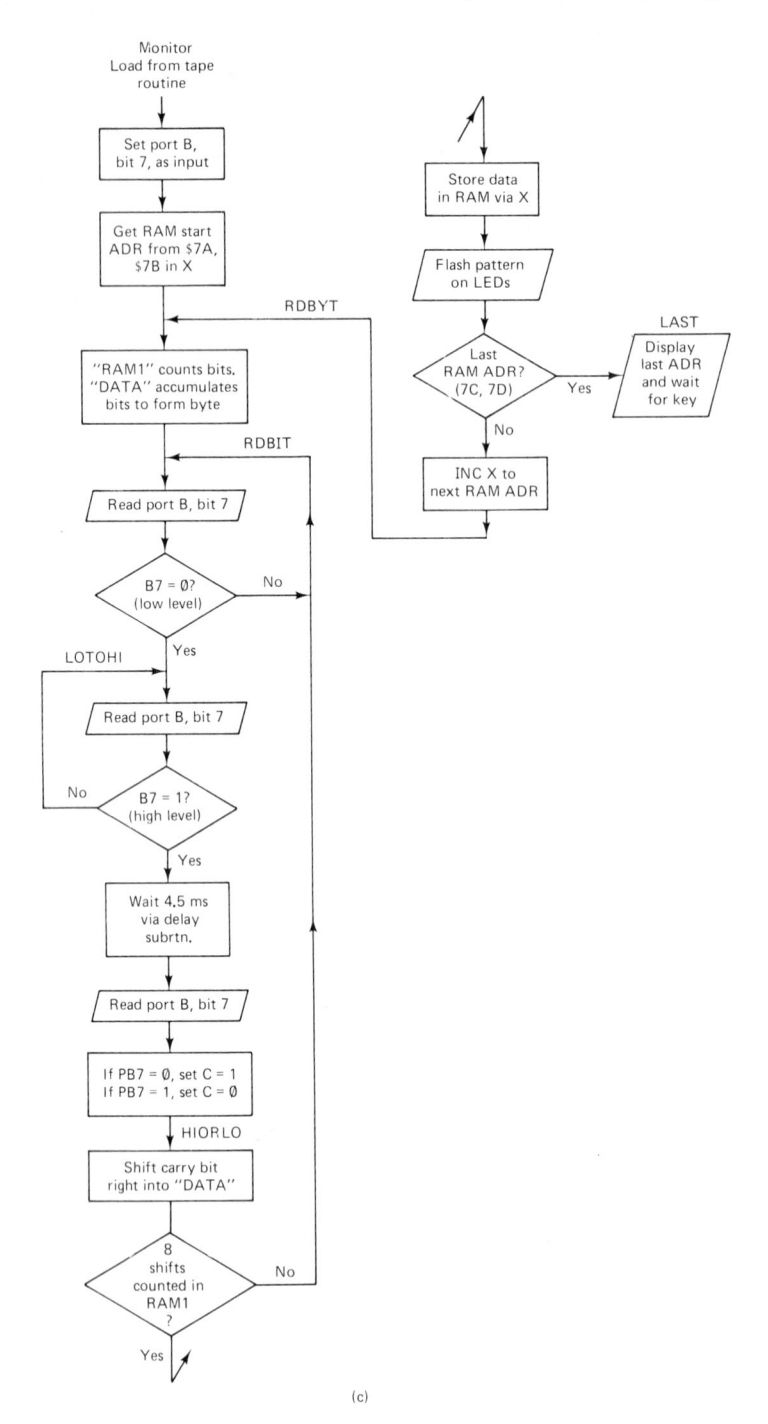

Figure 9-13 *(cont.)*

9.9 THE MICROCHICKEN TAPES: SAVE AND LOAD ROUTINES

The Microchicken Monitor saves programs on tape by recording a series of 3600-Hz tones interspersed with blank or "quiet" periods. Tones are recorded rather than raw binary because the frequency response of a portable cassette recorder is quite limited. A string of all 00 or all FF bytes, for example, would each produce extended dc levels, between which the recorder could not distinguish. The tone format also removes the need for accurate speed control of the tape in the playback mode. Each bit has its own time reference. Here's how it works.

A single bit is recorded in about 7.5 ms: 5 ms of tone followed by a 2.5-ms quite period for a binary 0, or 2.5 ms of tone followed by 5 ms of quiet for a binary 1. This is illustrated in Fig. 9-13(a). On playback, a timing loop is started when the tone begins. The timer runs for 4.5 ms, and then input line PB7 is read. If the tone is still present (logic 1) the bit recorded was a 0. If the tone is absent (logic 0 on PB7), the bit was a 1. One byte takes about 8 × 7.5 ms, or 60 ms to record. A page takes 15 seconds and 2K takes about 2 minutes to record.

The Save-on-Tape routine is flowcharted in Fig. 9-13(b). Bytes are picked up, starting at the address placed by the user in RAM locations $7A and 7B. The 8 bits are shifted out, least-significant first, and used to set a flag byte, RAM2, which equals 0 for a 0-bit, or 1 for a 1-bit.

Nine cycles at 3600 Hz are then output via PB6, and RAM2 is checked. If it is zero, nine more cycles are made and a 2.5-ms quiet period follows. If RAM2 = 1, no more cycles are sent, but a 5-ms quiet period follows immediately. The next-higher bit is then shifted out of the data bytes and another 7.5-ms tone/quiet period is generated.

At the end of each 7.5-ms bit period, RAM1 is checked to see if the entire byte has been sent. If so, the current RAM address (in 7A, 7B) is compared with the ending RAM address (in 7C, 7D) to see if the SAVE has been completed. If not completed, the byte at the next higher address is fetched and sent bit by bit in the same manner. As each byte is fetched it is latched into port C, where it produces a pattern on one or the other LED. This pattern is not a readable digit and it changes at 16 Hz, but it does provide the user with an indication that the *record* function is being performed. Upon completion of the SAVE the address of the last RAM location saved is displayed.

The Load-from-Tape routine should be examined after reviewing the hardware of Fig. 9-4(b). The flowchart for tape LOAD is given in Fig. 9-13(c). The routine starts by reading PB7 and waiting until a low (no tone) is sensed. It then waits for a high level (tone) and assumes this to be the start of the bit-0 field for the first byte, whose address is given in RAM locations 7A, 7B.

After a 4.5-ms delay PB7 is read again, a binary 1 is shifted into the

DATA buffer if PB7 is low at this time, and a 0 is shifted in if PB7 is high. RAM1 counts the number of bits shifted in to DATA, and loops the program back to read another bit until DATA is full. Next, DATA is stored in the RAM location pointed to by the X register, which is then incremented to point to the next RAM location in the developing file.

As in the SAVE routine, an unreadable pattern based on the data being read flashes on the display during the read process. A flaw in the process will usually cause the display to show a blank or a single "8" digit. The flashing display provides some reassurance that data is being read. When the value in the X register matches the ending address stored in RAM 7C, 7D, the program stops reading input data and displays the ending address.

"Microchicken" Montior: Program Listing

```
1000  *-----------------------------------------------------------------------
1010  **** MICROCHICKEN 6802 MONITOR **** COPYRIGHT 1984 BY D. L. METZGER ****
1020  *-----------------------------------------------------------------------
1030  * THIS IS AN OPERATING PROGRAM FOR A 6802 MICROCOMPUTER.
1040  * IT PERMITS COMMANDS AND DATA TO BE INPUT VIA HEX KEYBOARD.
1050  * DATA IS DISPLAYED IN HEX ON TWO 7-SEGMENT LEDS.
1060  *
1070  * PRESSING "RESET" CAUSES THE PROGRAM TO SCAN THE KEYBOARD
1075  * FOR THE FUNCTION TO BE PERFORMED. SUBSEQUENT KEY ENTRIES
1077  * ACCESS NEW FUNCTIONS.
1078  *
1080  * FCN 0  ENTER NEW CURRENT ADR & DISPLAY IT (4 KEY INPUTS,
1090  *          THEN NEW FUNCTION).
1092  * FCN 1  DISPLAY DATA OF CURRENT ADR ON FIRST PRESS;
1094  *          INCREMENT CURRENT ADR ON SUBSEQUENT PRESSES.
1100  * FCN 2  DISPLAY DATA OF CURRENT ADR ON FIRST PRESS OF "2".
1105  *          ENTER NEW DATA & INCR CRNT ADR ON SUBSEQUENT
1107  *          PAIRS OF KEYSTROKES. USE "RESET" TO CHANGE FCN.
1110  * FCN 3  DISPLAY DATA OF CURNT ADR ON FIRST PRESS. DECR
1115  *          CURNT ADR ON SUBSEQUENT PRESSES OF "3".
1120  * FCN 4  RUN PROGRAM STARTING AT CURRENT ADDRESS.
1130  * FCN 5  JUMP TO ADDRESS 0001.
1140  * FCN 6  BURN EPROM FROM RAM   * PUT ADDRESSES IN RAM FIRST:
1150  * FCN 7  DUMP EPROM TO RAM     * RAM START -- $007A   7B
1160  * FCN 8  SAVE RAM ON TAPE      * RAM END   -- $007C,  7D
1170  * FCN 9  LOAD RAM FROM TAPE    * EPROM START- $007E,  7F
1175  *
1180  * FCN A  DISPLAY ACCUM A            **
1190  * FCN B  DISPLAY ACCUM B            **   USE AFTER
1200  * FCN C  DISPLAY COND-CODE REGISTER **   SINGLE
1210  * FCN D  DISPLAY INDEX REGISTER     **   STEP
1220  * FCN E  DISPLAY PROGRAM COUNTER    **   FUNCTION
1225  *        (ADR OF NEXT INSTRUCTION)  **
1230  * FCN F  EXECUTE A SINGLE INSTRUCTION IN RAM (AT CURNT ADR)
1240  *
1260  *
4001-         1000 CRA   .EQ  $4001   CONTROL REGISTER, PIA PORT A
4000-         1010 PA    .EQ  $4000   PORT A, PIA: KEYBD & EPROM ADR LO
4003-         1020 CRB   .EQ  $4003   CONTROL REGISTER, PIA PORT B
4002-         1030 PB    .EQ  $4002   PORT B, PIA: TAPE & EPROM DATA
2000-         1040 PRTC  .EQ  $2000   PORT C, OUTPUT LATCH TO LED DISPLAY
A000-         1050 PRTD  .EQ  $A000   PORT D, OUTPUT TO EPROM CTRL & ADR HI
007F-         1060 PCLO  .EQ  $7F        HOLD SEVEN
007E-         1070 PCHI  .EQ  $7E     MACHINE REGISTERS
007D-         1080 XLO   .EQ  $7D     SAVED ON STACK
```

Sec. 9.9 Microchicken Monitor: Program Listing

```
007C-            1090 XHI    .EQ   $7C      BY INTERRUPT (IRQ)
007B-            1100 ACCA   .EQ   $7B      AND REPLACED BEFORE
007A-            1110 ACCB   .EQ   $7A      EACH SINGLE-STEP
0079-            1120 CCR    .EQ   $79      OPERATION
0078-            1130 COUNT  .EQ   $78      COUNTS UP TO KEYIN VALUE
0077-            1140 CHECK  .EQ   $77      BUFFER CHECKS 1ST KEYIN AGAINST 2ND
0076-            1150 CLOCK  .EQ   $76      TIME-DELAY VALUE & OUTER-LOOP COUNTER
0075-            1160 INRBUF .EQ   $75      TIME-DELAY COUNTER INNER LOOP
0074-            1170 BYTE   .EQ   $74      HOLDS 2 KEY INPUTS & 2 DISPLY DIGITS.
0073-            1180 LONIB  .EQ   $73      HOLDS LOW 4 BITS OF BYTE (HI 4 = 0)
0072-            1190 PATLO  .EQ   $72      HOLDS ADDRESS OF DESIRED
0071-            1200 PATHI  .EQ   $71        BIT PATTERN FOR LED DISPLAY.
0070-            1210 LODIS  .EQ   $70      HOLDS 4 DIGITS FOR "DISFOR"
006F-            1220 HIDIS  .EQ   $6F        DISPLAY ROUTINE.
006E-            1230 LOADR  .EQ   $6E      HOLDS CURRENT ADDRESS.
006D-            1240 HIADR  .EQ   $6D        (AS ENTERED VIA KEY OR SNGLSTEP)
006C-            1250 JUMP   .EQ   $6C      GETS JMP (7E); SNGLSTP TO HIADR, LOADR.
006B-            1260 BKBYT  .EQ   $6B      DATA ONE ADR BEFORE SNGLSTEP INSTR.
006A-            1270 TIMER  .EQ   $6A      BREAKS DELAYS IN "DISFOR" DISPLAY INTO
0069-            1280 LOOPS  .EQ   $69        2-MS CHUNKS TO ALLOW SCAN FOR KEYIN.
0068-            1290 DATA   .EQ   $68      BYTE BEING SENT OR RCVD IN TAPE OR EPROM
0067-            1300 RAM1   .EQ   $67      BUFFERS FOR DISDTA, EPROM,
0066-            1310 RAM2   .EQ   $66        AND TAPE ROUTINES.
0065-            1320 RAM3   .EQ   $65      BUFFER FOR BYTIN.
0064-            1330 RAM4   .EQ   $64      BUFFERS HOLD XLO AND
0063-            1340 RAM5   .EQ   $63        XHI IN DISPLY ROUTINE.
                 1350 *
                 1360        .OR   $FC00    * FILE OF PATTERNS FOR HEX DISPLAY
                 1370        .TA   $4400    *   ON 7-SEG LEDS STARTS AT $FC00.
FC00- 80 F2 48
FC03- 60 32 24
FC06- 04 F0 00
FC09- 30 10 06
FC0C- 8C 42 0C
FC0F- 1C         1380        .HS   80F24860322404F0003010068C420C1C
                 1390 *
                 1400        .OR   $FC20    * SUBROUTINES & PROGM START AT $FC20.
                 1410        .TA   $4420
                 1420 *
                 1430 * ----------------------------------------------------------
                 1440 * SUB TO LOOK FOR KEY PRESS. C FLAG CLEARED IF KEY SENSED.
                 1450 * ROWS 1 - 4 ARE PULLED LOW IN SUCCESSION WHILE COLUMNS 1 -
                 1460 * 4 ARE SCANNED. LEAVES KEY VALUE IN RAM LOCATION "COUNT".
                 1470 *
FC20- 36         1480 KEY    PSHA
FC21- 37         1490        PSHB
FC22- 7F 40 01   1500        CLR   CRA      GET DATA-DIR REGISTER
FC25- 86 F0      1510        LDAA  #$F0     BITS 4 - 7 ARE OUTPUTS
FC27- B7 40 00   1520        STAA  PA       BITS 0 - 3 INPUTS VIA PORT A
FC2A- 86 04      1530        LDAA  #$04     GET OUTPUT REGISTER
FC2C- B7 40 01   1540        STAA  CRA
FC2F- 7F 00 78   1550        CLR   COUNT    START WITH 0
FC32- 86 EF      1560        LDAA  #$EF     ESTABLISH 1-BIT-LOW PATTERN
FC34- 16         1570        TAB              AND SAVE.
FC35- B7 40 00   1580 PULLOW STAA  PA       OUTPUT 1-BIT-LOW (PORT A, 4 - 7).
FC38- B6 40 00   1590        LDAA  PA       LOOK FOR A LOW COLUMN
FC3B- 8A F0      1600        ORAA  #$F0       (BITS 0 - 3)
FC3D- 81 FF      1610        CMPA  #$FF     IF ALL HIGH, NEXT ROW;
FC3F- 26 14      1620        BNE   PRESSD   IF NOT, ONE IS PRESSED
FC41- 7C 00 78   1630        INC   COUNT
FC44- 7C 00 78   1640        INC   COUNT    ADD 4 TO COUNT
FC47- 7C 00 78   1650        INC   COUNT      IN GOING TO NEXT ROW.
FC4A- 7C 00 78   1660        INC   COUNT
FC4D- 59         1670        ROLB           PUT 0 IN NEXT HIGHER ROW
FC4E- 17         1680        TBA              AND TRANSFER TO OUTPUT ACCUM.
FC4F- 25 E4      1690        BCS   PULLOW   IF WASN'T LAST ROW, DO NEXT ROW.
```

```
FC51- 0D        1700          SEC              IF WAS LAST, SET CARRY TO SHOW
FC52- 33        1710 LEAVE    PULB             "NO KEY", RESTORE ACCUM A, B,
FC53- 32        1720          PULA
FC54- 39        1730          RTS              AND LEAVE ROUTINE.
                1740 *
FC55- 46        1750 PRESSD   RORA             YOU FOUND THE ROW,
FC56- 24 FA     1760          BCC    LEAVE     NOW SHUFFLE THRU THE COLUMNS
FC58- 7C 00 78  1770          INC    COUNT     UNTIL THE LOW FALLS INTO
FC5B- 7E FC 55  1780          JMP    PRESSD    THE CARRY BIT.
                1790 *
                1800 *------------------------------------------------------------
                1810 * SUBROUTINE TO CHECK & DEBOUNCE KEY. RETURNS $0X IN COUNT
                1820 * CLEARS C IF VALID KEY INPUT; SETS C IF NOT. TAKES 25 MS
                1830 * MIN IF KEY IN; ABOUT 200 US IF NO KEY.
                1840 *
FC5E- 36        1850 KEYIN    PSHA
FC5F- 86 FF     1860 READ     LDAA   #$FF      INIT WITH AN IMPOSSIBLE CHECK.
FC61- 97 77     1870          STAA   CHECK
FC63- BD FC 20  1880          JSR    KEY       VALID KEY INPUT LEAVES C CLEAR.
FC66- 25 14     1890          BCS    QUIT
FC68- 96 78     1900          LDAA   COUNT
FC6A- 97 77     1910          STAA   CHECK
FC6C- 86 26     1920          LDAA   #$26      APPROX 25 MS DELAY
FC6E- 97 76     1930          STAA   CLOCK
FC70- BD FC 8B  1940          JSR    DELAY     FOR DEBOUNCE
FC73- BD FC 20  1950          JSR    KEY       GET SECOND INPUT.
FC76- 96 78     1960          LDAA   COUNT     COMPARE 2 INPUTS 25 MS APART
FC78- 91 77     1970          CMPA   CHECK     IF NOT SAME, IGNORE INPUT
FC7A- 26 E3     1980          BNE    READ      AND TRY INPUT AGAIN.
FC7C- 32        1990 QUIT     PULA
FC7D- 39        2000          RTS
                2010 *
                2020 *------------------------------------------------------------
                2030 * SUBROUTINE TO WAIT UNTIL KEY IS RELEASED.
                2040 *
FC7E- BD FC 20  2050 KEYUP    JSR    KEY       IF KEY STILL DOWN, WAIT IN
FC81- 24 FB     2060          BCC    KEYUP     LOOP UNTIL IT'S UP.
FC83- 0C        2070          CLC              CLEAR C MEANS VALID KEY.
FC84- 36        2080          PSHA
FC85- 96 77     2090          LDAA   CHECK     RESTORE PROPER VALUE TO
FC87- 97 78     2100          STAA   COUNT     "COUNT" VIA "CHECK".
FC89- 32        2110          PULA
FC8A- 39        2120          RTS              CARRY SET, NO KEY IN.
                2130 *------------------------------------------------------------
                2140 * SUBROUTINE FOR UNIVERSAL TIME DELAYS VIA VALUE IN "CLOCK".
                2150 * DELAY = (C * C * 18) + (C * 14) + (16) MICROSECONDS.
                2160 * MAX DELAY = 1.2 SEC ON 1-MHZ CLOCK.
                2170 *
FC8B- 37        2180 DELAY    PSHB
FC8C- D6 76     2190          LDAB   CLOCK     OUTER AND INNER LOOPS EACH
FC8E- D7 75     2200 OTRLOP   STAB   INRBUF    DECREMENT "CLOCK" TIMES.
FC90- 01        2210 INRLOP   NOP
FC91- 01        2220          NOP              NO-OPERATION JUST
FC92- 01        2230          NOP              TO BURN TIME.
FC93- 01        2240          NOP
FC94- 7A 00 75  2250          DEC    INRBUF
FC97- 26 F7     2260          BNE    INRLOP    LEAVE INNER LOOP WHEN INRBUF = 0
FC99- 7A 00 76  2270          DEC    CLOCK
FC9C- 26 F0     2280          BNE    OTRLOP    LEAVE OUTER LOOP WHEN CLOCK = 0
FC9E- 33        2290          PULB
FC9F- 39        2300          RTS
                2310 *------------------------------------------------------------
                2320 * SUBROUTINE TO PUT 2 KEYSTROKES INTO RAM LOCATION "BYTE"
                2330 * ROUTINE HANGS UP AND WAITS FOR 2 VALID KEY INPUTS.
                2340 * USES KEYIN SUB WHICH USES KEY SUB (10 BYTES STACKED).
                2350 *
```

Sec. 9.9 Microchicken Monitor: Program Listing

```
FCA0- 36            2360 BYTIN  PSHA
FCA1- BD FC 5E      2370 HANGUP JSR   KEYIN    GET FIRST NIBBLE
FCA4- 25 FB         2380        BCS   HANGUP   WAIT FOR VALID KEY INPUT
FCA6- BD FC 7E      2390        JSR   KEYUP    WAIT FOR KEY TO BE RELEASED.
FCA9- 78 00 78      2400        ASL   COUNT    SHIFT 1ST DIGIT TO HI 4 BITS
FCAC- 78 00 78      2410        ASL   COUNT
FCAF- 78 00 78      2420        ASL   COUNT
FCB2- 78 00 78      2430        ASL   COUNT    LOW 4 BITS FILL WITH 0000
FCB5- 96 78         2440        LDAA  COUNT
FCB7- 97 65         2450        STAA  RAM3     SAVE IN "RAM3"
FCB9- 96 6E         2460        LDAA  LOADR    DISPLAY LOW DIGIT OF
FCBB- 97 74         2470        STAA  BYTE      CURRENT ADDRESS AFTER
FCBD- BD FC D0      2480        JSR   DISPLY    FIRST KEYSTROKE.
FCC0- BD FC 5E      2490 SECND  JSR   KEYIN    GET 2ND NIBBLE
FCC3- 25 FB         2500        BCS   SECND    WAIT FOR KEY
FCC5- BD FC 7E      2510        JSR   KEYUP    WAIT FOR KEY RELEASE.
FCC8- 96 78         2520        LDAA  COUNT    ADD INTO LOW 4 BITS
FCCA- 9B 65         2530        ADDA  RAM3     SAVED IN "RAM3"
FCCC- 97 74         2540        STAA  BYTE     STORE 8 BITS IN "BYTE".
FCCE- 32            2550        PULA
FCCF- 39            2560        RTS
                    2570 *------------------------------------------------------------
                    2580 * SUBROUTINE TO DISPLAY THE 2 DIGITS FROM RAM "BYTE" ON LEDS
                    2590 *   TAKES 6 MS (3 MS ON EACH LED). USES BIT-PATTERN FILE.
                    2600 *
FCD0- 36            2610 DISPLY PSHA
FCD1- DF 63         2620        STX   RAM5
FCD3- 86 FC         2630        LDAA  #$FC     BASE ADR OF FILE IS $FC00
FCD5- 97 71         2640        STAA  PATHI
FCD7- 96 74         2650        LDAA  BYTE     GET LOW 4 BITS OF BYTE IN RAM LONIB
FCD9- 84 0F         2660        ANDA  #$0F
FCDB- 97 73         2670        STAA  LONIB
FCDD- 96 74         2680        LDAA  BYTE     GET HI 4 BITS OF BYTE IN
FCDF- 44            2690        LSRA            LOW 4 BITS OF RAM "PATLO"
FCE0- 44            2700        LSRA
FCE1- 44            2710        LSRA
FCE2- 44            2720        LSRA           LEFT 4 BITS FILL IN WITH 0000
FCE3- 97 72         2730        STAA  PATLO    GET BIT PATTERN FOR HI DIGIT
FCE5- DE 71         2740        LDX   PATHI     FROM FILE VIA X. (BIT 0 = 0 TO LITE
FCE7- A6 00         2750        LDAA  00,X      HI LED)
FCE9- B7 20 00      2760        STAA  PRTC     OUTPUT HI DIGIT PATTERN TO PORT C
FCEC- 86 0C         2770        LDAA  #$0C
FCEE- 97 76         2780        STAA  CLOCK
FCF0- BD FC 8B      2790        JSR   DELAY    DELAY FOR APPROX 3 MS:
FCF3- 96 73         2800        LDAA  LONIB    PICK UP LOW-DIGIT NUMBER
FCF5- 97 72         2810        STAA  PATLO
FCF7- DE 71         2820        LDX   PATHI    GET BIT PATTERN FOR LOW DIGIT FROM
FCF9- A6 00         2830        LDAA  00,X      FILE VIA X REGISTER AND OUTPUT
FCFB- 4C            2840        INCA            TO PORT C.
FCFC- B7 20 00      2850        STAA  PRTC     (INC MAKES BIT 0 = 1 TO LITE LO LED)
FCFF- 86 0C         2860        LDAA  #$0C
FD01- 97 76         2870        STAA  CLOCK
FD03- BD FC 8B      2880        JSR   DELAY    DELAY FOR APPROX 3 MS
FD06- DE 63         2890        LDX   RAM5
FD08- 32            2900        PULA
FD09- 39            2910        RTS
                    2920 *------------------------------------------------------------
                    2930 * SUBROUTINE TO DISPLAY 2 DIGITS FROM CURNT ADR UNTIL KEYIN.
                    2940 *
FD0A- DF 66         2950 DISDTA STX   RAM2
FD0C- 36            2960        PSHA
FD0D- DE 6D         2970        LDX   HIADR    PUT CONTENTS OF CURRENT ADR IN BYTE
FD0F- A6 00         2980        LDAA  00,X
FD11- 97 74         2990        STAA  BYTE
FD13- BD FC D0      3000 STAY   JSR   DISPLY   DISPLAY AND LOOK FOR KEY INPUT
FD16- BD FC 5E      3010        JSR   KEYIN    (3 LEVELS OF SUBRTN NESTING; 10 BYTES)
```

```
FD19- 25 F8      3020         BCS  STAY    EXIT SUB WHEN KEY INPUT SENSED
FD1B- DE 66      3030         LDX  RAM2
FD1D- 32         3040         PULA
FD1E- 39         3050         RTS
                 3060  *-----------------------------------------------------------
                 3070  * SUBROUTINE TO DISPLAY 4 DIGITS - HI, LO, BLANK - 1 SEC EA
                 3080  *   LOOK FOR KEY INPUT EVERY 5 MS OR SO.
                 3090  *
FD1F- 36         3100  DISFOR PSHA
FD20- 96 6F      3110  AGAIN  LDAA HIDIS   PUT HIDISPLAY BUFFER IN BYTE
FD22- 97 74      3120         STAA BYTE
FD24- 86 A0      3130         LDAA #$A0    DISPLAY 2 HI DIGITS 160 TIMES
FD26- 97 69      3140         STAA LOOPS
FD28- BD FC D0   3150  HITWO  JSR  DISPLY  @ 6 MS EA, OR 1 SEC.
FD2B- BD FC 5E   3160         JSR  KEYIN   CHECK FOR KEY INPUT.
FD2E- 24 33      3170         BCC  EXIT     LEAVE DISPLAY IF FOUND.
FD30- 7A 00 69   3180         DEC  LOOPS
FD33- 26 F3      3190         BNE  HITWO
FD35- 96 70      3200         LDAA LODIS
FD37- 97 74      3210         STAA BYTE    THEN DISPLAY LOW 2 DIGITS
FD39- 86 A0      3220         LDAA #$A0
FD3B- 97 69      3230         STAA LOOPS
FD3D- BD FC D0   3240  LOTWO  JSR  DISPLY  FOR ABOUT 1 SEC
FD40- BD FC 5E   3250         JSR  KEYIN
FD43- 24 1E      3260         BCC  EXIT
FD45- 7A 00 69   3270         DEC  LOOPS
FD48- 26 F3      3280         BNE  LOTWO
FD4A- 86 FF      3290         LDAA #$FF    BLANK DISPLAY FOR ABOUT 0.5 SEC
FD4C- B7 20 00   3300         STAA PRTC     BY PULLING ALL PORT C LINES HI.
FD4F- BD FC 5E   3310  LOOK   JSR  KEYIN   CHECKING FOR KEY INPUT
FD52- 24 0F      3320         BCC  EXIT
FD54- 86 0A      3330         LDAA #$0A    EVERY 2 MS.
FD56- 97 76      3340         STAA CLOCK
FD58- BD FC 8B   3350         JSR  DELAY
FD5B- 7C 00 6A   3360         INC  TIMER   256 TIMES.
FD5E- 26 EF      3370         BNE  LOOK    EXIT SUB WHEN KEY INPUT IS SENSED.
FD60- 7E FD 20   3380         JMP  AGAIN
FD63- 32         3390  EXIT   PULA
FD64- 39         3400         RTS
                 3410  *-----------------------------------------------------------
                 3420  *
                 3430  * END SUBROUTINES  *****  START MAIN PROGRAM
                 3440  *
                 3450  *-----------------------------------------------------------
                 3460  * INITIALIZE STACK, EPROM; DISPLAY CURRENT ADR. (RESET)
                 3470  *
FD65- 8E 00 62   3480  START  LDS  #$0062  INIT STACK.
FD68- 7F A0 00   3490         CLR  PRTD    DISABLE EPROM IF CONNECTED.
FD6B- DE 6D      3500  DISADR LDX  HIADR   TRANSFER 2 ADR BYTES TO DISPLAY
FD6D- DF 6F      3510         STX  HIDIS    BUFFERS AND DISPLAY 4 DIGITS.
FD6F- BD FD 1F   3520         JSR  DISFOR
                 3530  *
                 3540  *-----------------------------------------------------------
                 3550  * ENTER CURNT ADR (4 DIGITS, THEN NEXT FUNCTION)   (FCN 0)
                 3560  *
FD72- BD FC 7E   3570  FUNCN  JSR  KEYUP   WAIT UNTIL KEY UP; DETERMINE FUNCTION.
FD75- 96 78      3580         LDAA COUNT   IF COUNT = 0,
FD77- 26 11      3590         BNE  ONE      (IF NOT, TRY FCN 1)
FD79- BD FC A0   3600  INADR  JSR  BYTIN
FD7C- 96 74      3610         LDAA BYTE    PUT 2 DIGITS IN HIADR,
FD7E- 97 6D      3620         STAA HIADR
FD80- BD FC A0   3630         JSR  BYTIN
FD83- 96 74      3640         LDAA BYTE    2 DIGITS IN LOADR
FD85- 97 6E      3650         STAA LOADR   VIA "BYTE" AND DISPLAY
FD87- 7E FD 6B   3660         JMP  DISADR  NEW ADR.
                 3670  *-----------------------------------------------------------
```

Sec. 9.9   Microchicken Monitor: Program Listing   **199**

```
                 3680 * DISPLAY CURRENT-ADR DATA & INCR ADR WITH KEY = 1 (FCN 1)
                 3690 *
FD8A- 81 01      3700 ONE    CMPA #01      IF KEY RETURNS COUNT OF 1
FD8C- 26 14      3710        BNE  TWO      DISPLAY DATA OF CURRENT ADR
FD8E- BD FD 0A   3720 DISNXT JSR  DISDTA   LOOKING FOR KEYIN EVERY FEW MS.
FD91- 96 78      3730        LDAA COUNT    IF KEY NOT = 1,
FD93- 81 01      3740        CMPA #01      DETERMINE NEW FUNCTION.
FD95- 26 DB      3750        BNE  FUNCN
FD97- BD FC 7E   3760        JSR  KEYUP    IF KEY = 1, WAIT FOR KEYUP.
FD9A- DE 6D      3770        LDX  HIADR
FD9C- 08         3780        INX           INCR ADR VIA X REGISTER.
FD9D- DF 6D      3790        STX  HIADR
FD9F- 7E FD 8E   3800        JMP  DISNXT   AND DISPLAY NEW DATA.
                 3810 *-----------------------------------------------------------------
                 3820 * DISPLAY DATA OF CURRENT ADR. INPUT PAIRS OF DIGITS AND
                 3830 * INCR CURNT ADR FOR EVERY 2 KEYSTROKES.  DISPLAY LOWEST
                 3840 * ADR DIGIT AFTER FIRST KEY INPUT.                     (FCN 2)
FDA2- 81 02      3850 TWO    CMPA #02      IF KEY RETURNS FUNCTION 2
FDA4- 26 12      3860        BNE  THREE
FDA6- BD FD 0A   3870 INDTA  JSR  DISDTA   DISPLAY DATA (6 MS) UNTIL KEY IN
FDA9- BD FC A0   3880        JSR  BYTIN    GET 2 DIGITS IN "BYTE"
FDAC- 96 74      3890        LDAA BYTE     (PICK UP INPUT BYTE;
FDAE- DE 6D      3900        LDX  HIADR    PICK UP CURRENT ADR;
FDB0- A7 00      3910        STAA 00,X     STORE BYTE IN ADR.)
FDB2- 08         3920        INX           INCR TO NEXT ADDRESS.
FDB3- DF 6D      3930        STX  HIADR
FDB5- 7E FD A6   3940        JMP  INDTA    DISPLAY DATA AT [HIADR,LOADR]
                 3950 *-----------------------------------------------------------------
                 3960 * DISPLAY DATA OF CURNT ADR; DECR ADR WITH KEY = 3  (FCN-3)
                 3970 *
FDB8- 81 03      3980 THREE  CMPA #03      IF KEY RETURNS 03
FDBA- 26 14      3990        BNE  FOUR
FDBC- BD FD 0A   4000 DISBAK JSR  DISDTA   DISPLAY DATA AT CURRENT ADR
FDBF- 96 78      4010        LDAA COUNT    WHILE CHECKING FOR KEY. IF KEY
FDC1- 81 03      4020        CMPA #03      NOT = 3, DETERMINE NEW FUNCTION.
FDC3- 26 AD      4030        BNE  FUNCN
FDC5- BD FC 7E   4040        JSR  KEYUP    IF KEY = 3, WAIT FOR KEYUP.
FDC8- DE 6D      4050        LDX  HIADR
FDCA- 09         4060        DEX           DECREMENT ADR ON KEY INPUT = 3.
FDCB- DF 6D      4070        STX  HIADR
FDCD- 7E FD BC   4080        JMP  DISBAK
                 4090 *-----------------------------------------------------------------
                 4100 * RUN PROGRAM STARTING AT CURRENT ADR          (FCN 4)
                 4110 *
FDD0- 81 04      4120 FOUR   CMPA #04      IF KEY RETURNS 04
FDD2- 26 04      4130        BNE  FIVE
FDD4- DE 6D      4140 RUNPGM LDX  HIADR    JUMP TO CURRENT ADR
FDD6- 6E 00      4150        JMP  00,X     AND RUN PROGRAM.
                 4160 *-----------------------------------------------------------------
                 4170 * RUN USER PROGRAM AT ADR 0001.                (FCN 5)
                 4180 *
FDD8- 81 05      4190 FIVE   CMPA #$05     IF KEY RETURNS 05
FDDA- 26 03      4200        BNE  SIX      (IF NOT, TRY 6)
FDDC- 7E 00 01   4210        JMP  01       RUN PROGRAM AT ADR 0001.
                 4220 *-----------------------------------------------------------------
                 4230 * BURN EPROM FROM RAM. STORE STARTING RAM ADR AT $7A (HI) &
                 4240 * $7B (LO); ENDING RAM ADR AT $7C, 7D; STARTING ROM ADR AT
                 4250 * $7E, 7F. TAKES 50 MS / BYTE. DISPLAYS ROM LOW ADR WHILE
                 4260 * PROGRAMMING; RAM END ADR WHEN DONE. CHECK FOR FAILURE
                 4270 * TO PROG & DISPLAY BAD EPROM ADR IF FAILED.   (FCN 6)
                 4280 *
FDDF- 81 06      4290 SIX    CMPA #$06     IF KEY RETURNS $6
FDE1- 26 74      4300        BNE  SEVEN    (TRY 7 IF NOT)
FDE3- 7F 40 01   4310 BURN   CLR  CRA      ASK FOR PIA DIRECTION REGISTERS.
FDE6- 7F 40 03   4320        CLR  CRB
FDE9- 86 FF      4330        LDAA #$FF
```

```
FDEB- B7 40 00  4340         STAA  PA
FDEE- B7 40 02  4350         STAA  PB      SET ALL PORTS FOR OUTPUTS.
FDF1- 86 04     4360         LDAA  #$04
FDF3- B7 40 01  4370         STAA  CRA     ACCESS PORTS (NOT DIR REG) NEXT.
FDF6- B7 40 03  4380         STAA  CRB
FDF9- DE 7A     4390         LDX   $7A     PUT RAM ADR IN X.
FDFB- E6 00     4400         LDAB  00,X    PICK UP BYTE FROM RAM.
FDFD- 96 7F     4410         LDAA  $7F     PICK UP LOW BYTE ROM ADR
FDFF- B7 40 00  4420         STAA  PA       AND OUTPUT VIA PORT A.
FE02- 96 7E     4430         LDAA  $7E     PICK UP HI BYTE ADR AND
FE04- 97 67     4440         STAA  RAM1     SAVE IN RAM FOR LATER.
FE06- 8A 10     4450         ORAA  #$10    BIT 4 III DISABLES EPROM OUTPUT.
FE08- B7 A0 00  4460         STAA  PRTD    OUTPUT ROM HI 3 BIT ADR.
FE0B- F7 40 02  4470         STAB  PB      OUTPUT DATA BYTE TO ROM.
FE0E- D7 68     4480         STAB  DATA    (SAVE IN RAM FOR LATER)
FE10- 8A 18     4490         ORAA  #$18    BRING PROG PULSE (PIN 18)
FE12- B7 A0 00  4500         STAA  PRTD     & OE (PIN 20) BITS HIGH.
FE15- 96 7F     4510         LDAA  $7F     SET TO DISPLAY LOW
FE17- 97 74     4520         STAA  BYTE     ROM ADR.
FE19- C6 08     4530         LDAB  #$08    EIGHT LOOPS
FE1B- D7 69     4540         STAB  LOOPS
FE1D- BD FC D0  4550  PROM   JSR   DISPLAY (8 DISPLYS AT 6 MS EACH
FE20- 7A 00 69  4560         DEC   LOOPS    = 48 MS BURN TIME)
FE23- 26 F8     4570         BNE   PROM
FE25- 96 67     4580         LDAA  RAM1    RETRIEVE HI ADR WITH BITS 3 & 4
FE27- B7 A0 00  4590         STAA  PRTD    LO TO TURN OFF PROG PULSE & VERFY.
FE2A- DE 7E     4600         LDX   $7E     HOLD EPROM ADR IN X REGISTER.
FE2C- 7F 40 03  4610         CLR   CRB     ASK FOR DIRECTION REG B.
FE2F- 7F 40 02  4620         CLR   PB      SET ALL INPUTS.
FE32- 86 04     4630         LDAA  #04     ASK FOR PORT B.
FE34- B7 40 03  4640         STAA  CRB
FE37- B6 40 02  4650         LDAA  PB      GET DATA FROM EPROM.
FE3A- 91 68     4660         CMPA  DATA    SAME AS PROGRAMMED?
FE3C- 27 05     4670         BEQ   NEXT    YES? CONTINUE.
FE3E- DF 6D     4680         STX   HIADR   NO? THEN DISPLAY EPROM ADR
FE40- 7E FD 6B  4690         JMP   DISADR   AT WHICH FAILURE OCCURRED.
FE43- 08        4700  NEXT   INX            MOVE TO NEXT EPROM ADR
FE44- DF 7E     4710         STX   $7E      AND SAVE IN RAM.
FE46- DE 7A     4720         LDX   $7A     IF CURRENT RAM ADR EQUAL
FE48- 9C 7C     4730         CPX   $7C      TO END RAM ADR
FE4A- 27 06     4740         BEQ   BURNED   YOU'RE DONE.
FE4C- 08        4750         INX           IF NOT, MOVE TO NEXT RAM ADR
FE4D- DF 7A     4760         STX   $7A      AND SAVE.
FE4F- 7E FD E3  4770         JMP   BURN    NEXT BYTE.
FE52- DF 6D     4780  BURNED STX   HIADR   IF EQUAL DISPLAY RAM END ADR
FE54- 7E FD 6B  4790         JMP   DISADR   AND WAIT FOR ADR (FCN 0).
                4800  *------------------------------------------------------------
                4810  * DUMP EPROM TO RAM.  RAM START ADR AT $007A (HI) & 7B (LO).
                4820  * RAM END ADR AT 7C, 7D.  ROM START AT 7E, 7F.  (FCN-7)
                4830  *
FE57- 81 07     4840  SEVEN  CMPA  #$07    IF KEY RETURNS A 7
FE59- 26 3D     4850         BNE   EIGHT    (IF NOT, TRY 8)
FE5B- 7F 40 01  4860         CLR   CRA     ASK FOR DIRECTION REGISTERS.
FE5E- 7F 40 03  4870         CLR   CRB
FE61- 86 FF     4880         LDAA  #$FF    SET PORT A FOR OUTPUTS
FE63- B7 40 00  4890         STAA  PA       (LO ADR LINES OF EPROM)
FE66- 7F 40 02  4900         CLR   PB      PORT B FOR INPUTS (DATA)
FE69- 86 04     4910         LDAA  #$04
FE6B- B7 40 01  4920         STAA  CRA     ACCESS PORTS NEXT TIME.
FE6E- B7 40 03  4930         STAA  CRB
FE71- 96 7E     4940  LOAD   LDAA  $7E     GET ROM HI ADR,
FE73- 84 07     4950         ANDA  #$07    MASK OFF ALL BUT LO 3 BITS.
FE75- B7 A0 00  4960         STAA  PRTD    OUTPUT HI ADR; OE & PROG = 0.
FE78- 96 7F     4970         LDAA  $7F     PICK UP ROM LO ADR
FE7A- B7 40 00  4980         STAA  PA       AND OUTPUT.
FE7D- DE 7E     4990         LDX   $7E
```

Sec. 9.9 Microchicken Monitor: Program Listing

```
FE7F- 08          5000           INX            MOVE TO NEXT ROM ADR
FE80- DF 7E       5010           STX    $7E     AND SAVE.
FE82- B6 40 02    5020           LDAA   PB      GET ROM DATA AND
FE85- DE 7A       5030           LDX    $7A     PUT IN RAM ADR GIVEN
FE87- A7 00       5040           STAA   00,X    IN $7A, 7B.
FE89- 9C 7C       5050           CPX    $7C     IS THIS LAST RAM ADR?
FE8B- 27 06       5060           BEQ    LOADED  YES? THEN DONE.
FE8D- 08          5070           INX            NO? THEN MOVE TO
FE8E- DF 7A       5080           STX    $7A     NEXT RAM ADR AND
FE90- 7E FE 71    5090           JMP    LOAD    DO NEXT BYTE.
FE93- DF 6D       5100   LOADED  STX    HIADR   DISPLAY ENDING RAM ADR
FE95- 7E FD 6B    5110           JMP    DISADR  & WAIT FOR KEY (FCN 0).
                  5120   *------------------------------------------------------------
                  5130   * SAVE RAM TO TAPE. STORE STARTING ADR IN RAM ADR $7A (HI) &
                  5140   *  $7B (LO); ENDING ADR AT $7C (HI) & $7D (LO). TAKES 64 MS
                  5150   *: PER BYTE; 16 SEC/PAGE. DISPLAY END RAM WHEN DONE. (FCN-8)
                  5160   *
FE98- 81 08       5170   EIGHT   CMPA   #08     IF KEY RETURNS 08,
FE9A- 26 67       5180           BNE    NINE
FE9C- 7F 40 03    5190   TAPE    CLR    CRB     ASK FOR PORT B DIRECTION REG.
FE9F- C6 40       5200           LDAB   #$40    SET BIT 6 AS OUTPUT.
FEA1- F7 40 02    5210           STAB   PB
FEA4- C6 04       5220           LDAB   #04     SET CONTROL REG TO
FEA6- F7 40 03    5230           STAB   CRB     ACCESS PORT B NEXT TIME.
FEA9- DE 7A       5240           LDX    $7A     STARTING ADR OF DUMP TO TAPE.
FEAB- A6 00       5250   NXTBYT  LDAA   00,X    PICK UP BYTE.
FEAD- 97 68       5260           STAA   DATA    SAVE IN "DATA".
FEAF- B7 20 00    5270           STAA   PRTC    FLASH PATTERN ON DISPLAY.
FEB2- 7F 00 67    5280           CLR    RAM1
FEB5- 7C 00 67    5290   NXTBIT  INC    RAM1    COUNT OFF ONE SHIFT IN "RAM1".
FEB8- 7F 00 66    5300           CLR    RAM2    (00 = 0 BIT; 01 = 1 BIT)
FEBB- 74 00 68    5310           LSR    DATA    PUT BIT INTO CARRY.
FEBE- 24 03       5320           BCC    BITOUT  IF C = 0 KEEP "RAM2" = 0.
FEC0- 7C 00 66    5330           INC    RAM2    IF C = 1, SET "RAM2" = 1.
                  5340   *
                  5350   * THIS PART OF ROUTINE OUTPUTS ONE BIT TO TAPE. 18 CYCLES
                  5360   * OF 3600-HZ FOR A 0 OR 9 CYCLES FOR A 1, IN 8-MS FIELD.
                  5370   *
FEC3- 4F          5380   BITOUT  CLRA           A COUNTS NO. OF CYCLES.
FEC4- C6 40       5390   TONE    LDAB   #$40    PUT A HI ON PORT B, BIT 6.
FEC6- F7 40 02    5400           STAB   PB
FEC9- C6 17       5410           LDAB   #23     DELAY 23 X 6 = 138 US
FECB- 5A          5420   OUTHI   DECB           WITH OUTPUT HI.
FECC- 26 FD       5430           BNE    OUTHI
FECE- F7 40 02    5440           STAB   PB      B WILL BE = 00.
FED1- C6 17       5450           LDAB   #23     PUT LOW ON PB6 AND
FED3- 5A          5460   OUTLO   DECB           DELAY 138 US.
FED4- 26 FD       5470           BNE    OUTLO
FED6- 4C          5480           INCA           "A" = NO. CYCLES COMPLETED.
FED7- 81 09       5490           CMPA   #09     9 CYCLES DONE? BORROW FLAG = 0?
FED9- 25 E9       5500           BCS    TONE    NO; MAKE ANOTHER.
FEDB- 7D 00 66    5510           TST    RAM2    YES; STOP TONE
FEDE- 26 09       5520           BNE    HIBIT   IF BIT = 1.
FEE0- 81 12       5530           CMPA   #18     IF BIT = 0, FINISH
FEE2- 26 E0       5540           BNE    TONE    18 CYCLES, THEN
FEE4- C6 0B       5550           LDAB   #11     STOP TONE FOR 2.37 MS,
FEE6- 7E FE EB    5560           JMP    QUIET   AND GET NEXT BIT.
FEE9- C6 10       5570   HIBIT   LDAB   #16     IF BIT = 1, STOP TONE
FEEB- D7 76       5580   QUIET   STAB   CLOCK
FEED- BD FC 8B    5590           JSR    DELAY   FOR 4.97 MS.
                  5600   *
FEF0- 96 67       5610           LDAA   RAM1    HOW MANY BITS SENT?
FEF2- 81 08       5620           CMPA   #08     ALL 8?
FEF4- 26 BF       5630           BNE    NXTBIT  NO; SEND NEXT BIT.
FEF6- 9C 7C       5640           CPX    $7C     YES; THEN IS THIS
FEF8- 27 04       5650           BEQ    FINSHD  THE LAST DATA BYTE?
```

202   Microchicken: A General-Purpose Computer with Monitor   Chap. 9

```
FEFA- 08            5660            INX             NO; MOVE TO NEXT ADR.
FEFB- 7E FE AB      5670            JMP   NXTBYT
FEFE- DF 6D         5680  FINSHD    STX   HIADR     YES; DISPLAY END ADR
FF00- 7E FD 6B      5690            JMP   DISADR    AND WAIT FOR KEYIN.
                    5700  *
                    5710  *------------------------------------------------------------
                    5720  * LOAD RAM FROM TAPE. STORE STARTING RAM ADR AT $7A (HI) &
                    5730  * 7B (LO); ENDING ADR AT $7C, 7D. TAKES 64 MS/BYTE. (FCN-9)
                    5740  *
FF03- 81 09         5750  NINE      CMPA  #$09      IF KEY RETURNS 09
FF05- 26 51         5760            BNE   ADISP     (ELSE CHECK KEYS A - F)
FF07- 7F 40 03      5770            CLR   CRB       ASK FOR PORT B DIRECTION REGISTER.
FF0A- 7F 40 02      5780            CLR   PB        SET PORT B FOR ALL INPUTS.
FF0D- 86 04         5790            LDAA  #$04      SET CTRL REG TO ACCESS
FF0F- B7 40 03      5800            STAA  CRB       PORT B NEXT TIME.
FF12- DE 7A         5810            LDX   $7A       STARTING ADR AT $7A.
FF14- 7F 00 67      5820  RDBYT     CLR   RAM1      NO BITS SHIFTED IN YET;
FF17- 7F 00 68      5830            CLR   DATA      DATA BYTE = 0 TO START.
FF1A- B6 40 02      5840  RDBIT     LDAA  PB        READ BIT AT PORT B, BIT 7
FF1D- 84 80         5850            ANDA  #$80      MASK OFF ALL BUT BIT 7.
FF1F- 26 F9         5860            BNE   RDBIT     WAIT FOR LOW LEVEL
FF21- B6 40 02      5870  LOTOHI    LDAA  PB        THEN WAIT FOR LOW-TO-HI
FF24- 84 80         5880            ANDA  #$80        TRANSITION,
FF26- 27 F9         5890            BEQ   LOTOHI
FF28- C6 0F         5900            LDAB  #15       AND DELAY FOR 4.5 MS.
FF2A- D7 76         5910            STAB  CLOCK
FF2C- BD FC 8B      5920            JSR   DELAY
FF2F- B6 40 02      5930            LDAA  PB        READ INPUT BIT.
FF32- 84 80         5940            ANDA  #$80
FF34- 0D            5950            SEC             IF BIT IN = 0,
FF35- 27 01         5960            BEQ   HIORLO    LEAVE C = 1;
FF37- 0C            5970            CLC             ELSE SET C = 0.
FF38- 76 00 68      5980  HIORLO    ROR   DATA      SHIFT CARRY BIT INTO
FF3B- 7C 00 67      5990            INC   RAM1      DATA AND COUNT OFF
FF3E- 96 67         6000            LDAA  RAM1      A SHIFT.
FF40- 81 08         6010            CMPA  #08       8 BITS SHIFTED IN YET?
FF42- 26 D6         6020            BNE   RDBIT     NO? READ NEXT BIT.
FF44- 96 68         6030            LDAA  DATA      YES? STORE 8 BITS IN
FF46- A7 00         6040            STAA  00,X        RAM AT ADR X.
FF48- B7 20 00      6050            STAA  PRTC      FLASH PATTERN ON DISPLAY.
FF4B- 9C 7C         6060            CPX   $7C       LAST ADDRESS?
FF4D- 27 04         6070            BEQ   LAST      YES...
FF4F- 08            6080            INX             NO? GO TO NEXT ADR
FF50- 7E FF 14      6090            JMP   RDBYT       FOR NEXT BYTE.
FF53- DF 6D         6100  LAST      STX   HIADR     ELSE DISPLAY LAST ADR
FF55- 7E FD 6B      6110            JMP   DISADR    AND WAIT FOR KEYIN.
                    6120  *
                    6130  *------------------------------------------------------------
                    6140  * DISPLAY ACCUM A. USE AFTER SNGLSTP.              (FCN-A)
                    6150  *
FF58- 81 0A         6160  ADISP     CMPA  #$0A      IF KEY RETURNS $0A
FF5A- 26 0F         6170            BNE   BDISP
FF5C- 96 7B         6180            LDAA  ACCA      PICK UP A BUFFER
FF5E- 97 74         6190            STAA  BYTE      DISPLAY 2 DIGITS FROM ACCUM A
FF60- BD FC D0      6200  DISBYT    JSR   DISPLY
FF63- BD FC 5E      6210            JSR   KEYIN     LOOK FOR KEY IN
FF66- 25 F8         6220            BCS   DISBYT    CONTINUE DISPLAY
FF68- 7E FD 72      6230            JMP   FUNCN     OR EVALUATE KEY FOR NEW FUNCTION.
                    6240  *------------------------------------------------------------
                    6250  * DISPLAY ACCUM B                                  (FNC-B)
                    6260  *
FF6B- 81 0B         6270  BDISP     CMPA  #$0B      IF KEY RETURNS $0B
FF6D- 26 07         6280            BNE   CCRDIS
FF6F- 96 7A         6290            LDAA  ACCB      PICK UP B BUFFER
FF71- 97 74         6300            STAA  BYTE
FF73- 7E FF 60      6310            JMP   DISBYT    DISPLAY & LOOK FOR KEY AS ABOVE
```

Sec. 9.9   Microchicken Monitor: Program Listing

```
                 6320  *----------------------------------------------------------------
                 6330  * DISPLAY CONDITION-CODE REGISTER                     (FCN-C)
                 6340  *
FF76- 81 0C      6350  CCRDIS CMPA #$0C      IF KEY RETURNS $0C
FF78- 26 07      6360         BNE  XDISP
FF7A- 96 79      6370         LDAA CCR       PICK UP CCR BUFFER
FF7C- 97 74      6380         STAA BYTE
FF7E- 7E FF 60   6390         JMP  DISBYT    DISPLAY & LOOK FOR KEY AS IN ADISP
                 6400  *----------------------------------------------------------------
                 6410  * DISPLAY X-INDEX REGISTER                            (FCN-D)
                 6420  *
FF81- 81 0D      6430  XDISP  CMPA #$0D      IF KEY RETURNS $0D
FF83- 26 0A      6440         BNE  PCDIS     PICK UP 2 BYTES (HI & LO)
FF85- DE 7C      6450         LDX  XHI       OF X-INDEX BUFFER VIA X INDEX
FF87- DF 6F      6460  DISDBL STX  HIDIS     AND STORE IN DISPLAY BUFFERS
FF89- BD FD 1F   6470         JSR  DISFOR    DISPLAY FOUR DIGITS (1 SEC EA BYTE)
FF8C- 7E FD 72   6480         JMP  FUNCN     EXIT DISFOR WHEN KEYIN.
                 6490  *----------------------------------------------------------------
                 6500  * DISPLAY PROGRAM COUNTER (ADR OF NEXT INSTR)         (FCN-E)
                 6510  *
FF8F- 81 0E      6520  PCDIS  CMPA #$0E      IF KEY RETURNS $0E
FF91- 26 05      6530         BNE  ONESTP
FF93- DE 7E      6540         LDX  PCHI      PICK UP 2 BYTES OF PROG CTR
FF95- 7E FF 87   6550         JMP  DISDBL    AND DISPLAY 4 DIGITS AS ABOVE
                 6560  *----------------------------------------------------------------
                 6570  * EXECUTE SINGLE INSTR IN RAM STARTING AT CURNT ADR. (FCN-F)
                 6580  * 1) SAVE THE BYTE PRECEDING THE USER INSTRUCTION IN
                 6590  *    "BKBYT", & INSERT A CLR-INTRUPT-MASK (0E)THERE.
                 6600  * 2) JUMP TO THE "CLI" INSTRUCTION. ONE USER INSTRUCTION
                 6610  *    WILL EXECUTE BEFORE THE IRQ IS RECOGNIZED. IRQ SAVES
                 6620  *    ALL MACHINE REGISTERS ON STACK & VECTORS TO "RETURN".
                 6630  * 3) PULL MACHINE REGISTERS OFF STACK & SAVE IN RAM BUFRS.
                 6640  * 4) REPLACE "CLI" IN RAM WITH ORIGINAL BYTE FROM "BKBYT".
                 6650  * 5) PUT PROG CTR IN CURRENT ADR (READY FOR NEXT STEP).
                 6660  *
FF98- 81 0F      6670  ONESTP CMPA #$0F      IF KEY RETURNS OTHER THAN $0F
FF9A- 27 03      6680         BEQ  CONT      JUMP TO START FOR NEW COMMAND.
FF9C- 7E FD 65   6690         JMP  START
FF9F- DE 6D      6700  CONT   LDX  HIADR     PICK UP BYTE AT ADR ONE
FFA1- 09         6710         DEX            BEFORE CURRENT USER INSTRUCTION
FFA2- DF 6D      6720         STX  HIADR
FFA4- A6 00      6730         LDAA 00,X      AND STORE IN RAM "BKBYT".
FFA6- 97 6B      6740         STAA BKBYT
FFA8- 86 0E      6750         LDAA #$0E      STORE A "CLI" COMMAND AS THE INSTR
FFAA- A7 00      6760         STAA 00,X      PRECEDING THE CURRENT INSTR
FFAC- 86 7E      6770         LDAA #$7E      SET UP A "JMP" INSTR TO VECTOR TO
FFAE- 97 6C      6780         STAA JUMP      "CLI" PRECEDING USER INSTRUCTION.
FFB0- D6 7A      6790         LDAB ACCB      RESTORE MACHINE REGISTERS
FFB2- DE 7C      6800         LDX  XHI       AS SAVED BY "IRQ" INTERRUPT.
FFB4- 96 7B      6810         LDAA ACCA
FFB6- 36         6820         PSHA           (USE STACK TO RELOAD ACCUM A
FFB7- 96 79      6830         LDAA CCR       WITHOUT ALTERING CCR)
FFB9- 06         6840         TAP
FFBA- 0F         6850         SEI            ENSURE INTERRUPT MASK BIT IS HIGH.
FFBB- 32         6860         PULA
FFBC- 7E 00 6C   6870         JMP  $006C     JUMP TO NEXT USER INSTR VIA RAM
                 6880  *                     COMMANDS AT $6C,6D,6E (JMP HIADR).
                 6890  *
                 6900  * HERE YOU WILL DO ONE INSTR FROM RAM AND BE INTERRUPTED.
                 6910  * INTERRUPT VECTOR LANDS YOU AT "RETURN".
                 6920  *
FFBF- 32         6930  RETURN PULA           PLACE 7 MACHINE REGISTERS IN
FFC0- 97 79      6940         STAA CCR       RAM BUFFERS.
FFC2- 32         6950         PULA
FFC3- 97 7A      6960         STAA ACCB
FFC5- 32         6970         PULA
```

```
FFC6- 97 7B    6980        STAA  ACCA
FFC8- 32       6990        PULA
FFC9- 97 7C    7000        STAA  XHI
FFCB- 32       7010        PULA
FFCC- 97 7D    7020        STAA  XLO
FFCE- 32       7030        PULA
FFCF- 97 7E    7040        STAA  PCHI
FFD1- 32       7050        PULA
FFD2- 97 7F    7060        STAA  PCLO
FFD4- DE 6D    7070        LDX   HIADR   RETRIEVE ADR OF "CLI" AND REPLACE
FFD6- 96 6B    7080        LDAA  BKBYT      ORIGINAL DATA.
FFD8- A7 00    7090        STAA  00,X
FFDA- DE 7E    7100        LDX   PCHI    PUT PROGM CNTR IN CURRENT ADR
FFDC- DF 6D    7110        STX   HIADR   DISPLAY PROG CTR (ADR OF NEXT INSTR)
FFDE- 7E FF 87 7120        JMP   DISDBL  AND LOOK FOR KEY IN.
               7130 *-------------------------------------------------------
FFE1- DE 61    7140 BREAK  LDX   $0061   GET ADR FOLLOWING SWI INSTR FROM
FFE3- 09       7150        DEX             STACK; GO BACK TO ADR OF INSTR.
FFE4- DF 61    7160        STX   $0061   PUT RETURN ADR OF ORIG INSTR IN STACK.
FFE6- DF 6D    7170        STX   HIADR   ORIG INSTR FROM BKBYT GOES IN HIADR (X)
FFE8- 20 D5    7180        BRA   RETURN  AFTER ENTERING SST MODE.
               7190 *-------------------------------------------------------
               7200 * STORE VECTORS AT END OF EPROM.
               7210        .OR   $FFF8
               7220        .TA   $47F8
FFF8- FF BF    7230        .DA   RETURN  IRQ VECTOR
FFFA- FF E1    7240        .DA   BREAK   SWI VECTOR
FFFC- 00 20    7250        .HS   0020    NMI VECTOR
FFFE- FD 65    7260        .DA   START   RESET VECTOR
               7270 * EPROM START $0400, END $07FF.   WORKSPACE START $0400
               7280 * APPLE TARGET ADDRESS START $4400
               7290        .EN
```

10

Chicken Pickin': An Industrial Microcomputer Application

This chapter presents a striking example of how a microcomputer can bring otherwise-unattainable levels of efficiency to a rather ordinary business—in this case, a chicken ranch. The project will be implemented on the Microchicken system detailed in Chapter 9 to permit step-by-step development by changing the program in RAM. We will meet the 1408 D/A converter again, this time seeing how it can be used to perform analog-to-digital conversion under computer control. We will also become acquainted with a very popular serial-data interface chip—the 6850 ACIA. We will use a pair of these chips to interface our computer with a desktop microcomputer, and illustrate some of the advantages that can be obtained by enabling computers to communicate with each other.

10.1 THE PROBLEM AND THE PROGRAM

Imagine that you own a chicken ranch. You have a contract with Corporal Saunders to deliver a continuing supply of chickens in boxes containing a minimum of 12 pounds, net. You are paid a flat rate of $4.00 per box. The boxes must contain whole chickens only—no parts. Boxes weighing less than 12 pounds are not accepted. However, nothing extra is paid for boxes weighing over 12 pounds. Obviously, it is to your advantage to find a combination whose weights, when added, will total exactly 12 pounds. If you try to picture a human operator attempting to do this with a scale, you will see that it could develop into quite a comedy. The computer can do it in less than a tenth of a second.

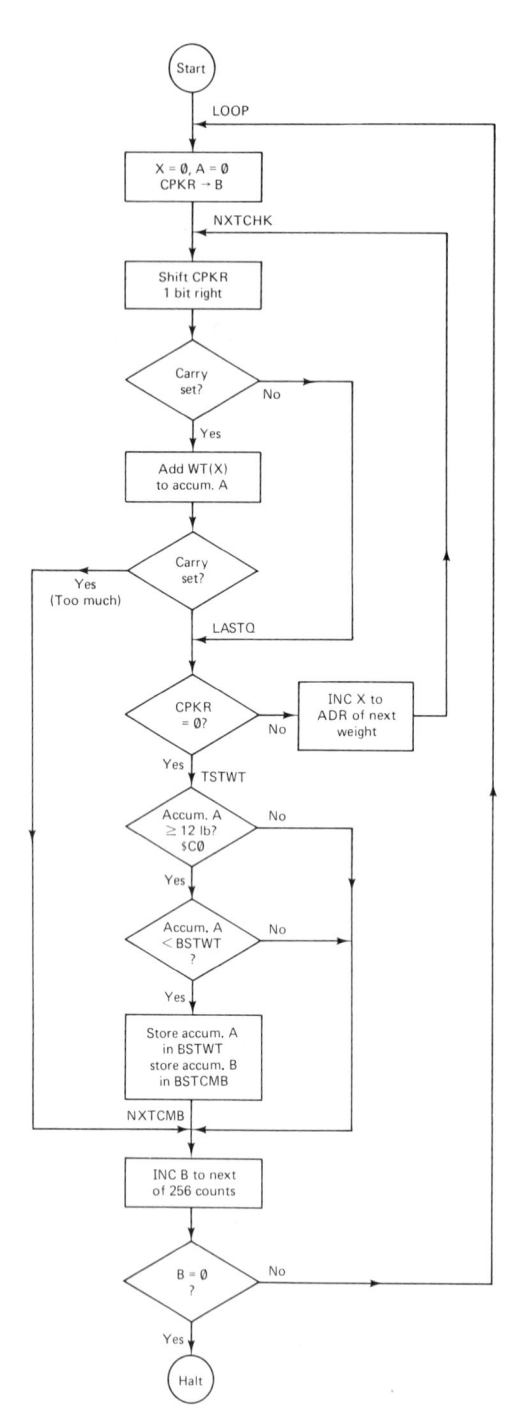

206   Chicken Pickin': An Industrial Microcomputer Application   Chap. 10

Figure 10-1 Flowchart for the basic Chicken Pickin' program. There are 256 possible ways to select from eight chickens. The program finds the "best combination": at least 12 pounds, but no more in excess of that than necessary.

Sec. 10.1 The Problem and the Program

The program that makes this possible is flowcharted in Fig. 10-1. Before beginning, the weights of eight randomly picked chickens are stored in eight RAM locations 0000 through 0007. The weights are stored in pounds (high nibble) and ounces (low nibble), which is particularly convenient since "pounds and ounces" is a base-sixteen number system and requires no conversion from the usual hexadecimal display.

The program computes the total weight for each of the 256 possible combinations of the eight weights stored. These combinations are determined by the 256 binary counts of an 8-bit register, whose contents are stored in RAM *CPKR*. Bits 0 through 7 of CPKR correspond to weights stored at locations 0000 through 0007, respectively. A binary 1 in CPKR means "Add in the weight of this chicken." A binary 0 means "Don't add this one." The decision is made by shifting CPKR right into the carry bit. If *C* is set (binary 1), the weight is added to a total accumulated in register A. If *C* = 0, the ADD is bypassed. The weight to be added (or not) is pointed to by *X*, which starts at 0000 and is incremented after each shift-and-add.

If the total exceeds 15 pounds 15 ounces ($FF), a BCS aborts the accumulation for that combination and the next binary combination is tried. When all weights corresponding to "1" bits have been added (CPKR = 0), register A is tested to see that its contents are:

1. 12 pounds or more, and
2. less than the previous accumulated "best weight."

If both of these conditions are true, the old "best weight" in RAM "BSTWT" is replaced by the new accumulated total from register A, and the old "best combination" in RAM "BSTCMB" is replaced by the new binary-select combination from register B. Otherwise, the "best weight" and "best combination" buffers are left alone and register B is incremented to try the next binary combination.

The program halts when binary-select register B counts all the way around through $FF to 00. At this point RAM locations $0A (best combination) and $0B (best weight) can be examined for the optimum selection of the eight available chickens. If you preload several random sets of weights between 2 and 4 pounds, you may be surprised to see how frequently an ideal or nearly ideal combination (totaling $C0 or $C1) is found. Here is the complete program listing. It can be loaded into the unexpanded microcomputer described in Chapter 9. Implementing it as an independent breadboarded system would involve extensive modification because of the keyboard input and hex-display output requirements.

Chicken Pickin': Program Lising

```
                        1000  *  -----------------------------------------------------------
                        1010  *         CHICKEN PICKIN'  ****  MANUAL DATA ENTRY
                        1020  *
0009-                   1030  CPKR   .EQ   $09       CHICKEN PICKER HOLDS TEMP BINARY COMB.
000A-                   1040  BSTCMB .EQ   $0A       ANSWER (BINARY COMBINATION TO CHOOSE)
000B-                   1050  BSTWT  .EQ   $0B       BEST WEIGHT TOTAL (LBS & OZ.)
                        1060         .OR   $10       START PROG ASSEMBLY AT RAM $0010
                        1065         .TA   $4010     STORE CODE IN APPLE RAM AT $4010
                        1070  *
0010- 86 FF             1080  START  LDAA  #$FF      START WITH EXCESSIVE "BEST WEIGHT"
0012- 97 0B             1090         STAA  BSTWT
0014- 7F 00 0A          1100         CLR   BSTCMB    AND "CHOOSE NONE" AS BEST COMB.
0017- C6 07             1110         LDAB  #$07      START PICKING 3 CHICKENS (0000 0111)
0019- CE 00 00          1120  LOOP   LDX   #0000     FILE OF CHICKEN WEIGHTS STARTS AT 0000
001C- 4F                1130         CLRA            TOTAL "SO FAR" = 0.
001D- D7 09             1140         STAB  CPKR      RAM "CPKR" HOLDS BINARY COMBINATION.
001F- 74 00 09          1150  NXTCHK LSR   CPKR      SHIFT BIT PATTERN INTO CARRY.
0022- 24 04             1160         BCC   LASTQ     (0 IN CARRY MEANS DON'T ADD THIS ONE)
0024- AB 00             1170         ADDA  00,X      (1 = ADD THIS WEIGHT FROM FILE)
0026- 25 15             1180         BCS   NXTCMB    IF WT > 15 LB, 15 OZ, TOO MUCH!
0028- 7D 00 09          1190  LASTQ  TST   CPKR      ALL BINARY 1'S (ADD THIS) SHIFTED OUT?
002B- 27 04             1200         BEQ   TSTWT     IF SO, IS THIS TOTAL WT LOWEST?
002D- 08                1210         INX             IF NOT, MOVE TO NEXT WT IN FILE AND
002E- 7E 00 1F          1220         JMP   NXTCHK    CHECK IF CPKR SAYS TO ADD IT IN.
0031- 81 C0             1230  TSTWT  CMPA  #$C0      IS TOTAL WT 12 LBS OR MORE?
0033- 25 08             1240         BCS   NXTCMB    NO? THEN TRY ANOTHER COMBINATION.
0035- 91 0B             1250         CMPA  BSTWT     YES, THEN IS NEW TOTAL LESS THAN
0037- 24 04             1260         BCC   NXTCMB    OLD BEST WEIGHT? IF SO,
0039- 97 0B             1270         STAA  BSTWT     REPLACE OLD BEST WEIGHT AND
003B- D7 0A             1280         STAB  BSTCMB    BEST COMB WITH NEW.
003D- 5C                1290  NXTCMB INCB            COUNT TO NEXT BINARY COMBINATION.
003E- 26 D9             1300         BNE   LOOP      IF NOT = 00, TRY IT
0040- 7E 00 40          1310  DONE   JMP   DONE      IF = 00, YOU TRIED THEM ALL.
```

10.2 ANALOG CHICKEN: ADDING AN A/D CONVERTER

In a real-life application it would be inconvenient to load the chicken weights manually from a hex keyboard. This section describes an advanced Chicken Picker in which the weights are loaded directly from a scale which drives a potentiometer shaft. The resulting analog voltage is proportional to weight, and is converted to a digital value with the help of the circuit shown in Fig. 10-2.

Analog-to-digital conversion. In operation, the data lines of the D/A converter are driven by the port D data latch. The binary output of this port starts at 0 and is incremented every 25 μs by the program. The voltage at pin 4 of the 1408 thus builds negative, and is applied to the inverting input of a comparator, after noise filtering. The 1-kΩ pot attached to the spring scale applies a negative voltage to the noninverting input. When the count makes the output of the 1408 more negative than the scale output voltage, the output of the comparator switches positive.

This output is connected to port B, line 5, which is programmed as an input. PB5 is checked after each increment of port D, and when it switches

Sec. 10.2   Analog Chicken: Adding an A/D Converter

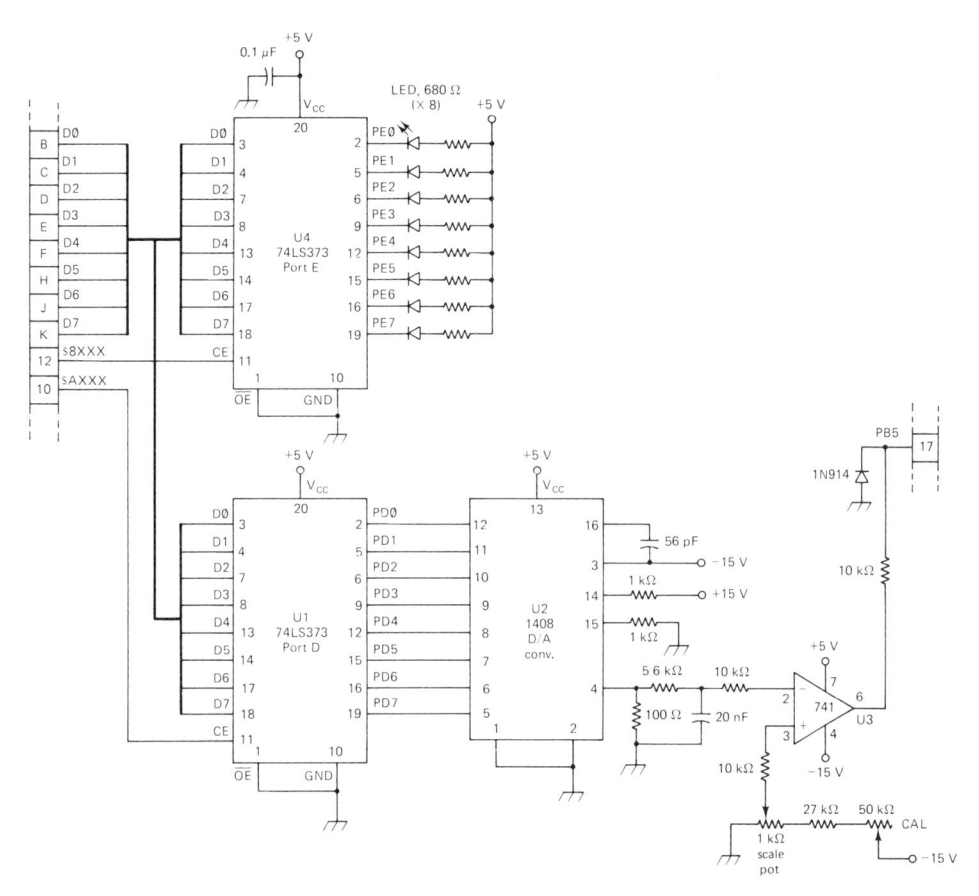

Figure 10-2 Hardware for Chicken Picker hanger display and A/D-converter scale, showing connections to Microchicken circuit board.

high, counting stops. The value in the counting register is now a digital representation of the analog voltage from the scale potentiometer.

Fast A/D conversion is not required in this application, and a count of 255 takes nearly 7 ms. If necessary the conversion time could be reduced to about 0.3 ms (for a 1-MHz clock) by a simple change in programming. In this technique, PD7 is first set to 1 with PD6 through PD0 set to 0. Comparator output PB5 is then checked: if PB5 = 0, PD7 is left at 1; if PB5 = 1, PD7 is reset to 0 (since the count 1000 0000 apparently exceeds the desired count). Bit 6 of port D is next tested and set high or low as dictated by the comparator output. Bits 5 through 0 are likewise tested and set in succession, and the binary count homes in on the desired value in eight checks (as opposed to 255 counts).

Processor independent A/D converters are available (at a somewhat higher price) in which the counting or bit testing is done by an internal register. This frees the processor for other functions while the conversion is being done. *Real-time* or *flash* A/D converters are built around a series of level comparators rather than a D/A converter. They are not clocked, internally or externally, and are very fast.

The analog-input Chicken Picker displays the selected chickens on a string of eight discrete LEDs, rather than on the hex display. Another octal latch (port E, at address $8000) is shown in Fig. 10-2 to drive these LEDs.

The analog input routine is flowcharted in Fig. 10-3(a). The program listing appears at the end of this section. Accumulator B and RAM "CPKR" are used as shift registers to point to one of the eight hangers at a time (binary 1 in bit position). The complemented register value (a single binary 0) is stored in port E to light the LED by the hanger pointed to.

To start, BSTCMB is set at $FF, indicating that *all* the chickens were selected on the "last" run, so all hangers now need to be filled. The LOAD routine compares the pointer (accumulator B) with the chickens taken (BSTCMB) and enters the SCALE routine for each bit position where a refill is needed.

SCALE counts RAM location BYTE up from 00 and outputs the values to the D/A converter until a read of input PB5 shows that the 1408 output equals the scale output voltage. The increment loop covers lines 1380 through 1430 in the program listing, and takes 25 μs. The SCALE A/D conversion and display are run repeatedly until a key input (any key) is pressed by the operator. The count is then stored in the file of weights ($C000 to $C007) and displayed for 1 second.

Pointer register CPKR is then shifted to the next hanger, X is incremented to the next address in the weight file, and the LOAD routine is reentered to see if the next hanger needs to be filled. When all hangers have been checked, the basic Chicken Pickin' module (Section 10.1, Figure 10.1) is entered.

User options. Upon completing Selection-Module 2, the program enters Display-Module 3, which is flowcharted in Fig. 10-2(b). Here the best weight total is displayed in hex and the combination selected is shown on the port-E LEDs. The operator then has the options of:

- Rejecting the selection and replacing the chicken on hanger 8 (*key F*—fail)
- Accepting the selection and weighing in chickens for the hangers thus emptied (*key 0*—OK), or
- Reviewing the weights on each of the eight hangers (any key, 1 through E).

The primary purpose of this last option is to permit the skeptical to perform an independent check of the machine's total. The weight on each

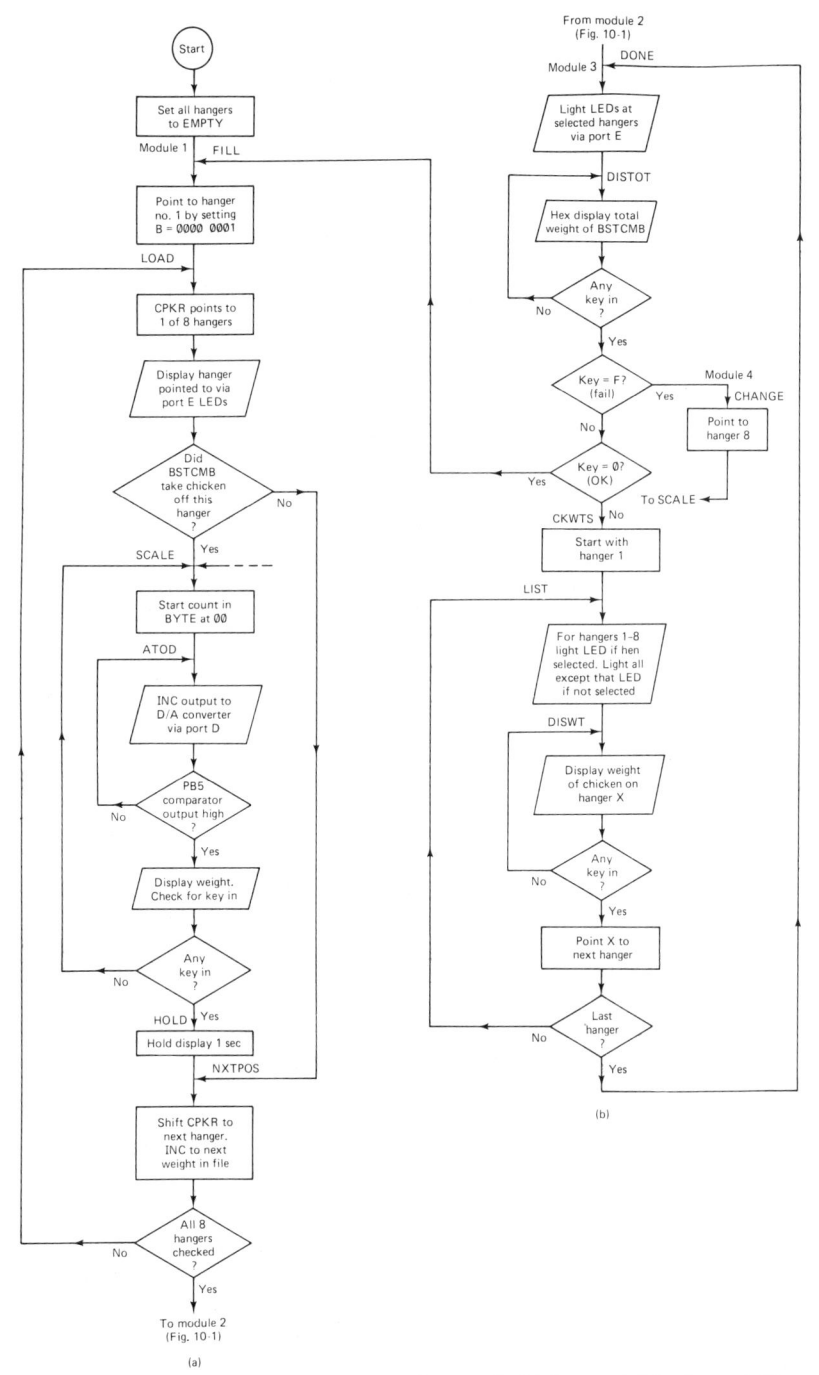

Figure 10-3 Software for automatic input of chicken weights via an A/D converter (a), and display of selection and refill options (b).

hanger is displayed in hex, starting with hanger 1 and advancing through hanger 8 to a redisplay of the total. At each hanger, the single corresponding LED is lit if that chicken was selected by BSTCMB. If not selected, that LED remains dark and the seven *other* LEDs light to indicate which hanger is being displayed.

Analog-Input Chicken Pickin': Program Listing

```
                1000 * ------------------------------------------------------------
                1010 *        CHICKEN PICKIN' 2  ***  ANALOG DATA INPUT
                1020 *
C009-           1030 CPKR    .EQ   $C009    CHICKEN PICKER HOLDS TEMP BINARY COMB.
C00A-           1040 BSTCMB  .EQ   $C00A    ANSWER (BINARY COMBINATION TO CHOOSE)
C00B-           1050 BSTWT   .EQ   $C00B    BEST WEIGHT TOTAL (LBS & OZ.)
FCD0-           1070 DISPLY  .EQ   $FCD0    MONITOR DISPLAY ROUTINE; 6 MS.
FC5E-           1080 KEYIN   .EQ   $FC5E    MONITOR CLEARS CARRY IF KEY IN.
FC7E-           1090 KEYUP   .EQ   $FC7E    MONITOR WAITS FOR KEY RELEASE.
0074-           1100 BYTE    .EQ   $74      RAM USED BY MONITOR FOR DISPLY.
0078-           1105 COUNT   .EQ   $78      RETURNS VALUE OF KEY INPUT.
4002-           1110 PB      .EQ   $4002    PIA PORT B.
4003-           1120 CRB     .EQ   $4003    CONTROL REGISTER FOR PORT B.
A000-           1130 PRTD    .EQ   $A000    OUTPUT-ONLY PORT.
8000-           1140 PRTE    .EQ   $8000    8 LED OUTPUTS.
6000-           1144 SERC    .EQ   $6000    SERIAL I/O CONTROL/STATUS.
6001-           1146 SERD    .EQ   $6001    SERIAL I/O DATA.
C00C-           1150 XBUF    .EQ   $C00C    SAVES X DURING DISPLY SUB.
C00E-           1160 LOOPBF  .EQ   $C00E    COUNTS DISPLAY LOOPS.
                1170         .OR   $C010    START PROG ASSEMBLY AT RAM $C010
                1180         .TA   $4010    STORE CODE IN APPLE RAM AT $4010
                1190 * ------------------------------------------------------------
                1200 *
C010- 7F 40 03  1210 START   CLR   CRB      GET DIRECTION REGISTER.
C013- 7F 40 02  1220         CLR   PB       SET ALL LINES AS INPUTS.
C016- 86 04     1230         LDAA  #04      ACCESS DATA REGISTER
C018- B7 40 03  1240         STAA  CRB      NEXT TIME.
C01B- C6 FF     1250         LDAB  #$FF     INDICATE "ALL HANGERS EMPTY"
C01D- F7 C0 0A  1260         STAB  BSTCMB   TO START.
C020- C6 01     1270 FILL    LDAB  #01      FILL ALL EMPTY HANGERS.
C022- F7 C0 09  1280         STAB  CPKR
C025- CE C0 00  1290         LDX   #$C000   FILE STARTS AT C000.
                1295 *
                1297 * MODULE 1 *** INPUT WEIGHTS AT EMPTY LOCATIONS ***
                1298 *
C028- F6 C0 09  1300 LOAD    LDAB  CPKR     IDENTIFY 1 OF 8 HANGERS.
C02B- 53        1310         COMB           DISPLAY 1 OF 8 LEDS
C02C- F7 80 00  1320         STAB  PRTE
C02F- 53        1330         COMB           IF NO CHICKEN LEFT AT
C030- F4 C0 0A  1340         ANDB  BSTCMB   THIS LOCATION,
C033- 27 31     1350         BEQ   NXTPOS   (SKIP IF ONE IS THERE)
                1360
C035- 7F 00 74  1370 SCALE   CLR   BYTE     WEIGH IN A CHICKEN.
C038- 7C 00 74  1380 ATOD    INC   BYTE     RAM "BYTE" COUNTS UP WEIGHT.
C03B- 96 74     1390         LDAA  BYTE     A/D TAKES 5 MS MAX.
C03D- B7 A0 00  1400         STAA  PRTD     OUTPUT COUNT TO A/D CONV.
C040- B6 40 02  1410         LDAA  PB       CHECK COMPARATOR OUTPUT
C043- 84 20     1420         ANDA  #$20     ON BIT 5 ONLY.
C045- 27 F1     1430         BEQ   ATOD     LOW = KEEP COUNTING.
C047- BD FC D0  1440         JSR   DISPLY   6 MS OF WEIGHT DISPLAY,
C04A- 7F A0 00  1450         CLR   PRTD     LET COMPARATOR RECOVER,
C04D- BD FC D0  1460         JSR   DISPLY   AND DISPLAY SOME MORE
C050- BD FC 5E  1470         JSR   KEYIN    LOOK FOR KEY PRESS (CRY CLR).
C053- 25 E0     1480         BCS   SCALE    ANY KEY WILL LOAD WEIGHT.
```

Sec. 10.2 Analog Chicken: Adding an A/D Converter 213

```
C055- 96 74      1490          LDAA   BYTE     PICK UP WEIGHT,
C057- A7 00      1500          STAA   00,X     PUT IN FILE.
C059- C6 A0      1510          LDAB   #$A0     160 LOOPS X 6 MS/LOOP
C05B- F7 C0 0E   1520          STAB   LOOPBF   (KEEP COUNT OF LOOPS IN RAM)
C05E- BD FC D0   1530 HOLD     JSR    DISPLY   HOLDS WEIGHT DISPLAY
C061- 7A C0 0E   1540          DEC    LOOPBF   FOR 1 SEC.
C064- 26 F8      1550          BNE    HOLD
C066- 08         1560 NXTPOS   INX             MOVE TO NEXT SLOT IN FILE.
C067- 78 C0 09   1570          ASL    CPKR     IF END OF FILE
C06A- 27 03      1580          BEQ    RUN      RUN CHICKEN PICKER.
C06C- 7E C0 28   1590          JMP    LOAD     IF NOT, GET NEXT WT.
                 1600 *
                 1604 * MODULE 2 *** SELECT BEST COMBINATION OF CHICKENS ***
                 1607 *
C06F- 86 FF      1610 RUN      LDAA   #$FF     START WITH EXCESSIVE "BEST WEIGHT"
C071- B7 C0 0B   1620          STAA   BSTWT
C074- 7F C0 0A   1630          CLR    BSTCMB   AND "CHOOSE NONE" AS BEST COMB.
C077- C6 07      1640          LDAB   #$07     START PICKING 3 CHICKENS (0000 0111)
C079- CE C0 00   1650 LOOP     LDX    #$C000   FILE OF CHICKEN WEIGHTS STARTS AT C000
C07C- 4F         1660          CLRA            TOTAL "SO FAR" = 0.
C07D- F7 C0 09   1670          STAB   CPKR     RAM "CPKR" HOLDS BINARY COMBINATION.
C080- 74 C0 09   1680 NXTCHK   LSR    CPKR     SHIFT BIT PATTERN INTO CARRY.
C083- 24 04      1690          BCC    LASTQ    (0 IN CARRY MEANS DON'T ADD THIS ONE)
C085- AB 00      1700          ADDA   00,X     (1 = ADD THIS WEIGHT FROM FILE)
C087- 25 18      1710          BCS    NXTCMB   IF WT > 15 LB, 15 OZ, TOO MUCH!
C089- 7D C0 09   1720 LASTQ    TST    CPKR     ALL BINARY 1'S (ADD THIS) SHIFTED OUT?
C08C- 27 04      1730          BEQ    TSTWT    IF SO, IS THIS TOTAL WT LOWEST?
C08E- 08         1740          INX             IF NOT, MOVE TO NEXT WT IN FILE AND
C08F- 7E C0 80   1750          JMP    NXTCHK   CHECK IF CPKR SAYS TO ADD IT IN.
C092- 81 C0      1760 TSTWT    CMPA   #$C0     IS TOTAL WT 12 LBS OR MORE?
C094- 25 0B      1770          BCS    NXTCMB   NO? THEN TRY ANOTHER COMBINATION.
C096- B1 C0 0B   1780          CMPA   BSTWT    YES, THEN IS NEW TOTAL LESS THAN
C099- 24 06      1790          BCC    NXTCMB   OLD BEST WEIGHT?  IF SO,
C09B- B7 C0 0B   1800          STAA   BSTWT    REPLACE OLD BEST WEIGHT AND
C09E- F7 C0 0A   1810          STAB   BSTCMB   BEST COMB WITH NEW.
C0A1- 5C         1820 NXTCMB   INCB            COUNT TO NEXT BINARY COMBINATION.
C0A2- 26 D5      1830          BNE    LOOP     IF NOT = 00, TRY IT
                 1832 *
                 1834 * MODULE 3 *** DISPLAY BEST COMBINATION AND TOTAL WEIGHT ***
                 1836 *
C0A4- F6 C0 0A   1840 DONE     LDAB   BSTCMB   PICK UP BEST PATTERN
C0A7- 53         1850          COMB            AND PULL LEDS LOW
C0A8- F7 80 00   1860          STAB   PRTE     BY SELECTED HENS.
C0AB- B6 C0 0B   1865          LDAA   BSTWT
C0AE- 97 74      1870          STAA   BYTE     DISPLAY BEST TOTAL WEIGHT
C0B0- BD FC D0   1880 DISTOT   JSR    DISPLY   UNTIL KEYIN SENSED.
C0B3- BD FC 5E   1882          JSR    KEYIN
C0B6- 25 F8      1884          BCS    DISTOT
C0B8- BD FC 7E   1886          JSR    KEYUP
C0BB- 86 0F      1890          LDAA   #$0F     IF KEY IS "F" (FAIL)
C0BD- 91 78      1900          CMPA   COUNT      OPERATOR HANGS A NEW HEN
C0BF- 27 38      1910          BEQ    CHANGE     AT SLOT 8 & TRIES AGAIN
C0C1- 7D 00 78   1920          TST    COUNT    IF KEY IS NOT = 0,
C0C4- 26 03      1930          BNE    CKWTS    CHECK ALL WEIGHTS ON HANGERS.
C0C6- 7E C0 20   1940          JMP    FILL     (IF 0, IT'S OK; FILL NEXT BOX)
C0C9- CE C0 00   1950 CKWTS    LDX    #$C000   FOR NONZERO KEY, DISPLAY
C0CC- C6 01      1960          LDAB   #01      ALL WEIGHTS:
C0CE- F7 C0 09   1970          STAB   CPKR     START WITH HANGER #1,
C0D1- F6 C0 09   1980 LIST     LDAB   CPKR     LIGHT ALL LEDS BUT N IF
C0D4- F4 C0 0A   1990          ANDB   BSTCMB   N NOT SELECTED; LIGHT
C0D7- 26 04      2000          BNE    POINT    ONLY N IF N SELECTED.
C0D9- F6 C0 09   2010          LDAB   CPKR
C0DC- 53         2020          COMB
C0DD- 53         2030 POINT    COMB            (LOW BITS LIGHT LEDS)
C0DE- F7 80 00   2040          STAB   PRTE
C0E1- E6 00      2050          LDAB   00,X     PUT EACH WEIGHT IN
```

```
C0E3- D7 74       2060            STAB BYTE        BYTE AND
C0E5- BD FC D0    2070  DISWT     JSR  DISPLY      DISPLAY UNTIL
C0E8- BD FC 5E    2080            JSR  KEYIN       KEY IS SENSED.
C0EB- 25 F8       2085            BCS  DISWT
C0ED- BD FC 7E    2088            JSR  KEYUP
C0F0- 08          2090            INX              MOVE TO NEXT OF 8.
C0F1- 78 C0 09    2100            ASL  CPKR        IF NOT LAST,
C0F4- 24 DB       2110            BCC  LIST        LIST NEXT WEIGHT,
C0F6- 7E C0 A4    2120            JMP  DONE        DISPLAY SELECTION AND
                  2130  *                          BEST WEIGHT AGAIN.
                  2134  * MODULE 4 *** CHANGE CHICKEN ON HANGER 8 ***
                  2136  *
C0F9- CE C0 07    2140  CHANGE    LDX  #$C007      POINT TO HANGER 8.
C0FC- C6 80       2150            LDAB #$80        REPLACE HEN #8
C0FE- F7 C0 09    2160            STAB CPKR        AND TRY AGAIN.
C101- 53          2170            COMB
C102- F7 80 00    2180            STAB PRTE        LIGHT LED AT HANGER 8.
C105- 7E C0 35    2190            JMP  SCALE       WEIGH A NEW CHICKEN.
                  2200  *
```

10.3 SERIAL CHICKEN: THE RS-232 INTERFACE

Let us imagine that our chicken ranch has been very successful—we now have five operators running chicken pickers. Record keeping is beginning to be a problem. We would like to wire all of the Chicken Pickin' computers to our accounting computer in the main office and have them report directly the total weight packed in each box. We will then be able to identify such things as the number of boxes per day and the average weight per box for each station, as well as for the ranch as a whole.

In fact, this situation is fairly representative of requirements for communication between machines. Where the rate of data transmission is relatively low (thousands of bits per second, rather than the millions handled by the computer's data bus), and the distance between machines is more than a few feet, serial data transmission is the universal choice. Figure 10-4 illustrates serial data transmission.

Serial data transmission. Only one wire plus ground is required for serial data transmission, making it easier to connect and less expensive than parallel (eight-wire) interface systems. A byte of data is sent one bit at a time, least-significant bit first, by switching this line *high* or *low* after predetermined intervals of time. In our interface these intervals will be 64 μs long, allowing a data rate of 1/64 μs or 15 625 bits per second. This is called the *baud rate* of the data transmission. Ours is not a standard rate; it was chosen to minimize our system's hardware. Standard rates are 75, 110, 150, 300, 600, 1200, 2400, 4800, 9600, and 19200 baud.

The bit stream. The rest state of the transmission line is a *logic-1* voltage. The beginning of a byte of data is signaled by a transition to a *logic-0* level for one time interval. This is called the *start bit*, and data bits 0 through 7 occupy the eight time intervals following it.

Sec. 10.3 Serial Chicken: The RS-232 Interface

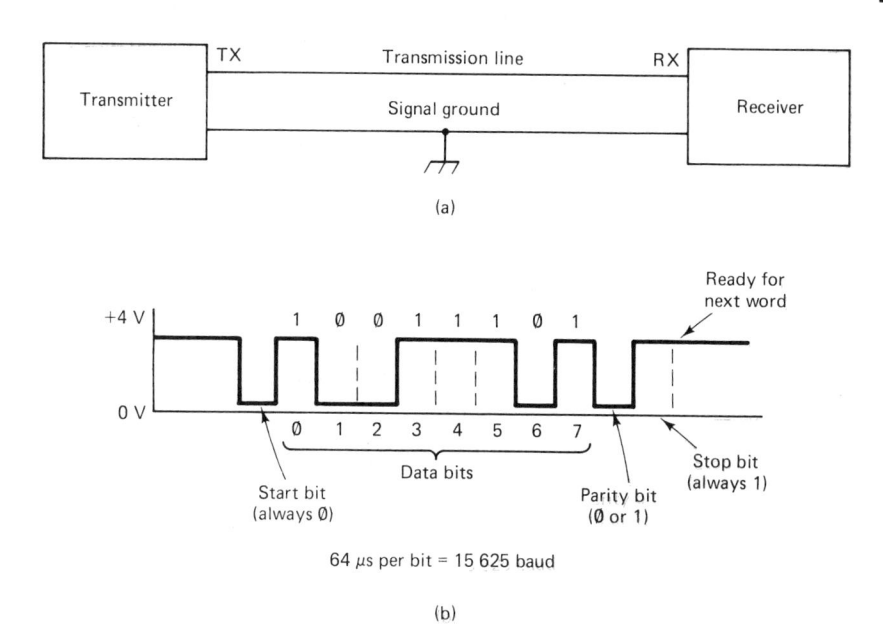

Figure 10-4 Basic wiring (a) and bit-stream structure (b) for serial data transmission with the ACIA.

A tenth bit, the *parity* bit, is transmitted after the data byte. We will be using odd parity, so if the number of 1 bits in the preceding byte is odd, the parity bit will be 0. If the number of 1 bits in the data is even, the parity bit will be 1. Thus the total number of 1 bits (including parity) is always odd for any word transmitted. The receiving computer can be programmed to test the parity of all incoming words. If any are received with an even number of 1 bits, the receiver will recognize that there has been an error in transmission and can request a correction from the transmitting computer.

The end of the data word is indicated by a *stop* bit, during which the line stays at logic 1 for one time interval. Any time after these 11 bits are completed, a new data word, beginning with a logic-0 *start* bit, can begin.

Each bit is read near the middle of its interval. There are 10 intervals from the middle of the *start* bit to the middle of the *stop* bit. The maximum timing difference between transmitter and receiver is therefore

$$\frac{\pm \frac{1}{2} \text{ interval}}{10 \text{ intervals}} = \pm 5\%$$

Specification RS-232-C, published by the Electronic Industries Association, has become the accepted standard for serial data links. Briefly, the specification requires:

- Logic 1 (called *mark*) between -5 and -15 V.
- Logic 0 (called *space*) between +5 and +15 V.

- Transmitter output not greater than +25 V open circuit. Source impedance such that a short between any two lines will cause a current not greater than 0.5 A. Signal switching transition not faster than 30 V/µs.
- Receiver load between 3000 and 7000 Ω, noninductive. Shunt capacitance of up to 2.5 nF permitted. Voltages from -3 to -25 V recognized as logic 1; +3 to +25 V as logic $\emptyset$.
- Connector pinout as shown in Fig. 10-5.

The RS-232-C specification leaves several connector pins free for user-determined applications. In addition, many of the specified pins are optional lines intended for handshaking and modem (phone line) applications. Our interface will not, strictly speaking, be an RS-232 line, because we will be using TTL levels ($\emptyset$ = 0 V; 1 = +4 V) rather than the RS-232 levels. ICs are available to translate TTL levels to RS-232 (type 75150) and the reverse (type 75154).

10.4 THE ACIA SERIAL INTERFACE CHIP

The 6850 serial interface chip takes most of the work out of linking 8-bit microcomputers with serial lines. Motorola calls the chip an ACIA—Asynchronous Communications Interface Adapter. Other manufacturers refer to a similar chip as a UART—Universal Asychronous Receiver/Transmitter. The term *asynchronous* means that the two computers need not operate on

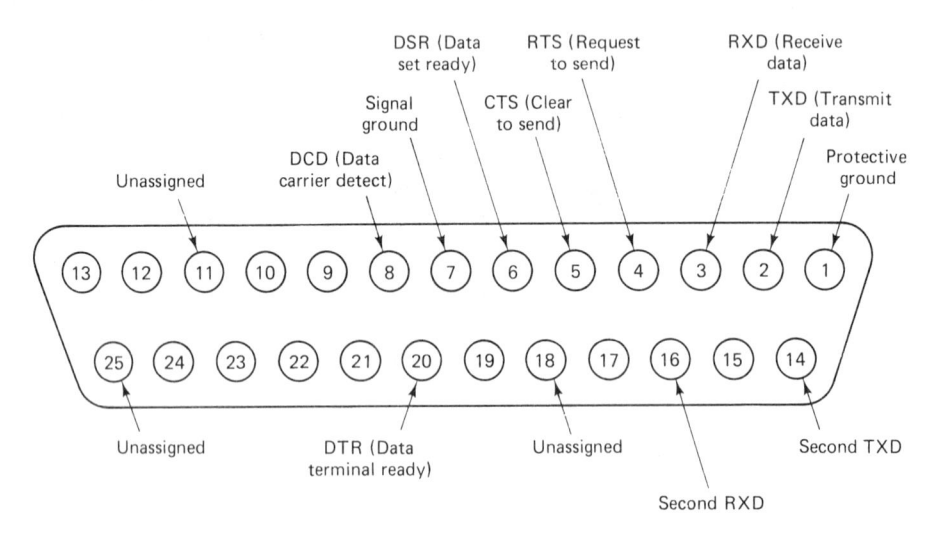

Figure 10-5 Standard RS-232C serial interface connector pinout.

Sec. 10.4   The ACIA Serial Interface Chip   217

the same clock. Figure 10-6 shows the pinout of the ACIA. The chip is activated for transmitting or receiving by decoding the address bus of the microcomputer to drive the chip-select lines at pins 8, 9, and/or 10. We will drive pin 9 ($\overline{CS2}$) from connecter pin 11 of our Microchicken computer, placing the ACIA at base address $6000. The receiver, transmitter, and E clocks of the ACIA (pins 3, 4, and 14) are all driven from the microcomputer's E clock.

Transmit mode. The eight ACIA data lines read data from the computer data bus in the transmit mode, which is selected when R/$\overline{W}$ goes high.

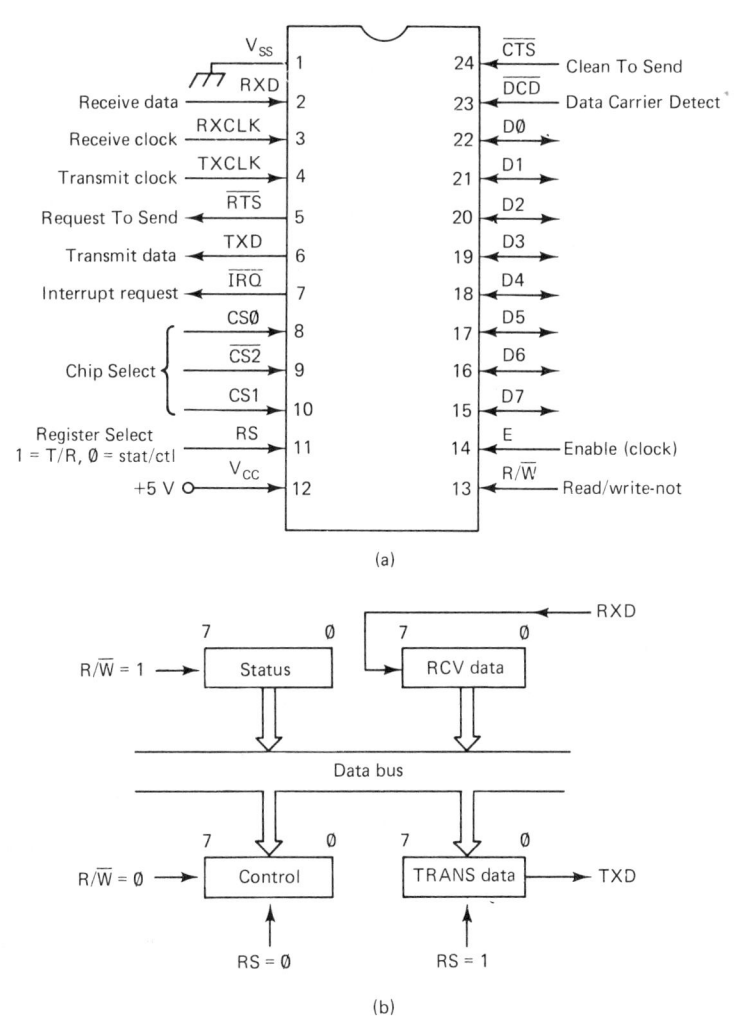

Figure 10-6 The 6850 serial interface chip: (a) pin functions and (b) register access.

This data must then be formatted for serial transmission with *start, parity,* and *stop* bits. The format shown in Fig. 10-5 is only one of a variety of data formats available with the ACIA. The transmitter and receiver must use the same data format, of course, and this is selected by writing a control word into the ACIA control register.

The control register is selected when RS (register select, pin 11) is *low* and R/W̄ is low. RS is usually connected to address line A0, so the control register is accessed in our system by writing to address $6000.

Bits 0 and 1 of the control register select the *reset* function (a mandatory chip-initialization procedure), and determine the clock division ratio, (*clock rate/baud rate*).

Control Bit		Function
1	0	(Baud/Reset)
0	0	Baud = CLK
0	1	CLK ÷ 16
1	0	CLK ÷ 64
1	1	Master reset

We will drive the CLK inputs from the 1-MHz *E clock* for convenience, resulting in a baud rate of 1 MHz/64 = 15 625 Hz. More extensive systems would use external clocks or dividers to achieve a standard baud rate.

The format of the bit string is selected by control-register bits 2, 3, and 4, according to the following table.

Control Bit			Bit Functions
4	3	2	(Word Format)
0	0	0	7 data, even parity, 2 stop
0	0	1	7 data, odd parity, 2 stop
0	1	0	7 data, even parity, 1 stop
0	1	1	7 data, odd parity, 1 stop
1	0	0	8 data, no parity, 2 stop
1	0	1	8 data, no parity, 1 stop
1	1	0	8 data, even parity, 1 stop
1	1	1	8 data, odd parity, 1 stop

All formats have one start bit (low level) preceding the bits listed. The total number of bits transmitted per word, including the start bit, can be 10 or 11. In the 7-data-bit modes the high-order bit (D7) is stripped off before transmitting.

Bits 5, 6, and 7 of the control register select the transmit and receive conditions under which the ACIA's IRQ output will signal the processor for

Sec. 10.4 The ACIA Serial Interface Chip

an interrupt. We will not be using interrupts, so we will keep all three bits at 0.

Our control word to address $6000 will then be 0000 0011 or $03 to initialize the ACIA, and 0001 1110 or $1E to format for 8 data bits, odd parity, baud rate = $E \div 64$.

The ACIA's data register is accessed by pulling the RS line (via A0) high and writing a word to the *transmit data register*. A STORE command to address $6001 does it. The bit stream is automatically sent out the TXD pin, picked up by the RXD pin on the receiving computer's ACIA, and stored in its *receive data register*.

The receive mode is entered by simply reading the ACIA data register. With R/$\overline{W}$ high it is actually the separate *receive data register* that is accessed. The ACIA data lines then output the data received via the RXD line. In 7-data-bit modes, bit 7 = 0.

It may have occurred to you that the computer can execute several hundred instructions during the 0.7 ms that it takes to transmit one byte, serially, at 15 625 baud. How do we keep the receiving computer from reading bytes faster than the transmitter sends them? The answer lies in the ACIA status register.

The ACIA status register is accessed by a *read* with the RS pin (line A0) low. It contains 8 independent bits, with logic 1 indicating the following conditions.

Status Bit	Condition
0	Receive data register full; new data available to read.
1	Transmit data register empty; clear to send next byte.
2	Data carrier detect. } Interface with modem chip for telephone connection
3	Clear to send.
4	Framing error; stop bit not received.
5	Receiver overrun; second word loaded into recieve data register before first word read out.
6	Parity error; number of 1 bits received not as selected.
7	Interrupt request generated ($\overline{IRQ}$ output low).

To ensure that new data is being read, the receiving computer simply monitors the status register bit 0 every few milliseconds. When it goes high, the ACIA has received a new word. When the *receive data register* is read, bit 0 of the status register is automatically reset to 0 until the transmitter delivers another word. To minimize the possibility of reading erroneous data, the receiving computer should also check status bits 4, 5, and 6 for the error flags listed above.

In our application the 6802 computer sends one word at a time, and that only after a fairly extensive selection process involving several delays by the human operator. There is, therefore, no danger that the transmitter will attempt to send new words before the old words have had time to be shifted out. In rapid-transmission systems we would have the transmitting computer check that status bit 1 was high before loading a new word into the *transmit data register*. This bit goes low automatically as the serial data is sent.

10.5 THE APPLE CONNECTION

This section presents hardware details and programming for serial data transmission from the Chicken Pickin' computer to an Apple II or an Apple-compatible computer.[1] The interface is quite straightforward, and should be easy to adapt to any desktop computer with these features:

- BASIC language
- Access to data lines $\emptyset$—7
- Access to address line A$\emptyset$
- Access to an output-select line (high or low active)
- Access to a R/$\overline{W}$ line
- Access to a 1-MHz (±3%) clock signal

Figure 10-7 shows the wiring diagram for the Chicken-to-Apple interface. Figure 10-8(a) and (b) is a true-size master art for an ACIA interface board which can be plugged directly into an Apple peripheral slot. Socket space is provided for an optional IC which could be a divider to achieve a standard baud rate or a buffer to convert the output to RS-232-standard voltages. Note that the card is to be inserted in the peripheral slot with the components on the operator's right-hand side. This is opposite from commercial boards, but it permits an easier-to-etch, easier-to-wire board.

The software for the Chicken Picker requires only a one-line modification and seven added lines to the Analog Chicken program of Section 10-2. Here is a listing of the changes.

[1] *Apple* is a registered trademark of Apple Computer Co.

Sec. 10.5   The Apple Connection

Modifications to Analog Chicken Listing

```
                1000 *  -----------------------------------------------------------
                1010 *         CHICKEN APPLE ***** SERIAL REPORT TO APPLE *****
                1020 *

                        :Modify line 1940:

C0C6- 7E C1 08  1940           JMP    REPORT   IF ACCEPTED, SEND VIA ACIA.

                        .. .. .. .. .. ..

                2210 * MODULE 5 *** OUTPUT TOTAL WEIGHT VIA ACIA ***
                2220 *
C108- 86 03     2230 REPORT    LDAA   #$03     MASTER RESET VIA ACIA
C10A- B7 60 00  2290           STAA   SERC     SERIAL CONTROL RESISTER.
C10D- 86 1E     2300           LDAA   #$1E     SET FORMAT FOR 8 BITS,
C10F- B7 60 00  2310           STAA   SERC     ODD PARITY (0001 1110)
                2320 *
C112- B6 C0 0B  2330           LDAA   BSTWT    OUTPUT BEST WEIGHT
C115- B7 60 01  2340           STAA   SERD     TO SERIAL DATA REGISTER.
                2360 *
C118- 7E C0 20  2410           JMP    FILL     FILL EMPTY HANGERS.
```

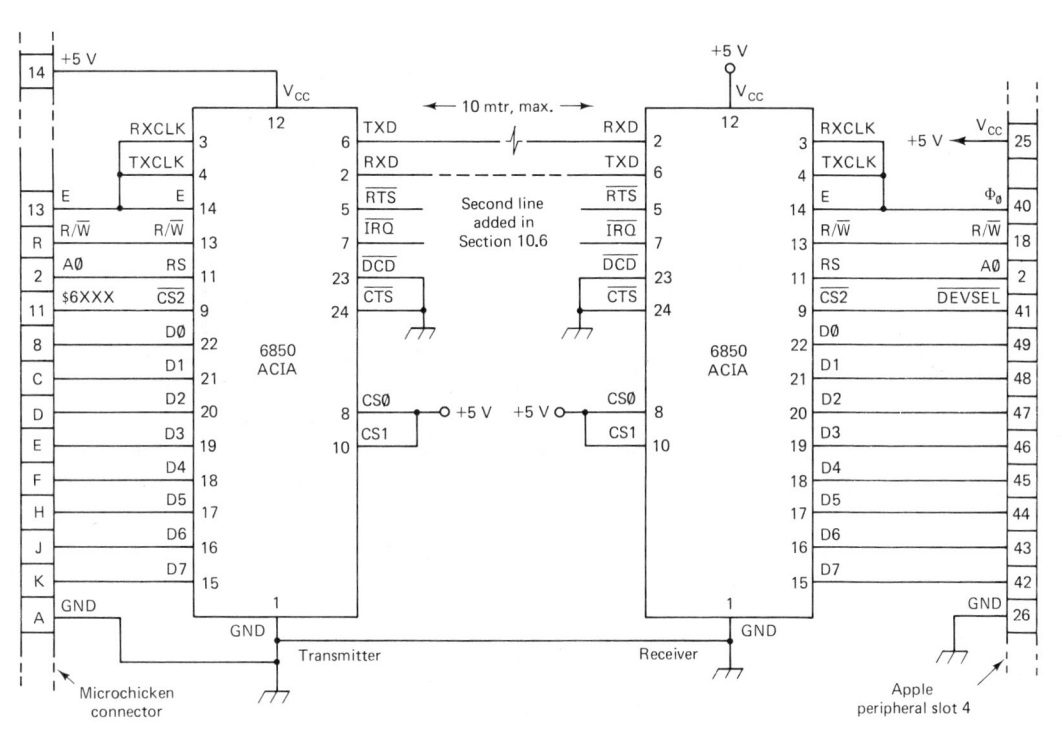

Figure 10-7 Serial interface hardware to permit Microchicken to send data to an Apple II computer.

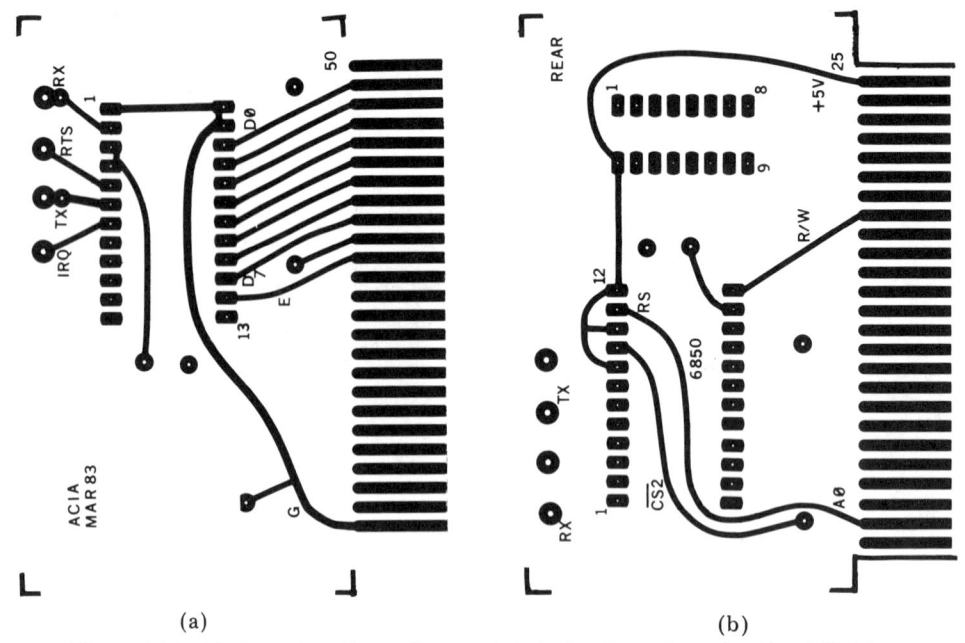

Figure 10-8 Master art patterns for a printed-circuit card to plug the ACIA into an Apple peripheral slot; component side (a) and foil side (b).

The program for the Apple is written in BASIC. It receives the total weights from the Chicken Picker and displays them, together with the box number, on the CRT. The POKE of data 03 to address 49 344 (decimal) resets the Apple's ACIA. This address ($C0C0) is the base address for peripheral slot 4, and accesses the ACIA control register. The POKE of decimal 30 ($1E) sets the 8-bit, odd-parity, ÷ 64 mode for compatability with the transmitting computer. The Apple clock is actually 1.023 MHz, but this difference does not exceed the ACIA timing tolerance.

The PEEK command is BASIC's way of reading a byte of data from a specified memory location. PEEK (49 344) reads the status register. The IF statement produces a result of a 0 if SR bit 0 = 0, or 0.5 if bit 0 = 1. It keeps the computer in a *wait* loop until the status register shows the *receive data register full*, whereupon the *receive data register* is read at address 49 345 ($C0C1). Here is the BASIC program listing.

BASIC Listing: Apple Reads ACIA

```
 5   N = 1
10   POKE 49344, 03
20   POKE 49344, 30
```

```
30  SR = PEEK (49344)
40  IF SR / 2 - INT (SR / 2) < 0.1 THEN GOTO 30
50  DA = PEEK (49345)
60  PRINT "WEIGHT NO. ";N;" EQUALS ";DA
70  N = N + 1
80  GOTO 30
```

10.6 LINEAR CHICKEN: A COMPUTER BRAIN TRANSPLANT

If we are realistic, we will have to admit that the scale we have designed for the Chicken Picker is likely to be either very expensive or very inaccurate. This is because the potentiometer, the spring and pulley used to drive it, and the A/D converter are likely to be nonlinear. Thus, if the scale is calibrated so that 2 pounds 0 ounces registers a count of $20, it is not likely that 4 pounds 0 ounces will register a count of $40. We could improve the linearity by using a linear wirewound potentiometer, a more sophisticated spring and drive mechanism, and a faster comparator in the A/D converter, but there is an easier way.

A graph of weight versus counts for the A/D converter is shown in Figure 10-9 for a hypothetical system. The counts may not equal—or even bear a linear relationship to—the weights, but each count does correspond to a unique weight. We have plenty of RAM left in our Chicken Pickin' computer. Why not store a table of weights versus counts in RAM? Then we could read the D/A converter and go into the table to find the corresponding weight, completely bypassing the problem of component nonlinearity.

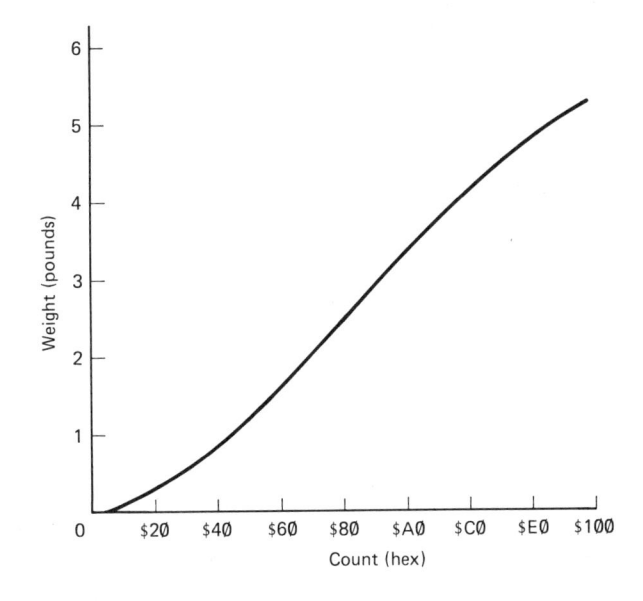

Figure 10-9 Representative weight versus count for an A/D converter scale. Nonlinearity is inevitable.

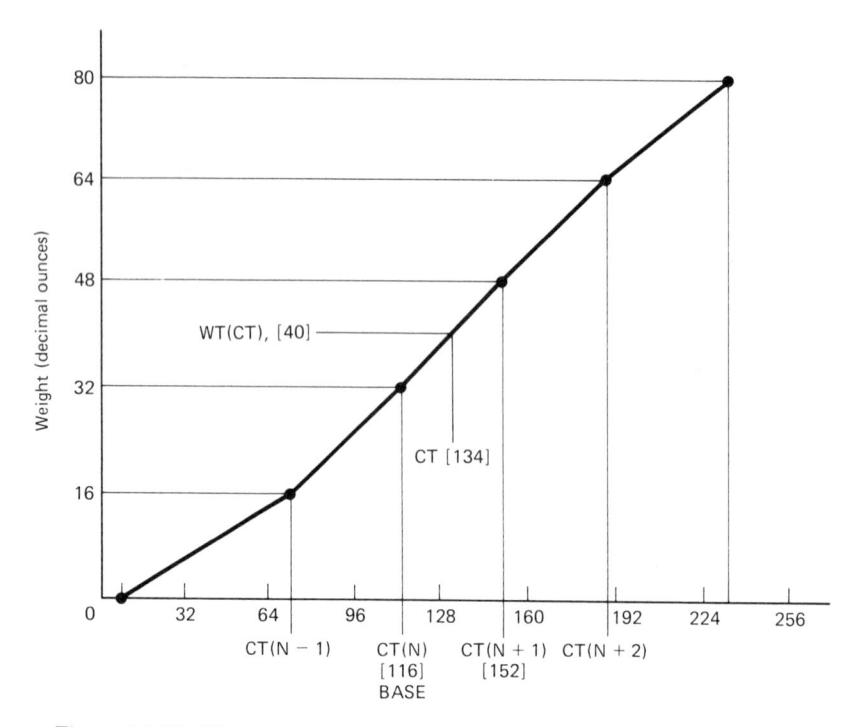

Figure 10-10 Linear segments approximate the curve of Fig. 10-9. A BASIC language program develops a file of weights, WT(CT), for each numeric count, CT, from the A/D converter. Example numbers appear in brackets.

Thinking a little further, it becomes clear that this lookup-table idea will allow us to read out the scale in just about any units we like—pounds and ounces this morning, pounds and tenths of a pound this afternoon, tenths and hundredths of a kilogram tomorrow. All we have to do is reload the data in the RAM table.

Automated calibration. Loading 256 values in the table by hand could prove quite tedious, even if we save it on tape so that it only needs to be done once. Generating the table could prove even more tedious. Aren't computers supposed to be able to automate this sort of thing? Absolutely!

Look at Fig. 10-10. The previous graph has here been approximated by five straight-line segments. With the computational power of BASIC we could have the Apple *compute* all 256 table values from only six data points. And with the serial data link we could have them automatically loaded into the Chicken Picker's RAM. Here is the procedure.

1. The operator places standard weights of 0, 1, 2, 3, 4, and 5 pounds, in succession, on the scale. The Chicken Picker transmits the six corresponding counts from the A/D converter to the Apple via the ACIA.

2. The Apple stores the six counts as CT(∅) through CT(5).
3. The Apple calculates the weights corresponding to all counts between CT(∅) and CT(5) using

$$WT(CT) = BASE + 16 \frac{(CT - CT(N))}{CT(N+1) - CT(N)}$$

where BASE is the weight of the last 1-pound mark, CT(N) is the count at the last 1-pound mark, and CT(N+1) is the count at the next 1-pound mark. As an example, if BASE = 32 ounces ($2∅) and current count CT is halfway between CT(N) and CT(N+1), current weight WT(CT) = 32 ounces + 8 ounces ($28).
4. The Apple stores all values of WT(CT) as they are calculated, and when finished, displays them on the screen as they are sent to the Chicken Picker via the ACIA.
5. The Chicken Picker stores the values in a RAM table and uses the table for weight display and optimum packaging selection.

The complete listings for the BASIC program and the 6802 program are given below. Lines 1540 through 1620 of the 6802 SCALE routine are alterations to exchange the A/D converter count (RAMP) for the weight from the file (stored in BYTE).

The LINEARIZER LOADER module outputs the counts for each standard weight via the ACIA (lines 2700 through 3050) and stores the data sent back from the Apple in the weight file (lines 3070 through 3180). CALIB initializes the PIA and ACIA. STDWT and ADCON is a rewrite of the earlier SCALE routine to weigh the 1-pound standards. It also outputs the corresponding counts via the ACIA. BYPAS loops back to the scale routine until the counts for all standard weights are transmitted. LOOK waits for the ACIA status bit ∅ to indicate a *receive data register full* condition, wherepon it reads the receive data register and stores the data word in the weight file.

The 6802 listing is given for loading into RAM starting at $C∅1∅. It can be transferred to the low half of a 2716 EPROM if the seven underlined bytes are changed, C∅ to F8 and C1 to F9. A copy of the system monitor can then be burned into the high half of this EPROM, which can now serve as a monitor with coresident chicken picker.

The BASIC program sends data as quickly as it can, checking only that the transmit data register is empty before poking the next weight byte. Still, there is no danger of an overrun (transmitted word rate exceeding receiver read rate) because BASIC is very much slower than machine language. A single POKE instruction, for example, takes about 5 ms. Where two machines of comparable speed are interfaced it will be necessary to either slow down the transmitter or employ some form of handshaking.

BASIC Program to Linearize Chicken Scale

```
100 REM  - *****  SCALE LINEARIZER WITH AUTOMATIC INPUT. ******
105 REM  -         USE WITH "LINEAR CHICKEN" 6802 PROGRAM
110 REM  - OPERATOR PLACES WEIGHTS OF 0, 1, 2, 3, 4, & 5 POUNDS
120 REM  - ON SCALE, PRESSING ANY KEY AFTER EACH WEIGHT SETTLES.
130 REM  - PROGRAM INPUTS ASSOCIATED HEX COUNTS FROM SCALE (PEEK)
140 REM  - AND CALCULATES A TABLE OF WEIGHTS (LBS & OZS) VS. COUNTS.
150 REM  - TABLE IS THEN POKED INTO REMOTE COMPUTER MEMORY.
200 DIM CT(255),WT(255)
210 POKE 49344,03: REM      - ACIA MASTER RESET (0000 0011)
220 POKE 49344,30: REM - ACIA 8 BITS, ODD PARITY, 1/64 CLOCK (0001 1110)
230 FOR N = 0 TO 5
240 SR = PEEK (49344): REM     - PICK UP ACIA STATUS REGISTER.
250 IF SR / 2 -  INT (SR / 2) < 0.1 THEN  GOTO 240: REM  - HANG UP UNTIL
    BIT 0 = 1 (RECEIVE DATA REGISTER FULL).
255 IF SR > 15 THEN  PRINT "RECEIVE ERROR; STATUS READS DECIMAL ";SR
260 CT(N) =  PEEK (49345): REM     - PICK UP DATA ON 1-LB INCREMENTS.
270 PRINT "COUNT FOR ";N;" LBS IS ";CT(N)
280 NEXT N
300 REM  - CALCULATE TABLE
310 BASE = 0:ACCUM = 0: REM     - ACCUM IS CURRENT ACCUMULATED COUNT.
320 FOR N = 0 TO 4
330 BASE = ACCUM: REM      - BASE IS COUNT AT LAST 1-LB MARK.
340 FOR CT = CT(N) TO CT(N + 1)
350 ACCUM = BASE + 16 * (CT - CT(N)) / (CT(N + 1) - CT(N))
360 WT(CT) =  INT (ACCUM + .5): REM   - INTERPOLATE WEIGHT BETWEEN MARKS.
370 IF CT / 5 =  INT (CT / 5) THEN   PRINT "COUNT = ";CT,"WEIGHT = ";WT(CT
    ): REM - PRINT WEIGHT FOR EVERY 5TH COUNT.
380 NEXT CT: REM     - NEXT COUNT.
390 NEXT N: REM     - NEXT 1-LB MARK.
500 REM  - OUTPUT TABLE TO REMOTE COMPUTER:
510 FOR CT = CT(0) TO CT(N)
520 TD =  PEEK (49344): REM - PICK UP ACIA STATUS REGISTER.
530 TD =  INT (TD / 2): REM - SHIFT BIT 1 TO BIT-0 POSITION.
540 IF TD / 2 -  INT (TD / 2) < 0.1 THEN  GOTO 520: REM   - IF BIT 2 (TRA
    NS DATA REG EMPTY) = 0, WAIT UNTIL REGISTER IS EMPTY.
550 POKE 49345,WT(CT): REM     - TRANSMIT WEIGHT FOR EACH COUNT.
560 CLICK =  PEEK ( - 16336): REM     - CLICK SPEAKER ON EACH BYTE SENT.
570 NEXT CT
595 N = 1
600 POKE 49344,03
610 POKE 49344,30: REM - RESET ACIA; FORMAT 8 BIT, ODD PARITY.
620 SR =  PEEK (49344)
630 IF SR / 2 -  INT (SR / 2) < 0.1 THEN  GOTO 620: REM   WAIT FOR RECEIVE
    DATA FULL.
640 DA =  PEEK (49345): REM     - PICK UP TOTAL WEIGHT.
650 IF DA < 200 THEN  GOTO 700
660 FOR CYCLE = 1 TO 40
670 CLICK =  PEEK ( - 16336): REM - CLICKS IF OVER 8 OZ EXCESS.
680 NEXT CYCLE
700 PRINT "WEIGHT NO. ";N;" EQUALS ";DA
710 N = N + 1
720 GOTO 620
```

Linear Chicken Program (Start at $C150 to Calibrate)

```
              1000 *  ---------------------------------------------------------
              1010 *       LINEAR CHICKEN  *****  APPLE CALIBRATES SCALE  *****
              1020 *       USE WITH APPLESOFT "SCALE LINEARIZER" PROGRAM.
              1030 *
C008-         1040 RAMP    .EQ   $C008    COUNTS UP UNTIL COMPARATOR SWITCHES.
C009-         1050 CPKR    .EQ   $C009    CHICKEN PICKER HOLDS TEMP BINARY COMB.
```

Sec. 10.6 Linear Chicken: A Computer Brain Transplant

```
C00A-               1060    BSTCMB  .EQ     $C00A       ANSWER (BINARY COMBINATION TO CHOOSE)
C00B-               1070    BSTWT   .EQ     $C00B       BEST WEIGHT TOTAL (LBS & OZ.)
C00C-               1080    HIX     .EQ     $C00C       POINTS TO FILE OF WEIGHTS
C00D-               1090    LOX     .EQ     $C00D       VIA X REGISTER.
C00E-               1100    HIBUF   .EQ     $C00E       SAVES HI X & COUNTS DISPLY LOOPS.
C00F-               1110    LOBUF   .EQ     $C00F       SAVES LO X & COUNTS NO. OF STD WTS.
FC8B-               1120    DELAY   .EQ     $FC8B       MONITOR TIME DELAY VIA "CLOCK"
FCD0-               1130    DISPLY  .EQ     $FCD0       MONITOR DISPLAY ROUTINE; 6 MS.
FC5E-               1140    KEYIN   .EQ     $FC5E       MONITOR CLEARS CARRY IF KEY IN.
FC7E-               1150    KEYUP   .EQ     $FC7E       MONITOR WAITS FOR KEY RELEASE.
0074-               1160    BYTE    .EQ     $74         RAM USED BY MONITOR FOR DISPLY.
0076-               1170    CLOCK   .EQ     $76         PASSES VALUE TO DELAY SR (FF = 1.2 S)
0078-               1180    COUNT   .EQ     $78         RETURNS VALUE OF KEY INPUT.
4002-               1190    PB      .EQ     $4002       PIA PORT B.
4003-               1200    CRB     .EQ     $4003       CONTROL REGISTER FOR PORT B.
A000-               1210    PRTD    .EQ     $A000       OUTPUT-ONLY PORT.
8000-               1220    PRTE    .EQ     $8000       8 LED OUTPUTS.
6000-               1230    SERC    .EQ     $6000       SERIAL I/O CONTROL/STATUS.
6001-               1240    SERD    .EQ     $6001       SERIAL I/O DATA.
                    1250            .OR     $C010       START PROG ASSEMBLY AT RAM $C010
                    1260            .TA     $4010       STORE CODE IN APPLE RAM AT $4010
                    1270    * ------------------------------------------------------------
                    1280    *
C010- 7F 40 03      1290    START   CLR     CRB         GET DIRECTION REGISTER.
C013- 7F 40 02      1300            CLR     PB          SET ALL LINES AS INPUTS.
C016- 86 04         1310            LDAA    #04         ACCESS DATA REGISTER
C018- B7 40 03      1320            STAA    CRB         NEXT TIME.
C01B- C6 FF         1330            LDAB    #$FF        INDICATE "ALL HANGERS EMPTY"
C01D- F7 C0 0A      1340            STAB    BSTCMB      TO START.
C020- C6 01         1350    FILL    LDAB    #01         FILL ALL EMPTY HANGERS.
C022- F7 C0 09      1360            STAB    CPKR
C025- CE C0 00      1370            LDX     #$C000      FILE STARTS AT C000.
                    1380    *
                    1390    * MODULE 1 *** INPUT WEIGHTS AT EMPTY LOCATIONS ***
                    1400    *
C028- F6 C0 09      1410    LOAD    LDAB    CPKR        IDENTIFY 1 OF 8 HANGERS.
C02B- 53            1420            COMB                DISPLAY 1 OF 8 LEDS
C02C- F7 80 00      1430            STAB    PRTE
C02F- 53            1440            COMB                IF NO CH1CKEN LEFT AT
C030- F4 C0 0A      1450            ANDB    BSTCMB      THIS LOCATION,
C033- 27 4A         1460            BEQ     NXTPOS      (SKIP IF ONE IS THERE)
                    1470
C035- 7F C0 08      1480    SCALE   CLR     RAMP        WEIGH IN A CHICKEN.
C038- 7C C0 08      1490    ATOD    INC     RAMP        RAM "RAMP" COUNTS UP UNTIL COMPARATOR
C03B- B6 C0 08      1500            LDAA    RAMP        OUTPUTS A "1" (5 MS MAX).
C03E- B7 A0 00      1510            STAA    PRTD        OUTPUT COUNT TO A/D CONV.
C041- B6 40 02      1520            LDAA    PB          CHECK COMPARATOR OUTPUT
C044- 84 20         1530            ANDA    #$20        ON BIT 5 ONLY.
C046- 27 F0         1540            BEQ     ATOD        LOW = KEEP COUNTING.
C048- 86 C2         1550            LDAA    #$C2        FILE OF WEIGHTS STARTS AT $C200.
C04A- B7 C0 0C      1560            STAA    HIX         JUMP INTO FILE AS DEEP AS
C04D- B6 C0 08      1570            LDAA    RAMP        COUNTED OFF BY "RAMP" AND
C050- B7 C0 0D      1580            STAA    LOX         PICK UP CORRESPONDING WEIGHT
C053- FF C0 0E      1590            STX     HIBUF
C056- FE C0 0C      1600            LDX     HIX         VIA X INDEX,
C059- A6 00         1610            LDAA    00,X        AND STORE
C05B- 97 74         1620            STAA    BYTE        IN "BYTE" FOR DISPLAY.
C05D- FE C0 0E      1630            LDX     HIBUF       REPLACE VALUE OF X.
C060- BD FC D0      1640            JSR     DISPLY      6 MS OF WEIGHT DISPLAY,
C063- 7F A0 00      1650            CLR     PRTD        LET COMPARATOR RECOVER,
C066- BD FC D0      1660            JSR     DISPLY
C069- BD FC 5E      1670            JSR     KEYIN       LOOK FOR KEY PRESS (CRY CLR).
C06C- 25 C7         1680            BCS     SCALE       ANY KEY WILL LOAD WEIGHT.
C06E- 96 74         1690            LDAA    BYTE        PICK UP WEIGHT,
C070- A7 00         1700            STAA    00,X        PUT IN FILE.
C072- C6 A0         1710            LDAB    #$A0        160 LOOPS X 6 MS/LOOP
```

228   Chicken Pickin': An Industrial Microcomputer Application   Chap. 10

```
C074- F7 C0 0E  1720          STAB  HIBUF    (KEEP COUNT OF LOOPS IN RAM)
C077- BD FC D0  1730 HOLD     JSR   DISPLY   HOLDS WEIGHT DISPLAY
C07A- 7A C0 0E  1740          DEC   HIBUF    FOR 1 SEC.
C07D- 26 F8     1750          BNE   HOLD
C07F- 08        1760 NXTPOS   INX            MOVE TO NEXT SLOT IN FILE.
C080- 78 C0 09  1770          ASL   CPKR     IF END OF FILE
C083- 27 03     1780          BEQ   RUN      RUN CHICKEN PICKER.
C085- 7E C0 28  1790          JMP   LOAD     IF NOT, GET NEXT WT.
                1800 *
                1810 * MODULE 2 *** SELECT BEST COMBINATION OF CHICKENS ***
                1820 *
C088- 86 FF     1830 RUN      LDAA  #$FF     START WITH EXCESSIVE "BEST WEIGHT"
C08A- B7 C0 0B  1840          STAA  BSTWT
C08D- 7F C0 0A  1850          CLR   BSTCMB   AND "CHOOSE NONE" AS BEST COMB.
C090- C6 07     1860          LDAB  #$07     START PICKING 3 CHICKENS (0000 0111)
C092- CE C0 00  1870 LOOP     LDX   #$C000   FILE OF CHICKEN WEIGHTS STARTS AT C000
C095- 4F        1880          CLRA           TOTAL "SO FAR" = 0.
C096- F7 C0 09  1890          STAB  CPKR     RAM "CPKR" HOLDS BINARY COMBINATION.
C099- 74 C0 09  1900 NXTCHK   LSR   CPKR     SHIFT BIT PATTERN INTO CARRY.
C09C- 24 04     1910          BCC   LASTQ    (0 IN CARRY MEANS DON'T ADD THIS ONE)
C09E- AB 00     1920          ADDA  00,X     (1 = ADD THIS WEIGHT FROM FILE)
C0A0- 25 18     1930          BCS   NXTCMB   IF WT > 15 LB, 15 OZ, TOO MUCH!
C0A2- 7D C0 09  1940 LASTQ    TST   CPKR     ALL BINARY 1'S (ADD THIS) SHIFTED OUT?
C0A5- 27 04     1950          BEQ   TSTWT    IF SO, IS THIS TOTAL WT LOWEST?
C0A7- 08        1960          INX            IF NOT, MOVE TO NEXT WT IN FILE AND
C0A8- 7E C0 99  1970          JMP   NXTCHK   CHECK IF CPKR SAYS TO ADD IT IN.
C0AB- 81 C0     1980 TSTWT    CMPA  #$C0     IS TOTAL WT 12 LBS OR MORE?
C0AD- 25 0B     1990          BCS   NXTCMB   NO? THEN TRY ANOTHER COMBINATION.
C0AF- B1 C0 0B  2000          CMPA  BSTWT    YES, THEN IS NEW TOTAL LESS THAN
C0B2- 24 06     2010          BCC   NXTCMB   OLD BEST WEIGHT?  IF SO,
C0B4- B7 C0 0B  2020          STAA  BSTWT    REPLACE OLD BEST WEIGHT AND
C0B7- F7 C0 0A  2030          STAB  BSTCMB   BEST COMB WITH NEW.
C0BA- 5C        2040 NXTCMB   INCB           COUNT TO NEXT BINARY COMBINATION.
C0BB- 26 D5     2050          BNE   LOOP     IF NOT = 00, TRY IT
                2060 *
                2070 * MODULE 3 *** DISPLAY BEST COMBINATION AND TOTAL WEIGHT ***
                2080 *
C0BD- F6 C0 0A  2090 DONE     LDAB  BSTCMB   PICK UP BEST PATTERN
C0C0- 53        2100          COMB           AND PULL LEDS LOW
C0C1- F7 80 00  2110          STAB  PRTE     BY SELECTED HENS.
C0C4- B6 C0 0B  2120          LDAA  BSTWT
C0C7- 97 74     2130          STAA  BYTE
C0C9- BD FC D0  2140 DISTOT   JSR   DISPLY   DISPLAY BEST TOTAL WEIGHT
C0CC- BD FC 5E  2150          JSR   KEYIN    UNTIL KEYIN SENSED.
C0CF- 25 F8     2160          BCS   DISTOT
C0D1- BD FC 7E  2170          JSR   KEYUP
C0D4- 86 0F     2180          LDAA  #$0F     IF KEY IS "F" (FAIL)
C0D6- 91 78     2190          CMPA  COUNT    OPERATOR HANGS A NEW HEN
C0D8- 27 38     2200          BEQ   CHANGE   AT SLOT 8 & TRIES AGAIN.
C0DA- 7D 00 78  2210          TST   COUNT    IF KEY IS NOT = 0,
C0DD- 26 03     2220          BNE   CKWTS    CHECK ALL WEIGHTS ON HANGERS.
C0DF- 7E C1 21  2230          JMP   REPORT   (IF 0, TAKE IT; FILL NEXT BOX)
C0E2- CE C0 00  2240 CKWTS    LDX   #$C000   FOR NONZERO KEY, DISPLAY
C0E5- C6 01     2250          LDAB  #01      ALL WEIGHTS:
C0E7- F7 C0 09  2260          STAB  CPKR     START WITH HANGER #1,
C0EA- F6 C0 09  2270 LIST     LDAB  CPKR     LIGHT ALL LEDS BUT N IF
C0ED- F4 C0 0A  2280          ANDB  BSTCMB   N NOT SELECTED; LIGHT
C0F0- 26 04     2290          BNE   POINT    ONLY N IF N SELECTED.
C0F2- F6 C0 09  2300          LDAB  CPKR
C0F5- 53        2310          COMB
C0F6- 53        2320 POINT    COMB           (LOW BITS LIGHT LEDS)
C0F7- F7 80 00  2330          STAB  PRTE
C0FA- E6 00     2340          LDAB  00,X     PUT EACH WEIGHT IN
C0FC- D7 74     2350          STAB  BYTE     BYTE AND
C0FE- BD FC D0  2360 DISWT    JSR   DISPLY   DISPLAY UNTIL
```

Sec. 10.6 Linear Chicken: A Computer Brain Transplant

```
C101- BD FC 5E   2370          JSR    KEYIN     KEY IS SENSED.
C104- 25 F8      2380          BCS    DISWT
C106- BD FC 7E   2390          JSR    KEYUP
C109- 08         2400          INX              MOVE TO NEXT OF 8.
C10A- 78 C0 09   2410          ASL    CPKR      IF NOT LAST,
C10D- 24 DB      2420          BCC    LIST      LIST NEXT WEIGHT,
C10F- 7E C0 BD   2430          JMP    DONE      DISPLAY SELECTION AND
                 2440 *                         BEST WEIGHT AGAIN.
                 2450 * MODULE 4 *** CHANGE CHICKEN ON HANGER 8 ***
                 2460 *
C112- CE C0 07   2470 CHANGE   LDX    #$C007    POINT TO HANGER 8.
C115- C6 80      2480          LDAB   #$80      REPLACE HEN #8
C117- F7 C0 09   2490          STAB   CPKR      AND TRY AGAIN.
C11A- 53         2500          COMB
C11B- F7 80 00   2510          STAB   PRTE      LIGHT LED AT HANGER 8.
C11E- 7E C0 35   2520          JMP    SCALE     WEIGH A NEW CHICKEN.
                 2530 *
                 2540 * MODULE 5 *** OUTPUT TOTAL WEIGHT VIA ACIA ***
                 2550 *
C121- 86 03      2560 REPORT   LDAA   #$03      MASTER RESET VIA ACIA
C123- B7 60 00   2570          STAA   SERC      SERIAL CONTROL RESISTER.
C126- 86 1E      2580          LDAA   #$1E      SET FORMAT FOR 8 BITS,
C128- B7 60 00   2590          STAA   SERC      ODD PARITY (0001 1110)
                 2600 *
C12B- B6 C0 0B   2610          LDAA   BSTWT     OUTPUT BEST WEIGHT
C12E- B7 60 01   2620          STAA   SERD      TO SERIAL DATA REGISTER.
                 2630 *
C131- 7E C0 20   2640          JMP    FILL      FILL EMPTY HANGERS.
                 2650 * ---------------------------------------------------
                 2660 * LINEARIZER LOADER ***** INTERFACE WITH APPLE II *****
                 2670 *
                 2680          .OR    $C150
                 2690          .TA    $4150
                 2700 *
C150- 7F 40 03   2710 CALIB    CLR    CRB       GET DDRB
C153- 7F 40 02   2720          CLR    PB        ALL INPUTS
C156- 86 04      2730          LDAA   #04
C158- B7 40 03   2740          STAA   CRB       DATA REGISTER NEXT
C15B- 86 03      2750          LDAA   #$03      MASTER RESET ACIA
C15D- B7 60 00   2760          STAA   SERC
C160- 86 1E      2770          LDAA   #$1E      FORMAT = 8-BIT, ODD
C162- B7 60 00   2780          STAA   SERC      PARITY.
C165- 7F C0 0F   2790          CLR    LOBUF
C168- 7F 00 74   2800 STDWT    CLR    BYTE      SCALE ROUTINE
C16B- 7C 00 74   2810 ADCON    INC    BYTE      "BYTE" COUNTS UP UNTIL
C16E- 96 74      2820          LDAA   BYTE
C170- B7 A0 00   2830          STAA   PRTD      COMPARATOR APPLIES A "1"
C173- B6 40 02   2840          LDAA   PB        TO PORT B, BIT 5.
C176- 84 20      2850          ANDA   #$20
C178- 27 F1      2860          BEQ    ADCON
C17A- BD FC D0   2870          JSR    DISPLY    DISPLAY COUNT AND
C17D- 7F A0 00   2880          CLR    PRTD      LET COMPARATOR
C180- BD FC D0   2890          JSR    DISPLY    RECOVER.
C183- BD FC 5E   2900          JSR    KEYIN     LOOK FOR KEY (CLR CARRY)
C186- 25 E0      2910          BCS    STDWT     NO KEY? THEN WEIGH AGAIN.
C188- BD FC 7E   2920          JSR    KEYUP     KEY? WAIT FOR KEY RELEASE.
C18B- 96 74      2930          LDAA   BYTE      ANY KEY SENDS COUNT TO
C18D- B7 60 01   2940          STAA   SERD      MASTER COMPUTER.
C190- 7D C0 0F   2950          TST    LOBUF     PUT FIRST COUNT ONLY
C193- 26 03      2960          BNE    BYPAS     IN LOW X BUFFER.
C195- B7 C0 0D   2970          STAA   LOX
C198- 7C C0 0F   2980 BYPAS    INC    LOBUF     HOW MANY STD WTS LOADED?
C19B- F6 C0 0F   2990          LDAB   LOBUF
C19E- C1 06      3000          CMPB   #06       ALL 5 DONE?
C1A0- 26 C6      3010          BNE    STDWT     NO? DO ANOTHER.
C1A2- B7 C0 0F   3020          STAA   LOBUF     SAVE HIGHEST COUNT IN "LOBUF";
```

```
C1A5- 86 C2       3030           LDAA  #$C2     FILE STARTS ON PAGE $C2,
C1A7- B7 C0 0C    3040           STAA  HIX       WORD GIVEN BY FIRST COUNT IN LOX.
C1AA- B7 C0 0E    3050           STAA  HIBUF      HIBUF, LOBUF BECOMES HI, LO X BUFR.
C1AD- F6 60 01    3060           LDAB  SERD     READ ACIA TO CLEAR RCV-DTA-FULL BIT.
                  3070 *
C1B0- FE C0 0C    3080           LDX   HIX      START OF FILE.
C1B3- B6 60 00    3090 LOOK      LDAA  SERC     PICK UP ACIA STATUS.
C1B6- 84 01       3100           ANDA  #01      LOOK FOR A 1 IN BIT 0
C1B8- 27 F9       3110           BEQ   LOOK      (RCV-DTA FULL)
C1BA- B6 60 01    3120           LDAA  SERD     PICK UP CALCULATED WEIGHT.
C1BD- A7 00       3130           STAA  00,X     STORE IN FILE.
C1BF- 08          3140           INX
C1C0- BC C0 0E    3150           CPX   HIBUF    REACHED HIGHEST COUNT? (BY X BUFR)
C1C3- 26 EE       3160           BNE   LOOK     NO? GET NEXT.
C1C5- 7E C0 10    3170           JMP   START    YES? RUN PICKER.
```

10.7 PROGRAM PROLIFERATION

The first version of the Chicken Pickin' program, presented at the beginning of this chapter, occupied 50 bytes of memory. The last version occupied 415 bytes. This, in miniature, is farily typical of what happens to microcomputer systems. At the moment on-board automotive-engine-control programs average about 15 kilobytes. A controller for a modest bank of elevators uses perhaps 60 kilobytes. Give enough software engineers enough time and they will eventually come up with enough clever add-ons to fill all 65 536 memory bytes with a program to run a washing machine. The 68000 microprocessor has a 23-bit address bus which can access over 8 000 000 words of memory.

To get on the bandwagon of program proliferation, you might like to try your hand at some of the following add-ons.

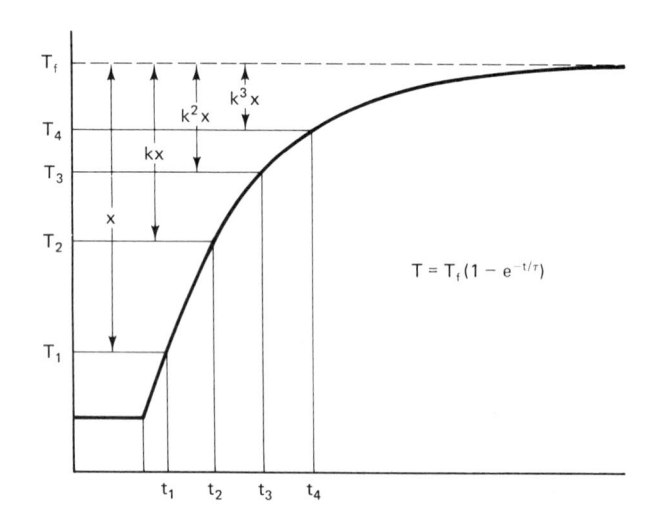

Figure 10-11 Temperature rises toward a final value according to a negative exponential curve. The final value can be predicted from any three values equally spaced in time.

$$T = T_f(1 - e^{-t/\tau})$$

Sec. 10.7 Program Proliferation

- Eliminate the need for the operator to press a button to record a chicken's weight. Write a routine to automatically accept any weight over 1 pound 8 ounces that remains stable for 0.5 second.
- Eliminate readout flash when the weight is midway between two values. Have the scale stick on the value that is read more frequently in each preceding 1-second period.
- Convert the scale to read pounds and hundredths of a pound. Use a rack of 16 hangers rather than 8 to extend the combinations available. This will require some research on programming for double-precision and binary-coded-decimal arithmetic. Programming books covering these topics are not hard to find.
- Program the Apple and 6802 systems to permit changing the net weight per box from the Apple keyboard.
- Program the Apple to display the total weights in pounds and ounces rather than in decimal ounces.

Or you may try some spin-off projects.

- A disk jockey has essentially the same problem as the chicken rancher. He has 7 minutes 40 seconds until the network news comes on. Help him find a combination of records that will exactly fill the available time. Of course, he wants to keep it commercial- and chatter-free. Keyboard input and minute/second data format are the major differences from the Chicken Picker.
- Thermistors make nice thermometer elements, but they are terribly nonlinear with temperature. Linearize one with a lookup table.
- Some fever thermometers display a final temperature in about 3 seconds by measuring three successive temperatures and predicting where the temperature-rise curve will level off. Study Fig. 10-11 and see if you can do it.

11

Video Chicken: Adding a TV Monitor

The two-digit hex display of the Microchicken system is certainly its major limitation. In this chapter we will see how to add a CRT which can display 512 characters at once (numerals 0-9, the capital letters, and 27 punctuation marks and symbols) plus color graphics.

Since this is the last chapter, we will also take a few moments to enumerate some of the many microcomputer chips and functions that we have not had time to cover thoroughly. This will make you aware of some important current topics in micro and personal computers, and it will give you a menu from which to select your next microcomputer project.

11.1 THE 6847 VIDEO DISPLAY GENERATOR

Video interfacing has become immensely less difficult with the introduction of chips dedicated to this purpose. Motorola's *6847* is available for about $12 and is one of the easiest to use. The story of how the VDG uses binary data to produce TV video signals is intricate and fascinating, but the chip can be used by those who have no detailed knowledge of the TV video process. We will concentrate on the external characteristics of the device and the circuit connections needed to make it work.

The VDG operates independently of the microprocessor most of the time. It is more akin to a microprocessor itself than to a peripheral device such as the PIA or ACIA. For example, it has a 13-line address bus which *outputs* addresses to its own display memory. This display memory contains data which the VDG reads to determine what character or graphics pattern to display next.

A scan of the CRT screen is made 60 times per second, and the 6847 reads the entire display memory at that rate to keep the display visible—essentially continuous read. By contrast, the *processor* accesses the display memory (RAM) only occasionally, when a new character needs to be written in.

VDG display mode is controlled by eight input lines to the 6847. These may be hard-wired, switch selected, or program controlled via an 8-bit data latch. There are 12 display modes with two color options on each mode. Table 11-1 lists all the modes for completeness, but don't panic—you will only need to use two of them for a while.

The format of the CRT display is shown in Fig. 11-1 for the alphanumeric and semigraphic modes. The other modes are similar, except that the memory bytes go to higher values.

Of the 40 pins on the 6847 package, we can now account for 31:

- 13 pins: address outputs (we will use nine for 512 bytes at first)
- 8 pins: data inputs
- 8 pins: mode-select inputs
- 2 pins: power supply (+5 V), and ground

We will now examine the remaining nine pins.

$\overline{\text{HS}}$ (horizontal sync) and $\overline{\text{RP}}$ (row preset) are outputs used primarily to implement external character generation, such as lowercase letters, non-English alphabets, and special symbols. We will not be using them, so they can be left unconnected.

CLK is an input that must be fed with a TTL-level clock at 3.579545 MHz, which is the television standard color-subcarrier frequency. For black-and-white-only video this frequency may vary by a few percent without harm. The duty cycle (high-to-total time) must be near 50% for good-quality character generation.

$\overline{\text{FS}}$ (field sync) is an output that goes low for about 2.0 ms at the end of each scan of the screen. This happens 60 times per second. The VDG is not accessing the display memory during these times, so you can use $\overline{\text{FS}}$ to signal the processor (via its $\overline{\text{IRQ}}$ input) that a memory write can be performed without interference.

$\overline{\text{MS}}$ (memory select) is an input that tells the VDG to stop accessing memory and let its address outputs float in the high-Z state. It can be used to interrupt the display while the processor writes to memory, although a noticeable flicker may result. If the processor and VDG clocks are not synchronous, a fight for the buses may develop, resulting in spurious displays.

The remaining four pins are video outputs. Y is the standard black-and-white composite video and sync signal. The sync peaks are at about +1 V

VDG Mode	Elements on Screen	Display Element Configuration (per byte). Each box is one element.	Data Bit Functions 7 6 5 4 3 2 1 0	Colors (B = Black)	Memory Bytes Required	Control Word 35 G/$\overline{A}$ / 34 S/$\overline{A}$ / 31 EX/IN / 27 GM2 / 29 GM1 / 30 GM0 / 39 CSS / 32 INV
Alphanumeric Internal	32 × 16	5 × 7-pixel character	X X A A A A A A (6-bit ASCII)	1 + B	512	0 0 0 X X X A A
Alphanumeric External	32 × 16	8 × 12-pixel (one of 12 rows)	L L L L L L L L	1 + B	512	0 0 1 X X X A A
Semigraphics Four	64 × 32	L_3 L_2 6 / L_1 L_0 (4)	X C$_2$ C$_1$ C$_0$ L$_3$ L$_2$ L$_1$ L$_0$ (4 elements, one color)	8 + B	512	0 1 0 X X X X X
Semigraphics Six	64 × 48	L_5 L_4 4 / L_3 L_2 / L_1 L_0	C$_1$ C$_0$ L$_5$ L$_4$ L$_3$ L$_2$ L$_1$ L$_0$ (6 elements, one color)	4 + B	512	0 1 1 X X X A X
Color Graphics One	64 × 64	E$_3$ E$_2$ E$_1$ E$_0$ 3 (16 × 3 pixels)	C$_1$C$_0$ C$_1$C$_0$ C$_1$C$_0$ C$_1$C$_0$ / E$_3$ E$_2$ E$_1$ E$_0$	4	1024	1 X X 0 0 0 A X
Resolution Graphics One	128 × 64	7 6 5 4 3 2 1 0 3 L L	L$_7$ L$_6$ L$_5$ L$_4$ L$_3$ L$_2$ L$_1$ L$_0$	1 + B	1024	1 X X 0 0 1 A X
Color Graphics Two	128 × 64	E$_3$ E$_2$ E$_1$ E$_0$ 3	C$_1$C$_0$ C$_1$C$_0$ C$_1$C$_0$ C$_1$C$_0$ / E$_3$ E$_2$ E$_1$ E$_0$	4	2048	1 X X 0 1 0 A X
Resolution Graphics Two	128 × 96	7 6 5 4 3 2 1 0 2 L L	L$_7$ L$_6$ L$_5$ L$_4$ L$_3$ L$_2$ L$_1$ L$_0$	1 + B	1536	1 X X 0 1 1 A X
Color Graphics Three	128 × 96	▢▢ 2 / E$_3$ E$_0$	C$_1$C$_0$ C$_1$C$_0$ C$_1$C$_0$ C$_1$C$_0$ / E$_3$ E$_2$ E$_1$ E$_0$	4	3072	1 X X 1 0 0 A X
Resolution Graphics Three	128 × 192	▭▭▭▭▭▭▭▭ 1 / L$_7$ L$_0$	L$_7$ L$_6$ L$_5$ L$_4$ L$_3$ L$_2$ L$_1$ L$_0$	1 + B	3072	1 X X 1 0 1 A X
Color Graphics Six	128 × 192	▭▭▭▭ 1 / E$_3$ E$_0$	C$_1$C$_0$ C$_1$C$_0$ C$_1$C$_0$ C$_1$C$_0$ / E$_3$ E$_2$ E$_1$ E$_0$	4	6144	1 X X 1 1 0 A X
Resolution Graphics Six	256 × 192	▭▭▭▭▭▭▭▭ 1 / L$_7$ L$_0$	L$_7$ L$_6$ L$_5$ L$_4$ L$_3$ L$_2$ L$_1$ L$_0$	1 + B	6144	1 X X 1 1 1 A X

Table 11-1 Display modes of the 6847 Video Display Generator.

Notes:
1. X indicates an inactive input or bit. No change for 1 or 0.
2. A indicates an active bit.
   - Data bits form alphanumeric characters by ASCII code.
   - Control bit INV gives bright character on black background for INV = 0, dark character on bright background for INV = 1.
   - Control bit CSS selects one of two color sets when active.

	CSS = 0	CSS = 1
Alphanumerics:	Green/Black	Orange/Black
Graphics (except Semi 4):	Green, Yellow, Blue, Red	Buff, Cyan, Magenta, Orange

3. L indicates illumination; 0 = dark, 1 = bright.
4. C indicates color-determining bit. E = element color.

C$_2$	C$_1$	C$_0$	Color (E)
0	0	0	Green
0	0	1	Yellow
0	1	0	Blue
0	1	1	Red
1	0	0	Buff (brownish yellow)
1	0	1	Cyan (greenish blue)
1	1	0	Magenta (purplish red)
1	1	1	Orange

Sec. 11.2 Stand-Alone VDG Test Circuits 235

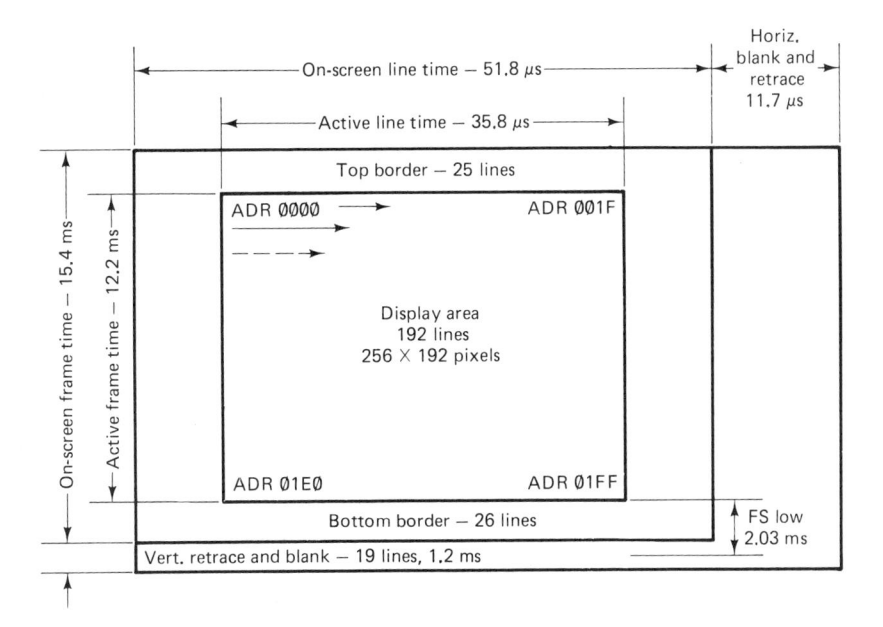

```
                          ┌── On-screen line time — 51.8 μs ──┐  Horiz.
                                                                 blank and
                             ┌── Active line time — 35.8 μs ──┐  retrace
                                                                 11.7 μs
       ┌─────────────────────────────────────────────────────┐
       │              Top border — 25 lines                   │
       │   ┌──────────────────────────────────────────┐       │
       │   │ ADR 0000  →                    ADR 001F  │       │
   On-screen│  ─ ─ ─ →                                │       │
   frame    │                                          │       │
   time     │          Display area                    │       │
   15.4 ms  │          192 lines                       │       │
       Active│         256 × 192 pixels                │       │
       frame │                                          │       │
       time  │                                          │       │
       12.2  │                                          │       │
       ms    │ ADR 01E0                       ADR 01FF  │       │
       │   └──────────────────────────────────────────┘       │
       │              Bottom border — 26 lines                │  FS low
       │  Vert. retrace and blank — 19 lines, 1.2 ms          │  2.03 ms
       └─────────────────────────────────────────────────────┘
```

Figure 11-1 Screen format for the 6847 Video Display Generator.

and the white level is at about +0.5 V. Color information is provided via outputs φA and φB, which are normally connected directly to corresponding pins of a type 1372 color TV modulator chip. CHB (chroma bias) also interfaces directly from the 6847 to the 1372.

11.2 STAND-ALONE VDG TEST CIRCUITS

The VDG can be made to put characters and graphics on the screen by simply connecting its low eight address lines to the data inputs. The mode-select pins can be hard-wired, or certain ones can be connected to the higher-order address lines for dynamic switching between modes. Figure 11-2 shows the connections, and you may fascinate yourself for quite some time just experimenting with the video effects that can be obtained with this circuit.

Simplicity was the major design objective for the circuit of Fig. 11-2, and it therefore drives a video monitor (not a TV receiver) with black-and-white signals only. Monitors generally require about 1 V p-p video signal with negative-going sync, and have a 75-Ω input impedance. The 6847 has a 0.5 V p-p, positive sync, high-impedance output, so dc amplifier Q_2 and emitter follower Q_3 amplify, invert, and buffer the signal. If you don't have a video monitor, but do have experience with TV receivers, you may be able to tap in to the video amplifier of a standard set so that it can be used with the circuit of Fig. 11-2. Working on TV receivers is dangerous—they generate tens of thousands of volts—so do not attempt to modify one unless you are experienced in the safety precautions required. If your receiver uses a transformerless power supply it will be necessary to add a line-isolation transformer to prevent shock and damaged components when connecting it to the computer system.

If you want color display, which, admittedly, makes the graphics modes much more impressive, you will have to use the 1372 modulator IC in the connection shown in Fig. 11-3(a). Notice that the 1372 includes an oscillator, so Q_1 of Fig. 11-2 is no longer needed. If you have modified a TV receiver for video input, but require a positive-sync signal, you can invert the signal

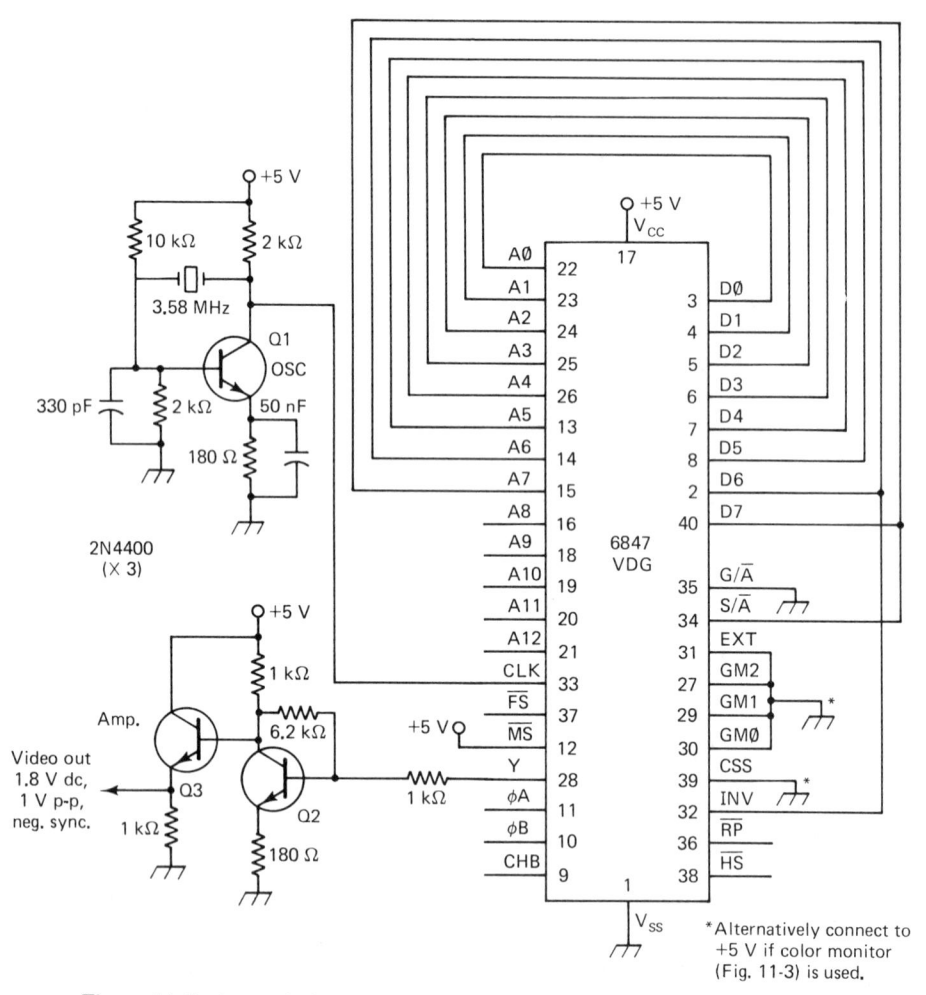

Figure 11-2 A stand-alone circuit for displaying the 6847's repertorie of characters and graphics on a black-and-white video monitor.

Sec. 11.2 Stand Alone VDG Test Circuits

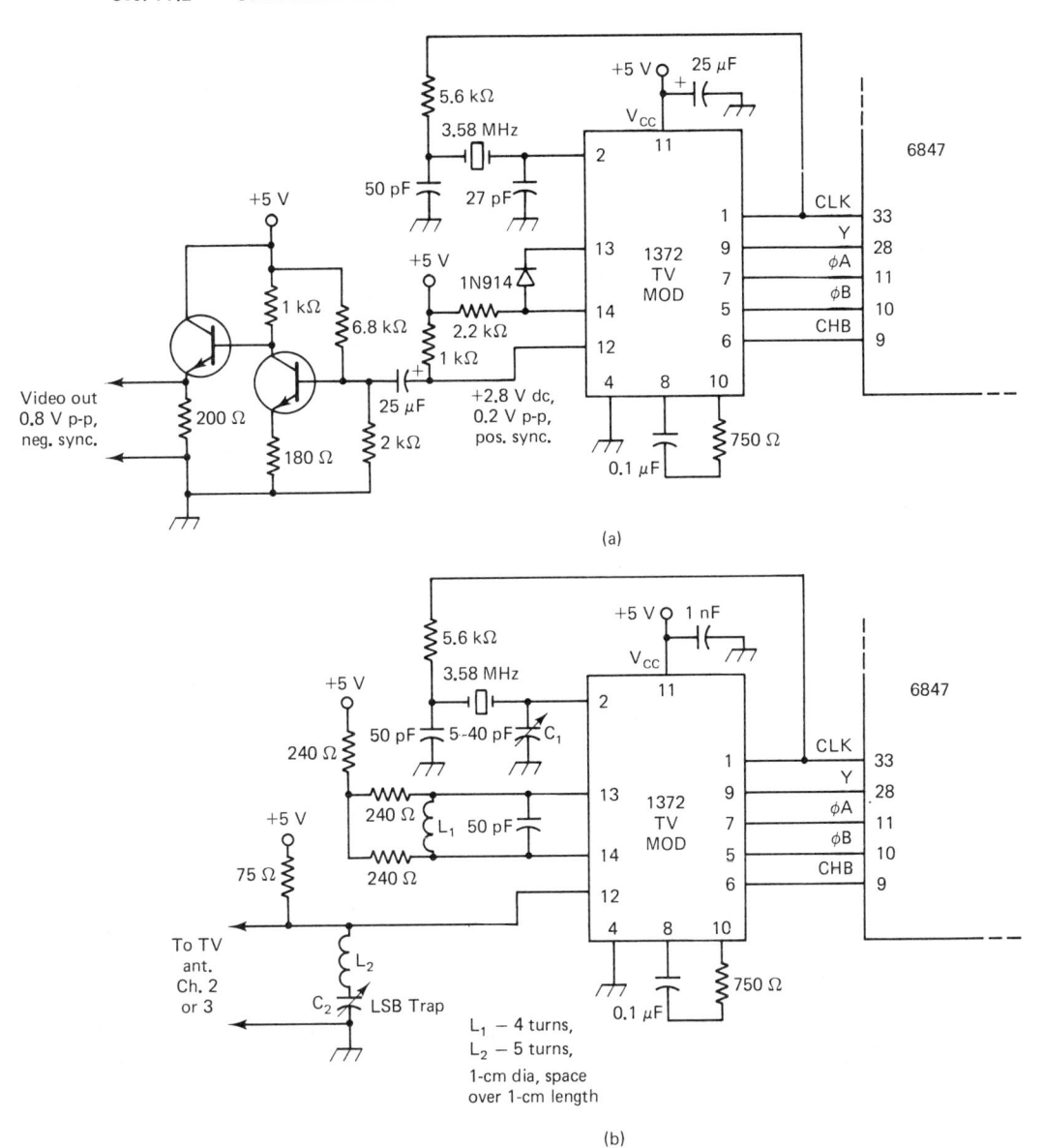

Figure 11-3 Circuits for driving a color video monitor (a) and a color or black-and-white TV receiver (b).

by reversing the *914* diode and moving the 2.2-kΩ resistor from pin 14 to pin 13.

If you must use a TV receiver, try the circuit of Fig. 11-3(b), but be aware that the resolution of the display will be much poorer and all sorts of annoying interference patterns will be present. Let coils L_1 and L_2 be self-supporting in air so that they can be adjusted by spreading their turns. Keep them shielded from one another. Adjust L_1 to place the signal at channel 2 or 3 as you prefer. Adjust L_2, C_2, and C_1 for best resolution with minimum interference.

TABLE 11-2

Hex	ASCII	Hex	ASCII	Hex	ASCII	Hex	ASCII
00	@	10	P	20	blank	30	0
01	A	11	Q	21	!	31	1
02	B	12	R	22	" (quote)	32	2
03	C	13	S	23	#	33	3
04	D	14	T	24	$	34	4
05	E	15	U	25	%	35	5
06	F	16	V	26	&	36	6
07	G	17	W	27	' (apostrophe)	37	7
08	H	18	X	28	(	38	8
09	I	19	Y	29	)	39	9
0A	J	1A	Z	2A	*	3A	: (colon)
0B	K	1B	[	2B	+	3B	; (semicolon)
0C	L	1C	\	2C	, (comma)	3C	<
0D	M	1D	]	2D	- (hyphen)	3D	=
0E	N	1E	↑	2E	. (period)	3E	>
0F	O	1F	←	2F	/ (solidus)	3F	?

A fixed message display or graphic image can be placed on the screen by connecting a 2716 EPROM to the VDG as shown in Fig. 11-4. You can program the first 512 bytes with your message using Table 11-2 for ASCII characters. You can mix normal and inverse characters (dark on a light background) by connecting INV input (pin 32) to D6 output (pin 2) of the VDG, and adding $40 to the ASCII code for characters to be inverted. You can mix graphics with alphanumerics by connecting $\overline{A}/S$ input (pin 34) to D7 output (pin 40), and loading data bytes between $80 and $FF into the EPROM. This is Semigraphics Four mode, and according to Table 11-1, the following color blocks (8 × 12 pixels) can be produced.

Data	Color	Data	Color	Data	Display
8F	Green	CF	Buff	X0	Black
9F	Yellow	DF	Cyan	X3	Bottom row
AF	Blue	EF	Magenta	XC	Top row
BF	Red	FF	Orange	X5	Right side

Sec. 11.3   Interfacing the Computer and the Video Display   239

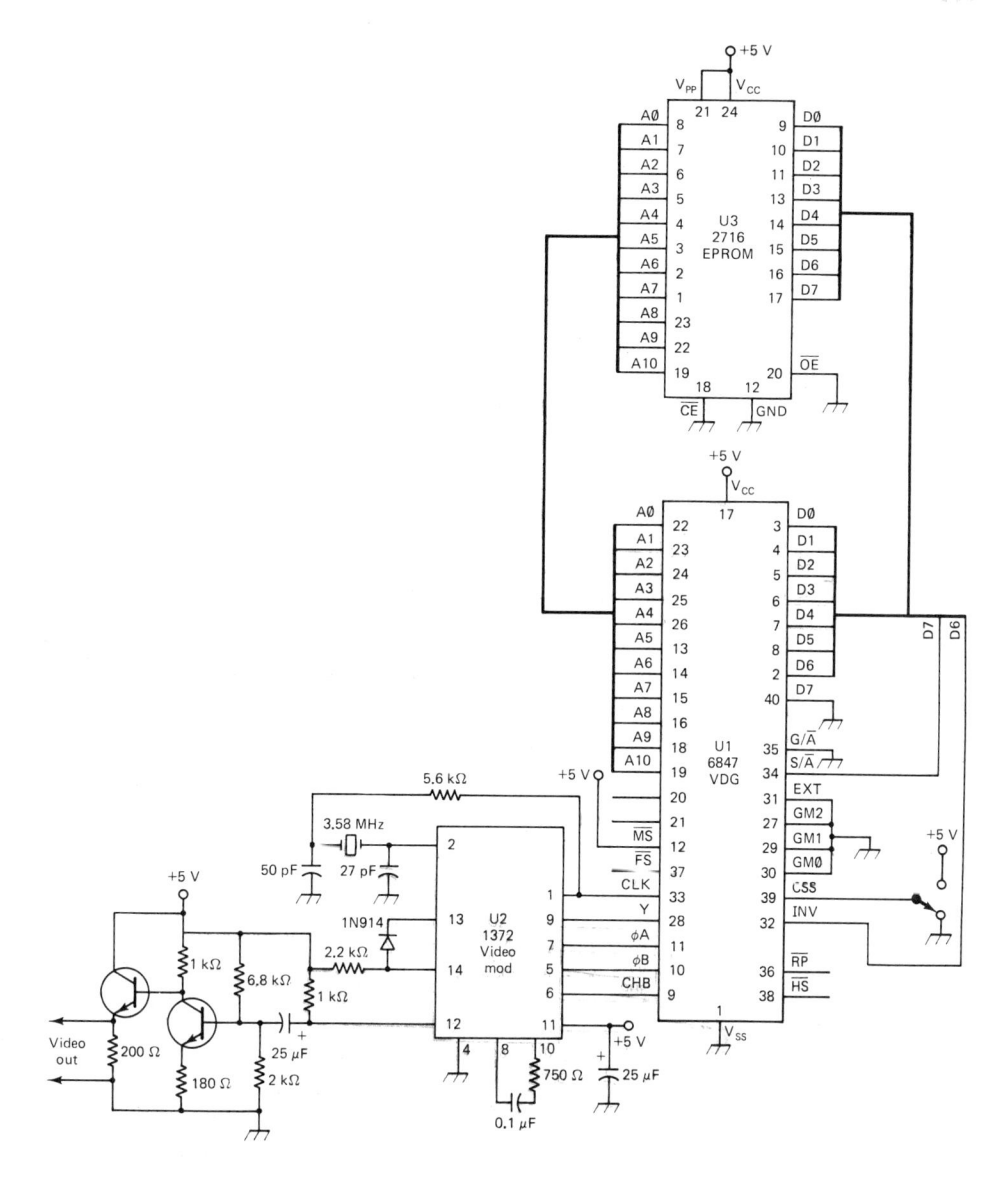

Figure 11-4 A fixed message or graphics pattern can be burned into EPROM and displayed with this circuit.

11.3 INTERFACING THE COMPUTER AND THE VIDEO DISPLAY

To get our Microchicken computer to display via the VDG, only three additional steps are needed.

1. Replace the EPROM of Fig. 11-4 with a RAM so that the computer can write to it.
2. Find a way to isolate the computer's data and address lines from the display memory during normal run-and-display time, but connect them during a computer write to display memory. The VDG must also be told not to output addresses, and the display RAM must be told not to output data during a computer write.
3. Develop the necessary software to translate results generated by the computer into ASCII and/or graphics codes and load them into the appropriate locations of display memory. This is really the only hard part.

The video interface is shown in Fig. 11-5. Two octal buffers provide isolation/connection for nine address lines (512 bytes) and seven of the eight data lines. This will allow display of the 64 different characters, normal or inverted, in a 32-character by 16-row format (alphanumeric mode). By switching S_1 this can be changed to mixed alphanumeric (normal only) and graphics (green, yellow, blue, red, black). Each graphics block occupies the space of one alpha character and consists of four elements, all the same color but individually on-off controllable (Semigraphics Four mode).

You may wish to add a third buffer for the remaining address lines and data line at some future time, but to start, let's keep it as simple as possible. If you are using a black-and-white monitor you may, of course, use the oscillator and buffer circuits of Fig. 11-2, and if you are using a TV receiver you may use Fig. 11-3(b).

If you have built the Microchicken computer all the way through the Chicken Picker and Scale Linearizer you will be out of address-decoder lines at this point, so something has to go to make room for the VDG interface. Since not everyone will have a desktop computer to interface to, we will delete the ACIA function and place the VDG at $6000. You may wish to delete the eight-LED display at $8000 instead. In any case, the processor's WRITE signal must be ANDed with the chip-select signal to prevent false writes to the display RAM. Note that the 74LS02 NOR is a negative-true NAND in this application.

This line ($\overline{CS}$ AND $\overline{W}$) turns off the VDG via the $\overline{MS}$ input, enables the two tri-state buffers, and puts the RAM in the write-to-memory mode.

Keyboard entries can be used to put characters on the screen by simply loading data to addresses $6000 through $61FF using the Microchicken's function 0 (load address) and function 2 (load data). Two simple software

Sec. 11.3   Interfacing the Computer and the Video Display   241

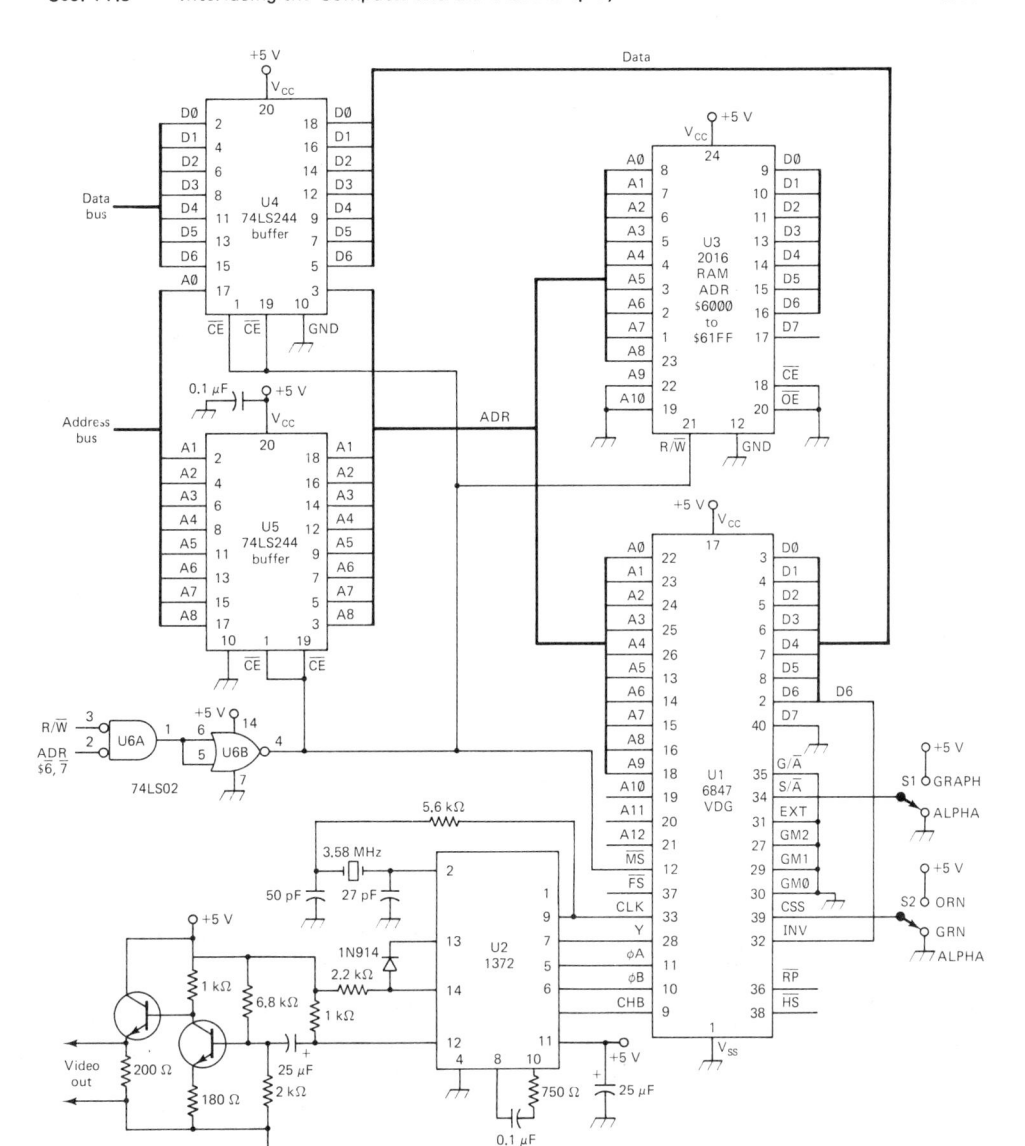

Figure 11-5 The complete hardware for interfacing the video display to the Microchicken computer. Note that the EPROM is replaced with a RAM.

routines to acquaint you with computer control of the screen are listed below. The first fills the screen with the VDG's repertoire of characters, in sequential but in changing positions. The second is just a video dazzler intended to mesmerize with streaks of color. You may prefer to wire $\overline{A}/S$ (pin 34) high and connect CSS (pin 39) to D6 for the latter program.

Character Font for the 6847

```
                1000  *------------------------------------------------------------
                1010  * VIDEO DISPLAY GENERATOR CHARACTER DISPLAY - 6847
                1020  *
                1030        .OR   $0001
                1040        .TA   $4001
0076-           1050  CLOCK .EQ   $0076
FC8B-           1060  DELAY .EQ   $FC8B
                1070  *
0001- CE 60 00  1080  START LDX   #$6000   TOP OF SCREEN
0004- A7 00     1090  LOOP  STAA  00,X     WRITE CHARACTER A AT X.
0006- 4C        1100        INCA           NEXT CHARACTER.
0007- C6 20     1110        LDAB  #$20     $20 = SPEED; VARY AT WILL.
0009- D7 76     1120        STAB  CLOCK    $20 -> 52 CHAR/SEC OR
000B- BD FC 8B  1130        JSR   DELAY    10 SEC TO WRITE WHOLE SCREEN.
000E- 01        1140        NOP            TRY DAA, ROLA, COMA FOR NEW PATTERNS.
000F- 08        1150        INX            NEXT SCREEN POSITION.
0010- 8C 62 00  1160        CPX   #$6200   END OF SCREEN?
0013- 27 03     1170        BEQ   NEW      YES:
0015- 7E 00 04  1180        JMP   LOOP     NO: WRITE NEXT CHARACTER.
0018- 8B 25     1190  NEW   ADDA  #$25     JUMP TO NEW CHARS AND
001A- 7E 00 01  1200        JMP   START    START AT TOP SCREEN.
                1210  *
                1220        .EN
```

Video Dazzler Program

```
                1000  *------------------------------------------------------------
                1010  * VIDEO DAZZLER !@#$%^&*(-)+={[';]|":/>.<,WILD COLORS ON CRT
                1020  *
                1030        .OR   $0002
                1040        .TA   $4002
0000-           1050  HIX   .EQ   $0000
0001-           1060  LOX   .EQ   $0001
0076-           1070  CLOCK .EQ   $0076
FC8B-           1080  DELAY .EQ   $FC8B
                1090  *
0002- C6 11     1100  START LDAB  #$11     $11 = GAP BETWEEN CHANGED CELLS; VARY
0004- CE 60 00  1110  RUN   LDX   #$6000    AT WILL.  $6000 = TOP OF SCREEN.
0007- DF 00     1120        STX   HIX      BUFFERS FOR X REGISTER ARE HIX, LOX.
0009- A7 00     1130  LOOP  STAA  00,X     WRITE TO CRT AT X.
000B- 37        1140        PSHB           SAVE GAP ON STACK.
000C- DB 01     1150        ADDB  LOX      ADVANCE POSITION ON SCREEN BY "B".
000E- D7 01     1160        STAB  LOX
0010- 24 08     1170        BCC   NOCARY   ADVANCE SCREEN HI BYTE TO BOTTOM
0012- 7C 00 00  1180        INC   HIX       IF CARRY APPEARS FROM LO BYTE.
0015- C6 0A     1190        LDAB  #$0A     SPEED OF DISPLAY SET TO $0A;
0017- D7 76     1200        STAB  CLOCK     (500 CELLS/SEC); VARY AT WILL.
0019- 33        1210        PULB           RETRIEVE GAP.
001A- BD FC 8B  1220  NOCARY JSR  DELAY    MONITOR SUBROUTINE. T ~ B*B*18 US.
001D- DE 00     1230        LDX   HIX
001F- 36        1240        PSHA
0020- 81 62     1250        CMPA  #$62     X BUFFER PASSED END OF
0022- 32        1260        PULA            VIDEO PAGE?
0023- 27 03     1270        BEQ   PAGE     YES:
0025- 7E 00 09  1280        JMP   LOOP     NO: WRITE MORE CELLS.
0028- 4C        1290  PAGE  INCA           CHANGE CELL CONTENTS.
0029- 5A        1300        DECB           DECREASE GAP BETWEEN CHANGED CELLS
002A- C1 04     1310        CMPB  #$04     TO MINIMUM OF 5.
002C- 26 03     1320        BNE   SKIP
002E- 7E 00 02  1330        JMP   START    (BACK TO ORIGINAL GAP)
0031- 7E 00 04  1340  SKIP  JMP   RUN      GO TO TOP OF SCREEN.
                1350  *
                1360        .EN
```

11.4 VIDEO CHICKEN

This section uses the hardware of the preceding section and the basic analog-input Chicken Pickin' program of Section 10.2. Additions are made to the program to allow it to display its results on the video monitor.

No provision has been made for synchronizing the VDG and processor clocks, so a fight for the bus will develop occasionally, resulting in spurious characters showing up on the screen. This can be avoided by removing the 6802 clock and connecting the CLK pin 33 of the VDG to the 6802 EXTL pin. However, this will throw the ACIA's baud rate off, making a separate clock for the ACIA necessary if interfacing to a microcomputer with a 1-MHz clock is contemplated. Another solution is to alter the program to store the data and target address in a RAM buffer until an interrupt is received (connect VDG output $\overline{FS}$ to 6802 input $\overline{IRQ}$). The interrupt routine then dumps the data at the appropriate display-RAM address while the VDG is between sweeps of the screen.

Figure 11-6(a) shows the flowchart for the video output routine. The first part of Module 1 simply displays an unchangeable sign-on message. The second part of Module 1 lists the chickens' weights by hanger number as they are weighed, and includes the analog-input *scale* routine. Module 2 is the basic Chicken Picker. Module 3 displays a text heading along with the hanger numbers of the selected chickens and the total weight in pounds and ounces.

At the start of the program the screen is cleared by loading an ASCII *blank* ($20) into all 512 memory bytes. The starting and final adresses of the message destination in display RAM are loaded into $007A through 007D. The ASCII codes for each character of the message are kept in a memory file whose starting address is loaded into address $007E (HI) and 007F (LO). Bytes are then loaded into accumulator A as the stack register increments through the file addresses, and stored as the X register increments through display-RAM addresses. Another file is used as a lookup table to convert hex digits to the ASCII codes for decimal pounds and ounces (for example, $F = ASCII 31, 35 to display 15 ounces). Figure 11-6(b) shows the video display.

Here is the program listing.

Video Chicken CRT Display: Program Listing

```
                1000 * ------------------------------------------------------------
                1010 *      VIDEO CHICKEN *** CRT DISPLAY AND ANALOG INPUT
                1020 *      **** COPYRIGHT 1984 BY D. L. METZGER ****
0029-           1030 CPKR   .EQ    $0029     CHICKEN PICKER HOLDS TEMP BINARY COMB.
002A-           1040 BSTCMB .EQ    $002A     ANSWER (BINARY COMBINATION TO CHOOSE)
002B-           1050 BSTWT  .EQ    $002B     BEST WEIGHT TOTAL (LBS & OZ.)
002C-           1060 XBUF   .EQ    $002C     SAVES X DURING DISPLY SUB (2 BYTES)
002E-           1070 LOOPBF .EQ    $002E     COUNTS DISPLAY LOOPS.
0030-           1080 CURSR  .EQ    $0030     CRT POSITION, 6000 - 6020; 61E0 - 61FF
0032-           1090 STKBFR .EQ    $0032     SAVE STACK WHILE MOVING FILE TO CRT.
0034-           1100 NUMRL  .EQ    $0034     POINTS TO ASCII DECIMAL NUMERAL CODES.
```

```
0036-              1110 NMBR   .EQ  $0036    HOLDS NUMBER TO BE WRIT TO CRT.
0037-              1120 LASTN  .EQ  $0037    NUMBER OF PREVIOUS HANGER.
FCD0-              1130 DISPLY .EQ  $FCD0    MONITOR DISPLAY ROUTINE; 6 MS.
FC5E-              1140 KEYIN  .EQ  $FC5E    MONITOR CLEARS CARRY IF KEY IN.
FC7E-              1150 KEYUP  .EQ  $FC7E    MONITOR WAITS FOR KEY RELEASE.
0074-              1160 BYTE   .EQ  $74      RAM USED BY MONITOR FOR DISPLY.
0078-              1170 COUNT  .EQ  $78      RETURNS VALUE OF KEY INPUT.
4002-              1180 PB     .EQ  $4002    PIA PORT B (BIT 5 = 1 FOR CMPRTR ON)
4003-              1190 CRB    .EQ  $4003    CONTROL REGISTER FOR PORT B.
A000-              1200 PRTD   .EQ  $A000    OUTPUT-ONLY PORT TO D/A CONVRTR.
8000-              1210 PRTE   .EQ  $8000    8 LED OUTPUTS.
                   1220        .OR  $F810    START PROG ASSEMBLY AT ROM $F810
                   1230        .TA  $4010    STORE CODE IN APPLE RAM AT $4010
                   1240 *
F810- 7F 40 03     1250 START  CLR  CRB      GET DIRECTION REGISTER.
F813- 7F 40 02     1260        CLR  PB       SET ALL LINES AS INPUTS.
F816- 86 04        1270        LDAA #04      ACCESS DATA REGISTER
F818- B7 40 03     1280        STAA CRB      NEXT TIME.
F81B- CE 00 08     1290        LDX  #$0008   FILL ADR 0008 THRU 000F WITH
F81E- 86 31        1300        LDAA #$31     ASCII CODES ($31 -$38) FOR
F820- A7 00        1310 ASCII  STAA 00,X     HANGER DIGITS 1 THRU 8.
F822- 08           1320        INX
F823- 4C           1330        INCA
F824- 81 39        1340        CMPA #$39
F826- 26 F8        1350        BNE  ASCII
                   1360 * --------------------------------------------------------
                   1370 * WRITE GREETING AND DATA HEADINGS ON CRT.
F828- BD F9 92     1380        JSR  CLEAR    CLEAR SCREEN
F82B- CE 60 01     1390        LDX  #$6001   WRITE HELLO MESSAGE AT
F82E- DF 7A        1400        STX  $7A        SCREEN LINE 1 (6000 - 601F)
F830- CE 60 1F     1410        LDX  #$601F
F833- DF 7C        1420        STX  $7C
F835- CE FA 20     1430        LDX  #$FA20   WITH ASCII CHAR'S FROM
F838- DF 7E        1440        STX  $7E      FILE AT FA20
F83A- BD F9 A0     1450        JSR  WRITE
F83D- CE 60 40     1460        LDX  #$6040   WRITE HEADING FOR
F840- DF 7A        1470        STX  $7A      HANGER NOS. & WEIGHTS.
F842- CE 60 60     1480        LDX  #$6060
F845- DF 7C        1490        STX  $7C
F847- CE FA 40     1500        LDX  #$FA40   FROM ASCII FILE AT FA40.
F84A- DF 7E        1510        STX  $7E
F84C- BD F9 A0     1520        JSR  WRITE
F84F- C6 FF        1530        LDAB #$FF     INDICATE "ALL HANGERS EMPTY"
F851- D7 2A        1540        STAB BSTCMB   TO START.
                   1550 * --------------------------------------------------------
                   1560 * MODULE 1 *** INPUT WEIGHTS AT EMPTY LOCATIONS ***
                   1570 *
F853- CE 60 64     1580 TOPAGN LDX  #$6064   SET CURSOR TO LINE ABOVE NO.1.
F856- DF 30        1590        STX  CURSR    SAVE X AS SCREEN POSITION.
F858- C6 01        1600 FILL   LDAB #01      FILL ALL EMPTY HANGERS.
F85A- D7 29        1610        STAB CPKR     CPKR SHIFTS 1 BIT RIGHT, HANGER 1 - 8.
F85C- CE 00 00     1620        LDX  #$0000   WEIGHT FILE STARTS AT 0000.
F85F- DF 2C        1630        STX  XBUF     XBUF HOLDS WT FILE & HANGER POINTER.
                   1640 *
                   1650 * --------------------------------------------------------
                   1660 * WRITE HANGER NUMBER TO CRT.
F861- 96 31        1670 LOAD   LDAA CURSR+1  SET TO START OF CURRENT
F863- 84 E0        1680        ANDA #$E0     LINE.
F865- 8B 24        1690        ADDA #$24     ADD A LINE AND INDENT 4 SPACES.
F867- 24 03        1700        BCC  PASS     IF CARRY OUT OF LO BYTE, ADD 1 TO
F869- 7C 00 30     1710        INC  CURSR    HIGH BYTE SCREEN ADR.
F86C- 97 31        1720 PASS   STAA CURSR+1
F86E- DE 2C        1730        LDX  XBUF
F870- A6 08        1740        LDAA 08,X    PICK UP ASCII FOR HANGER NO.
F872- DF 2C        1750        STX  XBUF    FROM FILE AT 0008 - 000F.
```

Sec. 11.4 Video Chicken

```
F874- DE 30        1760          LDX    CURSR
F876- A7 00        1770          STAA   00,X       OUTPUT AT CURSOR.
F878- 97 37        1780          STAA   LASTN
                   1790  * ------------------------------------------------------------
F87A- D6 29        1800          LDAB   CPKR       IDENTIFY 1 OF 8 HANGERS.
F87C- 53           1810          COMB              DISPLAY 1 OF 8 LEDS
F87D- F7 80 00     1820          STAB   PRTE       BY PULLING A PORT-E BIT LOW.
F880- 53           1830          COMB              RESTORE 1 = SELECT IN ACC B.
F881- D4 2A        1840          ANDB   BSTCMB     IF THIS HANGER IS FULL
F883- 27 5C        1850          BEQ    NXTPOS     SKIP THE SCALE ROUTINE.
                   1860  *                        IF WEIGHING, INVERSE SCALE NUMBER.
F885- DE 2C        1870          LDX    XBUF
F887- A6 08        1880  HILITE  LDAA   08,X       PICK UP ASCII DIGIT CODE
F889- 8B 40        1890          ADDA   #$40       AND INVERT VIDEO.
F88B- DE 30        1900          LDX    CURSR      OUTPUT AT CRT
F88D- A7 00        1910          STAA   00,X       CURSOR POSITION.
                   1920  *
F88F- 7F 00 74     1930  SCALE   CLR    BYTE       WEIGH IN A CHICKEN.
F892- 7C 00 74     1940  ATOD    INC    BYTE       RAM "BYTE" COUNTS UP WEIGHT.
F895- 96 74        1950          LDAA   BYTE       A/D TAKES 5 MS MAX.
F897- B7 A0 00     1960          STAA   PRTD       OUTPUT COUNT TO A/D CONV.
F89A- B6 40 02     1970          LDAA   PB         CHECK COMPARATOR OUTPUT
F89D- 84 20        1980          ANDA   #$20       ON BIT 5 ONLY.
F89F- 27 F1        1990          BEQ    ATOD       LOW = KEEP COUNTING.
F8A1- BD FC D0     2000          JSR    DISPLY     6 MS OF WEIGHT DISPLAY,
F8A4- 7F A0 00     2010          CLR    PRTD       LET COMPARATOR RECOVER,
F8A7- BD FC D0     2020          JSR    DISPLY     AND DISPLAY SOME MORE.
F8AA- BD FC 5E     2030          JSR    KEYIN      LOOK FOR KEY PRESS (CRY CLR).
F8AD- 25 E0        2040          BCS    SCALE      ANY KEY WILL LOAD WEIGHT.
                   2050  * STAY IN SCALE ROUTINE UNTIL KEY PRESSED.
F8AF- 96 37        2060          LDAA   LASTN      WRITE NORMAL NUMBER OVER
F8B1- A7 00        2070          STAA   00,X       INVERTED NO. AT CURSOR.
F8B3- 96 74        2080          LDAA   BYTE       PICK UP WEIGHT,
F8B5- DE 2C        2090          LDX    XBUF
F8B7- A7 00        2100          STAA   00,X       PUT IN FILE.
                   2110  * ------------------------------------------------------------
                   2120  * DISPLAY INDIVIDUAL CHICKEN WEIGHTS IN DECIMAL LBS & OZ.
F8B9- 86 FA        2130          LDAA   #$FA       PAGE OF ASCII NUMERAL FILE.
F8BB- 97 34        2140          STAA   NUMRL
F8BD- D6 74        2150          LDAB   BYTE       NMBR IS BUFR TO SAVE BOTH
F8BF- D7 36        2160          STAB   NMBR       NIBBLES. ACC B HANDLES
F8C1- 54           2170          LSRB              HI NIBBLE SEPARATELY.
F8C2- 54           2180          LSRB
F8C3- 54           2190          LSRB
F8C4- 54           2200          LSRB
F8C5- 96 31        2210          LDAA   CURSR+1    MOVE CURSOR RIGHT 16 SPC,
F8C7- 8B 10        2220          ADDA   #$10       UNDER WEIGHT HEADING.
F8C9- 97 31        2230          STAA   CURSR+1
F8CB- BD F9 B2     2240          JSR    SCRIB      SCRIBBLE HI NIBBLE.
F8CE- D6 36        2250          LDAB   NMBR       B GETS LO NIBBLE
F8D0- C4 0F        2260          ANDB   #$0F       ONLY THIS TIME.
F8D2- BD F9 B2     2270          JSR    SCRIB      SCRIBBLE LO NIBBLE
                   2280  * ------------------------------------------------------------
F8D5- C6 A0        2290          LDAB   #$A0       160 LOOPS X 6 MS/LOOP
F8D7- D7 2E        2300          STAB   LOOPBF     (KEEP COUNT OF LOOPS IN RAM)
F8D9- BD FC D0     2310  HOLD    JSR    DISPLY     HOLDS WEIGHT DISPLAY
F8DC- 7A 00 2E     2320          DEC    LOOPBF     FOR 1 SEC.
F8DF- 26 F8        2330          BNE    HOLD
                   2340  * ------------------------------------------------------------
                   2350  * THAT CHICKEN'S WEIGHED IN.  ANY MORE?
F8E1- DE 2C        2360  NXTPOS  LDX    XBUF
F8E3- 08           2370          INX               MOVE TO NEXT SLOT IN FILE.
F8E4- DF 2C        2380          STX    XBUF
F8E6- 78 00 29     2390          ASL    CPKR       IF END OF FILE
F8E9- 27 03        2400          BEQ    RUN        RUN CHICKEN PICKER.
F8EB- 7E F8 61     2410          JMP    LOAD       IF NOT, GET NEXT WT.
```

```
                  2420 * ------------------------------------------------------------
                  2430 * MODULE 2 *** SELECT BEST COMBINATION OF CHICKENS ***
                  2440 *
F8EE- 86 FF       2450 RUN    LDAA  #$FF       START WITH EXCESSIVE "BEST WEIGHT"
F8F0- 97 2B       2460        STAA  BSTWT
F8F2- 7F 00 2A    2470        CLR   BSTCMB     AND "CHOOSE NONE" AS BEST COMB.
F8F5- C6 07       2480        LDAB  #$07       START PICKING 3 CHICKENS (0000 0111)
F8F7- CE 00 00    2490 LOOP   LDX   #$0000     FILE OF CHICKEN WEIGHTS STARTS AT 0000
F8FA- 4F          2500        CLRA             TOTAL "SO FAR" = 0.
F8FB- D7 29       2510        STAB  CPKR       RAM "CPKR" HOLDS BINARY COMBINATION.
F8FD- 74 00 29    2520 NXTCHK LSR   CPKR       SHIFT BIT PATTERN INTO CARRY.
F900- 24 04       2530        BCC   LASTQ      (0 IN CARRY MEANS DON'T ADD THIS ONE)
F902- AB 00       2540        ADDA  00,X       (1 = ADD THIS WEIGHT FROM FILE)
F904- 25 15       2550        BCS   NXTCMB     IF WT > 15 LB, 15 OZ, TOO MUCH!
F906- 7D 00 29    2560 LASTQ  TST   CPKR       ALL BINARY 1'S (ADD THIS) SHIFTED OUT?
F909- 27 04       2570        BEQ   TSTWT      IF SO, IS THIS TOTAL WT LOWEST?
F90B- 08          2580        INX              IF NOT, MOVE TO NEXT WT IN FILE AND
F90C- 7E F8 FD    2590        JMP   NXTCHK     CHECK IF CPKR SAYS TO ADD IT IN.
F90F- 81 C0       2600 TSTWT  CMPA  #$C0       IS TOTAL WT 12 LBS OR MORE?
F911- 25 08       2610        BCS   NXTCMB     NO? THEN TRY ANOTHER COMBINATION.
F913- 91 2B       2620        CMPA  BSTWT      YES, THEN IS NEW TOTAL LESS THAN
F915- 24 04       2630        BCC   NXTCMB     OLD BEST WEIGHT?  IF SO,
F917- 97 2B       2640        STAA  BSTWT      REPLACE OLD BEST WEIGHT AND
F919- D7 2A       2650        STAB  BSTCMB     BEST COMB WITH NEW.
F91B- 5C          2660 NXTCMB INCB             COUNT TO NEXT BINARY COMBINATION.
F91C- 26 D9       2670        BNE   LOOP       IF NOT = 00, TRY IT
                  2680 * ------------------------------------------------------------
                  2690 * MODULE 3 *** DISPLAY BEST COMBINATION AND TOTAL WEIGHT ***
                  2700 *
F91E- D6 2A       2710 DONE   LDAB  BSTCMB     PICK UP BEST PATTERN
F920- 53          2720        COMB             AND PULL LEDS LOW
F921- F7 80 00    2730        STAB  PRTE       BY SELECTED HENS.
                  2740 *
                  2750 * WRITE HEADING FOR BOTTOM OF SCREEN RESULTS:
                  2760 *
F924- CE 61 A0    2770        LDX   #$61A0     SCREEN START
F927- DF 7A       2780        STX   $7A
F929- CE 61 BF    2790        LDX   #$61BF     SCREEN END ADR.
F92C- DF 7C       2800        STX   $7C
F92E- CE FA 60    2810        LDX   #$FA60     START OF ASCII FILE
F931- DF 7E       2820        STX   $7E        WITH MESSAGE.
F933- BD F9 A0    2830        JSR   WRITE
                  2840 *
                  2850 * LIST CHICKENS SELECTED BY HANGER NUMBERS:
                  2860 *
F936- CE 61 E0    2870 ANSR   LDX   #$61E0     START OF BOTTOM LINE.
F939- 86 30       2880        LDAA  #$30       ASCII NUMERAL 0 TO START:
F93B- 53          2890        COMB
F93C- 4C          2900 VIDSEL INCA             NEXT NUMERAL
F93D- 54          2910        LSRB             B CONTAINS BINARY COMBINATION;
F93E- 24 FC       2920        BCC   VIDSEL     1 = SELECT, 0 = NO.
F940- A7 00       2930        STAA  00,X       WRITE HANGER NO. IF SELECTED.
F942- 08          2940        INX
F943- 08          2950        INX              SKIP 2 SPACES.
F944- 08          2960        INX
F945- 5D          2970        TSTB             LEAVE LOOP IF B = 00.
F946- 26 F4       2980        BNE   VIDSEL     NEXT HANGER SELECTED ?
                  2990 *
                  3000 * DISPLAY TOTAL WEIGHT IN LBS & OZ.
                  3010 *
F948- CE 61 FA    3020 VIDWT  LDX   #$61FA     POINT CURSOR NEAR END OF
F94B- DF 30       3030        STX   CURSR      BOTTOM LINE OF SCREEN.
F94D- D6 2B       3040        LDAB  BSTWT      PICK UP TOTAL WEIGHT.
F94F- 54          3050        LSRB
F950- 54          3060        LSRB             MOVE HI NIBBLE TO
F951- 54          3070        LSRB             ACCUM B LOW 4 BITS.
```

Sec. 11.4   Video Chicken   **247**

```
F952- 54            3080          LSRB
F953- BD F9 B2      3090          JSR   SCRIB     SCRIBBLE HI NIBBLE.
F956- D6 2B         3100          LDAB  BSTWT
F958- C4 0F         3110          ANDB  #$0F      LEAVE LO NIBBLE ONLY;
F95A- BD F9 B2      3120          JSR   SCRIB     SCRIBBLE LO NIBBLE.
                    3130 *
F95D- 96 2B         3140          LDAA  BSTWT
F95F- 97 74         3150          STAA  BYTE      DISPLAY BEST TOTAL WEIGHT
F961- BD FC D0      3160 DISTOT   JSR   DISPLY    UNTIL KEYIN SENSED.
F964- BD FC 5E      3170          JSR   KEYIN
F967- 25 F8         3180          BCS   DISTOT
F969- BD FC 7E      3190          JSR   KEYUP
                    3200 *
F96C- CE 61 E0      3210          LDX   #$61E0    CLEAR LAST LINE (SELECTIONS
F96F- 86 20         3220          LDAA  #$20      AND TOTAL WT) TO ASCII
F971- BD F9 97      3230          JSR   SCRUB     BLANKS AFTER CHOICE MADE.
                    3240 *
F974- 86 0F         3250          LDAA  #$0F      IF KEY IS "F" (FAIL)
F976- 91 78         3260          CMPA  COUNT     OPERATOR HANGS A NEW HEN
F978- 27 03         3270          BEQ   CHANGE    AT SLOT 8 & TRIES AGAIN.
F97A- 7E F8 53      3280          JMP   TOPAGN    IF NOT "F", TAKE IT & GO.
                    3290 *------------------------------------------------------------
                    3300 * MODULE 4 *** CHANGE CHICKEN ON HANGER 8 ***
                    3310 *
F97D- CE 61 64      3320 CHANGE   LDX   #$6164    HANGER "8" CHAR POSITION
F980- DF 30         3330          STX   CURSR     ON CRT SCREEN.
F982- CE 00 07      3340          LDX   #$0007    POINT TO HANGER 8.
F985- DF 2C         3350          STX   XBUF
F987- C6 80         3360          LDAB  #$80      REPLACE HEN #8
F989- D7 29         3370          STAB  CPKR      AND TRY AGAIN.
F98B- 53            3380          COMB
F98C- F7 80 00      3390          STAB  PRTE      LIGHT LED AT HANGER 8.
F98F- 7E F8 87      3400          JMP   HILITE    WEIGH A NEW CHICKEN.
                    3410 * -----------------------------------------------------------
                    3420 * SUBROUTINE TO CLEAR CRT SCREEN
F992- CE 60 00      3430 CLEAR    LDX   #$6000
F995- 86 20         3440          LDAA  #$20      ASCII BLANK
F997- A7 00         3450 SCRUB    STAA  00,X
F999- 08            3460          INX
F99A- 8C 62 00      3470          CPX   #$6200
F99D- 26 F8         3480          BNE   SCRUB
F99F- 39            3490          RTS
                    3500 *------------------------------------------------------------
                    3510 * SUBROUTINE TO WRITE ASCII CHAR'S FROM FILE TO CRT.
                    3520 *  START ADR HELD AT 7A (HI), 7B (LO); CRT END AT 7C (HI),
                    3530 *  7D (LO). ASCII FILE START ADR HELD AT 7E (HI), 7F (LO).
                    3540 *
F9A0- DE 7A         3550 WRITE    LDX   $7A
F9A2- 9F 32         3560          STS   STKBFR    SAVE STACK
F9A4- 9E 7E         3570          LDS   $7E
F9A6- 34            3580          DES
F9A7- 32            3590 LETTR    PULA            STACK LOADS ASCII CODES
F9A8- A7 00         3600          STAA  00,X      COUNTING UP FILE.
F9AA- 08            3610          INX             X STORES CODES COUNTING
F9AB- 9C 7C         3620          CPX   $7C       UP DISPLAY RAM ADRS.
F9AD- 26 F8         3630          BNE   LETTR
F9AF- 9E 32         3640          LDS   STKBFR
F9B1- 39            3650          RTS
                    3660 * ----------------------------------------------------------
                    3670 * SUBROUTINE TO WRITE LO NIBBLE OF ACC B IN DECIMAL ON CRT.
                    3680 *
F9B2- D7 35         3690 SCRIB    STAB  NUMRL+1   LO BYTE OF ADR FILE
F9B4- 86 20         3700          LDAA  #$20      ASCII BLANK
F9B6- C1 0A         3710          CMPB  #$0A      BELOW TEN?
F9B8- 25 02         3720          BCS   BLANK     YES; KEEP BLANK CHAR.
F9BA- 86 31         3730          LDAA  #$31      ASCII "1"
```

```
                                                    248                     Video Chicken: Adding a TV Monitor    Chap. 11

F9BC- DE 30        3740 BLANK   LDX   CURSR
F9BE- A7 00        3750        STAA  00,X    WRITE BLANK OR 1
F9C0- 08           3760        INX
F9C1- DF 30        3770        STX   CURSR   ADVANCE CURSOR
F9C3- DE 34        3780        LDX   NUMRL   GO INTO ASCII NUMERAL
F9C5- A6 00        3790        LDAA  00,X     FILE
F9C7- DE 30        3800        LDX   CURSR   WRITE DIGIT AT
F9C9- A7 00        3810        STAA  00,X     CURSOR LOCATION.
F9CB- 08           3820        INX
F9CC- 08           3830        INX            SKIP A SPACE.
F9CD- DF 30        3840        STX   CURSR
F9CF- 39           3850        RTS
                   3860        .OR   $FA00
                   3870        .TA   $4200
                   3880 * ASCII FILE FOR DECIMAL LSD FROM HEX NIBBLE 0 - F.
FA00- 30 31 32
FA03- 33 34 35
FA06- 36 37 38
FA09- 39 30 31
FA0C- 32 33 34
FA0F- 35           3890        .HS   303132333435363738393031323334 35
                   3900        .OR   $FA20
                   3910        .TA   $4220
                   3920 *
                   3930 * ASCII FILE FOR GREETING
FA20- 17 05 0C
FA23- 03 0F 0D
FA26- 05 20 14
FA29- 0F 20 04
FA2C- 01 0E 27
FA2F- 13 20 03
FA32- 08 09 03
FA35- 0B 05        3940        .HS   17050C030F0D0520140F2004010E271320030809030B05
FA37- 0E 20 12
FA3A- 01 0E 03
FA3D- 08 20 20     3950        .HS   0E2012010E03082020
                   3960        .OR   $FA40
                   3970        .TA   $4240
                   3980 *
                   3990 * ASCII FILE FOR HEADING
FA40- 08 01 0E
FA43- 07 05 12
FA46- 20 0E 0F
FA49- 2E 20 20
FA4C- 20 20 20
FA4F- 17 05 09
FA52- 07 08 14
FA55- 20 28        4000        .HS   08010E070512200E0F2E202020202017050907081420 28
FA57- 0C 02 13
FA5A- 20 26 20
FA5D- 0F 1A 29     4010        .HS   0C02132026200F1A29
                   4020        .OR   $FA60
                   4030        .TA   $4260
                   4040 *
                   4050 *     ASCII FILE FOR BOTTOM SCREEN HEADING.
FA60- 13 05 0C
FA63- 05 03 14
FA66- 20 03 08
FA69- 09 03 0B
FA6C- 05 0E 13
FA6F- 3A 20 20
FA72- 20 14 0F
FA75- 14 01        4060        .HS   13050C05031420030809030B050E133A202020140F1401
FA77- 0C 20 0C
FA7A- 02 13 2F
FA7D- 0F 1A        4070        .HS   0C200C02132F0F1A
                   4080        .EN
```

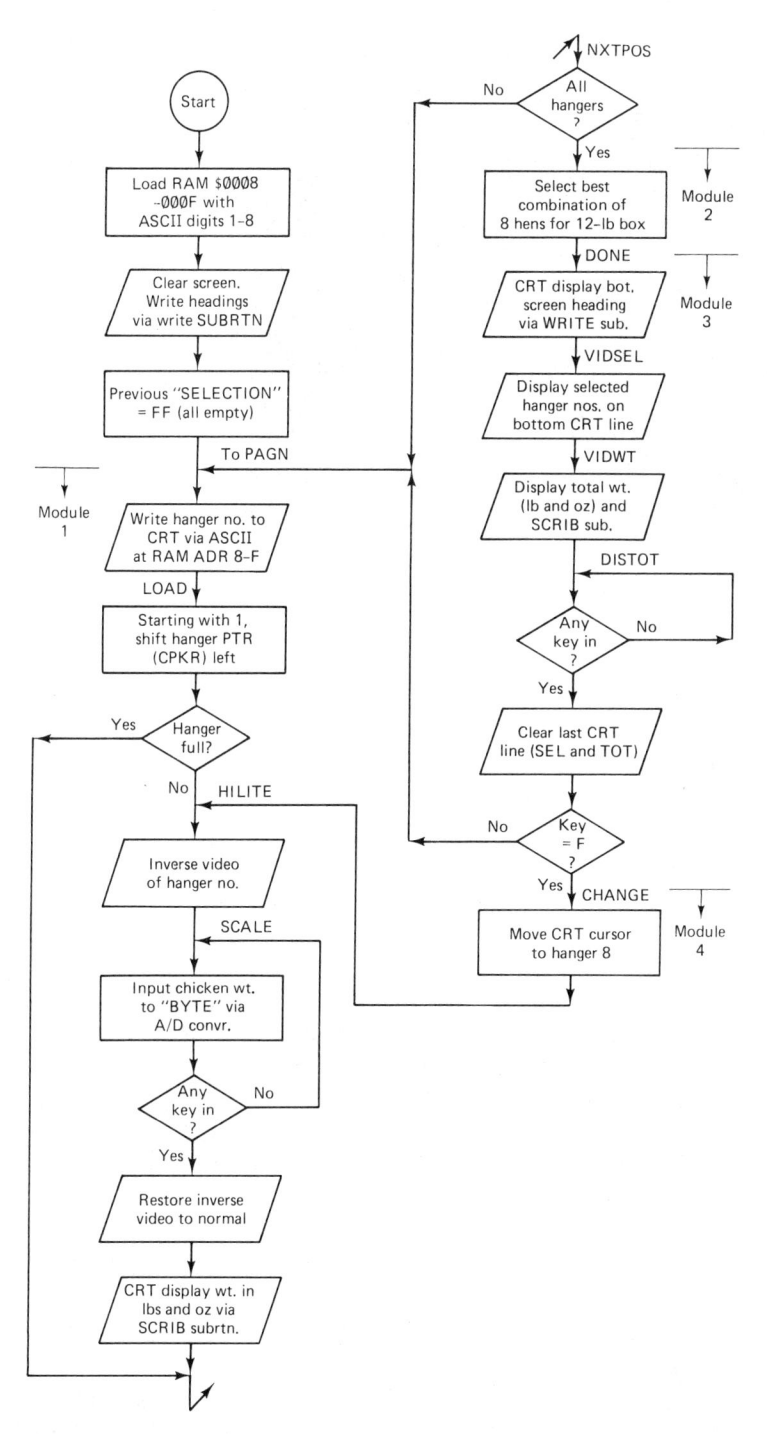

Figure 11-6 (a) Flowchart for program additions to display Chicken Pickin' data on the video monitor.

Figure 11-6 (b) The Video Chicken display on a black-and-white monitor.

11.5 THINGS LEFT UNDONE

Further expansion. At this point the obvious question is: "How far are we from building our own desktop microcomputer?" Unfortunately, we are still quite far. Here are the major obstacles.

1. *64-key input.* We have a 4 × 4 matrix keyboard routine. An 8 × 8 routine could be similarly constructed. ASCII codes for each character would have to be obtained from a lookup table.
2. *Memory.* Even a modest desktop micro has an 8-K ROM and 12 K of RAM. At 2 K per chip, that's 10 chips. The 6802 is capable of driving about 20 to 25 microcomputer components (memories, PIAs, VDG, etc.) or about five 74LSXX-type chips (latches, bus buffers, address decoders). Bidirectional bus buffering, using a chip such as the 74LS245, is common in larger systems. EPROM's of 4 K (2732) and 8 K (2764) are available to reduce component count. The 74154 four-to-16-line decoder can be used in place of the 74138 for accessing more memory and I/O chips.
3. *BASIC* language is the *sine qua non* for personal computers, and this is likely to be the insurmountable obstacle. Writing it yourself is out of the question—professional programmers compact a limited version into 4 K of memory. A beginner would need 8 K or more. Of course, the professionally done versions are proprietary, and very jealously guarded, so documentation is not generally available.
4. *An operating system* should include screen formatting, display scrolling, editing, backspace, shift, and repeat functions. A disk operating system

Sec. 11.5 Things Left Undone 251

is probably out of the question, but all serious computerists agree that it is essential.

Other microprocessors. We have dealt exclusively with the Motorola 6802 processor, but you should have at least a talking knowledge of the other major chips competing in the field.

- The 6800 was Motorola's original processor. It has exactly the same op codes as the 6802. It requires an external two-phase clock generator and it has no internal RAM.
- The Rockwell 6502 was an early 6800 spin-off. It is very similar to the 6800, but it has one accumulator and two 8-bit index registers, X and Y. It has additional indirect-addressing modes and a more convenient decimal-addition mode. It is the processor used in most of the early desktop microcomputers, such as the Apple II, Atari, and Commodore Pet.
- The Motorola 6809 is a significant advance over the 6800. It has two 16-bit index registers and two stack pointers. Its two accumulators can be concatenated to form a 16-bit double accumulator D, allowing double bytes to be loaded, stored, and swapped with index and stack registers. It has an 8-bit by 8-bit multiply instruction and seven or 12 addressing modes, depending on how you count them. It is used in the Radio Shack Color Computers.
- The Motorola 6805 is actually a family of single-chip microcomputers (not microprocessors). The ROM (1100 to 2508 bytes) and RAM (64 to 112 bytes) are internal, and the address and data lines are not brought out. The freed package pins are dedicated to I/O functions. The -P2 and -P4 versions come in 28-pin packages and have 20 PIA-type I/O lines and an internal timer. The other versions come in 40-pin packages and have 20 or more I/O lines. The -R2 and -U2 versions have integrated 8-bit A/D converters.
- The Motorola 6801 is a complete microcomputer system in a 40-pin package. It uses the basic 6800 instruction set, with the addition of double-accumulator and 8-bit multiply instructions. It includes 2 K of ROM and 128 bytes of RAM, 29 I/O lines, a timer, and a serial (6850-like) interface. Its I/O lines can be reconfigured to function as address and data lines to access external memory and I/O devices.
- The Intel 8080 was the chip that started it all. It comes in a 40-pin package, but requires three power supplies (+5 V, -5 V, and +12 V) and an external clock. In addition to the accumulator, it contains six general-purpose registers, two of which can function as a 16-bit double accumulator. 8080 programs make extensive use of a MOVE instruction which transfers data between registers and from registers to memory.

- The Zilog Z-80 is a spin-off of the 8080. It requires a single +5-V supply and a single-phase TTL-level clock. It follows the 8080 instruction set, with several additions for moving and searching large blocks of memory. It contains two identical sets of 8080-type registers, so interrupts can often be handled by switching to the other set without bothering to save-on-stack. It is used in the very popular CP/M (Control Program/ Microprocessor) disk operating system.
- The Intel 8085 is an advanced version of the 8080, and uses the same instruction set. It uses a single +5-V supply, has an internal clock generator, and contains an integrated serial I/O port. Its low eight address lines are multiplexed with its data lines, the pins being labeled AD∅ through AD7. An external address latch, triggered by an *address-latch enable* (ALE) output, holds the address while data appears on the multiplexed bus.
- The 8048 is Intel's single-chip microcomputer. It contains 1 K of ROM, 64 bytes of RAM, and an internal timer. It has 27 I/O lines, some of which can be used to access external memory. The 8035 is an 8048 without the internal mask-programmed ROM.

Comparisons between Motorola- and Intel-type processors are of doubtful validity, because each has its advantages and each can, in the end, compute any computable function. Note, for example, processor speed comparisons. The 8085A-2 has a 5-MHz clock, whereas the 68B09 has a 2-MHz clock. But an 8085 machine cycle is normally three clock cycles. An *add immediate* or *add to memory* takes seven clock cycles for the 8085, whereas the 6800 *add immediate* takes two clock cycles, and the *add extended* takes three clock cycles.

Sweet Sixteens. Intel calls its 16-bit processors the iAPX family. Motorola's is the 68000. The battle is on!

- The Intel 8086 comes in a 40-pin package. It uses a multiplexed address-and-data bus and therefore requires an external address latch. It operates at up to 10 MHz and requires an external clock generator. It has 14 internal 16-bit registers. The 8088, a version with an 8-bit data bus, is used in the IBM PC and Peanut microcomputers.
- The Motorola 68000 comes in a 64-pin package and uses separate address and data buses. It operates up to 12 MHz and requires an external single-phase clock. It has sixteen 32-bit internal registers, so four bytes can be processed internally with one instruction. It incorporates the data MOVE instruction. The 68000 is used in Apple's Lisa and Macintosh computers, and is widely used with Bell Laboratory's UNIX disk operating system.

Appendices

appendix

A

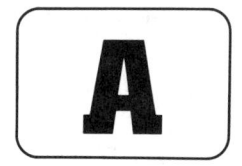

Microcomputer Wiring Techniques

1. Have a complete system diagram with all IC pin numbers marked before you start building.
2. The ICs come with their pins bent out at an angle to facilitate machine insertion in industrial settings. Lay the pins on a table top and carefully bend each row straight.
3. Position the ICs on your breadboard in approximately the same relative positions as they appear on the system diagram. Keep pin 1 at the top for all of them. This will make it easier to locate test points later.
4. Use the stick-on labels printed in Appendix B to make pin identification easier.
5. Use new No. 22 solid wire for breadboarding. Cut each wire about $\frac{1}{2}$ to 1 inch longer than it needs to be to reach. This will allow you to move it without pulling out one end. Strip $\frac{3}{8}$ inch of insulation from each end. If you strip too little, you run the risk of a missed connection; too much and you may get a short between two wires.
6. Use different-color wires for each function. This will be a tremendous help in troubleshooting. Using different colors for odd- and even-numbered address and data lines helps you spot wiring errors as you make them, rather than later. A suggested color code is given at the end of this appendix.
7. Wire all V_{CC} and ground pins first. Use the power strips that run vertically down the breadboards. Use an ohmmeter to check that the power

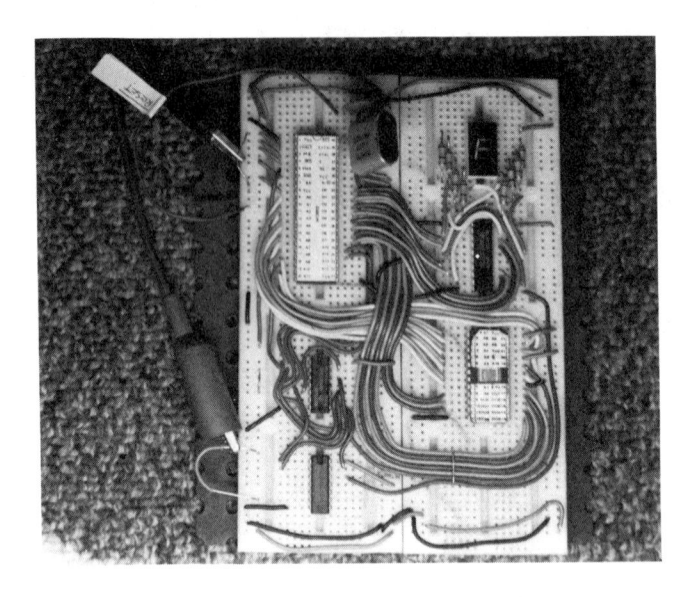

Figure A-1 A well-planned and wired microcomputer system on a breadboard.

strips are connected as one long bus. On some breadboards they are not. Put several 0.1-μF bypass capacitors between V_{CC} and ground.

8. Have a copy of the system diagram for notes. Brite-line every connection as you make it to avoid missing a connection.
9. Wire the address and data buses next. Route the wires in bundles such that they pass around (not over the top of) the ICs. You will want to be able to remove the ICs and get a probe on their pins.
10. Wire the clock, control, and I/O lines last. Cut resistor and capacitor leads short to avoid shorts and dangling components. Again, don't route wires over the chips. Figure A-1 shows a typical breadboard microcomputer system.
11. Hook a 2-inch-long bare wire along the ground bus for test-instrument ground chips. Bring commonly accessed test points out to the edge of the breadboard for easy access.
12. Check that V_{CC} *at the chips* is not below +4.9 V. Long thin lines from the power supply can drop excessive voltage.
13. Don't pull chips out of their sockets with your thumb and forefinger. You'll get the leads spiked into your finger when it pulls out. Pry the chip up from underneath, or use an IC extractor tool.
14. When going from one project to the next, it is generally easier to tear the old one down and wire the new one from scratch. Attempts to modify one microprocessor system into another invariably lead to wiring errors.

Appendix A

MICROCOMPUTER COLOR CODE

Black	Ground
Brown	Clock, chip-select, and control
Red	V_{CC} supply; +5 V
Orange	Supply lines other than V_{CC}
Yellow	Address bus, even numbers
Green	Address bus, odd numbers
Blue	Data bus, even numbers
Violet	Data bus, odd numbers
Gray	I/O bus, even numbers
White	I/O bus, odd numbers

appendix

B

IC Labels

Cut out and paste on to facilitate wiring and troubleshooting your projects.

```
 1 Vss    RST 40
 2 HLT    EXT 39
 3 MR     XTL 38
 4 IRQ    E→37
 5←VMA    RE 36
 6 NMI    VR 35
 7←BA     RW→34
 8 Vcc    D0 33
 9 A0     D1 32
10 A1     D2 31
11 A2     D3 30
12 A3  6802  D4 29
13 A4     D5 28
14 A5     D6 27
15 A6     D7 26
16 A7     A15 25
17 A8     A14 24
18 A9     A13 23
19 A10    A12 22
20 A11    Vss 21
```

```
 1 A7    Vcc 24
 2 A6    A8 23
 3 A5    A9 22
 4 A4    Vpp 21
 5 A3    OE 20
 6 A2    A10 19
 7 A1    CE 18
 8 A0 2716 D7 17
 9 D0    D6 16
10 D1    D5 15
11 D2    D4 14
12 Vss   D3 13
```

```
 1 Vss    CA1←40
 2 PA0    CA2↔39
 3 PA1    IRQA→38
 4 PA2    IRQB→37
 5 PA3    RS0←36
 6 PA4    RS1←35
 7 PA5    RST 34
 8 PA6    D0 33
 9 PA7    D1 32
10 PB0    D2 31
11 PB1    D3 30
12 PB2 6821 D4 29
13 PB3    D5 28
14 PB4    D6 27
15 PB5    D7 26
16 PB6    E←25
17 PB7    CS1 24
18←CB1    CS2 23
19←"2     CS0 22
20 Vcc    RW→21
```

258

Appendix B

```
 ┌──┐
─│OE  Vc│
 │Q0  Q7│
 │D0  D7│
 │D1  D6│
 │Q1  Q6│
 │Q2  Q5│
 │D2  D5│
 │D3  D4│
 │Q3  Q4│
 │G   CE│
 └──────┘
 74LS373
```

```
      ┌──┐
 │1 GND    V_CC 24│
 │2 D0       A0 23│
 │3 D1       A1 22│
 │4 D2       A2 21│
 │5 D3   6   A3 20│
 │6 D4   8   A4 19│
 │7 D5   1   A5 18│
 │8 D6   0   A6 17│
 │9 D7      R W̄ 16│
 │10 CS0   C̄S̄5̄ 15│
 │11 C̄S̄1̄   C̄S̄4̄ 14│
 │12 C̄S̄2̄    CS3 13│
 └────────────────┘
```

```
      ┌──┐
 │1 V_SS    C̄T̄S̄ ← 24│
 │2 → RD   D̄C̄D̄ ← 23│
 │3 → RCK    D0 22│
 │4 → TCK    D1 21│
 │5 ← R̄T̄S̄  6 D2 20│
 │6 ← TD   8 D3 19│
 │7 ← ĪR̄Q̄  5 D4 18│
 │8 → CS0  0 D5 17│
 │9 → C̄S̄2̄    D6 16│
 │10 → CS1   D7 15│
 │11 → RS    E ← 14│
 │12 V_CC   R W̄ 13│
 └──────────────────┘
```

```
      ┌──┐
 │1 V_SS       D7 40│
 │2 D6       CSS ← 39│
 │3 D0       H̄S̄ ← 38│
 │4 D1       F̄S̄ ← 37│
 │5 D2   7   R̄P̄ ← 36│
 │6 D3   4   ĀḠ ← 35│
 │7 D4   8   ĀS̄ ← 34│
 │8 D5   6   CLK ← 33│
 │9 → CHB   INV ← 32│
 │10 → φB   ĪN̄T̄ ← 31│
 │11 → φA   GM0 ← 30│
 │12 → M̄S̄   GM1 ← 29│
 │13 A5       Y ← 28│
 │14 A6     GM2 ← 27│
 │15 A7       A4 26│
 │16 A8       A3 25│
 │17 V_CC     A2 24│
 │18 A9       A1 23│
 │19 A10      A0 22│
 │20 A11     A12 21│
 └──────────────────┘
```

259

appendix C

Summary of Cycle-by-Cycle Operation

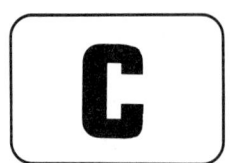

Table 8 provides a detailed description of the information present on the address bus, data bus, valid memory address line (VMA), and the read/write line (R/$\overline{W}$) during each cycle for each instruction.

This information is useful in comparing actual with expected results during debug of both software and hardware as the control program is executed. The information is categorized in groups according to addressing modes and number of cycles per instruction. (In general, instructions with the same addressing mode and number of cycles execute in the same manner; exceptions are indicated in the table.)

TABLE 8 — OPERATIONS SUMMARY

Address Mode and Instructions	Cycles	Cycle #	VMA Line	Address Bus	R/$\overline{W}$ Line	Data Bus
IMMEDIATE						
ADC EOR ADD LDA AND ORA BIT SBC CMP SUB	2	1	1	Op Code Address	1	Op Code
		2	1	Op Code Address + 1	1	Operand Data
CPX LDS LDX	3	1	1	Op Code Address	1	Op Code
		2	1	Op Code Address + 1	1	Operand Data (High Order Byte)
		3	1	Op Code Address + 2	1	Operand Data (Low Order Byte)
DIRECT						
ADC EOR ADD LDA AND ORA BIT SBC CMP SUB	3	1	1	Op Code Address	1	Op Code
		2	1	Op Code Address + 1	1	Address of Operand
		3	1	Address of Operand	1	Operand Data
CPX LDS LDX	4	1	1	Op Code Address	1	Op Code
		2	1	Op Code Address + 1	1	Address of Operand
		3	1	Address of Operand	1	Operand Data (High Order Byte)
		4	1	Operand Address + 1	1	Operand Data (Low Order Byte)
STA	4	1	1	Op Code Address	1	Op Code
		2	1	Op Code Address + 1	1	Destination Address
		3	0	Destination Address	1	Irrelevant Data (Note 1)
		4	1	Destination Address	0	Data from Accumulator
STS STX	5	1	1	Op Code Address	1	Op Code
		2	1	Op Code Address + 1	1	Address of Operand
		3	0	Address of Operand	1	Irrelevant Data (Note 1)
		4	1	Address of Operand	0	Register Data (High Order Byte)
		5	1	Address of Operand + 1	0	Register Data (Low Order Byte)
INDEXED						
JMP	4	1	1	Op Code Address	1	Op Code
		2	1	Op Code Address + 1	1	Offset
		3	0	Index Register	1	Irrelevant Data (Note 1)
		4	0	Index Register Plus Offset (w/o Carry)	1	Irrelevant Data (Note 1)
ADC EOR ADD LDA AND ORA BIT SBC CMP SUB	5	1	1	Op Code Address	1	Op Code
		2	1	Op Code Address + 1	1	Offset
		3	0	Index Register	1	Irrelevant Data (Note 1)
		4	0	Index Register Plus Offset (w/o Carry)	1	Irrelevant Data (Note 1)
		5	1	Index Register Plus Offset	1	Operand Data
CPX LDS LDX	6	1	1	Op Code Address	1	Op Code
		2	1	Op Code Address + 1	1	Offset
		3	0	Index Register	1	Irrelevant Data (Note 1)
		4	0	Index Register Plus Offset (w/o Carry)	1	Irrelevant Data (Note 1)
		5	1	Index Register Plus Offset	1	Operand Data (High Order Byte)
		6	1	Index Register Plus Offset + 1	1	Operand Data (Low Order Byte)

TABLE 8 — OPERATIONS SUMMARY (CONTINUED)

Address Mode and Instructions	Cycles	Cycle #	VMA Line	Address Bus	R/W̄ Line	Data Bus
INDEXED (Continued)						
STA	6	1	1	Op Code Address	1	Op Code
		2	1	Op Code Address + 1	1	Offset
		3	0	Index Register	1	Irrelevant Data (Note 1)
		4	0	Index Register Plus Offset (w/o Carry)	1	Irrelevant Data (Note 1)
		5	0	Index Register Plus Offset	1	Irrelevant Data (Note 1)
		6	1	Index Register Plus Offset	0	Operand Data
ASL LSR ASR NEG CLR ROL COM ROR DEC TST INC	7	1	1	Op Code Address	1	Op Code
		2	1	Op Code Address + 1	1	Offset
		3	0	Index Register	1	Irrelevant Data (Note 1)
		4	0	Index Register Plus Offset (w/o Carry)	1	Irrelevant Data (Note 1)
		5	1	Index Register Plus Offset	1	Current Operand Data
		6	0	Index Register Plus Offset	1	Irrelevant Data (Note 1)
		7	1/0 (Note 3)	Index Register Plus Offset	0	New Operand Data (Note 3)
STS STX	7	1	1	Op Code Address	1	Op Code
		2	1	Op Code Address + 1	1	Offset
		3	0	Index Register	1	Irrelevant Data (Note 1)
		4	0	Index Register Plus Offset (w/o Carry)	1	Irrelevant Data (Note 1)
		5	0	Index Register Plus Offset	1	Irrelevant Data (Note 1)
		6	1	Index Register Plus Offset	0	Operand Data (High Order Byte)
		7	1	Index Register Plus Offset + 1	0	Operand Data (Low Order Byte)
JSR	8	1	1	Op Code Address	1	Op Code
		2	1	Op Code Address + 1	1	Offset
		3	0	Index Register	1	Irrelevant Data (Note 1)
		4	1	Stack Pointer	0	Return Address (Low Order Byte)
		5	1	Stack Pointer − 1	0	Return Address (High Order Byte)
		6	0	Stack Pointer − 2	1	Irrelevant Data (Note 1)
		7	0	Index Register	1	Irrelevant Data (Note 1)
		8	0	Index Register Plus Offset (w/o Carry)	1	Irrelevant Data (Note 1)
EXTENDED						
JMP	3	1	1	Op Code Address	1	Op Code
		2	1	Op Code Address + 1	1	Jump Address (High Order Byte)
		3	1	Op Code Address + 2	1	Jump Address (Low Order Byte)
ADC EOR ADD LDA AND ORA BIT SBC CMP SUB	4	1	1	Op Code Address	1	Op Code
		2	1	Op Code Address + 1	1	Address of Operand (High Order Byte)
		3	1	Op Code Address + 2	1	Address of Operand (Low Order Byte)
		4	1	Address of Operand	1	Operand Data
CPX LDS LDX	5	1	1	Op Code Address	1	Op Code
		2	1	Op Code Address + 1	1	Address of Operand (High Order Byte)
		3	1	Op Code Address + 2	1	Address of Operand (Low Order Byte)
		4	1	Address of Operand	1	Operand Data (High Order Byte)
		5	1	Address of Operand + 1	1	Operand Data (Low Order Byte)
STA A STA B	5	1	1	Op Code Address	1	Op Code
		2	1	Op Code Address + 1	1	Destination Address (High Order Byte)
		3	1	Op Code Address + 2	1	Destination Address (Low Order Byte)
		4	0	Operand Destination Address	1	Irrelevant Data (Note 1)
		5	1	Operand Destination Address	0	Data from Accumulator
ASL LSR ASR NEG CLR ROL COM ROR DEC TST INC	6	1	1	Op Code Address	1	Op Code
		2	1	Op Code Address + 1	1	Address of Operand (High Order Byte)
		3	1	Op Code Address + 2	1	Address of Operand (Low Order Byte)
		4	1	Address of Operand	1	Current Operand Data
		5	0	Address of Operand	1	Irrelevant Data (Note 1)
		6	1/0 (Note 3)	Address of Operand	0	New Operand Data (Note 3)

TABLE 8 — OPERATIONS SUMMARY (CONTINUED)

Address Mode and Instructions	Cycles	Cycle #	VMA Line	Address Bus	R/W Line	Data Bus
EXTENDED (Continued)						
STS STX	6	1	1	Op Code Address	1	Op Code
		2	1	Op Code Address + 1	1	Address of Operand (High Order Byte)
		3	1	Op Code Address + 2	1	Address of Operand (Low Order Byte)
		4	0	Address of Operand	1	Irrelevant Data (Note 1)
		5	1	Address of Operand	0	Operand Data (High Order Byte)
		6	1	Address of Operand + 1	0	Operand Data (Low Order Byte)
JSR	9	1	1	Op Code Address	1	Op Code
		2	1	Op Code Address + 1	1	Address of Subroutine (High Order Byte)
		3	1	Op Code Address + 2	1	Address of Subroutine (Low Order Byte)
		4	1	Subroutine Starting Address	1	Op Code of Next Instruction
		5	1	Stack Pointer	0	Return Address (Low Order Byte)
		6	1	Stack Pointer − 1	0	Return Address (High Order Byte)
		7	0	Stack Pointer − 2	1	Irrelevant Data (Note 1)
		8	0	Op Code Address + 2	1	Irrelevant Data (Note 1)
		9	1	Op Code Address + 2	1	Address of Subroutine (Low Order Byte)
INHERENT						
ABA DAA SEC ASL DEC SEI ASR INC SEV CBA LSR TAB CLC NEG TAP CLI NOP TBA CLR ROL TPA CLV ROR TST COM SBA	2	1	1	Op Code Address	1	Op Code
		2	1	Op Code Address + 1	1	Op Code of Next Instruction
DES DEX INS INX	4	1	1	Op Code Address	1	Op Code
		2	1	Op Code Address + 1	1	Op Code of Next Instruction
		3	0	Previous Register Contents	1	Irrelevant Data (Note 1)
		4	0	New Register Contents	1	Irrelevant Data (Note 1)
PSH	4	1	1	Op Code Address	1	Op Code
		2	1	Op Code Address + 1	1	Op Code of Next Instruction
		3	1	Stack Pointer	0	Accumulator Data
		4	0	Stack Pointer − 1	1	Accumulator Data
PUL	4	1	1	Op Code Address	1	Op Code
		2	1	Op Code Address + 1	1	Op Code of Next Instruction
		3	0	Stack Pointer	1	Irrelevant Data (Note 1)
		4	1	Stack Pointer + 1	1	Operand Data from Stack
TSX	4	1	1	Op Code Address	1	Op Code
		2	1	Op Code Address + 1	1	Op Code of Next Instruction
		3	0	Stack Pointer	1	Irrelevant Data (Note 1)
		4	0	New Index Register	1	Irrelevant Data (Note 1)
TXS	4	1	1	Op Code Address	1	Op Code
		2	1	Op Code Address + 1	1	Op Code of Next Instruction
		3	0	Index Register	1	Irrelevant Data
		4	0	New Stack Pointer	1	Irrelevant Data
RTS	5	1	1	Op Code Address	1	Op Code
		2	1	Op Code Address + 1	1	Irrelevant Data (Note 2)
		3	0	Stack Pointer	1	Irrelevant Data (Note 1)
		4	1	Stack Pointer + 1	1	Address of Next Instruction (High Order Byte)
		5	1	Stack Pointer + 2	1	Address of Next Instruction (Low Order Byte)

Appendix C

TABLE 8 — OPERATIONS SUMMARY (CONCLUDED)

Address Mode and Instructions	Cycles	Cycle #	VMA Line	Address Bus	R/W̄ Line	Data Bus
INHERENT (Continued)						
WAI	9	1	1	Op Code Address	1	Op Code
		2	1	Op Code Address + 1	1	Op Code of Next Instruction
		3	1	Stack Pointer	0	Return Address (Low Order Byte)
		4	1	Stack Pointer − 1	0	Return Address (High Order Byte)
		5	1	Stack Pointer − 2	0	Index Register (Low Order Byte)
		6	1	Stack Pointer − 3	0	Index Register (High Order Byte)
		7	1	Stack Pointer − 4	0	Contents of Accumulator A
		8	1	Stack Pointer − 5	0	Contents of Accumulator B
		9	1	Stack Pointer − 6	1	Contents of Cond. Code Register
RTI	10	1	1	Op Code Address	1	Op Code
		2	1	Op Code Address + 1	1	Irrelevant Data (Note 2)
		3	0	Stack Pointer	1	Irrelevant Data (Note 1)
		4	1	Stack Pointer + 1	1	Contents of Cond. Code Register from Stack
		5	1	Stack Pointer + 2	1	Contents of Accumulator B from Stack
		6	1	Stack Pointer + 3	1	Contents of Accumulator A from Stack
		7	1	Stack Pointer + 4	1	Index Register from Stack (High Order Byte)
		8	1	Stack Pointer + 5	1	Index Register from Stack (Low Order Byte)
		9	1	Stack Pointer + 6	1	Next Instruction Address from Stack (High Order Byte)
		10	1	Stack Pointer + 7	1	Next Instruction Address from Stack (Low Order Byte)
SWI	12	1	1	Op Code Address	1	Op Code
		2	1	Op Code Address + 1	1	Irrelevant Data (Note 1)
		3	1	Stack Pointer	0	Return Address (Low Order Byte)
		4	1	Stack Pointer − 1	0	Return Address (High Order Byte)
		5	1	Stack Pointer − 2	0	Index Register (Low Order Byte)
		6	1	Stack Pointer − 3	0	Index Register (High Order Byte)
		7	1	Stack Pointer − 4	0	Contents of Accumulator A
		8	1	Stack Pointer − 5	0	Contents of Accumulator B
		9	1	Stack Pointer − 6	0	Contents of Cond. Code Register
		10	0	Stack Pointer − 7	1	Irrelevant Data (Note 1)
		11	1	Vector Address FFFA (Hex)	1	Address of Subroutine (High Order Byte)
		12	1	Vector Address FFFB (Hex)	1	Address of Subroutine (Low Order Byte)
RELATIVE						
BCC BHI BNE BCS BLE BPL BEQ BLS BRA BGE BLT BVC BGT BMI BVS	4	1	1	Op Code Address	1	Op Code
		2	1	Op Code Address + 1	1	Branch Offset
		3	0	Op Code Address + 2	1	Irrelevant Data (Note 1)
		4	0	Branch Address	1	Irrelevant Data (Note 1)
BSR	8	1	1	Op Code Address	1	Op Code
		2	1	Op Code Address + 1	1	Branch Offset
		3	0	Return Address of Main Program	1	Irrelevant Data (Note 1)
		4	1	Stack Pointer	0	Return Address (Low Order Byte)
		5	1	Stack Pointer − 1	0	Return Address (High Order Byte)
		6	0	Stack Pointer − 2	1	Irrelevant Data (Note 1)
		7	0	Return Address of Main Program	1	Irrelevant Data (Note 1)
		8	0	Subroutine Address (Note 4)	1	Irrelevant Data (Note 1)

NOTES:
1. If device which is addressed during this cycle uses VMA, then the Data Bus will go to the high-impedance three-state condition. Depending on bus capacitance, data from the previous cycle may be retained on the Data Bus.
2. Data is ignored by the MPU.
3. For TST, VMA = 0 and Operand data does not change.
4. MS Byte of Address Bus = MS Byte of Address of BSR instruction and LS Byte of Address Bus = LS Byte of Sub-Routine Address.

Courtesy of Motorola, Inc.

appendix D

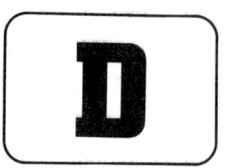

Object Code for *Ambulance Siren*

```
                    1000 ********* AMBULANCE SIREN ***********
                    1010 *
                    1020        .OR    $FFD4
                    1030        .TA    $47D4
                    1040 *
FFD4- 86 40         1050 START  LDAA   #$40      START WITH 64 DELAY LOOPS.
FFD6- CE 00 B0      1060 TONE   LDX    #$00B0    MAKE 176 CYCLES PER TONE.
FFD9- 16            1070 CYCLE  TAB              2 US/CY (9 CY/LOOP) 64 LOOP
FFDA- 5A            1080 ON     DECB             = 1.2 MS/HALF CYCLE,
FFDB- 27 03         1090        BEQ    SWITCH    OR 434 HZ HI FREQ.
FFDD- 7E FF DA      1100        JMP    ON        80 LOOPS = 347 HZ LOW FREQ.
FFE0- 16            1110 SWITCH TAB              FIRST LOOP KEEPS A4 HIGH.
FFE1- 5A            1120 OFF    DECB             THIS LOOP
FFE2- 27 03         1130        BEQ    LASTQ     KEEPS
FFE4- 7E FF E1      1140        JMP    OFF       A4 LOW.
FFE7- 09            1150 LASTQ  DEX              LAST CYCLE?
FFE8- 27 03         1160        BEQ    NEWF      YES: CHANGE FREQ.
FFEA- 7E FF D9      1170        JMP    CYCLE     NO: MAKE ANOTHER AF CYCLE.
FFED- 81 40         1180 NEWF   CMPA   #$40      ACCA SET FOR HI FREQ?
FFEF- 27 03         1190        BEQ    LOWER     YES: MAKE DELAY LONGER.
FFF1- 7E FF D4      1200        JMP    START     NO: START WITH HIGH FREQ.
FFF4- 8B 10         1210 LOWER  ADDA   #$10      ADD 16 LOOPS TO DELAY.
FFF6- 7E FF D6      1220        JMP    TONE      START WITH 176 AF CYCLES.
                    1230        .OR    $FFFE
                    1240        .TA    $47FE
FFFE- FF D4         1250        .DA    START
                    1260        .EN
```

appendix E

Program Listing For *Air Raid* Sound

```
                1000 *-----------------------------------------------------------
                1010 * AIR RAID GAME   COPYRIGHT 1984  BY D. L. METZGER
                1020 *
                1030 * PROGRAM CONTAINS SOUND EFFECTS; ILLUSTRATES MODULAR
                1040 *   STRUCTURED PROGRAMMING TECHNIQUE.
                1050 *
                1060 * FOUR ANTIAIRCRAFT BATTERIES SHOOT DOWN WAVES OF ATTACKING
                1070 * PLANES. HOW MANY HITS CAN YOU SCORE BEFORE THEY WIPE
                1080 * OUT ALL OF YOUR BATTERIES?
                1090 *-----------------------------------------------------------
                1100 *             -- RULES OF THE GAME --
                1110 * PLANE FLYING ACROSS INDICATED BY ROW OF 8 LIGHTS.
                1120 * PLANE DWELLS ON EACH LIGHT ABOUT 0.8 SEC TO START,
                1130 *   SPEEDING UP ON EACH PASS.
                1140 * PLANE IS VULNERABLE TO BE SHOT DOWN DURING THE
                1150 *   THIRD QUARTER OF EACH DWELL PERIOD.
                1160 * TWO POINTS PER HIT. PLANE SHOOTS AT BATTERY AT 3/4
                1170 *   THROUGH DWELL PERIOD. BATTERY (BUTTON) PROTECTED FROM
                1180 *   BEING SHOT BY PLANE FOR 1/2 A DWELL PERIOD
                1190 *   AFTER SHOT. IRQ BUTTON REDUCES PLANE-VULNERABLE
                1200 *   AND BATTERY-PROTECTED TIMES BUT ADDS 1 POINT
                1210 *   PER HIT TO SCORING.
                1220 * USE 6 TIMES MAX OR SHOTS BECOME DUDS.  LED DARKENS
                1230 *   OVER BATTERY AFTER IT IS SHOT OUT. PLANE IS LUCKY
                1240 *   ENOUGH TO HIT BATTERY ONLY EVERY 4TH CHANCE.
                1250 * SCORE DISPLAYED IN BINARY WHEN ALL BATTERIES SHOT OUT.
                1260 *
                1270 *-----------------------------------------------------------
                1280 *              MODULE 0 -- INITIALIZATION
                1290 *-----------------------------------------------------------
2000-           1300 INPUT  .EQ  $2000     INPUT BUFFER ADR
4000-           1310 OUTPUT .EQ  $4000     OCTAL LATCH FOR LED OUT
6000-           1320 OUTSND .EQ  $6000     LATCH FOR SPEAKER OUT
0000-           1330 SCORE  .EQ  00        COUNTS UP POINTS FOR HITS
0001-           1340 LUCK   .EQ  01        PLANE HITS BATT EVERY 4TH CHANCE
0002-           1350 DELAY  .EQ  02        SPEEDS UP SHIFT OF PLANE LEDS
```

```
0003-              1360 MASK    .EQ   03      HOLDS 0 BITS WHERE BATT SHOT OUT
0004-              1370 DWLCT   .EQ   04      DWELL SHIFTS TO NEXT LED WHEN = 0
0005-              1380 CHARGE  .EQ   05      HOLDS TIME OF LIVE SHOT; DECRSD BY IRQ
0006-              1390 SHPOS   .EQ   06      SHOT POSITION - BIT WHERE KEY PRESSED
0007-              1400 SHCT    .EQ   07      PICKED UP FROM CHARGE; COUNTED DOWN
0008-              1410 POINTS  .EQ   08      POINTS PER HIT; INCRSD BY IRQ
0009-              1420 FREQ    .EQ   09      MAKES PLANE-CRASH WHINE FREQ DECR.
000A-              1430 REPS    .EQ   10      NO. OF CYCLES AT EACH FREQ (CRASH SND)
000B-              1440 SNDBUF  .EQ   11      PICKED UP FROM FREQ & COUNTED DOWN
000C-              1450 GUNDLY  .EQ   12      GUNDELAY FOR MACHINE-GUN SOUND
000D-              1460 BURSTS  .EQ   13      NUMBER OF BURSTS OF MACHINE GUN
                   1470         .OR   $FD00   PROGRAM START ADR
                   1480         .TA   $4500   ASSEMBLER TARGET ADR
                   1490 *------------------------------------------------------
                   1500 * ACCUM B = PLANE POSITION. MASK DARKENS LEDS OVER
                   1510 *   SHOT-OUT BATTERIES. DELAY OF  $FF STARTS WITH ABOUT
                   1520 *   0.8 SEC PER SHIFT.  CARRY SAVED ON STACK FOR ROTATING
                   1530 *   PLANE POSITION THROUGH CARRY BIT.
                   1540 *------------------------------------------------------
FD00- 5F           1550         CLRB
FD01- 7F 00 00     1560         CLR   SCORE
FD04- 7F 00 01     1570         CLR   LUCK
FD07- 7F 00 04     1580         CLR   DWLCT
FD0A- 7F 00 06     1590         CLR   SHPOS
FD0D- 7F 00 07     1600         CLR   SHCT
FD10- 86 FF        1610         LDAA  #$FF
FD12- 97 03        1620         STAA  MASK
FD14- 97 05        1630         STAA  CHARGE
FD16- 97 02        1640         STAA  DELAY
FD18- 86 02        1650         LDAA  #$02
FD1A- 97 08        1660         STAA  POINTS
FD1C- 8E 00 7F     1670         LDS   #$007F
FD1F- 0D           1680         SEC
FD20- 07           1690         TPA
FD21- 36           1700         PSHA
                   1710 *------------------------------------------------------
                   1720 * MODULE 1 -- CHECK PLANE STATUS, OUTPUT PLANE POSITION,
                   1730 *   AND DELAY.  IF DWELL COUNT = 0, ROTATE PLANE RIGHT
                   1740 *   THRU CARRY, MASK IF OVER DEAD BATRY. DISPLAY POSITION,
                   1750 *   CHANGE LUCK COUNTER FOR MODULE 4, AND SPEED UP GAME.
                   1760 * IN ANY CASE, DELAY MAX OF 3 MS, MAKING A PLANE-MOTOR
                   1770 *   NOISE WITH MIN FREQ OF 160 HZ, INCREASING.
                   1780 *------------------------------------------------------
FD22- 7C 60 00     1790 PLAY    INC   OUTSND
FD25- 7A 00 04     1800         DEC   DWLCT
FD28- 26 12        1810         BNE   WAIT
FD2A- 32           1820         PULA
FD2B- 06           1830         TAP
FD2C- 56           1840         RORB
FD2D- 07           1850         TPA
FD2E- 36           1860         PSHA
FD2F- 37           1870         PSHB
FD30- D4 03        1880         ANDB  MASK
FD32- F7 40 00     1890         STAB  OUTPUT
FD35- 33           1900         PULB
FD36- 7C 00 01     1910         INC   LUCK
FD39- 7A 00 02     1920         DEC   DELAY
FD3C- 96 02        1930 WAIT    LDAA  DELAY
FD3E- 4A           1940 LOOP    DECA
FD3F- 26 FD        1950         BNE   LOOP
                   1960 *------------------------------------------------------
                   1970 * MODULE 2 - CHECK SHOT STATUS AND INPUT SHOT IF TIMED OUT.
                   1980 *------------------------------------------------------
                   1990 * IF SHOT COUNTER NOT = 0, DECREMENT IT.  IF = 0, PLACE
                   2000 *   KEY INPUT IN SHOT POSITION MASKING OUT NO-BATTERY AND
                   2010 *   DEAD-BATTERY BITS. IF THERE IS A VALID INPUT,
```

Appendix E

```
                    2020 *   RECHARGE SHOT COUNTER.
                    2030 *------------------------------------------------------------
FD41- 7D 00 07      2040          TST   SHCT
FD44- 27 03         2050          BEQ   KEY
FD46- 7A 00 07      2060          DEC   SHCT
FD49- 26 10         2070 KEY      BNE   EXIT
FD4B- B6 20 00      2080          LDAA  INPUT
FD4E- 43            2090          COMA
FD4F- 84 55         2100          ANDA  #$55
FD51- 94 03         2110          ANDA  MASK
FD53- 97 06         2120          STAA  SHPOS
FD55- 27 04         2130          BEQ   EXIT
FD57- 96 05         2140          LDAA  CHARGE
FD59- 97 07         2150          STAA  SHCT
FD5B- 01            2160 EXIT     NOP
                    2170 *------------------------------------------------------------
                    2180 * MODULE 3 -- FLASH ALL LEDS IF BATTERY HITS PLANE.
                    2190 *------------------------------------------------------------
                    2200 * IF PLANE IS 3/4 WAY THROUGH ITS DWELL, AND SHOT
                    2210 *   POSITION = PLANE POSITION, AND MASK SHOWS BATTERY NOT
                    2220 *   SHOT OUT, AND SHOT COUNT >= $C0, THEN FLASH ALL LEDS,
                    2230 *   MAKE PLANE-CRASH SOUND, & ADD TO SCORE.
                    2240 *------------------------------------------------------------
                    2250 *
FD5C- 96 04         2260          LDAA  DWLCT
FD5E- 81 40         2270          CMPA  #$40
FD60- 26 43         2280          BNE   NOHIT
FD62- D1 06         2290          CMPB  SHPOS
FD64- 26 3F         2300          BNE   NOHIT
FD66- D5 03         2310          BITB  MASK
FD68- 27 3B         2320          BEQ   NOHIT
FD6A- 96 07         2330          LDAA  SHCT
FD6C- 81 C0         2340          CMPA  #$C0
FD6E- 25 35         2350          BCS   NOHIT
FD70- 86 FF         2360          LDAA  #$FF
FD72- B7 40 00      2370          STAA  OUTPUT
                    2380 *
                    2390 * PLANE-CRASH SOUND; 400 HZ TO 200 HZ IN 3 SECONDS.
                    2400 *   SND BUF COUNTS DELAY PER HALF CYCLE.
                    2410 *   "FREQ" HOLDS INCREASING DELAY. $18 HALF CYCLES AT
                    2420 *     EACH FREQ.  DELAYS FROM $40 TO $80 LOOPS.
                    2430 *
FD75- 86 40         2440 WHINE    LDAA  #$40
FD77- 97 09         2450          STAA  FREQ
FD79- 86 18         2460 LOWRF    LDAA  #$18
FD7B- 97 0A         2470          STAA  REPS
FD7D- 96 09         2480 SAME     LDAA  FREQ
FD7F- 97 0B         2490          STAA  SNDBUF
FD81- 7A 00 0B      2500 HALF     DEC   SNDBUF
FD84- 26 FB         2510          BNE   HALF
FD86- 7A 00 0A      2520          DEC   REPS
FD89- 96 0A         2530          LDAA  REPS
FD8B- B7 60 00      2540          STAA  OUTSND
FD8E- 26 ED         2550          BNE   SAME
FD90- 7C 00 09      2560          INC   FREQ
FD93- 96 09         2570          LDAA  FREQ
FD95- 81 80         2580          CMPA  #$80
FD97- 26 E0         2590          BNE   LOWRF
                    2600 *
FD99- 7F 40 00      2610          CLR   OUTPUT
FD9C- 09            2620 TWO      DEX
FD9D- 26 FD         2630          BNE   TWO
FD9F- 96 00         2640          LDAA  SCORE
FDA1- 9B 08         2650          ADDA  POINTS
FDA3- 97 00         2660          STAA  SCORE
FDA5- 01            2670 NOHIT    NOP
```

```
                2680 *----------------------------------------------------------------
                2690 * MODULE 4 - IF PLANE HITS BATTERY FLASH ONE LED TEN TIMES.
                2700 *----------------------------------------------------------------
                2710 * IF PLANE IS 3/4 THROUGH DWELL, AND PLANE IS OVER ANY
                2720 * BATTERY, AND MASK SHOWS BATTERY IS LIVE, AND IF THERE
                2730 * IS NO SHOT AT THE PLANE OR SHOT COUNTER <80, AND LUCK
                2740 * COUNTER LOW TWO BITS ARE ZERO, THEN FLICKER PLANE LED
                2750 * 10 TIMES AT 8 HZ AND REMOVE BATTERY BIT FROM MASK.
                2760 *----------------------------------------------------------------
                2770 *
FDA6- 96 04     2780        LDAA  DWLCT
FDA8- 81 41     2790        CMPA  #$41
FDAA- 26 42     2800        BNE   SAFE
FDAC- C5 55     2810        BITB  #$55
FDAE- 27 3E     2820        BEQ   SAFE
FDB0- D5 03     2830        BITB  MASK
FDB2- 27 3A     2840        BEQ   SAFE
FDB4- D1 06     2850        CMPB  SHPOS
FDB6- 26 05     2860        BNE   LUCKY
FDB8- 7D 00 07  2870        TST   SHCT
FDBB- 2B 31     2880        BMI   SAFE
FDBD- 96 01     2890 LUCKY  LDAA  LUCK
FDBF- 84 03     2900        ANDA  #$03
FDC1- 26 2B     2910        BNE   SAFE
                2920 *
                2930 * ACC A IS USED TO COUNT OFF TEN FLICKERS OF PLANE LED
                2940 *
FDC3- 86 0A     2950        LDAA  #$0A
FDC5- 97 0D     2960        STAA  BURSTS
FDC7- F7 40 00  2970 CYCLE  STAB  OUTPUT
                2980 *
                2990 * MACHINE GUN SOUND; 160-HZ PULSES. 192 ($C0) LOOPS
                3000 * PER 16-US HALF CYCLE.  24 ($18) HALF CYCLES PER BURST.
                3010 *
FDCA- 86 C0     3020 STUTR  LDAA  #$C0
FDCC- 97 0C     3030        STAA  GUNDLY
FDCE- 86 18     3040        LDAA  #$18
FDD0- 7A 00 0C  3050 BANG   DEC   GUNDLY
FDD3- 26 FB     3060        BNE   BANG
FDD5- 4A        3070        DECA
FDD6- B7 60 00  3080        STAA  OUTSND
FDD9- 26 F5     3090        BNE   BANG
                3100 *
FDDB- 7F 40 00  3110        CLR   OUTPUT
FDDE- CE 0D 00  3120        LDX   #$0D00
FDE1- 09        3130 BACK2  DEX
FDE2- 26 FD     3140        BNE   BACK2
FDE4- 7A 00 0D  3150        DEC   BURSTS
FDE7- 26 DE     3160        BNE   CYCLE
FDE9- 96 03     3170        LDAA  MASK
FDEB- 10        3180        SBA
FDEC- 97 03     3190        STAA  MASK
FDEE- 01        3200 SAFE   NOP
                3210 *
                3220 *----------------------------------------------------------------
                3230 * MODULE 5 -- ACCEPT INTERRUPT AND DISPLAY SCORE.
                3240 *----------------------------------------------------------------
                3250 *
FDEF- 0E        3260        CLI
FDF0- 96 03     3270        LDAA  MASK
FDF2- 81 AA     3280        CMPA  #$AA
FDF4- 26 08     3290        BNE   GO
FDF6- 96 00     3300        LDAA  SCORE
FDF8- B7 40 00  3310        STAA  OUTPUT
FDFB- 7E FD FB  3320 HALT   JMP   HALT
FDFE- 0F        3330 GO     SEI
```

Appendix E

```
FDFF- 7E FD 22  3340          JMP  PLAY
                3350 *
                3360 *-----------------------------------------------------------
                3370 * INTERRUPT ROUTINE (IRQ) - REDUCES CHARGE, MAKING TIMING
                3380 * MORE CRITICAL AND PLANE HARDER TO HIT. INCREMENTS
                3390 * POINTS PER HIT.  IMPOSSIBLE TO HIT PLANE IF USED MORE
                3400 * THAN 4 TIMES.
                3410 * -----------------------------------------------------------
                3420 *
FE02- 0F        3430 BOOST    SEI
FE03- 96 05     3440          LDAA CHARGE
FE05- 80 0D     3450          SUBA #$0D
FE07- 97 05     3460          STAA CHARGE
FE09- 7C 00 08  3470          INC  POINTS
FE0C- CE C0 00  3480          LDX  #$C000
FE0F- 09        3490 HOLD     DEX
FE10- 26 FD     3500          BNE  HOLD
                3510
FE12- 0E        3520          CLI
FE13- 3B        3530          RTI
                3540 *
                3550 *-----------------------------------------------------------
                3560 *        INTERRUPT REQUEST AND RESET VECTORS.
                3570 *-----------------------------------------------------------
                3580 *
                3590          .OR  $FFF8       IRQ VECTOR
                3600          .TA  $47F8       CONTAINS ADR OF
FFF8- FE 02     3610          .DA  BOOST       "BOOST" ROUTINE.
                3620          .OR  $FFFE       RESET VECTOR
                3630          .TA  $47FE       CONTAINS ADR OF
FFFE- FD 00     3640          .HS  FD00        PROGRAM START.
                3650          .EN              END
```

Index

A

ACIA, 216
A/D conversion, 208
ADC instructions, 101
ADD instructions, 101
Address, 2, 7
Address bus, 2
Address decoding, 25, 35, 53
Address display, 75
Addresses, processor vs. EPROM, 40
Addressing modes, 9, 37, 41, 65, 71, 72
Address recognizer, 80
Air Raid game, 105, 265
Ambulance siren program, 46, 264
Analog/digital conversion, 208
AND instructions, 61
ASCII, 7, 238
Assemblers, 39
Automated calibration, 224

B

Back branching, 99
BASIC language, 63, 222, 226
Baud rate, 214
BCS instruction, 61
BEQ instruction, 41
BGE, BGT instructions, 101
BHI instruction, 101
Bidirectional bus, 6
Binary, 3
Bit, 2
Bit masking, 61, 180
BLE, BLS instructions, 101
BMI instruction, 101
BNE instruction, 100
BPL instruction, 101
Branch displacement, 100
Branch instructions, 41, 100
Branch table, 100
Breakpoints, 187
Bubble memory, 24
Bus, 2
Byte, 6

C

Carry flag, 100
CE (Chip Enable), 27
Checksum, 145
Chicken Pickin', 205
CLI instruction, 97, 183
Clock, 9
CLR instruction, 39
CMP instructions, 61
Color code, 257
COM instructions, 90
Comments, 39

Computer, 1, 165
Control register, 138, 218
Cross assembler, 85
Crystal, 10

D

Data bus, 5
Data-bus display, 78
Data-direction register, 137
Data qualification, 127
Data types, 6
Debounce circuit, 30
Debugging, program, 186
Decoder, 53
Decoding, software, 68
Delay routine, 174
DEX instruction, 44
Diagnostic program, 38
Digital advantage, 46
Digital/analog converter, 53
Direct addressing, 72
Disk, 23
Display memory, 233
Dynamic RAM, 23

E

E clock, 9
Echoing, 145
EPROM, 23
EPROM programmer, 29, 172, 188
Erasing, 28
Extended addressing, 9

F

Fight for the bus, 25, 243
Firmware, 23
Floppy disk, 23
Flowcharting, 44

G

Games, 57, 67, 87, 105
General-purpose computer, 165

H

H flag, 102
Half carry, 102
Halt, 75
Handshaking, 142

Hex Drill game, 67
Hexadecimal, 5

I

I flag, 102
IC pinout labels, 258
IC tester, 134
    data development for, 158
    hardware, 145
    software, 149, 154
Immediate instructions, 37
INC instruction, 14
Index register, 42
Indexed addressing, 65
Indirect addressing, 71
Inherent instructions, 9
Input buffers, 87
Instructions, 7, 8
Interfacing computers, 220, 240
Interrupt-mask flag, 102
Interrupt, non-maskable, 99
Interrupt request, 97
IRQ vector, 97

J

JMP instruction, 12
JSR instruction, 93

K

K (kilobyte), 27
Keyboard read routine, 176

L

Labels, IC stick-on, 258
Labels, program, 39, 44
Lamp-flasher program, 42
Latch, 52
LDA instructions, 37
LDX instruction, 42
Linearization routine, 223
Linear programs, 115
Logic analyzer, 126
Logic levels, 2
LSB, 12

M

MEM game, 87, 102
Microchicken monitor, 194
Microprocessor comparisons, 251

Index

Mirroring, 36
Modules, program, 111
Monitor, TV, 235
Monitor program, 174, 194
MSB, 12

N

N flag, 101
Nested loops, 90
Nested subroutines, 179
Nibble, 6
NMI, 99
Number game, 57

O

Object code, 39
OE (output enable), 27
Offset, address, 65
Overflow flag, 101

P

Parity bit, 215
PIA chip, 135
    port A vs. port B, 140
Police siren program, 44
Power supplies, 173
Printed circuits, 169, 222
Program counter, 5
Program debugging, 186
Program listing, 39
Program logic, 84
Programmer, EPROM, 29, 172, 188
Programmer's card, beginning, 49
Programmer's model, 96
Programming philosophy, 111
PROM, 23
Protocol, 145
PSH instructions, 95
PUL instructions, 95

Q

Qualification, data, 127

R

RAM, 2
Ramp generator, 56
Random-number generator, 58
Rat's nest programming, 108, 117
Relative addressing, 41

Reset, 10
Reset vector, 38
ROM, 23
Rotate instructions, 109
RS-232 interface, 214, 215
RTI instruction, 98
RTS instruction, 93
R/W (Read/Write-not), 10, 16

S

SBC instructions, 101
Scale linearizer, 223
Serial data transmission, 214
Shift instructions, 193, 201
Single stepping, 76, 183
Software decoding, 68
Sound effects, 121, 123
Source code, 39
STA instructions, 37
Stack, 93
Stack pointer, 93-95
Static RAM, 23
Strobing, 149
Structured programming, 112
STX instruction, 42
SUB instruction, 101
Subroutine, 93, 174
SWI instruction, 99

T

Tape-record function, 171, 193
Test program:
    memory interface, 39
    single-step, 187
    video display, 242
Time-delay routine, 41, 174
Top-down programming, 111
Trigger circuit, 40
Tristate devices, 24
Troubleshooting, 75, 82
TST instruction, 49, 57

U

UART, 216

V

V flag, 101
VDG (video display generator), 232
Vectors, 38, 97
Video chicken, 243

Video display, 232
VMA, 10, 14
Volatile memories, 21

W

Wiring hints, 255
Word recognizer, 127

X

X register, 42

Z

Z flat, 42
Zero-page addressing, 72

6802 Programmer's Reference

OPERATIONS	MNEMON	IMMED INHER OP ~ #	DIR/REL (2 byte) OP ~	EXTND (3 byte) OP ~	INDEX (2 byte) OP ~	OPERATION (All register labels refer to contents)	AFFECTS COND. CODE REG. Example: N = set, N̄ = cleared, n = set or cleared, n[7] = note 7 below.
Add Acmltrs	ABA	1B 2 1				A + B → A	h n z v c
Add with Carry	ADCA	89 2 2	99 3	B9 4	A9 5	A + M + C → A	h n z v c
	ADCB	C9 2 2	D9 3	F9 4	E9 5	B + M + C → B	h n z v c
Add	ADDA	8B 2 2	9B 3	BB 4	AB 5	A + M → A	h n z v c
	ADDB	CB 2 2	DB 3	FB 4	EB 5	B + M → B	h n z v c
And	ANDA	84 2 2	94 3	B4 4	A4 5	A · M → A	n z V̄
	ANDB	C4 2 2	D4 3	F4 4	E4 5	B · M → B	n z V̄
Arithmetic, Shift Left	ASL			78 6	68 7	M ⎫ Shift left into	n z v[6] c
	ASLA	48 2 1				A ⎬ carry; 0 to LSB	n z v[6] c
	ASLB	58 2 1				B ⎭ [□]←[□□□□□□□□]←0 C 7 ← 0	n z v[6] c
Arithmetic, Shift Right	ASR			77 6	67 7	M ⎫ Shift right into	n z v[6] c
	ASRA	47 2 1				A ⎬ carry; bit 7 stays	n z v[6] c
	ASRB	57 2 1				B ⎭ [→□□□□□□□□]→[□] 7 → 0 C	n z v[6] c
Branch:						Test:	
If Carry Clear	BCC		24 4			C = 0?	
If Carry Set	BCS		25 4			C = 1?	
If = Zero	BEQ		27 4			Z = 1?	
If ≥ Zero	BGE		2C 4			N ⊕ V = 0?	
If > Zero	BGT		2E 4			Z + (N ⊕ V) = 0?	
If Higher	BHI		22 4			C + Z = 0?	
Bit Test	BITA	85 2 2	95 3	B5 4	A5 5	A · M ⎫ Sets CCR	n z V̄
	BITB	C5 2 2	D5 3	F5 4	E5 5	B · M ⎭ bits only	n z V̄
Branch:						Test:	
If ≤ Zero	BLE		2F 4			Z + (N ⊕ V) = 1?	
If Lower Or Same	BLS		23 4			C + Z = 1?	
If < Zero	BLT		2D 4			N ⊕ V = 1?	
If Minus	BMI		2B 4			N = 1?	
If Not Equal Zero	BNE		26 4			Z = 0?	
If Plus	BPL		2A 4			N = 0?	
Always	BRA		20 4			None	
To Subroutine	BSR		8D 8			(Stack PCL, PCH)	
If Overflow Clear	BVC		28 4			V = 0?	
If Overflow Set	BVS		29 4			V = 1?	
Compare Acmltrs	CBA	11 2 1				A − B	n z v c
Clear Carry	CLC	0C 2 1				0 → C	C̄
Clear Intrpt Mask	CLI	0E 2 1				0 → I	Ī
Clear	CLR			7F 6	6F 7	00 → M	N̄ Z V̄ C̄
	CLRA	4F 2 1				00 → A	N̄ Z V̄ C̄
	CLRB	5F 2 1				00 → B	N̄ Z V̄ C̄
Clear Overflow	CLV	0A 2 1				0 → V	V̄
Compare	CMPA	81 2 2	91 3	B1 4	A1 5	A − M ⎫ Sets CCR	n z v c
	CMPB	C1 2 2	D1 3	F1 4	E1 5	B − M ⎭ bits only	n z v c
Complement, 1's	COM			73 6	63 7	M̄ → M	n z V̄ C
	COMA	43 2 1				Ā → A	n z V̄ C
	COMB	53 2 1				B̄ → B	n z V̄ C
Compare Index Reg	CPX	8C 3 3	9C 4	BC 5	AC 6	$(X_H/X_L) - (M/M+1)$	n[7] z v[8]
Decimal Adjust, A	DAA	19 2 1				Converts Add. of BCD to BCD Format	n z v c[3]
Decrement	DEC			7A 6	6A 7	M − 1 → M	n z v[4]
	DECA	4A 2 1				A − 1 → A	n z v[4]
	DECB	5A 2 1				B − 1 → B	n z v[4]
Decr Stack Pntr	DES	34 4 1				SP − 1 → SP	
Decr Index Reg	DEX	09 4 1				X − 1 → X	z
Exclusive OR	EORA	88 2 2	98 3	B8 4	A8 5	A ⊕ M → A	n z V̄
	EORB	C8 2 2	D8 3	F8 4	E8 5	B ⊕ M → B	n z V̄
Increment	INC			7C 6	6C 7	M + 1 → M	n z v[5]
	INCA	4C 2 1				A + 1 → A	n z v[5]
	INCB	5C 2 1				B + 1 → B	n z v[5]
Incrm Stack Pntr	INS	31 4 1				SP + 1 → SP	
Incrm Index Reg	INX	08 4 1				X + 1 → X	z
Jump	JMP			7E 3	6E 4	Oprnd H, L → PC	
Jump to Subrtn	JSR			BD 9	AD 8	Stack PCL, PCH	
Load Acmltr	LDAA	86 2 2	96 3	B6 4	A6 5	M → A	n z V̄
	LDAB	C6 2 2	D6 3	F6 4	E6 5	M → B	n z V̄
Load Stack Pntr	LDS	8E 3 3	9E 4	BE 5	AE 6	$M → SP_H, (M+1) → SP_L$	n[7] z V̄
Load Index Reg	LDX	CE 3 3	DE 4	FE 5	EE 6	$M → X_H, (M+1) → X_L$	n[7] z V̄
Logic, Shift Right	LSR			74 6	64 7	M ⎫ Shift right into	N̄ z v[6] c
	LSRA	44 2 1				A ⎬ carry; 0 to MSB	N̄ z v[6] c
	LSRB	54 2 1				B ⎭ 0→[□□□□□□□□]→[□] 7 → 0 C	N̄ z v[6] c
Complement, 2's (Negate)	NEG			70 6	60 7	00 − M → M ⎫ Complement	n z v[1] c[2]
	NEGA	40 2 1				00 − A → A ⎬ bits and	n z v[1] c[2]
	NEGB	50 2 1				00 − B → B ⎭ add 1	n z v[1] c[2]

6802 Programmer's Reference

ADDRESSING MODES — IMMED/INHER, DIR/REL (2 byte), EXTND (3 byte), INDEX (2 byte)

AFFECTS COND. CODE REG. — Example: N = set, $\overline{N}$ = cleared, n = set or cleared, n^7 = note 7 below.

OPERATIONS	MNEMON	IMMED/INHER OP ~ #	DIR/REL OP ~	EXTND OP ~	INDEX OP ~	OPERATION (All register labels refer to contents)	COND. CODE
No Operation	NOP	01 2 1				Inc. Prog. Cntr. Only	
Or, Inclusive	ORAA	8A 2 2	9A 3	BA 4	AA 5	A + M → A	n z $\overline{V}$
	ORAB	CA 2 2	DA 3	FA 4	EA 5	B + M → B	n z $\overline{V}$
Push Data on stack	PSHA	36 4 1				A → M_{SP}, SP − 1 → SP	
	PSHB	37 4 1				B → M_{SP}, SP − 1 → SP	
Pull Data off stack	PULA	32 4 1				SP + 1 → SP, M_{SP} → A	
	PULB	33 4 1				SP + 1 → SP, M_{SP} → B	
Rotate Left	ROL			79 6	69 7	M ⎫ Rotate left	n z v^6 c
	ROLA	49 2 1				A ⎬ through carry	n z v^6 c
	ROLB	59 2 1				B ⎭ ⎕ ← ⎕⎕⎕⎕⎕⎕⎕⎕ ←⎤ C 7 0	n z v^6 c
Rotate Right	ROR			76 6	66 7	M ⎫ Rotate right	n z v^6 c
	RORA	46 2 1				A ⎬ through carry	n z v^6 c
	RORB	56 2 1				B ⎭ ⎡→ ⎕⎕⎕⎕⎕⎕⎕⎕ → ⎕ C 7 0	n z v^6 c
Return From Intrpt	RTI	3B 10 1				Restore P, B, A, XH, XL, PCH, PCL from stack	h i n z v c
Return From Subrtn	RTS	39 5 1				Restore PCH, PCL from stack	
Subtract Acmltrs	SBA	10 2 1				A − B → A	n z v c
Subtr. with Carry	SBCA	82 2 2	92 3	B2 4	A2 5	A − M − C → A	n z v c
	SBCB	C2 2 2	D2 3	F2 4	E2 5	B − M − C → B	n z v c
Set Carry	SEC	0D 2 1				1 → C	C
Set Intrpt Mask	SEI	0F 2 1				1 → I	I
Set Overflow	SEV	0B 2 1				1 → V	V
Store Acmltr	STAA		97 4	B7 5	A7 6	A → M	n z $\overline{V}$
	STAB		D7 4	F7 5	E7 6	B → M	n z $\overline{V}$
Store Stack Pntr	STS		9F 5	BF 6	AF 7	SP_H → M, SP_L → (M + 1)	n^7 z $\overline{V}$
Store Index Reg	STX		DF 5	FF 6	EF 7	X_H → M, X_L → (M + 1)	n^7 z $\overline{V}$
Subtract	SUBA	80 2 2	90 3	B0 4	A0 5	A − M → A	n z v c
	SUBB	C0 2 2	D0 3	F0 4	E0 5	B − M → B	n z v c
Software Intrpt	SWI	3F 12 1				Stack PCL, PCH, XL, XH, A, B, P; Vector FFFA, B	I
Transfer Acmltrs	TAB	16 2 1				A → B	n z $\overline{V}$
	TBA	17 2 1				B → A	n z $\overline{V}$
Acmltr A → CCR	TAP	06 2 1				A → CCR	h i n z v c
CCR → Acmltr A	TPA	07 2 1				CCR → A	
Test, Zero or Minus	TST			7D 6	6D 7	M − 00 ⎫	n z $\overline{V}$ C
	TSTA	4D 2 1				A − 00 ⎬ Sets CCR bits only	n z $\overline{V}$ $\overline{C}$
	TSTB	5D 2 1				B − 00 ⎭	n z $\overline{V}$ $\overline{C}$
Stack Pntr → Index Reg	TSX	30 4 1				SP + 1 → X	
Index Reg → Stack Pntr	TXS	35 4 1				X − 1 → SP	
Wait for Intrpt	WAI	3E 9 1				Stack PC, X, A, B, CCR. Wait for NMI or valid IRQ. BA goes high.	

Programmer's Model

```
       7           0
      [   ACCA    ]  Accumulator A
       7           0
      [   ACCB    ]  Accumulator B
      15           0
      [     X     ]  Index Register
      15           0
      [    PC     ]  Program Counter
      15           0
      [    SP     ]  Stack Pointer
       7           0
P or CCR [1 1 H I N Z V C]  Condition-Code Register
                   │ │ │ │ │ └─ Carry from bit 7
                   │ │ │ │ └─── Overflow from bit 6
                   │ │ │ └───── Zero result
                   │ │ └─────── Negative (bit 7 = 1)
                   │ └───────── Interrupt mask
                   └─────────── Half carry from bit 3
```

- · Boolean AND
- + Boolean OR
- ⊕ Boolean Exclusive OR
- + Arithmetic Plus
- → Transferred into
- ~ Machine Cycles
- # Program Bytes

CONDITION-CODE REGISTER TESTS:
(Bit set if true and cleared otherwise)
1. (Bit V) Result = 10000000?
2. (Bit C) Result = 00000000?
3. (Bit C) Decimal value of most significant BCD character greater than nine? (Not cleared if previously set.)
4. (Bit V) Operand = 10000000 prior to execution?
5. (Bit V) Operand = 01111111 prior to execution?
6. (Bit V) Set equal to result of N ⊕ C after shift has occurred.
7. (Bit N) MS bit of result = 1?
8. (Bit V) 2's-complement overflow from subtraction of LS bytes?

DATE DUE		
MAY 1992		